CW01372128

NOTTINGHAM HIGH SCHOOL

John Knifton

NOTTINGHAM HIGH SCHOOL

The Anecdotal History of a British Public School

By John Knifton

Published by Lauren Knifton PhD

© John Knifton, 2016, www.johnknifton.com

All rights reserved. This book or any portion thereof may not be reproduced, stored in a retrieval system, or transmitted in any form or by any means, electronic, mechanical, photocopying, recording, or otherwise, or used in any manner whatsoever without the prior written permission of the publisher except for the use of brief quotations in a book review or scholarly journal.

Cover design by Lauren Knifton PhD

First Printing: 2016

ISBN: 978-1-329-67622-0

Published in Nottingham, England by Lauren Knifton PhD
www.laurenknifton.com

Table of Contents

Acknowledgements..9
Foreword 11
Chapter 1: Lost in the Mists of Time....................................14
Chapter 2: The Dame Agnes Mellers Years.........................17
Chapter 3: A Personal Friend of Guy Fawkes 23
Chapter 4: The School is Closed Today because of Plague 29
Chapter 5: Old Boy Cuts Off King's Head...........................31
Chapter 6: The Last Days of the Stoney Street School 36
Chapter 7: A New School and a New Name 58
Chapter 8: Dr Gow to the Rescue 77
Chapter 9: The D. H. Lawrence Years 94
Chapter 10: Major General Mahin: A Yank at the High School 113
Chapter 11: Albert Ball and the High School Go to War... 119
Chapter 12: The First Founder's Day and the Beginning of the Modern Era...152
Chapter 13: The Second World War 184
Chapter 14: Three Blackbirds Rising Proper: The School Grows 217
Chapter 15: Don't Let Examinations Ruin your Education...............234
Chapter 16: Out with the Old, In with the New: The Golden Age of Teachers...266
Chapter 17: The New Millennium 343
Afterword...391

This book is dedicated to the memory of Martin Jones, a teacher who gave more of his time to Nottingham High School than anybody else in its long history.

Acknowledgements

I first started writing a history of Nottingham High School during the 1990s, when it seemed that the impending New Millennium would provide a logical culmination to my account.

Alas, by the time I had finished my *magnum opus* in 1999, it seemed to be of little interest to anybody. Mentally, therefore, I forgot about the whole thing. Some years later, I mentioned that I had written what I thought was a readable account of the school's history, but for a second time, my masterpiece seemed to have very little appeal. Only in 2012 was any interest shown, and this came from Yvette Gunther, the School Librarian. Encouraged by her kind words, I decided to fill in the missing years, and to try to produce something for the 500th anniversary of the school in 2013.

This I have done, and what you are reading now is the result of that process. Originally, the ever helpful Marilyn Clarke pointed me in the direction of the School magazines such as *The Forester*, *The Nottinghamian*, *The Highvite*, and *The Merle*. I have made strenuous efforts to make it obvious when I am quoting from those worthy publications. In addition, I have used this opportunity to enliven my original accounts from the 1960s onwards by asking members of Staff for any contributions that they would care to make. Putting the emphasis firmly on humour and anecdote, a number of teachers replied, and I am grateful for the material contributed by John Allen, Mark Cleverley, Jim Cook, Kate Costante, Gerald Douglas, Carol Fletcher, Martin Jones, Stefan Krzeminski, Malcolm Saperia, John Swain, Les Wilkinson and Simon Williams. Current or former pupils who helped, some of them fairly inadvertently, included Adam Jaffe, Ian Jallands, Andrew McCarthy, Adrian Noskwith, Will Sanderson and Daniel Storey.

I owe my most sincere thanks of all, however, to Doctor Lauren Knifton, without whose expertise this work would never have been published for every Old Nottinghamian and his Golden Retriever to read. I would also like to thank Lauren for reading numerous drafts of this book and for rewriting the section on D.H. Lawrence in the light of more recent literary criticism, as well as bringing some interesting new conclusions to the table (so if this ruffles any feathers, blame her!).

Now you, dear reader, can read the book, and judge for yourself whether a success has been made of it.

Foreword

Over hundreds of years, what must be thousands of walking shadows and poor players have strutted and fretted their hour upon the High School stage, and then been heard no more. You can now spend just a few of your todays, perhaps, reading about all their yesterdays. This present work is certainly a tale told by an idiot, and it is occasionally full of sound and fury, although many of the juiciest anecdotes from modern times have had to be omitted.

It would be rather harsh, though, to say that the history of the High School signifies nothing. What used to be called the Dame Agnes Mellers' Free School has always stood on the side of the angels and has represented, fairly faithfully, the basic ideals of academic learning, good behaviour and caring concern for one's fellow man.

Strangely enough, though, throughout my years of intermittent historical research, I have always felt that the school was much older than we currently suppose, and that the figure of 500 years is being unduly pessimistic. Indeed, I would argue that, instead of the 500th anniversary, we should perhaps be looking at a minimum of 724 years, if my Maths is correct. Perhaps the 800th anniversary should be celebrated in 2089?

The reason for ideas which may seem, at first sight, rather strange is that I am far from convinced that Dame Agnes founded a completely brand new school. Rather, she funded a school which was already in existence, but which may have been on the point of financial oblivion. Certainly, in 1924, in Dr Gow's obituary, the writer spoke of "Nottingham High School, an ancient Grammar School, already existing in the thirteenth century, and refounded and endowed by Dame Agnes Mellers, under a Charter of King Henry VIII, in 1513." Similar ideas were expressed by the Duke of Portland in 1933, when he came to open officially the new Gymnasium and the new Library. This same interpretation was still current nearly thirty years later, when the then Headmaster, Mr.Reynolds, wrote his own brief history of "The Buildings of Nottingham High School". He described the events of 1513 as "the re-foundation or endowment of the School by Dame Agnes Mellers."

We may never know the truth, of course. It would be rather nice though, to think that the first entry in this lengthy diary, namely Thursday, June 30th 1289, the date which constitutes the earliest ever reference to a Grammar School in Nottingham, was describing a school where the cheeky, but clever, young Robin of Locksley sat on the back row in his Lincoln Green Hoodie, causing countless problems for the teacher as he tried to kiss that pretty girl Marian for the umpteenth time. Or perhaps attempted to steal young Tuck's enormous lunch, and then to spill ink on the elegant clothes of the young William Scarlet. Perhaps Robin was busy writing a new set of lyrics for Allan-a-Dale, or just trying to whack John Little very hard on the back of his enormous head.

Of all the High School's walking shadows and poor players, my own personal favourite is probably John Peck Hemm, the writing master who, from 1816-1833, exhibited the inventive accountancy and shady financial dealings which nowadays would surely lead him to high office either in politics or (more likely, perhaps) in a major bank. Suffice it to say, though, that his *Portraits of the Royal Family in Penmanship*, which appeared in 1831, are still on sale today at a minimum price of £500, and that for a book of no more than twelve pages.

Among those last syllables of recorded time, and all those yesterdays, the most wonderful day in the school's history must surely have been the morning of Tuesday, February 1st 1916 when the boys were able to enjoy eight inches of snow in the playground and, when they were eventually forced inside into their classrooms, were then able to discuss how a number of Zeppelins had overflown Nottingham the previous evening dropping a few, fairly inconsequential, bombs near Stapleford.

To continue the literary analogy, though, if that were the best of times, the worst of times was undoubtedly Tuesday, August 14th 1917 when, according to the High School's Roll of Honour, Second Lieutenant James Knowles Turpin was killed in action at Boundary Road behind the Brigade HQ at Hill Top Farm near St Jaan. Within hours, Lieutenant Harold Ballamy was also killed in action as the Battle of Passchendaele continued on its blood soaked course.

Judge for yourself though...

Which pupil was the cleverest?

And which one was the most famous?

Which servant of the school was the greatest of them all?

Who was the most wonderful sportsman?

Decide which teacher was the best.

And which was the most disreputable?

And most important of all, who was the school's most beautiful teacher?

No debate necessary. It's Miss Southall for me.

Chapter 1: Lost in the Mists of Time

Thursday, June 30th 1289

This date is the earliest reference to a Grammar School in Nottingham. It comes in a letter from the Archbishop of York, John Le Romeyn, which was sent both to the Master of the School and to a priest at Kinoulton. The priest had been running his own local school which was contrary to the accepted practice at the time when schools were not allowed to compete with one another. The Master of the Grammar School had made a complaint to the Archbishop about this breach of the unwritten rules. The Archbishop's compromise was that the school in Kinoulton should continue to operate but only with local clergy. The Nottingham establishment could use "external priests".

1307

John de Burton quit the post as Master of the Grammar School. Very little is known about who occupied teaching positions during this time period, except for the very occasional mention of who left his employment and when.

Tuesday, August 13th 1382

A possible new school building or perhaps a new Master's house, on "The Pavement", was conveyed to Robert de Retford, vicar of St Mary's, Nottingham and William de Adbolton "Scolemaster" of Nottingham Grammar School. The latter was to die around 1389 or 1390.

Thursday, January 15th 1395

Robert Fole, chaplain, sought on two occasions to recover the sum of 3s 4d, owed to him for teaching the son of William Cupper for five terms. He may well have been the successor to William de Adbolton. A few years later in 1401, Fole reappears in the borough records where he is referred to as a "master of the grammar school of Nottingham".

1423 - 1424

Robert Goldsmyth who was the "lately Usher of the Nottingham Grammar School" was fined two shillings for an unspecified offence.

Tuesday, January 26th 1430

George Mortimer sued Thomas Ridley, "Clerk and Master of the School at Nottingham" for the seven pence rent owed for a building called the "School House", and for four pence damages. Mortimer had repeatedly asked for the money but Ridley simply refused to pay. In court, Ridley denied the offence and said that he owed Mortimer nothing.

Monday, February 22nd 1430

Ridley admitted that he owed Mortimer the money.

A few years after 1430

On two separate occasions, George Mortimer again sued Thomas Ridley for the money owed to him as fees for tuition. It is thought that Mortimer may have been the Master at the school before Ridley who had been foolish enough to rent his house to the latter for use as a school. The outcome of the case remains unknown. Certainly, we know that Mortimer must have taught boys at some point as he also sued Robert Bennington for the six pence he owed for "schoolage" of his son.

Wednesday, February 29th 1432

Thomas Ridley went on to rent a building called the "Manse", from the St John's Hospital, at a cost of 26s 8d for nine months from Christmas 1429 to Holy Cross Day on September 14th, 1430. At the end of this period, Ridley was then sued for his failure to pay the rent properly, for breaking down the wall of the building, and for damaging it by fire. Ridley lost his case, which was heard by a court in session during the Fair of the Feast of *St.Peter in Cathedra*.

Tuesday, May 28th 1433

George Mortimer sued John Crophill, skinner, of Nottingham, for school fees of four pence, which should have been paid to him at Easter.

Monday or Wednesday, February 19th in, most probably, 1472 or 1473

An agreement was reached between Thomas Lacy, the Master at the grammar school in Nottingham, and Sir William Cowper in the town of Wollaton. Negotiated by a neutral party, the chapter at Southwell

Minster, Cowper was allowed to teach twenty-six boys or youths the art of grammar.

1477

The Southwell chapter summarily dismissed Lacy for neglect and absenteeism. Thomas Blakebourne may have been the man who succeeded him.

Thursday, September 15th 1496

Thomas Blakebourne, the Master at the grammar school and a B.A. from Cambridge University, sued Robert Oldham for the sixpence he was owed for tiling the roof of the almshouse. He lost his case. Disappointing, of course, to see a Cambridge *alumnus* and the local Headmaster reduced to doing odd jobs to make up his wages.

Chapter 2: The Dame Agnes Mellers Years

Sunday, June 16th 1507

On or about this date, Richard Mellers died. He is thought to have originated perhaps at Leicester where a man supposed to be his brother, William, was a famous bell founder. William, however, always wrote his surname as "Miller", although this was, of course, in the days when spelling was famously imprecise. In her will, Dame Agnes herself spelt her name as "Mellers".

Richard Mellers had been, at one time or another, Sheriff of Nottingham (1472-1473), Chamberlain (1484-1485), Royal Commissioner, and Mayor of Nottingham (1499-1500 and again in 1506). In 1499, it is known that he had paid £20 to be Mayor of the town for twelve months. In the same year, Mellers is known to have given twenty shillings to help repair the Hethbeth Bridge as Trent Bridge's predecessor was called. As well as being a brazier and probably a potter, dealing in metal pots and dishes, Mellers also owned the largest bell-foundry in the region. The site of his premises has long disappeared, but in fact, its exact geographical location is still known today. From 1888 onwards, just north of the city centre, steps began to clear away a "curious V-shaped slice of slum property" which "was a most unhygienic and immoral neighbourhood and nothing good could be said for it". This clearance took a number of years and resulted in the formation of Queen Street and King Street, the latter being opened on June 22nd, 1892. During this time it was inevitable that, along with the slums and the undesirable features, other more interesting premises were bound to disappear. Among these was Mellers' Bell Foundry, which is known to have stood on the site of the present day Queen Street Post Office.

Richard Mellers was certainly an unscrupulous businessman and during his lifetime, he had cheated many customers in his efforts to acquire great personal wealth. Shortly before his death we know that he received a pardon for having offended against the statutes of weights and measures. This pardon would only have been granted because of his previous position as Mayor of Nottingham. After his death his widow, Dame Agnes, became a "vowess", resolving never to remarry and instead to devote herself to the service of the church. She tried to repay many of her husband's victims and then decided to spend the rest of his money on charitable causes. She decided to found a Free School which would be independent of both church and state. This would require the creation of a corporation and the permission of King Henry VIII. To get the necessary licence, she turned for help to her old friend, Sir Thomas Lovell. He was a Knight of the Garter and a Privy Councillor, and had previously been Chancellor of the Exchequer, Speaker of the House of Commons, Treasurer of the King's Household, Constable of the Tower of London and Governor of Nottingham Castle. As might be imagined, he quickly and easily received the King's consent and Dame Agnes' project went ahead.

Many local worthies in the town were asked to make their own contribution to the school, Dame Agnes having herself offered four pieces of land in St Peter's Churchyard and one in Bridlesmithgate. Alderman Thomas Alestre, the mayor of the town, gave three acres of land at Todeholes. This was at St Ann's Hill, near Mapperley Road, an area which was called Toadhole Hill as recently as the last century. William Kirkby, a baker, gave two gardens near St Nicholas' church. The majority of the eighty subscribers, however, promised to pay a sum "by yere" for the rest of their lives. The amounts varied from ten shillings from Master Richard Taverner, to four pence from Henry Hopkyn, a local tanner, Robert Averell, Rychard Dalderbery, Wyllium Edmondson and Thomas Hewet.

Sunday, May 5th 1512

Bearing this date, a bill is still in existence for the repair of a children's school. It is in the handwriting of William Barwell, the Mayor's clerk, and may well refer to a primary school which sent pupils to the grammar school or, equally, it may have been the original grammar school, fallen on hard times. The school was in a "cottage bought of Thomas Sherwod at Notyngham standing in the Peperstreet at John' Howes' back gate". This would have been to the east of St Peter's church. The repairs were carried out by Rychard Halom, and threepence was paid for "a loade of clay to the tofalle (penthouse) that ye children lerne inne." The same amount was paid for "a bunche of stone lattice". This is the last of the eleven apparent references to the Nottingham Grammar School between 1289 and 1513. At this point in time, it is impossible to tell what connection, if any, there is with Dame Agnes Mellers' Free School, or even if the schools mentioned have a continuous linear history.

On the other hand, Dame Agnes may well have decided to develop an original grammar school into her own Free School. This original school may have depended solely on fees paid by the pupils and Dame Agnes thought it would be a good idea to establish a foundation which would ensure a better financial future for the school. Given that she was a vowess, she may well have wished to take control of an older school and then to bring it under the aegis of St Mary's church. It may even be that, having used much of the money which her husband had left her to pay back those whom he had cheated, she felt that one positive benefit that could come out of the whole situation would be to offer financial help to an ancient school which was clearly in need of assistance. We may well never know the true answer. It is interesting to see, however, that in *The Nottinghamian* for 1924 there was a clear connection in the writer's mind between these older schools from before 1513 and the present Nottingham High School. Dr Gow had died this year and in his obituary, it was said that "he was appointed Headmaster of the Nottingham High School, an ancient Grammar School, already existing in the thirteenth century and refounded and endowed by Dame Agnes Mellers, under a Charter of King Henry VIII, in 1513." Again in 1933, similar ideas were expressed by the Duke of Portland, when he came to open a number of recently completed school buildings. The very same interpretation was obviously still current nearly thirty years later, when the Headmaster, Mr Reynolds, wrote his own brief history called *The Buildings of Nottingham High School*. He described the events of 1513 as "the re-foundation or endowment of the School by Dame Agnes Mellers." This scenario would give the High School a history of some seven hundred years, making it one of the oldest schools in the country.

Friday, November 22nd 1512

The Royal Seal was attached to a charter granting permission for the "foundation and building of a certain school" for the "teaching of boys and their instruction in good manners and letters." At the very end of the lengthy handwritten document comes the first mention of the High School's present Latin motto "Lauda Finem". Perhaps the poor scribe felt exactly the same way that countless thousands of schoolboys have felt ever since that day "Praise the Lord, it's over!" A number of intriguingly ambiguous details occur around this time. One contemporary document says that what Dame Agnes was doing was to "unite, create and establysche oon Free Scole", as if there were some definite connection between the present day High School and the Nottingham schools of previous centuries. Similarly, a number of other early documents refer to her not as a "foundress" but as a "fundress", as if she were building and strengthening what was already there.

Sunday, February 2nd 1513

The school opened on this day which was known as Candlemas or the Feast of the Purification of the Blessed Virgin Mary. This holy day, in its turn, was a direct descendant of the ancient Celtic festival of Imbolc, when nature is first seen to stir, lambing begins and St Bridgit, goddess of healing and poetry, is celebrated at her wells and springs.

The very first classes were originally said to have been held in the nave, or perhaps the north transept, of St Mary's church. The very first Master was called John Smyth. He had previously been the "parson of Bylbrough", and it is known that he taught a number of pupils at the parsonage in Bilborough during this period. In 1505, for example, he had brought a civil action against Thomas Samon in order to recover the tuition fees of a boy called Thomas a Pole who had been a boarder with him from May 19th - August 15th 1505. Unfortunately, he failed and did not get his money. In the leaves of the Court Book, Smith had described himself as "Deane of Notyngham and parson off Bylbrough." Smith died in the summer of, probably, 1538, but it is not known whether he was still the Master of the Free School at this point. The first schoolwardens at the Free School were William English, Dame Agnes' son-in-law, and the Mayor's Clerk, William Barwell. The school taught good manners, grammar, and literature, and every day the pupils "beginn theire learnynge to saye with an high voyce whole Credo in Deum patrem etc." In all probability, the Free School would have taught similar things to what is known to have been taught in the recently founded St Paul's School (1509-1518). They would have included "good literature bothe Latin and Greeke, and good authors such as have the verye Romane eloquence with wisdom, specially Christen autors, that wrote their wisdome with clean and chaste Latin, other in verse or in prose to encrease knowledge and worshippinge of God and Our Lord

Christ Jesu, and good Christen life and manners in the Children". At St.Paul's School, hours were long. In the summer, the pupils studied from 6-8 a.m., and then from 9-11.30 a.m. In the afternoon, they worked from 1-3.30 p.m., and then from 4-6 p.m. In winter, it was 7-11.30 a.m., and then from 1-5 p.m.

Probably April, perhaps early May, 1514

Dame Agnes died, and was buried alongside her husband in St Mary's Church. She left much of her property to the school.

1522?

There is some evidence that in this year, the Free School occupied its own premises.

Around 1530-1570?

Within a few years of Dame Agnes' death, her very high standards of morality were more or less forgotten. Money went missing and both Masters and wardens neglected their duties. A number of Masters appeared in court on various charges which varied from failing to maintain the church windows to the theft of pupils' books.

January, perhaps, in 1532

The Master of the school, George Somers, was accused of detaining "a fetherbedd a bolster & two pyllows a Coveryng greene & Redd a Coverlett a paire of Flaxen Sheetes" to the value of 46s 8d. He also owed twelve pence for the hire of the same bed.

Friday, July 15th 1532

In a much more dramatic episode, George Somers, was now accused of murder. The Records tell how "We indicte the Skolle master of wilfull murdar." The incident took place on June 17th and Somers had supposedly assaulted John Langton, Chaplain of Nottingham, "by violence and weapons, namely a stick and daggers, of malice aforethought", and had then "feloniously killed and wilfully murdered the same John, against the peace of our Lord the King." The outcome of these events remains unknown, although hopefully, if convicted, he did not keep his post as Master of the school.

1548

This year gives the first definite proof that there was an actual schoolhouse, separate from St Mary's Church. King Edward VI's commissioners, inquiring into the wealth and duties of the country's chantries, found that, in Nottingham, the Guild of the Holy Trinity had been paying an annual sum of eight shillings for the upkeep of the Free School which was known to have had its own garden. When the royal commissioners dissolved the chantry, the school was given the house "called the Free Scole or the Scholehouse without anything paying for the same." They received the garden as well.

Sunday, October 11th 1553

A confirmation of the original licence issued by Henry VIII was granted by Queen Mary and King Phillip, "King and Queen of England, France, Naples, Jerusalem, and Ireland, Defenders of the Faith, Princes of Spain and Sicily, Archdukes of Austria, Dukes of Milan, Burgundy and Brabant, Counts of Hapsburg, Flanders and Tyrol."

Monday, September 29th 1558

Alderman John Heskey left to the school his tithes of Hay "within the meadowes and fields of the towne of Nottingham". They had previously belonged to Lenton Priory, and were one of the greatest gifts the school ever received, comprising some 1,265 acres. They formed a significant proportion of its revenues for the next three centuries.

Friday, March 22nd 1563 or, perhaps, 1564

Henry Cockrame, "schoolmaster of the Grammar School of the town of Nottingham", was summoned by the Archbishop of York to prove his qualifications to be a schoolmaster. He never answered the summons, and was excommunicated. In actual fact, Cockrame is believed to have had a degree in Canon Law from Oxford University.

Chapter 3: A Personal Friend of Guy Fawkes

1564 -1576

Brian Garnett, or Garnet, is thought to have been the Master of the school at some unknown point between 1564 and 1575. It is considered most probable that he took up the post between 1564 and 1567, and then retired in, probably, 1575. He may then have lived in Beeston, but he was certainly buried in Heanor in Derbyshire on December 21st 1576, as the Late Skoolemaster of Nottingham. With his wife, Alice Jay, he had at least three sons, Richard, John and Henry and three daughters, Margaret, Eleanor and Anne, all of whom became nuns at Louvain. Of the sons, Henry is the most notable, because he was eventually to become the Superior of the Jesuits in England, and, allegedly, an active member of the Gunpowder Plot or the so-called Jesuit Treason.

Garnet was not quite tasked with carrying the barrels of gunpowder into the cellars, but rather, he was deemed to have been made aware of the assassination attempt, because all the details were revealed to him through the plotters' confessions. Of course, by the strict rules of his Catholic religion, Garnet was automatically prevented from informing the authorities by the absolute confidentiality of the confessional. None of this alters the basic fact, though, that Henry Garnet was executed for treason, on May 3rd 1606. At his trial, the jury only had to consider the verdict for fifteen minutes.

One source says that young Henry came to the Free School during Henry Cockrame's time as Master (most probably 1563-1564), and possibly a year or so before Cockrame left in 1565 and was replaced by Henry's father, Brian Garnett of Heanor, Derbyshire. Henry is supposed to have studied for two years under his father's tutelage, before leaving for Winchester College. He had been well taught in Nottingham, and proved to be an able student at Winchester. According to Antonia Fraser in *The Gunpowder Plot*, and *The Oxford Dictionary of National Biography*, his love of music and "rare and delightful" voice were complemented by an ability to perform songs without preparation, and he was reportedly also skilled with the lute. Father Thomas Stanney wrote that Garnet was "the prime scholar of Winchester College, very skilful in music and in playing upon the instruments, very modest in his countenance and in all his actions, so much that the schoolmasters and wardens offered him very great friendship, to be placed by their means in New College, Oxford." Instead of the delights of New College, Oxford, when he left the school in 1571, Garnet moved to London to work for a publisher, and shortly afterwards, travelled to the continent to join the Society of Jesus. He moved to Rome to study for the priesthood with the Jesuits, and was finally ordained as a priest around 1582.

By virtue of the events of May 3rd 1606, Henry Garnet must surely remain the only Old Nottinghamian ever to have been convicted as a terrorist, and, indeed, one of the very few ever to have been hanged, drawn and quartered, and then to have had his severed head placed on a pole on London Bridge. Thankfully, the more lurid details of his execution have survived in Antonia Fraser's book *The Gunpowder Plot*:

> "Garnet said his prayers, and was then thrown off the ladder and hanged. Before the executioner could cut him down alive, many in the crowd pulled on his legs, and as a result, Garnet did not suffer the remainder of his grim sentence. There was no applause when the executioner held Garnet's heart aloft and said the traditional words, "Behold the heart of a traitor". His head was set on a pole on London Bridge, but crowds of onlookers fascinated by its pallid appearance eventually forced the government to turn the head upwards, so its face was no longer visible."

From this peculiar pallid appearance of course, came the widely held belief that Garnet's head did not suffer any signs of decay or change. Furthermore, a miraculous portrait of him apparently appeared on an ear of corn onto which drops of his blood had fallen at the time of his execution. This particular ear of corn was later credited with a number of miracles. At one point, it was taken secretly out of the country into the possession of the Society of Jesus, before, with its small size surely playing a part, it was lost during the French Revolution.

The Roman Catholic Church has a large number of saints who have done far less than Henry Garnet to earn their sainthoods. Names which spring to mind would include St.Buriana, St.Erc, St.Ia and any number of Cornish villages named after dimly remembered holy men. Perhaps one fine day, Henry Garnet may yet become the only Old Nottinghamian ever to be canonised.

Circa 1570

Before this date the most important school subjects had been Latin grammar, literature and other subjects which could be studied orally by rote just as easily as from a written text. Around this time, however, the increasing availability of printed books began to put an end to this almost exclusively oral method of teaching. Both reading and writing began to take on a new importance and, by the end of the century, the school was bringing in a writing Master from time to time to teach these new skills. Even so, boys were expected to learn writing privately, and most of them would have gone to a separate writing school. Simple arithmetic, however, was almost completely unknown. Even at Cambridge University, many scholars were unable to "tell the numbers of pages, sections, chapters or other divisions in their books."

1575 or 1576 - 1584

The master at this time was called John Depupp, the son of an "innholder" from London, although he was educated at Cambridge University. When he was a Fellow at Caius College, he was accused of being "a man notoriously vicious and suspected to be popish", and only lasted eighteen months in the post. At the Free School, he seems to have been a good teacher and in the year 1576-1577, he earned £13 6s 8d. He died on January 4th 1603.

1578 - 1579

A house was built for the schoolmaster. It cost £9 4s 0d for the timber frame, £3 14s 8d for the foundations and chimney and three labourers were paid 1s 6d for "helpyng to reare" the frame. Some 3s 3d was paid out for five doors and a penthouse and further monies were spent on timber, its transportation and labour costs at ten pence per man per day. In addition, "Frybus and his man" were paid 1s 4d per day for burning plaster, thereby earning a total of 6s 8d.

Sunday, October 28th 1579

The Borough Records tell how "We present to have an husher for the Free Skoole, a thing very needfull for this towne; and to geve him ten pounds a yeare to have a goode one; itt will be a credett to have a good maister and a good hussher in one skoole." Judging by the archaic spelling it would seem that one of the Usher's main jobs was to keep the boys quiet. The first Usher was called Richard Slacke, and his name appears in the Accounts for 1577-1578. He was paid £2 10s 0d per annum at a time when the master was paid £13 6s 8d or twenty marks.

1588 to February 1591-1592

Christopher Heylowe, a Master of Arts from St John's College, Cambridge, had given great satisfaction as the Master of the school until either 1591 or 1592 when he was accused of stealing the boys' books. The records of Heylowe's trial are still extant and he defended himself vigorously "Christofer Heyloe, examined, sayeth he stole no bookes of any his scholers and he sayethe he had Tully's *Orations* aboute Michaelmas laste of Humfrey Quermbye in this sorte: when he readde a lecture thereon in the schoole, he tooke it into his chamber, and broughte into ye schoole againe: and he gave to Maister Greyi some other Terence in exchange for his; the Ovides *Metamorphosocez* he sayeth he boughte it of the stacyoner aboute a year agone." Eventually, the charges appear to have been dropped, but Heylowe was sacked, and given ten pounds in lieu of proper notice. The Chamberlain also paid Heylowe 40 s 0d for some "implements", which was probably some apparatus that Heylowe had bought with his own money for use in the school and was now being kept for his successor. Humfrey Quermbyez is thought to have been the great-grandson of Dame Agnes Mellers.

Tuesday, May 11th 1593

Heylowe was again in trouble. This time he was charged with "slandring our towne with the sicknes which will be to our decaye." He thus became the only headmaster ever to be accused of being a bubonic plague carrier but, fortunately for him, perhaps, he was found not guilty because plague was already in the town before the accusations were made. In this era, fear of strangers bringing plague was a way of life in Nottingham. In 1582, ten pence had been "given to a poore man that was suspected to have the Plague to avoyd the towne."

The late 1500s

By now the Free School was quite rich but actually received very little of its annual income. Councillors, wardens and Masters regularly embezzled school funds and many of them had actually involved themselves in the Free School with the intention of making easy money.

1602

John Lowe, the Headmaster, was found guilty in court of failing to ensure that "Maister Powdrell and Maister Grene attended church." He was not punished, however, since the parents of the two boys were either Roman Catholics or Puritans and had refused to let their sons attend Church of England services.

Sunday, September 15th 1602

It is clear from a document that one of the Schoolwardens, Richard Welche could not write his own name but instead made a curious mark like a cross with a capital letter R attached to it. By 1605, when he became Mayor, he had learned to write his own name properly.

Sunday, January 25th 1604

More than once around the turn of this century the Free School had to be closed because of outbreaks of plague in the city. Classes were temporarily moved to the countryside where there was less chance of pupils catching the pestilence because of the lower population density. On this occasion, it is recorded that "Itt is agreed, that Maister Braithwayte, the Usher, shall teach at some place within a mile or 2 of the towne, if parents will board their children att such a place." Elsewhere in the county, eighty-three people died of plague in the small village of Colston Bassett between July-September 1604. As was the normal practice at the time, those suspected of having the plague were sent to live in special cabins at Gorsey Close on Mapperley Plains. The latter were eventually to be demolished in June 1624. Plague broke out again in 1609, and the town set a special watch "to looke to the passengers that shall come from any visited place, and to look to the takinge vpp of forayne wnderinge people etc".

Tuesday, April 3rd 1607- April 1616

The new master, Thomas Soresbie, was a local man, probably from Holme Pierrepont. He had a Master of Arts degree from Queen's

College, Oxford and seems to have been very successful in his job. The local mood at the time must have been particularly Puritan since Soresbie had to promise that "the children be restrayned from so oft playinge as heretofore they haue vsed, and herein Maister Soresbye is required to take a speciall care that they play not, in any case, vpon any Monday, Wednesday, or Fryday." Thomas Soresbie remains one of the few masters to have died in office.

Chapter 4: The School is Closed Today because of Plague

1611 - 1612

There was a severe "visitation" of plague throughout the county and the country as a whole. At Loughborough, over five hundred people died. The school was closed at least twice during this period.

1613

This year gives the first mention that the "Freescole" was in Stoney Street, when it was recorded that the street needed paving from "Saint Maries Church style towardes the Free Scolle."

Sunday, March 11th 1615

Despite his apparent success, Thomas Soresbie was about to leave his post as Master of the Free School but passed away before he could relinquish his post. He was buried at St Mary's church.

Sunday, May 29th 1616 – Saturday, April 29th 1628

The new master, Robert Theobald, was "an excellent scholar". Not too long afterwards, however, Mrs Lucy Hutchinson was to portray him as "an excellent scholar, but having no children, some wealth and a little living that kept his house, he first grew lazy, and after, left off his school." A former pupil recalled him as "a person once of great learning, but afterwards becoming a cynic."

Friday, April 28th 1628

Thomas Leake was appointed as headmaster thereby inaugurating a period of great prosperity and success for the school which lasted for at least sixty years. Most of Leake's pupils were the sons of local merchants, craftsmen and farmers. Some of their names which have survived were Bateman, Beardsley, Truman and Willoughby.

January 1634

After a schoolwardens stole the school funds Thomas Leake and his usher, Samuel Lightefoote, were forced to accept only £5 11s 3d as their wages, rather than the forty pounds due to them.

Monday, August 4th 1634

On this day, King Charles I and Queen Henrietta visited Nottingham on their way back from Scotland to London. The Free School's Usher, Samuel Lightefoote, was chosen to make a speech of welcome and for this he was given "a suit, hatt, stockings, garters, shoes and other Accooterments" to a total value of £8 6s 0d. It was on this occasion that the Mayor and Council made a resolution to wear red gowns every November 5th "for ever" to mark the king's "deliverance from the powder-treason". Anyone failing to do so was to forfeit a shilling. It would be interesting to know if this by-law has ever been repealed.

Friday, September 19th 1636

Samuel Lightefoote was to be asked to resign for "his neglecte in his place in teachings the Schollers under his tuition".

1641

This year is the first mention of the fact that the Free School stood at the corner of Stoney Street and Barkergate. Mr Francis Pierrepont, or "Collonell the Right Honourable Francis Pierepont", was having a large residence built next to the site and wanted certain windows of the school building "stopped up". Pierrepont's mansion was eventually to be the second largest in the town with forty-seven rooms containing fireplaces.

1647

Thomas Leake's carriage ran over and killed Bevill Verye. The carriage which caused his death was then declared a deodand (an object which has caused a person's death) and in keeping with the tradition of a deodand becoming forfeit and dedicated to God, the carriage was put up for sale. The sale produced £5, which was divided up, with Verye's widow receiving £1 10s 0d, the sheriff getting one pound, the town ten shillings and Leake himself, strangely enough, receiving two pounds.

Chapter 5: Old Boy Cuts Off King's Head

Saturday, January 30th 1649

On this date King Charles I was executed in London. One of those who had initially sat in judgement on the King was a member of the Long Parliament, Colonel John Hutchinson. Along with Oliver Cromwell and just under thirty others, Hutchinson had then signed the warrant for the King's execution. When King Charles II returned in 1660, the future looked bleak for all those who had signed this death warrant and indeed, Hutchinson was imprisoned for some time in the Tower of London awaiting execution. The influence of his friends led to his release, however, and he was allowed to live out his days at Sandown Castle in Kent, imprisoned there for his refusal to renounce his republican ideals. On the other hand, Hutchinson can hardly have been the typical Puritan. It is known, for example, that he had long hair and a love of art and he seems not to have been particularly in favour of the religious intolerance practised by Cromwell and his followers.

As boys, both John Hutchinson and his brother, George, had been scholars at the Free School, during the period of decay under Robert Theobald and William Burrows. Indeed the boys were so neglected that their angry father, Sir Thomas Hutchinson of Owthorpe, had them sent as boarders to Lincoln, where they unfortunately encountered a "cruel and supercilious pedant". When Robert Theobald left in 1628, the two boys returned to the Free School where Thomas Leake was now the Headmaster. Leake was, according to John Hutchinson's mother, Lucy, "a very honest man, who, using him with respect, advanced him more in one month than the other did in a year". As far as can be traced, John Hutchinson remains the only Old Boy ever to participate in regicide.

Friday, November 16th 1657

"Master Henrie Pitts" became the new master. He had to agree to a number of conditions. One was that he was not to hire himself out as a preacher. He was not "to grant or allow any play-days above one in every monthe, besides holidays and such usual times." Most of all, he could only have "two potacions yearely, and no more. And nott to take above a shilling from any of the Townes Children for those potacions."

"Potacions" were drinking parties, where the masters charged each pupil a small sum to attend. The money collected in this way could be used to pay for the alcohol consumed and, if there was to be any cock-fighting, then it could pay for suitable birds. Any cash left over from buying such vital supplies could be kept by the masters or, as often happened, passed on to the less well paid individuals on the school payroll.

1658-1660

According to Lucy Hutchinson, rioting broke out in Nottingham following the death of Oliver Cromwell:

> "The town of Nottingham began to grow mad, and to declare themselves so, in their desires of the King. The boys, set on by their fathers and masters, got drums and colours, and marched up and down the town, and trained themselves in a military posture, and offered many affronts to the soldiers of the army that were quartered there. These were two troops of Colonel Hacker's regiment. One night there were about forty of the soldiers hurt and wounded with stones, upon the occasion of taking away the drums when the youths were gathering together to make bonfires to burn the Rump, as was the custom in those mad days. The soldiers, provoked to rage, shot again, and killed in the scuffle two Presbyterians and an old professor; and one that had been a great zealot for the cause, and master of the magazine at Nottingham Castle. He was only standing at his own door, and whether shot by chance or purpose, or by whom, it is not certain; but true it is, that at that time the Presbyterians were more inveterately bitter against the fanatics than even the cavaliers themselves, and they set on these boys. But upon the killing of this man they were enraged, and prayed very seditiously in their pulpits, and began openly to desire the King; not for good will to him, but only for destruction to all the fanatics."

It is rather difficult to believe that no Free School boys were involved in any of this taunting of soldiers, beating their drums and throwing hails of stones. The man killed at his own door was called Richard Hawkins. Colonel Hacker, who came from East Bridgford, had commanded the soldiers who were on duty when Charles I was executed.

The 1660s

Even some hundred and fifty years after the foundation of the school, the students still began and ended every single day with a religious service. Each Sunday, the master would take them to church and in the period of Lent, they would go every Friday to St Mary's Church, kneel in front of the tombs of Richard and Agnes Mellers and say prayers for their souls and all their relatives.

1688 - 1689

The rebuilding of the west front of the school was completed at a total cost of some £63 5s 9d. A plaque was placed on the wall to commemorate the repairs:

> "This School, founded in the reign of Henry VIII by Agnes Mellers, and by Injury of Time much decay'd, was repaired Ann. Dom. 1689. George Langford, Major John Aste, James Huthwaite, Schoolwardens."

Tuesday, December 2nd 1687

Gowen Knight became the Master of the Free School, succeeding Jeremiah Cudworth. He was already the vicar at Ashby-de-la-Zouch, and soon became vicar of Ponteland in Northumberland, Thrumpton in Nottinghamshire and Langford in Derbyshire. His Usher was Samuel Byrch, the vicar of Basford, and between them, the two men appear to have been so busy that they had little, if any, time to deal with the school. The Council, therefore, attempted to dismiss them but after much complicated manoeuvring, Knight died on September 9th 1691 and was buried in St Mary's Church. Byrch managed to keep his job for another seventeen years.

Sunday, August 18th 1697

Edward Griffith, the Master who had succeeded Knight in 1691, was called to appear in court by the Council "for neglecting the schoole, whereby the schoole is much decayed in its reputacion."

Friday, December 19th 1698

The Council again told Edward Griffith to leave, alleging that "he haveing very much neglected his duty therein, whereby the said

Freeschoole is very much decayed and lessened, to the greate prejudice and damage of the said Towne in perticuler, and to the Inhabitants of this towne in generall, they beinge necessitated to send their Children to other Schooles in the Countrys for their Education, to their greate charge and expence. And that the Schoole Wardens do give him a discharge, which they have done accordingly. And if he shall refuse to leave the said Freeschoole by Lady Day next, that they shall withdrawe his Sallary." Griffith made no reply whatsoever to this decision to dispense with his services.

May 1699

The Council issued a second decree that Griffith should quit his post. Again, he took absolutely no notice of it.

Saturday, January 23rd 1700

Surprisingly, it was agreed that Griffith should keep his job and salary until further notice.

Friday, January 22nd 1705

The Council told Griffith that he was "discharged from being Schoolmaster any longer". Not surprisingly, he ignored this order, although he did make a promise to depart in the very near future.

Friday, June 26th 1705

Once again, it was decided that "the Schoolwardens for the time to come do not pay or allow the said Mr Griffith the Head-schoolmaster any Sallary till further notice."

Saturday, March 27th 1706

The schoolwardens were told to raise the £85 of Griffith's wages which had not been paid to him over the past two years. Once he had been given this cash settlement, Griffith had promised to leave.

Friday, March 25th 1707

The tenacious Mr Griffith at long last departed, a mere ten years after being told to do so.

1707

The new Master, Richard Johnson, seems to have been, for the first five years or so of his reign, a vast improvement on his two predecessors. Johnson was the author of two volumes of an ambitious Latin Grammar, and a long Latin poem describing a horse race on the Forest, which was then called "The Lings".

Chapter 6: The Last Days of the Stoney Street School

June 1718

The Council now sought to remove Johnson, alleging that "for all or most of the time he hath been Master, he very much omitted and neglected to teach and instruct the Sons of the Burgesses of the said Town of Nottingham." Furthermore, "for the space of three Months and upward, he hath been and is now Delirious and *Non compos mentis* Whereby he is incapable of performing and executing the Office and Duty of the Master of the said Free-School". In recent years, much of Johnson's mental energy had been expended on a prolonged and bitter academic quarrel with Richard Bentley, who had recently brought out his own savagely amended version of Horace's *Odes*, with which Johnson passionately disagreed. The latter had also been forced, for this reason, to postpone his plans for a new Latin grammar. Certainly, Johnson had fallen ill in 1714, and wrote that "I suffered such pains in my limbs that for a whole year I could not sleep without using opium."

While Johnson seems to have indeed suffered some ill health, the Council's motivation for removing him may have had more to do with politics than their concern for the school's success. It may well be that Johnson's ill health was exaggerated to create a trumped-up charge of incompetence to remove a political thorn in the council's side.

Analysts have pointed out that Johnson's apparent problems with the Council members seem to have begun not long after the Old Pretender's rebellion in 1715. Nottingham at this time was, for the most part, a Whig town and it is not inconceivable that Johnson may have been a Jacobite. Certainly, many other schoolmasters throughout England lost their jobs around this time for their pro-Jacobite sympathies. When the Council tried to throw him out, however, like some of his predecessors, Johnson just refused point blank to go. On August 11th 1718, the Council went as far as to appoint William Smeaton to Johnson's position but Johnson still refused physically to leave either the school, or his house, something, of course, which went with the job.

Smeaton thereupon resigned, and left the town. The Council next appointed a local man, William Saunders, and an "action for ejectment" was taken out against Johnson. In court he seems to have conducted his defence with great skill and is known to have won his case. Johnson explained to the court how unreasonable it was to leave a man of his age penniless in the world and asked that he be given a testimonial so that at the very least he could go elsewhere and earn an honest living.

At one point Councillor Abney, knowing of Johnson's previous mental frailty, accused him "that has happened to you, which Felix imputed to St Paul; much learning hath made thee mad." Johnson replied to the Councillor that "the gentleman who made this remark would never be mad from the same cause." By now, though, the school had only five pupils with the Usher, George Bettinson, teaching two and Johnson doing the lion's share of the work with the other three. By this time, the Council was again repeating its charge that Johnson had been delirious for the last eighteen months.

Finally a petition was drawn up by the council, listing Johnson's many faults. He was asked to appear before the Council on November 19th 1719 to answer the charges before the petition was sent to the Archbishop of York. Johnson is known to have been prepared to answer the charges but he could see which way the wind was blowing. It was therefore decided that Johnson would leave his position, the school, and his house, before the following Lady Day, or forfeit two hundred pounds. In return, he would be paid a pension for life.

William Saunders was now told to leave, and Thomas Miles made headmaster at a reduced salary of forty pounds which would increase to fifty pounds on Johnson's death. Miles, though, did not ever take up the post. Perhaps he feared working in an atmosphere of what was obviously considerable confusion and in any case, numbers were still exceedingly low. His replacement was John Womack, a Bachelor of Arts from Corpus Christi College, Cambridge. The latter did not hold the poisoned chalice for long and died in April 1722. By now, the school had had five headmasters in little over two years.

Johnson himself fared little better. His story ended in misery, and his life came to an end in mysterious circumstances:

> "Some time afterwards, in a fit of despondency, he drowned himself in a small stream, which runs through Nottingham Meadows. The Reverend Timothy Wylde has heard Mr Chapel

speak of the extreme horror with which he was impressed, on meeting one evening, as he was walking in the meadows, a venerable grey-haired man, carried on a bier. It was Johnson. He appeared to have been sitting on the bank of the rivulet, and was found in shallow water with his head downward."

The incident was even reported in London newspapers:

"They write from Nottingham that some days since, the Rev Mr Richard Johnson, lately Master of the Free School there, being a little Melancholly, took a walk into the Meadows, and drowned himself in a Pit near the Old Trent."

Despite his apparent suicide, Johnson was eventually to be buried in consecrated ground. It may be that he was given the benefit of the doubt and his death was considered an unfortunate accident. He may have had some kind of seizure or fit. Equally, if it were suicide, then it may have been decided that he was insane at the time he committed the act.

It has been suggested by a number of analysts that Johnson's burial in consecrated ground may indicate that his death was not self-inflicted, but was actually murder. Consider some (admittedly) circumstantial evidence. Johnson was an awkward figure, a political problem and a financial burden to the establishment. It may have been the case that somebody's life was easier if Johnson were no longer around. His drowning was extremely mysterious. He was seriously infirm and racked with pain in all his limbs. Why did he then go for a long walk alone at the side of the river? And how did he then manage to drown in the "shallow water" of a "small stream"? Johnson's unexplained death remains one of the most intriguing aspects of Nottingham's history.

This era marks probably the lowest level to which the school has ever sunk. For years afterwards, wary of appointing another highly qualified and learned man who would turn out to be a second Johnson, the Council limited itself to local men whose characters were well known, even if that meant that they did not have any university experience.

1718

One textbook that the boys are known to have used was Corderius' *Colloquies*, which was in relatively simple Latin and contained dialogues between a Master and his pupils on a number of different topics. It was designed to teach morals and good behaviour.

Monday, January 3rd 1718

A plaque in St Mary's Church is believed to describe the education given at the Free School:

> "Here lyes Interr'd HENRY eldest son of John Plumptre Esq, Born 22 July 1708. deceased Janry 3, 1718/9 In these few and tender Years he had to a great Degree made himself Master of the *Jewish, Roman* and *English* HISTORY, the HEATHEN MYTHOLOGY and the French Tongue: and was not inconsiderably advanced in the *Latin*".

Circa 1725

In the summer, classes began at 7 a.m. and continued until 11 a.m. The afternoon began at 1 p.m. and finished at 5 p.m. or later, if the Master so decided. From October 14th to February 14th school began at 8 a.m. and finished at 4 p.m. It was a six day week but the Master was allowed to grant holidays and extra playtimes up to twelve hours per week.

1736

The school purchased a pair of globes but around 1799 they were stolen by Alderman Worthington. When he died, the executors of his will seized them and they were lost to the school.

Sunday, November 15th 1750

An advertisement was placed in the *Nottingham Weekly Courant* to the effect that in the Free School "those Boys, who have not Time or Capacity to become well acquainted with Latin and Greek, before they are removed to Trades, should be well instructed in their Own language; in order to render the Free Grammar School of Nottingham as beneficial as possible to the Sons of Burgesses and others, the Masters thereof have resolved, besides the usual Exercises of the School, to teach them English-Grammar, and a proper and elegant Manner of reading the most polite English Authors.-Those parents also, who desire it, may have their Children taught French, Geography, and the use of the Globes, with everything that is necessary, to qualify them for any genteel Employment or Profession, without any additional Fee or Reward."

This marked a radical departure from the curriculum as it had existed in the school for the past two hundred and fifty years.

Thursday, August 24th 1758 - Friday, February 1st 1793

Timothy Wylde became the longest serving Master in the history of the Free School (1758 – 1793). He did not have a degree but was a learned man who had a personal library of well over two hundred books, mainly on classical subjects, theology, history and literature. He was fond of tobacco and snuff and spent large sums on wine and other drinks. His shopping list included articles such as lump-sugar, nutmeg, mustard and honey. He wrote many letters and duly received replies from all over the country. Most interesting of all, perhaps, is that when he lived in Winchester he spent many hours every week on the bowling green. He regularly played for money, but lost most of the time with his usual stakes being anything from sixpence to 5s 6d. Only comparatively rarely did he win. As far as the Free School was concerned, Wylde seems to have been happy to leave things as they had been under his predecessor, John Henson. He did not reverse Henson's decision to introduce more modern subjects and actually allowed the classical subjects to decline considerably. By the time he left, hardly any of the boys was going on to university to pursue an academic career. The school had around fifty boys at this time. On average they entered at the age of eight and left at around fifteen.

1763

Gilbert Wakefield, in his memoirs, recalled his treatment at the hands of the Reverend Samuel Berdmore, who was the Usher at this time:

> "Soon after I went to this School, the reception which a request for leave of absence, inspected and approved by my father, met with from this gentleman, I shall not hastily forget. He threatened, with great snappishness, to flog me. I was alarmed beyond measure at a threat equally inhuman and unjust... the efforts of near thirty years have not been able to soothe the sore."

Wakefield was later to die of sunstroke at an advanced age, having sat on Brighton Beach, on "a warm, treacherous, sun-shining day."

Saturday, November 22nd 1766

The school's Usher, the Reverend William Fell had been in the job for only two years when the *Nottingham Journal* announced that "On Tuesday morning last, the Reverend William Fell married at St Mary's Mrs Newsam, a widow with a fortune of £10,000."

April 1776

The Reverend George Wayte was Usher at the Free School from 1732-1747, as well as being Vicar of Radford and Curate of Lenton where he lived. He was an enthusiastic worker for his parishioners and was known as a bit of a local character. He excelled himself in his seventieth year, however, when along with three other men, all from Radford, he was charged at the Quarter Sessions with breaking and entering. The victim was Samuel Eaton and all four defendants were found guilty of "expelling and keeping out the said Samuel Eaton and his wife and spoiling and detaining one Flock Bed, one chair, one Coal Pick, three wood planks, and one stocking-frame of the value of £9 10s 0d." All four men were fined a penny each. Even now, two centuries later, Wayte remains the oldest deputy headmaster to be convicted of burglary.

Friday, February 1st 1793

Timothy Wylde finally retired. For the last eighteen months there had been some dissatisfaction with the eighty-five year old's work. Eventually, a deputation arrived from the Nottingham Corporation, for a discussion of the terms under which the Master would leave. It included his son, Thomas, and his nephew, Isaac. The package was that Wylde would receive his salary for the rest of his life and either free use of the school house or twenty pounds per annum. Amazingly, Wylde wanted time to think about this fabulous offer but he finally resigned and went to live in High Pavement. He died on January 26th 1799.

An unknown date in the eighteenth century

A fight between boys of the Lower and Upper Schools spilled onto the street and became so violent that troops were summoned to break it up. In what might nowadays be considered a slight over-reaction, the soldiers opened fire and four boys were killed.

1804-1805

During this financial year the Free School spent one hundred pounds on the Schoolmaster's salary, and one pound on the school horse. The horse had the important job of collecting the many tithes to which the school was entitled and may well have had a much higher level of performance than the Schoolmaster himself.

1807

The Corporation drew up a constitution for the school. The hours of work were listed carefully and so were the holidays. An attempt at an exact curriculum was made, with the subjects to be taught all set down. A minimum age of eight was established for entry to the school and the maximum number of pupils was to be sixty. At this time each member of the Corporation was allowed to nominate in turn a specific boy for entry to the school at a special meeting. Boys tended to leave the school in a rather haphazard way but when there were a number of vacancies, a list of nominees could be drawn up and they would then fill the gaps. Quite often boys would be nominated and accepted but would then fail to take up the place for some reason. Occasionally, as in the case of Henry Strelley, the son of a butcher in Pepper Street, the reason was their premature death.

Tuesday, April 7th 1807

The Borough Records complain that "Scholars are unable to read. Ordered that the Schoolwardens be Authorized and Directed by this Hall to reject and not admit any Scholars into the Freeschool if it shall appear that they are not able to read."

Sometime after Friday, June 16th 1808

From this date onwards, the Schoolwardens' annual balance sheets were placed in a leather bound volume, instead of merely being kept on various separate sheets of parchment or paper. On an unknown date, an unknown clerk has decorated the title page of the new volume with the coat of arms presumably associated with Dame Agnes Mellers at that time, namely three black birds on a widow's lozenge. This is the first known instance of this coat of arms being linked with the school.

1811

During this year, Mr Toplis taught thirty-two pupils and Dr Robert Wood, the Usher, had twenty-four. The boys learned writing, accounts and a little Latin. The Mayor, Aldermen and Councillors made their usual annual inspection and, highly delighted with the school, awarded Toplis the customary bonus of one hundred pounds and Wood his forty pounds. Toplis, however, was expected to use fifty pounds of his own gratuity to pay the writing master. The latter was a Quaker named Charles Watson. Around this time, Mr Watson refused for religious reasons to serve in the Nottingham militia. He was fined twenty-five pounds by the overseers of St Mary's parish but refused to pay. For this reason the money was deducted by the Schoolwardens from his wages. Later that year, for the excellence of their work, Toplis, Wood and Watson were all made Freemen of the Borough. This honour usually cost a fee of some thirty guineas.

1812

The Master and Usher complained that a large number of books had been stolen. The Corporation circulated a leaflet to all the boys at the school that anybody caught doing this would be expelled.

January 1814

Dr Wood wrote a letter of complaint to the Schoolwardens that they should not admit any boys who would not be able to cope with work at the school. As Usher, it was Wood's job to teach the younger boys and he had recently turned away individuals who were under eight years of age or who could merely recite the letters of the alphabet.

1816

The writing master was now John Peck Hemm, a master of "penmanship" and an accomplished illustrator and engraver. He was also a spendthrift and seemed incapable of living within his means, whatever they might be. At this time, the writing master was entitled to claim his expenses back either from the Headmaster or the Schoolwardens. Hemm therefore requested payment for two thousand quills at £1 2s 0d a thousand, and three thousand quills at £1 12s 0d. If true, this would have meant that every boy was using a hundred pens a year. The writing master could make even more profit by buying the items in as quills and then cutting them into pens in his own spare time.

1818

By now, the school was teaching English Grammar, reading, writing and arithmetic:

> "Its former celebrity in Classical Learning is at an end."

1819

During the course of the academic year, the Free School spent £164 3s 8d on joiners to repair the building, a rather bizarre £11 19s 7d on police officers and a completely understandable £32 9s 6d on alcohol for the Staff and Governors.

1827-1828

The Schoolmaster's salary was still fixed at £100 and a grand total of £3 6s 0d was spent on candles and coal to light and heat the school.

1828

The Charity Commissioners made several criticisms of the school. On the one hand, they felt that it should be offering a better classical education as had been the intention of the original foundress, Agnes Mellers. They fully understood that the majority of the boys were the sons of tradesmen who would have very little use for either Latin or Greek but felt that, with only a little reorganisation, the boys could learn the Classics as well as Reading, Writing and Arithmetic. Secondly they felt that the accounts of the school could have been kept more carefully. As a relatively minor point, the Commissioners drew attention to the inventive ways by which Mr Hemm, the school's writing master, supplemented his admittedly meagre salary. As well as selling quills therefore, he charged all of his pupils 2s 6d every quarter for the fact that he taught them. He also received 1d commission from a local shop for every exercise book which his pupils purchased there. Within six months the Corporation took the Commissioners' advice, and increased John Hemm's annual salary to £70.

Monday, April 13th 1829

This date marked the entrance to the Free School of Edwin Woodhouse. He was eventually to be expelled, "having inflicted a serious wound with a knife" on a fellow pupil.

July 1829

Despite his new salary of £70, Hemm was still in serious financial straits. In 1821, he had started up a private school for young ladies in Castlegate and had run it as a completely commercial venture, even advertising in the Nottingham Review on several occasions. He now decided to stop coming to the Free School completely so that he could concentrate on his young ladies. What he did not do was to stop taking his seventy pounds per annum salary and the Town Clerk was forced to write to him to remind him of his obligations. Hemm obviously knew what was more rewarding financially and resigned from the Free School on March 30th 1830.

Thursday, September 8th 1831

To celebrate the coronation of William IV, all 56 boys were treated to a special dinner at a cost of 1s 3d each. The three teachers had a 2s 0d dinner and two bottles of wine at 5s 0d and punch to the value of 5s 0d were consumed. The total was £4 11s 0d.

1831

Mr Hemm the former writing Master published the second volume of his three volume work, *Portraits of the Royal Family in Penmanship*. It contained portraits of George IV, William IV and six royal dukes. Hemm's books were published by subscription, with up to two hundred and fifty people promising to purchase the finished work. One of those who bought his *Portraits of the Royal Family in Penmanship* was George Green, the famous mathematician who lived in the windmill at Sneinton. Others to buy his works were the King of Belgium, the Duchess of Cambridge and the Lord Chancellor. Hemm was a fine advertiser of his own works and persuaded Queen Adelaide to allow him to dedicate one of his books to her, thereby making it much more likely that some of the many minor courtiers and nobles would find it incumbent upon themselves to buy a copy. On the other hand, Hemm's work must have been of good quality if the reviews are to be believed: "these splendid specimens confer no trifling distinction on the Grammar School of Nottingham, where this talented penman was engaged." (*The Imperial Magazine*); "the grace, freedom and delicacy of the flourishes have never been equalled" (*The Manchester Guardian*). Hemm had left

Nottingham in 1830, and had gone to Manchester where he seemed to have disappeared from prominence.

June 1832

The new writing master, Mr Dudley, is thought to have shouldered much of the burden of running the school while the Master and Usher were either arguing or simply absent. In recognition of this, in September, his salary was raised to one hundred pounds per annum.

Late 1833

When the Reverend Butler became Headmaster, many changes quickly took place. The number of boys went up from sixty to eighty and they were divided into the English and Classical departments. Four masters were now employed, with two classrooms, one above the other, lit by candles in the dark days of winter. The English boys worked in the downstairs classroom from 8-11 a.m., and then from 2-4 p.m. After 11 a.m. and 4 p.m., the Classical boys came downstairs and worked under the supervision of the English teachers for a further hour. There were half holidays on Wednesdays and Saturdays. In addition, the Master was also the Chaplain to the Town Gaol and his duties there often clashed with his lessons. In that case, the boys might get a half day holiday.

Mid-June 1835

One of the boys' favourite occupations was "land measuring". To do this they went out to survey pieces of land with the English masters. On one occasion they went to a meadow beside the River Trent, and on another to some land next to the General Cemetery. Ironically, this particular area was later to be laid out as Waverley Street. This year, just before the Midsummer Examinations, the whole school spent an entire "field day" on the Forest. This cost a total of ten shillings for the refreshments given to the four masters and eighty boys.

During this era, the boys spent much of their leisure time in vigorous exercise, quite often of a fairly violent nature. There were continual fights, for example, with the lads who worked in a small factory in nearby Barkergate. On half days, such as Wednesday or Saturday, the boys would usually go off to the Park which at the time was "a fine open, breezy place where cows grazed and bluebells grew." The boys would divide themselves into groups and play "games to their hearts' content". A large rock at the foot of what was called the "Bay of Biscay" was the scene for many vigorous games of attack and siege and was stoutly defended at all times. The boys loved to play in the little caves in the rock at the side of the River Leen and one of their favourites, nicknamed the "Doctor's Shop" was seldom quiet or deserted for long. Any games and disputes among the boys often reflected the differences between their parents. One source of argument, for example, was whether citizens should pay rates to the church or not. Boys frequently formed sides between Church and Chapel. Very often, inside the school, these two warring groups would then fight for possession of the central stairs, which led from the Lower School to the Upper School. It was around this time that, as an old boy, Canon Lacey, recollected, when the boys all had a candle each in the winter, they "would extinguish their candles and while the wax was still fluid, they would throw them up with the purpose of making them stick to the roof."

Spring 1836

William R. Stevenson, who was later to reminisce in *The Forester*, joined the school. William Butler was still the Headmaster, with the Reverend Manners "a superior man", as the second Classical master. The two classrooms on the top floor of the school were used by Messrs Butler and Manners for the forty or so Classical scholars. The two downstairs classrooms were used for the forty boys of the English side. In one English room, Mr Sparey was in charge, a "splendid writer, and a fair arithmetician and grammarian, but a rather rough man with a love for the cane". He was assisted by Mr Hewson, "a teacher of a more patient temper". He taught not just English but also French, teaching grammar, setting exercises and marking them. A "foreigner" used to come in to teach the boys correct pronunciation of the language. Among the first to do this was Count Assolari, a "handsome figure, bronzed face and fierce moustachios, looked like a fine Cavalry Officer, but was no good as a teacher." The next incumbent was Monsieur Vogue, "most polite and courteous, at times unable to understand the rough blunt ways of English boys and yet too gentle spirited to rebuke us."

As regarded the teaching standards, Butler "was in his prime". Mr Manners was "eccentric, but his teaching was stimulating". Boys did not often stay on beyond fourteen or fifteen years of age, and did not therefore reach the same standards that they were destined to reach by the end of the century. In Latin they studied Cicero and Virgil, in Greek, mainly the New Testament, and selections of Xenophon. In Maths, it was Euclid, Mensuration, and Algebra as far as Quadratic Equations. No Science was taught. In general parents were indifferent to all of these subjects, and were merely anxious that their sons should obtain a plain English education in which initiation into the three R's was regarded as chiefly important. The boys were also asked to compose short essays or poems in English Composition lessons. At the end of every six months, there was an examination, which was always conducted orally, either by the masters in the presence of some of the gentlemen of the town, or by William Enfield, who was later to be the Town Clerk. The History examination was always keenly contested, and varied between English, Roman or Bible History. Prizes were offered for the best Essay and Poem, with the subject being chosen from the period of history which was studied during that particular half year. The best essay and poem would both be read out aloud on Prize Day.

There was no playground, but boys would play in Stoney Street, which was, at the time, a very quiet thoroughfare. On one side, where Adams and Company's warehouse was built in later years, there were a number of good-sized private houses, one or two with gardens enclosed with walls. On the other side, between Barker Gate and Woolpack Lane, there was a row of very ancient Almshouses. Half an hour before afternoon school began, the boys would all assemble in this street and "passers-by had the opportunity of witnessing some lively scenes, no doubt, residents in the houses voted us a great nuisance."

Half way down Barker Gate was "Titterton's famous toffy shop, where a roaring trade was often done". Fights still occurred, as they always had, with the boys who worked at a small factory in this street, as the latter annoyed the Free School boys and usurped their territory in Stoney Street. One day, Walter Yates became the school's champion and gave a severe thrashing to one of the factory's biggest bullies. That episode kept them quiet for quite some time afterwards. In later life, Yates became a surgeon, but was destined to die young.

Thursday, June 22nd 1837

At Prize Day, which was later reported in the *Nottingham Journal*, eighteen of the eighty-six boys in the school won prizes. They were for achievements such as the best essay in verse, the best writing, the best ciphering, top of the class in Classics, the history of England, or French. The only boy to win two prizes was William Stevenson, who was an exceptionally gifted student. Unfortunately, he was unable to go to either Oxford or Cambridge because he was a Baptist.

Friday, February 23rd 1838

Another gifted pupil was John Russell Hind who, as a hobby, studied the influence of the moon and other planets on the weather. While still at school, he wrote weather forecasts for the Nottingham Journal and these appeared on a weekly basis. He later became President of the Royal Astronomical Society and discovered the sun's corona, ten asteroids and two comets, tracking their appearances back to 11 B.C.

June 1838

John Manners left the Free School to become Headmaster of Wesley College in Sheffield. He was "eccentric but his teaching was stimulating. He would set us thinking by asking questions, and then listening with great interest to our replies as though he were learning from us. But he simply wanted to draw us out as Socrates did the sharp lads of his time."

Manners was replaced by Samuel Langworth, a local man, who does not seem to have had a degree, and it was not long before the school's academic standards began to slip.

Thursday, November 8th 1838

On this day John Thompson entered the Free School. He had only one leg and his mother wished him "to qualify as a schoolmaster." Despite his disabilities, the boy was "diligent and intelligent". Eventually, he was to gain employment as a School Assistant with Mr Keyworth at another (unnamed) school in Nottingham.

November, 1853

Edward Thurman left the Free School. According to the register, he had "played truant, and made little progress." At this time, truancy, very often aided and abetted by the boy's parents, seems to have been a not infrequent problem. In some cases, the boys' absences may have been to work in their father's business, perhaps in times of family illness.

Late 1854

Great scandal was caused in the town when the two writing masters, Messrs Sparey and Hewson, decided one Saturday evening to seek refreshment together in a local tavern on Long Row. They grew progressively more and more drunk and eventually managed to disgrace themselves thoroughly. This was an escapade which they might well have got away with, had it not been for the fact that their appalling behaviour coincided more or less exactly with the arrival of a Government Inspector who had recently come to the area. He found out about the episode and, as might be imagined, a great deal of embarrassment was caused for the school. Mr Sparey was told that if the offence was ever repeated, he would be instantly dismissed. Hewson fared even worse. A witness in the subsequent inquiry actually said "I do not send my boys to this School. I should not like to so long as a character like Hewson taught there." Hewson was then forced to resign.

July 1855

The Trustees made a number of other suggestions, namely that the Headmaster should work only at the school and should cease being the Chaplain at the Gaol. He should cease to take private pupils for his own profit. Examinations should be written rather than oral, and prizes should be stamped with the crest of the Corporation. Religious instruction should be introduced to the school curriculum. Every day should begin with a prayer and that prayer should be written by the Headmaster, and approved by the Trustees. The latter were also rather unhappy that the Headmaster had abused his power by purchasing twenty-four inkwells without their prior knowledge. Most important of all, perhaps, the Trustees asked the Commissioners for permission to sell the Stoney Street School and to move to a new site. This would be in what was then called the "Sand Fields", an area of roughly triangular shape, between Trinity Church and Forest Road.

Michaelmas 1857

James Tomlinson entered the school. He was later to leave, the register recording that he was "very slow, removed by his father rather than comply with the Rule not to let him be absent without previous leave."

Michaelmas 1858

According to the register, Charles Frederick Ingoldby "played truant and was idle and was sent away because he would not ask pardon for misconduct."

May 1858

William Butler's son was so ill that he begged the Trustees to allow him to vacate the Master's house so that the whole family could go and live in the country, far from the pollution of the narrow streets of the Broadmarsh. To their credit, the trustees agreed and the Butlers moved to Belvoir Terrace in Sneinton. It was a vain act, however, as their poor son died soon afterwards. The Master's house does not seem to have ever been occupied again.

December 1858

After almost five years of, presumably, temperance and model behaviour, Mr Sparey, the remaining member of the Long Row Two resigned. The Trustees' minutes give no reason for his departure. It was not, however, as if Mr Sparey was unused to criticism. In 1856, the Headmaster had written to the Trustees about "Mr Sparey's bad English", and then, when it was suggested that no member of staff should be allowed to keep a public house, it was (again) Mr Sparey's name that cropped up. The latter countered the accusation by saying that that the inn was held in the name of his wife's sister.

The late 1850s

Mr Martin Inett Preston recollected that the Free School "was a rough school, it was a bad school, it was lighted by farthing dips, it was badly warmed and worse ventilated. Our code of honour contained only one rule: 'Thou shalt not betray thy school-fellow'. But we loved the place."

Circa 1860

In 1931, the school magazine published a brief reminiscence of the Free School in Stoney Street. It came from the oldest Old Nottinghamian of the era, Mr John Braithwaite of Bournemouth:

> "There were two rooms, one above the other, about 30 by 20 feet in area. The upper school was on the first floor, the lower on the ground floor. The rooms were low and badly lighted and contained four or five desks, into each of which five or six boys were cramped. The windows looked out on to lank walls, the only artificial light was tallow candles, the ceiling and other walls were whitewashed and grimy, the flooring was worn and old, the desks deeply furrowed and carved, the playground a mere backyard covered with stones, the sanitary arrangements inadequate and all other comforts such as seats, shelves and drinking water entirely lacking. The form-room, however, contained two rows of pegs and some miniature lockers for the first form, and the front facade was of stone and the entrance from Stoney Street was a wide door with windows on each side."

Mr Braithwaite recounted "with a boyish delight of the games they played, top-spinning and marbles and rough games like "King of the Castle", besides stone throwing "at anything in sight." He concluded with the happy times spent in the school of two rooms and an "attic"; but he also said that he often thinks of the increased advantages afforded by the "new" school and hopes they will long continue.

June 1860

Very little had yet been done about the physical details of constructing the new school. The Bowling Alley Field had just been divided up into fifteen separate building lots, and was being advertised with a lease for ninety-nine years. The site was on a sandstone ridge which ran from west to east. To the south, was the recently established Arboretum Park. To the north was the Forest, which was a vast open space, preserved by the Enclosure Act of 1845, and used for drilling troops, cricket, and horse racing. Another contemporary description said that the site was "on the recently enclosed Lammas Lands, between the Arboretum and the Racecourse, so that however much the town extends, it is not likely to be enclosed by buildings. There is ground enough for a large playground." At the time, Forest Road ran along the top of a gorse covered ridge, and some of the famous windmills may still have been there. The greatest pity, of course, was that the Trustees did not take the opportunity to acquire enough land for the school to have its own games fields on site. While, in retrospect, this seems regrettable, it should not be forgotten that these events all happened well before team sport was organised in schools and that the Arboretum Street site must have seemed ideal for an absolute maximum of only two hundred boys.

Thursday, July 19th, 1860

At the age of eleven years and one month, Jessy Boot (sic) was elected to the Free School. He was born as Jessie Boot in Nottingham on June 2nd 1850. His father was a farm labourer called John, and his mother was originally Mary Wells. The family lived in an area of the town called variously Hockley or Goosegate, which at that time was extremely poor and overcrowded. His father opened a herbal remedy shop locally in 1849, but unfortunately passed away in early 1860. His mother, by now the Widow Mary Boot, decided to enrol her son in the Free School. On Thursday, July 19th, of that year, at the age of eleven years and one month, Jessy (sic) Boot was included on the register as a pupil at the Free School. He was to remain in Mr Field's English Department until his departure in August 1863, a period of just over two years. Meanwhile, Mrs Boot continued with the shop, helped out by her family and friends, and, from 1863 onwards, by her son Jesse. By 1871, Jesse was a co-partner with his mother in the imaginatively named "M & J Boot", and in 1883 the shop became "Boot and Company Limited". The business then expanded to Sheffield in 1884, and by 1900 there were Boots' shops over the whole country, reaching their peak with 560 branches in 1913. The business was sold by Sir Jesse Boot, who became 1st Baron Trent in 1917. It was bought by the Americans for £2.25 million. In 1933, however, during the Great Depression, the company was re-acquired by a British syndicate. Its head was the grandson of the founder, John Boot, who had inherited the title Baron Trent from his father, who had himself died in Jersey in 1931.

Wednesday, August 1st 1860

Although Master of the Free School, William Butler also acted as Chaplain to the Town Gaol. On one occasion, recalled Mr Braithwaite in later years:

"A man named Fenton was sentenced to death at the Notts. Assizes for a murder in the northern part of the county. Our headmaster, the Rev. W.Butler, as Chaplain of the County Gaol, was required to read the burial service at the execution, which was fixed for 8 o'clock one morning at the Gaol in the High Pavement. The second master read prayers, and we waited, silent and awed. Presently the door was burst open, and poor Mr Butler, with face white and drawn, stumbled in and staggered to his pew, almost spent. After resting awhile he stood up and said, "Boys, I have just come from" and then he broke down. After recovering himself, he began again, and preached us a more impressive sermon than I have heard from any pulpit. As no one was in the mood for lessons we were sent home for the day."

John Fenton, a blacksmith and publican, was hanged at the age of thirty-seven for the murder of Charles Spencer at Walkeringham on March 6th 1860. This was a public execution, held on the front steps of what is now the Shire Hall in High Pavement. The crowd, however, was a lot smaller than expected. This was because, fourteen years previously, the last public hanging had resulted in the crushing to death of seventeen people, almost all of them children.

1860

The Reverend William Butler, his physical constitution already somewhat weakened by the stresses and strains of the Sir Thomas White's Loan Money scandal in 1856 and the death of his son in 1858, finally resigned on the grounds of poor health. He was clearly a tired man and had himself suggested a year before that the move to a new school would be better carried out under a new headmaster.

December 1860

After Butler's resignation, it was hoped that the school would transfer to a new site within the next couple of years. For this reason the Trustees asked the Reverend Frederick Teeling Cusins (the Usher) to act as Headmaster until the move was completed. As might be anticipated, things did not go as planned and Cusins was to be kept hanging on, hoping one day to be Headmaster, for almost seven years.

Christmas 1860

Mr Braithwaite reminisced about a famous fight inside the Stoney Street building:

> "One breaking-up day (I think it was Christmas 1860) there was a bit of a riot in the lower school. One of the pupils, a big hulking fellow, who was leaving that quarter, had some kind of a grievance against the Master, and for revenge he set to and smashed everything in the room that was breakable, and incited the younger boys to help him. In a very short time, the room was a complete wreck, and when the master, Mr Hall, returned to see what the row was all about, they seized him and locked him in the room amid the ruins. Then they thought they would serve the upper room in the same way, but we had been watching their proceedings from above and were ready for them. When they attempted to mount the staircase to our room we met them at the bottom and a battle royal began. Though they exceeded us in numbers we had the advantage of position, and after a regular fight, which lasted over half-an-hour, we made a concerted rush, and cleared them out at the front door. Only fists were used, and though there were many bruises no bones were broken, and the lower boys had the most casualties. But it was a grand fight!
>
> And with jesting and with laughter still is the story told,
>
> How well the top boys kept the stairs in the brave days of old. "

Monday, August 1st 1864

The Charity Commissioners approved the plans for the new school. It was to have two sections, the Upper School and the Lower School, the latter managed by the Under Master. There would be fixed fees and the Headmaster and Usher would receive a pre-determined percentage of this money in addition to their ordinary salary. Anybody who wished could pay fifty pounds and have a boy of their choice admitted.

Sometime shortly after 8 a.m. on Wednesday, August 10th 1864

Like many of the previous Masters of the Free School, Frederick Cusins acted as Chaplain to the Town Gaol. An old boy reminisced how on one occasion: "looking very pale, he entered the room and said, "Boys, I have just seen a man hanged. I cannot teach you today. You may all go home." It may have been episodes like this which led to the rather grim tradition that every time a criminal was executed in Nottingham Gaol, only some two hundred metres from the Free School, the boys had a holiday. The man who was hanged on this day was Richard Thomas Parker, aged twenty-nine. After a lifetime of being overindulged by his parents, he went to a cricket match at Newark-on-Trent, and consumed, as was his wont, too much alcohol. He came home and shot both his parents from the window of the house. His father, Thomas Parker, recovered from his wounds, but his seventy-six-year old wife did not. This was the last public execution in Nottingham, and the executioner was Mr Asken of York. Parker was buried inside the gaol.

Early 1865

A competition was held to design the new school and the winning architect was Mr Arthur Wilson of Castlegate. His design, however, was rejected by the Charity Commissioners, as unsuitable. The runner up, Mr R. C. Sutton of Bromley House, Angel Row was then named as Architect of the school building. When construction work got under way, however, virtually no progress was made and Sutton was quickly dismissed.

The next architect was Thomas Simpson, who had not even taken part in the original competition. His plans, which contained, apparently, substantial contributions from Messrs T. C. Hull and Evans, were deemed satisfactory by the Trustees and the Charity Commissioners although insofar as he was by now the third architect to be engaged, the town was swept by increasingly wild rumours about what had happened.

Thursday, March 22nd 1866

In 1865, William Henry Revis had participated at the meeting of the local shinty club, when it was proposed that Nottingham Forest Foot Ball Club be formed. Shinty is nowadays played mainly in Scotland but at this time it was much more widespread throughout England. It is a hockey type sport, derived, it is thought, from the original Irish sport of Hurling. The momentous event took place at the Clinton Arms Hotel, in Sherwood Street. Revis was later to serve on the fledgling club's founding committee, along with Thomas George Howitt.

Revis soon became a regular player for the new club, and is credited with their first ever "goal", a "match winning try against the Notts Club in March 1866" scored after a close race with W. Browne. The match, watched by hundreds of curious spectators, was billed as "The Garibaldis v The Lambs" and the full story appears in a booklet entitled *History of Nottingham Forest Football Club* published in 1891, in connection with a bazaar held to raise funds for the club at the Mechanics' Hall in Nottingham. Events were recalled, albeit nearly twenty five years later:

> "The first series of matches between the Notts and Forest Clubs was played on the Forest towards the end of the season of 1866. Neither side had scored until close upon time, when after a sort of steeplechase race across the goal line and over the railings nearest the grand stand, between Hugh Browne and W. H. Revis, the ball was touched down by the latter and the place kick, 15 yards at right angles from the goal line, being taken by the same player, the first of many games between the two clubs in after years, ended in a win of one goal to nothing for the Forest. In order to obtain the goal a ball had to be kicked between the goal posts, there being no cross bar at that time. Mr J.S.Scrimshaw was Umpire."

William Henry Revis was born in 1849. His father was William Revis, a corn dealer of Bilbie Street, Nottingham. Revis entered the Free School on July 26th 1859 at the age of ten years six months, initially as a member of the Classical Department. William's elder brother, Joseph Revis, had already entered the school on July 29th 1845, at the age of nine years five months. He was placed "on trial", and left at Midsummer 1850. At this time, his father's profession is listed as a baker in Mansfield Road. William Revis had rather more academic success than his elder brother, however, and proved to be an intelligent student who won the Mayor of Nottingham's Prize for an English Essay in 1862. The following year he was awarded the Headmaster's Prize for Latin Composition and received a Second Class in the Oxford Local Examinations. He left the Free School in March 1864.

Chapter 7: A New School and a New Name

Noon, Thursday, October 18th 1866

The Foundation Stone for the new school was laid by the Right Honourable Lord Belper. The guests had been asked to assemble in the "Eastern Corridor of the Arboretum" at 11.30 a.m., and the ceremony itself followed half an hour later. It took place in heavy rain, and was watched by the whole school, the Trustees and around a hundred and twenty Old Boys. Eventually, it proved impossible to continue in the open air of the "Centre Corridor" of the Arboretum, and the whole party was forced to move to the Arboretum Rooms, where they were entertained with a series of speeches and "Wine and Biscuits". Strangely enough, the Foundation Stone appears to have soon been lost, and it has never been rediscovered. It contained "an aperture, with various documents in a bottle." Presumably, it was overlain with other stones, and its whereabouts were, quite simply, forgotten.

Problems and disputes were continually to dog the erection of the new building. It was still considered that the school was "quite in the outskirts of the town, and inconvenient of access." Much of the stonework would eventually be found to be well below standard.

April 1867

Joseph Frederick Hull, aged ten years and eleven months, failed to return to school after the Easter break, having "died of fever". The Free School register records many such sad events, with the victims perishing from the most unspecific and vague of causes.

June 1867

An eleven year old boy, Benjamin Arthur Heald, who had entered the English School in January 1866, is recorded as having "died from the effects of sunbathing". It is not known if this occurred at the Free School or at his home.

November 1867

Despite the success of Frederick Cusins as Acting Headmaster, his job was widely advertised.

1868

A Charity Commissioner reported on the High School under Frederick Cusins:

> "He is doing good work at this time. Under the present master a higher class of boys have begun to frequent the school, and their discipline and demeanour appears to be thoroughly satisfactory."

Overall, the standards under Frederick Cusins rose considerably. It was completely due to his "self-sacrificing energy" that the school was constantly overflowing with pupils during the seven years of his temporary leadership.

January 1868

The people of Nottingham were dismayed to hear that all boys would now have to pay fees. A writer to the *Nottingham Journal* complained that "would-be recipients of this splendid charity are refused admittance to make room for sons of well-to-do tradesmen and manufacturers".

Wednesday, March 11th 1868

A prize giving was held at which Frederick Cusins acted as Headmaster. The awards were based on the pupils' performances in the Oxford Local Examinations. The prizes were presented by Dr Vaughan, the former Headmaster of Harrow, and he said that the people of Nottingham were fortunate in "having such a master as the gentleman who was now at the head of their Grammar School." This was greeted with loud cheering. The man who had marked the examination papers, Canon Melville of Worcester, said that he hoped that Cusins' appointment would be confirmed, and that his position would be strengthened by the further success of the School.

The Trustees had postponed their announcement of the new Headmaster at least once, and at this time, no decision had yet been revealed. The Stoney Street School would close in a fortnight's time, and most people thought that this would mark the beginning of Cusin's reign as the Headmaster.

Friday, March 13th 1868

A shocking announcement was made. Mr Robert Dixon, the second master at Hereford Cathedral School, was named as the new Headmaster. This news "electrified the inhabitants of Nottingham from one end of the town to the other." It was considered a slur on Cusins' abilities, a shock to his pupils, and an act which would jeopardise his future career. After seven years of faithful service, he was being cast off without any thanks whatsoever. The Trustees were accused of a "mean and cowardly deception", as they had dismissed Cusins with only twelve days' notice. Dr Dixon was a fine scholar, both of Classics and Mathematics and his hobbies were Geology, History, and Literature.

Tuesday, March 17th 1868

The *Nottingham Journal* declared that Cusins was "a gentleman who for the past ten years has conducted (the school) with success." The new headmaster was "an unknown man, younger in years and less experienced." With the decision, the Trustees were "following their policy of doing everything in their power to destroy the usefulness of a noble institution." The outrage was to rumble on for many weeks, and to attract letters from Nottingham and beyond. Immense speculation grew as to the reasons for the Trustees decision. They varied from "sectarian rancour" to "party spite", from "personal hostility" and "despotic tyranny", to "ignorant presumption". Overall, it was judged "a very foolish, cruel and wicked thing".

Wednesday, March 25th 1868

This was the last day of the Stoney Street School. In later years, M.I.Preston recollected how "when prayers, broken by the sobs of the reader, were read for the last time, there were very few dry eyes even among us hardened boys." With its closure, Cusin's rule as Acting Headmaster came to an end. The man who had inspected the school annually since 1860, Mr George Hale of Sidney Sussex College, Cambridge, had always been most enthusiastic about Cusins' leadership. He said that his dismissal in favour of Dr Dixon was "cruel and perfectly incomprehensible conduct of the Trustees". The boys gave Mr Cusins "a beautiful ormolu time piece", and his wife received a biscuit box. The head-boy, John Russell, gave an address, which was later printed out on vellum. Great sorrow was expressed at Mr Cusin's departure, both for him, and the boys themselves. Cusins was dignified in his reply. He said that had received a "tremendous disappointment, but that was neither the time nor the place to enter upon it."

10.00 a.m. on Thursday, April 16th 1868

The boys of the Free School assembled at their new school, many of them accompanied by their parents. The Headmaster explained that the boys would receive a "thorough commercial and a thorough classical education" which would be "as complete as possible". He impressed upon them "the duties and advantages of punctuality and regularity, purposing to enforce strict discipline and strict obedience." He intended to govern "not by caprice, but by law and order."

The *Nottingham Journal* only found out about the ceremony by accident, and its reporter rushed up from the town, only to find the proceedings all but over. The *Nottingham Guardian* carried a long and enthusiastic account, although even as the High School's keenest supporter, it expressed its great regret that Dame Agnes Mellers' instructions were being ignored, and that the school was no longer a "Free Scole".

In the register for the Upper School, the first boy is listed as Henry Barber, who was born on September 30th 1857, and who formally entered the school on March 31st 1868. His father was John Barber, a grocer of Long Row, Nottingham. The Headmaster has added, in black ink, to Henry's entry in the register, "The 1st Boy Admitted into the New School" (sic). Henry left at Christmas 1873. The first boy in the new register for the Lower School was Arthur Sidney Maltby, aged thirteen, who was born on August 13th 1854, and who entered the school on the same day as Henry Barber. Maltby's father was Charles Maltby, a shopkeeper of Clumber Street. Arthur left at Midsummer 1869. In 1931, at the age of seventy-seven, he was to be one of the guests of honour at the school's Speech Day.

The Under Master in the new school was Alexander Irving and in the Upper School, the First Assistant Master was the Reverend Charles Yeld. Mr Charles Bray was the Second Assistant Master. In the Lower School, the First Assistant Master was Mr Henry Seymour, who also taught Drawing, and the Second Assistant Master was Mr James Chester. It was thought that foreign languages could only be taught by native speakers so Monsieur J.L.E.Durand was the French Master and

Herr Forest taught German. Only Mr Bray, who had been Usher under Mr Cusins, had previously worked at Stoney Street.

The finished building contained, to the west, the Upper or Classical School, and to the east, the Lower, or English School. Both rooms measured sixty feet long and thirty feet wide, and had an open timbered roof. There were also sliding doors, which could be pulled back to turn the two schools into one enormous expanse, some 160 feet long, and thirty feet wide. Each school was entered separately by porches right and left of the rear, while the main entrance was by steps from the terrace to the south. In later years, the Upper School at least was to be divided in two with a curtain, to make it easier to teach two classes. Classes would certainly have looked very different in those days. In each corner of the room a master would sit in a high chair, surrounded by his pupils, who would be on benches. Within a few weeks of the school's opening, the Chairman of the Trustees and the Clerk visited Birmingham to see a gas lighting system, intended to replace the candles used at Stoney Street. A special gas supply had to be used for this innovation.

The two schools were completely separate: each had its own "Head of the School", its own head boy and its own prefects. Fees in the Lower School were four guineas per year, and in the Upper School eight guineas per year. This monetary difference caused enormous friction between the two groups, which for many years amounted to a feud. Between the two schools was the splendidly Gothic tower, with two private rooms for the masters, which, in later years, would have other occupants, including the Headmaster and either the School Secretary or the Drill Serjeant. Next to the western porch was a porter's lodge, with a parlour, kitchen, scullery, three bedrooms and cellarage, with the masters' toilets adjoining the eastern porch. Eventually, the cellar of the porter's quarters became a boiler house, and the parlour became a storeroom where generations of caretakers brewed tea until Mr Boot drank the last cup shortly before demolition in 1939.

Most interesting of all, perhaps, was the fact that underneath the main building was a huge cellar where the sandstone base of the building had been hollowed out into a gigantic playroom which occupied the same area as the school above. It was reached by an archway from the terrace at the front of the school, and then by a passageway, along which coal was brought in carts, to avoid damage to the school gardens. The boys were allowed into the cellar to play in winter, or when there was bad weather. The cellar was lit by round windows, high up from inside, but at ground level when viewed from the outside of the building. Underneath the corridor which ran to the classrooms in the north arm was a corresponding tunnel. To the side of this were the boys' toilets, which were dry closets, a primitive kind of toilet, a dining room, and a number of storage rooms. This tunnel would eventually be continued and, as a cutting, link the school with Forest Road.

When the building was completed, it was found to be full of major faults. The architect was accused by the Trustees of passing parts of the structure as sound when they clearly were not, of carrying out work without the authority to do so, and of disobeying his instructions from the Trustees. No explanation was forthcoming and the Trustees decided to undertake legal proceedings. One planned feature which was destined never to be built was a large detached Headmaster's house, in the same architectural style as the rest of the complex. Instead, the Trustees added £100 to the £1,500 gift from Samuel Morley to buy a pair of semi-detached houses on the north east corner of Clarendon Road (Waverley Mount), the nearer of which was let to the Headmaster, Dr Dixon.

There were 192 pupils, all of them fee payers. The school had cost £6,000 to build and the principal contractor was a Mr Johnson.

June 1868

Mr Sutton, the architect, presented his bill to the Trustees. It was for £485 11s 0d. They decided to pay him three hundred guineas for the school and ten guineas for valuing the land. They insisted that he returned the plans to them. Twenty years later, Sutton was to design the Drawing and Writing School and a famous landmark in the centre of Nottingham, the Walter Fountain.

July 1868

A large group of local worthies, led by the Reverend Francis Morse (the Vicar of St Mary's) expressed their own regrets to Mr Cusins. Morse described him as "a manly, honest, straightforward, courteous gentleman." Eventually, Cusins went to live in North Hykeham near Lincoln, where he became Diocesan Inspector of Schools for the Archdeaconry of Nottingham. Not surprisingly, perhaps, he did not ever inspect the High School. He died on August 30th 1900, and is buried at North Hykeham. After Cusin's death, the one-time head boy, John Russell, set up a memorial fund to pay for the Cusins Prize for History.

July 1868

The Trustees gave the boys of the High School the right to wear mortar boards if they wished. It was thought that this measure would improve the new school's image, and enhance its improved status. At this time, both schools studied History, Latin, Mathematics, Science and Scripture, and the Lower School studied Elementary Free-hand, English Grammar, Mechanical Drawing, Reading and Spelling. The Upper School studied Book-keeping, Drawing and Designing, English and foreign literature, Greek and the principles of Civil Engineering.

Midsummer 1868

Disappointingly, the new school's first inspector reported that "the present standard of attainment is by no means high."

Wednesday, September 9th 1868

Wearing mortar boards made every High School boy immediately identifiable. Every single one became a target for every street urchin with a witty rejoinder, or worse still, a stone in his hand. On this particular day two boys were on trial at the Guildhall accused of assaulting an "intelligent boy", named Charles Barber. All six parents were in court, and the assaulted boy's father was keen to point out that he was not being particularly vindictive but merely wished to protect his son. The defendants' parents expressed their regret, but clearly not very well and both defendants were fined 15s 0d, a considerable sum in those days.

December 1868

Permission was granted for boarders to lodge at masters' houses. Thirty-eight boys were immediately accepted, at a cost of sixteen guineas in the Upper School and eight guineas in the Lower. They stayed with the Headmaster, the Second Master and two other teachers.

January 1869

Because of the distance of the school from the pupils' homes, dinners now had to be provided on site. The kitchens and dining rooms in the basement could offer "hot or cold meat or soup, vegetables, bread etc." for eight pence. Boys could bring their own dinners to school, and then use the dining room for a penny or, with vegetables, for two pence.

Circa 1870

About two acres of land were purchased to enlarge the playground, and they took the school's northern boundary as far as Forest Road. The tunnel underneath the school was continued as a cutting further northwards to permit access from Forest Road. A cart could comfortably be driven along it and it became gradually deeper towards the northern door of the school. At this point, it measured some six feet in height.

April 1870

Dr Dixon founded a new school magazine called *The Forester*. It contained for the most part learned pieces such as *The Suez Canal*, *Holman Hunt's Light of the World*, and even *The Life of the Monkey*, but also introduced a short section entitled *Our Chronicle*, designed to allow reports of "the honours, the work, or the sports of the School." In this particular edition, there was only enough room remaining to report that Lacey, the Head Boy, had gained a First Class with Honours in the Cambridge Senior Local Examinations in English, Latin and Geology.

Early Summer Term, 1870

In the school's first recorded cricket match, the Upper School Eleven played Mount Vernon School. The Upper School batted first, and made 227 all out, with Frank Ashwell scoring 97. In reply, Mount Vernon had made 12-2 when the match finished, for an unrecorded reason.

June 1870

After writing letters to the Charity Commissioners and to the local press, Mr James Morley of Lenton took the Trustees to court over the unsanitary condition of the boys' toilets, which were, of course, at this time, underground, as well as being dry earth closets. His own son had recently been ill and he wanted changes to be made before an epidemic arose. Mr H.O.Tarbotton, the Corporation Surveyor, was then instructed to look into the problem, and plans were drawn up. This did much to quell the rumours which were sweeping the town about an epidemic of cholera at the school, in which a boy had died. People during this era were very concerned about cholera. There had been a severe national epidemic as recently as 1865-1866.

Wednesday and Thursday, September 28th and 29th 1870

The Annual School sports were again held at Trent Bridge. Events on the first day included the popular "High Leap with a Pole", won by Woodhouse with a jump of 7ft 6ins, "a good jump for a man". A total of thirty-six boys also entered the stone gathering race, and the sack race was won by Darby, who had the bright idea of inserting a toe tightly into each corner of the sack, and then "shuffled along capitally". On the second day there was a "Stranger's Race" where, presumably, people not directly connected with the school were allowed to compete. There was reluctance to enter this race, because of the presence of Mr Sam Weller Widdowson, the famous captain of the Nottingham Forest Football Club, but a number of gentlemen finally took part, running in top hats and overcoats. As expected, Mr Widdowson was in first place, with Mr Frederick Rothera second. To finish, there was then a "blind donkey race" with the large boys blindfolded, and the small boys riding piggyback, giving them directions. It was won by Purchase and Brown.

Wednesday, October 5th 1870

The first recorded school football match took place, most probably on the Forest. The Fifth Form beat the Fourth Form by two goals to one.

Wednesday, October 12th 1870

On the Forest, the "First Ten" beat the "Next Twenty" by two goals to one. There cannot have been many football matches played between two teams, one of which was twice as large as the other.

Saturday, November 19th 1870

The school's first recorded away fixture was played at Mansfield against Mansfield Grammar School XV. The school won by 3-0, and the home side is known to have scored a goal to reduce the deficit to 1-3 only for the referee to disallow it.

Wednesday, November 30th 1870

In a return match on the Forest, the First XI beat Mansfield Grammar School by 4-0, the first recorded home victory for the team.

Christmas 1870

In the "Our Chronicle" section of the school magazine, the first descriptions of High School football appeared, with brief accounts of just five matches. During this first recorded season of 1870-1871, the school were to play representative fixtures against Mansfield Grammar School (3-0 and 4-0), Trent College (0-3) and Mount Vernon High School, a home game played on the Forest in dense fog throughout the entire afternoon, a defeat through "good play and good luck".

The early 1870s

It took a long time to excavate the playground to the same level as Forest Road. Sometimes builders paid sixpence and were allowed to take away a cartload of sand. On other occasions, the Trustees had to pay for the job to be done. Work began on the eastern side and the front of the school was not completed until about 1880.

Thursday, May 4th 1871

Eleven year old Thomas Wigley was playing in the yard before school, when he fell and hit his chest on a horizontal bar. Within a short time he was dead "as the result of epilepsy, superinduced by a fall." The School Register lists him as simply "died".

Early Summer Term, before Wednesday, June 7th 1871

A cricket match took place on the Forest between the "First 11" and the "Next 22" which had been strengthened by the presence of a member of staff, Mr Yeld. The latter team batted first and scored a grand total of 31 between them, with nine ducks, Mr Yeld being bowled by Towlson for seven. The First XI then made 113 to win, with Frank Ashwell scoring 44 runs.

September 1872

The price of a school meal was increased to ten pence. The Headmaster quite reasonably wanted a glass of beer to be included in the price, but the Trustees rejected this idea as "objectionable".

1873

Only a short time after they had opened in 1868, the new school buildings were now perceived as being inadequate in size. A third "School", therefore, was erected to the north, roughly where the cutting from Forest Road had previously met the tunnel which ran under the northern arm. It had a hammer beam roof, and Gothic windows. Two classrooms were then excavated downwards from the new building. After the Second World War, one of these was to become the staff room.

1873 onwards

Around this time, in view of the school's ever increasing numbers, it was decided to extend all of the school's existing buildings downwards, while at the same time excavating the sandstone surrounding them on the outside. This ingenious scheme would create an entire new floor for the school, provided, of course, that the huge structure did not collapse as the process took place. Indeed, large numbers of huge iron girders had to be inserted, to take the weight of the thousands of tons of masonry above them. The net result of this daring process was that, over a hundred years later, the original damp course of the 1868 building can still be seen some four metres or so above the present ground level. What had previously been the school's first floor now became the second, and three huge staircases had to be built to permit the boys to get to the upstairs classrooms. The only one which still survives is at the very front of the school. The process, of course, was never going to be a rapid one. It took a number of years and the first two rooms to emerge were a dining room and a chemical laboratory. Interestingly enough, one of the school's earliest ever groups of pupils, photographed probably soon after its opening in 1868, is still in existence. Nowadays, the boys would be some five or six metres off the ground! What may be the original level of the whole site may well be reflected in the present height of the staff car park, and the houses on the western side of Balmoral Road. They are all at least five or six metres above the school playground.

1874

A.E.Cullen won the school's first ever scholarship in Natural Sciences to Cambridge University.

Before 1875

The Second Master, Mr Irving was the subject of several complaints that he had struck boys in class. It was decided that in future, no boy could be corporally punished at the time of the offence.

1875

A large wall was erected along Forest Road and a magnificent Gothic fives court was built in the north eastern corner of the playground. It was named after Mr William Enfield, the former Town Clerk, in whose memory his friends had collected some £600 to fund a scholarship.

1876

The school year, which for the previous 350 years had been divided into four, was now changed to the more modern three term structure.

Saturday, March 4th 1876

Old Boy Arthur William Cursham made his début for England against Scotland at Glasgow. He played as an outside right, displaying "skill and dash" throughout, and playing "in pretty style on the right wing". England lost, however, by 0-3.

Monday, May 29th 1876

The Headmaster's wife, Ada, died "of the effects of a chill", or as his daughter was later to recall, "of pneumonia. My father never recovered from the loss." Dr Dixon had already taken a month's leave of absence in May, presumably to care for his dying wife. Her death was a great blow to him, and the subsequent stress and illness over the next two years would take a great toll on him.

Dr Dixon was left with five children, who were "Robert, Charles, Harold, Sydney and one daughter". The latter was named after her mother, and eighty years later, as Sister Ada at St Denys Convent, Warminster, could still recall her early years around the High School:

> "Workmen were always at work on building and making alterations and improvements. We had the free run of the buildings out of school hours. We had lovely singing lessons. For these, the school was divided into two divisions. I sat in front of the smaller boys & we sang most lustily the Harrow School Songs. A balloon was once let off quite near the school

with a most important person aboard, but I never can remember who he was."

May 1876 onwards

A new north "School" was to be joined to the original 1868 building by a new Drawing and Writing School. It was to be built as a huge room on top of the five classrooms which had been constructed in 1868. The most amazing feature about this new room was its roof, which was so startling that it was usually referred to as the "upturned boat". It was thought to have been inspired by the home of the Peggotty family in Dicken's *David Copperfield*. During the daytime, four massive curved windows let in an even, unchanging light, making the room ideally suited for drawing classes. Internal sliding shutters were fitted to the windows, and access to the room was by an ornate, but somewhat perilous winding spiral staircase. This was thought to be a possible fire risk, and a second entrance was added in the early 1880s.

The "Victoria History of the County of Nottingham", first published in 1906, tells how "As a great admirer of Dickens, one of Mr Patchitt's ambitions was to build an imitation of the upturned boat which is described in *David Copperfield* as the abode of Mr Peggotty. The net result was that, for the next fifty or so years, the High School was likened to "three small churches joined by an upturned boat.

1876

Difficulties were caused by staffing problems and parents were beginning to complain of "unsatisfactory teaching and the want of Masters".

Tuesday, April 17th, 1877

John Dane Player entered the High School at the age of twelve. He was born on November 29th 1864. He was No.541 in the Lower School Register, and in the Upper School, No.563. His father was John Player, a tobacconist of Belgrave Square, All Saints Street, Nottingham.

1877

What had previously been playrooms under the original school could now no longer be used for this purpose. The Trustees therefore built a couple of very large, long, covered sheds along the length of the Forest Road wall. The front of the School was tidied up, and shrubs and flowers planted. The large wrought iron gates were bought from the Coventry Iron Company for £150.

Wednesday, October 31st 1877

The First Eleven played football against Tudor House in a game where the opposition did not once get the ball into the High School half at any point during the game. The High School won by 15-0.

Monday, April 8th 1878

The Annual Athletic Sports took place at Trent Bridge, in front of a "numerous gathering", entertained by the playing of the Sax Tuba Band. The events included throwing the cricket ball, a 220 yard football dribbling race, a 100 yard three-legged race, a 100 yard sack race (with preliminary heats), a one mile bicycle race, and an Old Boys' race. One of the highlights must surely have come in the 220 yards open race when, because the course had been marked out incorrectly, one of the eleven runners, Sulley, took the wrong turning and "effectually disposed of his chance". The other runners also went wrong, but because they were trailing so far behind Sulley, they were able to run back, and get onto the correct route. Unfortunately, Small was knocked over in the confusion, and eliminated from the race, which was eventually won by G.F.Chalcraft. He won a desk, donated by the teaching staff. Keen students of tactics would also have delighted in the originality of F.Bailey, who, in the final of the sack race, finished second behind "the younger Walker", having decided not to jump inside his sack, but instead, to lie down and roll along the ground. Most interesting of all, though, must be the open "Bumping Match" the rules of which, unfortunately, have not survived. It must surely have consisted of a huge circle marked out by a rope, and the last boy left in it was the winner. In any case, the "contest caused great merriment among the spectators, who greeted the overturned combatants with roars of laughter. Finally two, varying greatly in size, were left in and after a prolonged struggle, W.A.Walker, who showed great quickness and dexterity in avoiding the attacks of his tall opponent, R.E.Fletcher, succeeded in knocking the latter over the line, amidst loud applause."

Monday, May 27th 1878

Monsieur Durand, a visiting French teacher, read a paper to the Nottingham High School Natural History Society (the N.H.S.N.H.S.). It was about butterflies, including those of his native land.

Christmas 1878

In *The Forester*, an Old Boy mentions an old custom which had existed in at least one of the Upper Forms at the school for a number of years. This was that when boys returned after their holidays, they were all given a sheet of paper and asked to write about the interesting or exciting experiences that they had had. The Form-master would then collect them all in, and the best two or three would be read aloud to the class, while the rest were corrected and handed back.

Wednesday, March 12th 1879

The First XI again played Tudor House, this time in an extremely high wind which encouraged the Tudor House players merely to kick the ball out of play as far as possible at every opportunity. *The Forester* lamented "Unfortunately there is no rule which provides for occurrences of this kind, but we should have thought there would have been a better spirit prevailing to prevent such unsatisfactory proceedings." The match finished 0-0.

Monday, May 5th 1879

The Forester contained an obituary for T.F.Littlewood, who had been one of the first hundred boys in the new school. Despite his "retentive memory and bright intellectual powers, indomitable perseverance and application", he had fallen victim to "that foul disease consumption." "His pure bright life may be held up as an example to those who are now where he once was."

Wednesday, December 10th 1879

In honour of Mr Bray's twenty-one years of service at the school, his pupils presented him with a handsome armchair.

Around 1880

The front of the school was finally levelled down, and what had originally been the cellars now became the ground floor of a three storey edifice. To accomplish this complex process, new foundations and windows had been inserted, and the school was soon able to put its new rooms to constructive use.

Saturday, January 10th 1880

A report of the Old Boys' dinner in the *Nottingham Guardian* bemoaned the fact that only some six students were at Oxford or Cambridge. The three currently at Oxford were all in their last year, and there were none in the pipeline to replace them.

Summer Term 1880

Faced with fierce competition from the Arboretum Rooms which could provide boys with whatever meals they wanted, school dinners were discontinued.

Wednesday, September 29th 1880

The annual swimming contests took place at Gedling Street Baths, in the presence of Alderman Gripper, the Second Master and a large number of parents and boys. Events included a number of races over two and four lengths. The last race was over one length, with three competitors fully clothed and still wearing their boots, much to the amusement of the spectators. In the diving contest, Colonel Seely dropped a large number of balls into the pool, and boys competed to see who could retrieve the most, the winner managing eleven balls in his three dives.

Thursday, November 11th 1880

The school First XI beat the Bank at football by 4-1. The High School team included Old Boy Harry Cursham, who was at the time a current Notts County and England footballer.

Wednesday, November 17th 1880

The First Team lost to Trent College at football by 0-14. *The Forester* described the conditions as "the slopes of the Forest were under water". The Trent team were "heavier and faster" than the High School and by half time led 4-0. After the interval, a strong wind across the pitch made "good cross-play" impossible for the High School forwards, and the Trent backs were just "too heavy and fast to get by". To quote *The Forester*, "Those who took the trouble to count, say that the Trent forwards obtained 10 more goals after half-time". *The Forester* described the team as "paralysed", although, to give them credit, they did look forward optimistically to the return fixture in the hope that the High School might at least "hold our own, if not to balance the account".

November 1881

The school presented Monsieur Adolphe Brunner with the £50 that they had collected as a mark of respect for their old teacher. Monsieur Brunner had taught German during the 1870s and was a much loved figure. He had been born in Paris in 1852 and educated at the Lycée Charlemagne from 1863-1869, and then at the Lycée Buonaparte. He received his Bachelier ès Lettres in November 1871, and was crowned best student in all France on three occasions by the Emperor Napoléon III. He came to England, and received a Bachelor of Arts degree from London University in 1875. The following year, he achieved a Master of Arts degree. Brunner had taught at the High School from 1872-1879. In 1879, he fell ill and as sick pay received £127 collected by friends, well-wishers and parents. In 1880, he was sufficiently recovered to return to the High School, but he left for good at Christmas 1881. Walking along on a winter's day in 1882, he slipped over on a children's icy slide. What nobody realised at the time was that he had splintered a rib, and this undiagnosed injury brought on pneumonia. This eventually developed into emphysema, and Brunner was to die on the operating table as doctors sought vainly to remedy their previous error.

Wednesday, November 24th 1881

Old Nottinghamian Leonard Lindley gained notoriety when he refereed a second round F.A.Cup tie between Notts County and Wednesbury Strollers at the Castle Ground, Nottingham. An own goal, plus two each from Arthur and Harry Cursham looked to have given Notts a 5-3 victory but Wednesbury were not at all happy that they had had two hotly contested goals awarded against them by a referee who came from the same town as their opponents. They protested to the F.A. who ordered a replay, on a neutral ground, with a neutral referee, Mr Pierce Dix of Sheffield. Leonard Lindley, therefore, contributed substantially to the idea that all cup ties and, eventually, all football matches, should be controlled by a neutral referee appointed by the governing body of that particular competition.

Saturday, February 17th 1883

While still a schoolboy, Tinsley Lindley made his début for the Nottingham Forest First Team, scoring four goals in a 6-1 home victory over Wolverhampton. He made four further appearances that season, scoring at least four more goals.

November 1883

School numbers were continuing to fall, and over a quarter had now left. The Governors decided "that the School Committee do enquire into the causes of the decline of the School and report thereon." Their conclusion was to draw Dr Dixon's particular attention to the contents of the midsummer examiners' report.

1884

C.W.Gowthorpe won the National 120 yards Hurdles Championship.

March 1884

Dr Dixon became seriously ill and was given three months off school. The stresses and strains of falling numbers of pupils no doubt exacerbated Dr Dixon's condition, in addition to his own personal grief and the burden of running his own household. His wife had died in May 1876, and Dr Dixon was still looking after five children, including a young daughter of only seven. He had also carried out for seventeen years a number of tasks about which Dr Gow, within weeks of his appointment, was to protest vigorously. During Dr Dixon's illness, the acting headmaster was the Reverend J.G.Easton.

June 1884

Dr Dixon had now recovered, but the lack of a housekeeper meant that he still spent a great deal of time at home looking after his children.

Midsummer 1884

Mr Harris, the Examiner, reported that the average levels of the school were very poor. Professor Reinold criticised both Mathematics and Science, "the School is at present not in an efficient or satisfactory state"

October 1884

The Headmaster was asked to make a reply to the Examiners' Report. Dr Dixon spoke of his illness, the difficulties of trying to teach pupils whose demands were all very different, and the immense difficulties of "the two distinct schools." He was able to add that the buildings had never been satisfactory at any point. For every one of his seventeen years at the High School, building operations and alterations had been in progress. He had never been free of "the sound of the carpenter's hammer, or the mason's trowel, or the labourer's pickaxe."

November-December 1884

The general perception throughout Nottingham was that the overall standards of the High School were growing steadily lower and lower. Both boys and staff seemed to be deteriorating badly, and the Headmaster, Dr Dixon, was in failing health. His representations to the Governors fell on deaf ears, and he resigned only a few days afterwards. He left the school in December 1884, a month after his job was advertised. He was offered a payment of £500 instead of a pension.

November 1884

A hundred and twelve people replied to the Governors' advertisement, of whom some thirty seven were already headmasters.

Chapter 8: Dr Gow to the Rescue

Tuesday, December 23rd 1884

The Governors, with the exception of Mr Blain and Mr Pratt, met to interview the candidates for Headmaster and to hold a ballot. Dr Gow was their choice. It was a very daring one, however, as Gow was not a schoolmaster, but a twenty-nine-year-old lawyer. He was a highly qualified Classicist and a fellow of Trinity College, Cambridge. After this, he had studied at Weimar, but since 1879 had worked mainly as a Chancery barrister. He had some experience of Classical teaching at St Paul's School, and knew Nottingham from having visited a number of Midland towns as a Cambridge University Lecturer in Literature from 1875-1878. At the time of his appointment, he was the only school teacher in the country who was a Doctor of Literature.

1885

The school was finally finished. According to *The Forester*, "an army of painters, glaziers, carpenters were engaged in white-washing, putting in new windows, completing the wainscoting and making foundations."

Early 1885

The entire staff was under notice of dismissal, but Dr Gow asked only two to leave. He decided to "try the rest for a time, and give them an opportunity of showing what they could do under tolerable conditions."

Early 1885

Reminiscing many years after the event, an Old Boy recollected how Gow was "blunt and brusque, but very human under the frigid armour of scholarship and authority. In the first hours of our acquaintanceship, we voted him "straight as a die", and took him to our hearts with an implicit confidence that soon ripened into an affection, which we never allowed to appear on the surface, save in a full-throated roar of approval on Speech Days." This quality of directness was to characterise Gow in his dealings with Governors, staff, parents and boys for the next sixteen years. On the other hand, at least one Old Boy reminisced that what they admired most about Dr Gow was "his skill in breaking large lumps of coal with a small poker. "Must have a bit more muscle than you'd think." we decided."

The first two terms of 1885

Dr Gow taught every class in the school for a few days and carried out two thorough examinations. Years later, Bernard Heald, who was by then himself the Headmaster of Midhurst Grammar School, Sussex, was to reminisce about how Dr Gow was different from other teachers. He never called boys up to his desk to go through their work, but always went to sit alongside them. Lessons usually finished with the customary phrase, "I think that just about finishes our dose."

March 1885

Dr Gow, who had strong views on the value of regular sport and physical activity, introduced the first of two "Examinations in Athletic Sports". This was a series of "football exercises", carried out in the school playground and including a number of "brilliant and exciting" football dribbling races. A few months later, a new Drill Serjeant, George Holmes, an ex-army man, arrived. He was responsible for "the usual manual exercise and marching drill, bayonet exercise, sword drill for infantry and cavalry and Indian club exercise." His appointment was "to the great advantage of all our games."

July 1885

Dr Gow told the Governors that the school was in a parlous state, which would take years to improve. This had been caused by the previous system of moving classes up at the end of the year, whether or not they were capable, and whether or not their teachers thought they should be moved. The net result was a situation where the teachers soon realised that they were wasting their time, and grew increasingly disillusioned. The few boys who were keen to learn soon stopped bothering, and gave up. In an elementary Arithmetic test, the boys in the highest form could not score 4%. This had a toxic effect on the school's intake, because the parents of clever boys did not send their sons to the High School.

July 1885

Dr Gow spoke up for the teaching staff:

"There is not a cupboard in the whole School: only four masters have desks: the blackboards are white and greasy with age. About £60 spent on trifling conveniences would do more than an extra £100 a year, distributed in increased salaries to give the masters new spirit for their work."

In the autumn, Dr Gow wrote to the Governors about a proper pay scale for the staff, something which had never existed before. The Masters of the Senior School were to receive a minimum of £180, rising in ten pound increments to a maximum of £250. The maximum for a Junior School master was to be £200.

Late 1885

Dr Gow reorganised many of the forms and persuaded a fair number of the less talented older boys to leave. He introduced a new curriculum with properly graded objectives. He made great efforts to improve discipline, and refused to tolerate bad behaviour or poor appearance. The boys responded very well to Gow's urgings and he had little reason to be particularly strict with any of them.

Dr Gow also separated the Classical scholars from the students of the more modern and commercial subjects. He thought that it was these boys who would stand the best chance of going to universities such as Oxford and Cambridge, and that they needed the right academic atmosphere in which to flourish. When they achieved academic success, it would be to the credit of the school.

The end of 1885

The school's first ever prospectus came out. It had 22 pages, and listed the Governors and staff, with information on everything from school fees to sports, and from scholarships to dining arrangements.

1886

The playground was finally level. Attempts were made to turf about an acre of it for tennis, cricket and football, but this did not stand much chance, given the continuous wear and tear to the surface. The playground then became "a sandy waste. It became steadily dustier and dirtier."

1886

New lavatories were built against the east wall of the playground, and a gymnasium was set up in the sheds on the northern side of the playground. A number of paths and gates were added to the school grounds and plans were made to record on the walls of the main school building the names of its various benefactors and distinguished pupils.

Easter 1886

At the suggestion of Dr Gow, a Six-a-side football competition was held. This attracted forty entries, and was won by "a very light team", captained by H Palmer. The Six-a-side Competition was to last until 1914, although it was to change to an Eight-a-side tournament from 1904-1905 onwards.

July 1886

The Forester reappeared after a gap of some six years. It cost 6d and contained 44 pages and reported that "No school of its class in the country is so cheap or is better provided with the means both for work and for play. It ought to have a brilliant future before it." The editors hoped that the magazine "will carry the record of the School down to a far distant posterity".

Saturday, July 3rd 1886

Running at Stamford Bridge, London, Charles F. Daft retained the National 120 Yards Hurdles Championship which he had already won in 1885. A member of the school staff, Mr Samuel Palmer had already won this title in 1878 and had retained it in 1879. He won again in 1882 and then defended the title in 1883. Palmer was therefore National Champion for four years out of six. A third Old Boy, C.W.Gowthorpe had triumphed in 1884. This meant the High School had won the National Hurdles Championship for seven years out of nine.

The end of 1886

Dr Gow reorganised the school for a second time. It was divided into the Junior School and the Senior School and the latter was divided into the Classical and the Modern sides. Around this time, the school day was lengthened to 12.30 p.m., and a half hour was deducted from afternoon school.

Thursday, May 19th 1887

Playing cricket on the Forest for the First XI against University College, R.H.Brett took nine wickets for sixteen runs in the College's overall total of 64 all out as they fell three runs short of victory. This match-winning performance was to remain a record for over fifty years.

Wednesday, May 25th 1887

The First XI played against Trent College on the Forest. Appearing for Trent College was the Essex county player, Mr Owen, who made 176 not out, including one seven, one six, six fives, five fours and 12 threes, in a final total of 310 all out. The High School's score remains unrecorded although Dr Gow made a lucky 42 and French batted well for his 29 not out.

Tuesday, June 21st 1887

The school celebrated the Jubilee of Queen Victoria with two days' holiday and the erection of a brand new flagpole on the tower.

The late 1880s

A short novel entitled *The Three Merles* appeared just after the First World War. It was written by a former pupil, Richard St Clair Page, and was a thinly veiled description of his years at the High School in the late 1880s. Very reminiscent of *Tom Brown's Schooldays* and other school tales of the Victorian era, it described how a new headmaster arrived at a quiet, comfortable school, and changed it completely by the very force of his personality. The Headmaster was Dr Govan (Dr Gow), and other teachers were called "Sammy" Horner (Sammy Corner) and "Old Mr Bray", (Charles Bray). The imaginary school, like the real one, had a Mr Lupton and a Serjeant Holmes as its School Porter. The younger Mr Jennings, Form Master of the Lower Second, and the elder Mr Jennings, Form Master of the Upper Third, were amalgams of the High School's Mr I.H.Jennings and the two Ryles brothers, "Jumbo" and "Nipper".

Saturday, April 7th 1888

In football, the School Six played the Masters' Six. *The Forester* carried the full story:

> "The School Six defeated the Master's (sic) Six by 3-1. The masters, who, like Hamlet, were somewhat "fat and scant of

breath", then demanded to play two fat men extra, to compensate for their want of nimbleness. This unfortunate challenge was accepted, and the School won again by 10-1."

Friday, June 29th 1888

The Athletic Sports, "for many years in abeyance", were revived and were held in "very unfavourable weather" on the Castle Ground. There was a good attendance of spectators and among the events was a three-legged race, won by W.A.Möller and C.P.S.Sanders, a sack race won by J.Blake and a bicycle race over one mile, won by W.A.Möller in 3 mins 45.4 seconds. F.Bramley won the "Throwing the Cricket Ball (for boys under 14)" with a distance of 57 yards. The Masters' Race was won by the Reverend T.W.Peck, with Mr W.T.Ryles in second place, two yards behind. There was also an Old Boys' Race, a handicap, run over 220 yards and a Tug of War, won by Team No 1 who defeated Team No 2 in the final. The prizes for the day were presented by Mrs Gow.

Thursday, July 12th 1888

The Forester provided one of its most absurdly boastful moments in its report of the Nottinghamshire Show, held at Wollaton Park. This was the "first shilling day" and *The Forester* reported that over 90,000 people turned up, "of whom the High School contributed a large proportion".

Thursday, November 22nd 1888

The High School played what appears to be their first football fixture on Nottingham Forest's Gregory Ground, running out easy winners against Derby School by 7-2. There had long been many problems with the Forest Recreation Ground, and it was probably because there were so many Old Boys in the ranks of Nottingham Forest at this time that the club made this generous offer to share their home ground. As well as football, the High School was to play its cricket fixtures "at the Gregory" for nine years, although games against other schools still continued both on the Forest (on Wednesdays) and at Trent Bridge (on Saturdays).

In actual fact, contemporary opinion was that the Gregory Ground was one of the best in the whole country. It hosted a number of top games, including an England trial match in March 1890. The record attendance was 11,500 for an F.A.Cup game between Nottingham Forest and Notts County. The Gregory Ground has now mostly disappeared but it used to stand roughly between Derby Road, Faraday Road and Salisbury Street. The school playing fields still there reveal the history of the site.

Saturday, December 8th 1888

Henry Alfred "Harry" Cursham scored his last goal for Notts County in the F.A.Cup, in a 3-1 victory over Staveley. Depending on interpretation, it was either his 49th, 52nd or 54th goal in the competition. Either of these would remain a record for the competition, well over a hundred years later. Cursham scored six goals in a single game against Wednesbury Strollers, although he claimed nine, and he played eight times for England, scoring five goals.

Saturday, December 22nd 1888

A Thomas White's scholar, C.P.S.Sanders, died of typhoid after a very short illness.

Tuesday, February 26th 1889

The Debating Society held its first ever meeting, at which Dr Gow was elected President. In its early days, the society held more musical evenings, or "soirées", than debates, including, for example, Mrs Bowman-Hart's class singing *Holiday on the Rhine*. These events formed an important part of the school's social life at the time.

A Thursday in the Easter Term 1889

A group of boys went to see the Tar and Sulphuric Acid Works at Giltbrook. The acid chambers were inspected, and produced huge fits of coughing, but the most glorious moment came when a retriever dog, which had attached itself to the party, fell into the tar oil well, presenting a "rather woe-begone appearance". Most of the school party then "rushed away in a rather undignified manner, fearing that they might carry with them undesirable evidence of their visit to a Tar Works."

Tuesday, June 18th 1889

E Knowles, "a boy of whom we were justly proud, though he did not stand very high in the school", died on June 14th. The poor little boy was buried on what would have been his birthday.

Saturday, September 28th 1889

The Cycling Club went to Dale Abbey. Dr Gow rode a tandem with P.W.Oscroft until they crashed and the School Captain, Paton, was then able to accompany the Headmaster.

Wednesday, November 27th 1889

The First XI played Trent College at football at Long Eaton. The hosts won the toss and kicked off down the slope. An unlucky own goal by Currie gave them their first score with a second goal before half time. After the interval the High School "played splendidly" and scored two goals in the first twenty minutes. Trent then scored through Sharples but the High School again equalised. There then followed what *The Forester* called "two very doubtful goals", one after the ball had allegedly gone out of play by several yards and the second from a very offside looking Sharples. The High School again "played up" and a splendid shot from Goodacre reduced the deficit to 4-5 but despite dominating the last few minutes they had to concede defeat. The best players in the game were Mr "Nipper" Ryles for the High School and the excellent Mr Owen, the Trent College goalkeeper. A return fixture on the Gregory Ground was turned down by Trent College, making "a very paltry protest against our playing four masters, while they only played three, the probable cause being that they were afraid of a beating." This quarrel marked the end of football fixtures between the two schools for well over a century, and they were only resurrected in the 1997-1998 season.

Winter 1889 - 1890

The school was ravaged by scarlet fever, and by "a curious influenza, which has lately come to us from Russia".

Monday, December 30th 1889

Dr Gow wrote to the Governors, and insisted that Charles Bray, who had worked at the Free School since 1859, should remain at the High School, "as long as I can in any way employ him." Bray was given lighter work to do, more in keeping with his age, and was paid half salary. Another veteran, Henry Seymour, was given a pension. His wife was so grateful that she endowed a scholarship after his death in 1903. In a similar fashion, "the caretakers, Knowles and his wife, very old and faithful servants" had good reason to be grateful to Dr Gow when he intervened on their behalf.

1890

Old Boy, C.F.Daft won the National 120 yards Hurdles Championship for the third time. He had previously won it in 1885 and 1886.

Saturday, April 5th, 1890

In the wonderfully titled article *A Short Account of the Runs*, *The Forester* tells how the Cycling Club went to Newark. Twenty seven riders set out from Forest Road at 10.30 a.m., and misfortune seems to have occurred with frightening frequency. Mr W.P.Paton fell off his safety cycle while riding down a steep hill into Woodborough and A.H. Goodliffe then crashed into him. A tandem-tricycle ridden by R.B.Brown and R.B.Paton then smashed into the wreckage, and finished up on the far side of the hedge. L.Allen avoided further disaster by jumping off his own bicycle, before he too became part of this amazing pile up. Minutes later, A.H.Lymn attempted the same treacherous descent, only to have his bicycle disintegrate into two separate sections as he reached top speed. His fall was so bad that he had to be sent home in a cart with the pieces of wreckage. After a delay of an hour and a half to repair Brown and Paton's tandem, the survivors set off, only for Miss Corner and T.B.Durose to be thrown off their own tandem. Newark was reached by 3.45 p.m., and dinner was heartily enjoyed at the Ossington Coffee Palace. During the return journey, tea was provided by Mr Corner at Radcliffe-on-Trent at 5 p.m., and the party finally reached Nottingham at 9 p.m.

The Forester records the casualties rather like a list of kills in a First World War air battle as "tandem smashed tandem and safety bicycle smashed safety bicycle. Thrown, more or less violently, without however, serious damage to their machines were Mr Corner, M.B.Paton, S.A.Wallis (twice), J.A.Wolverson (twice), B.Horner (twice), A.H.Goodliffe, Miss Corner and Durose (twice) and Mr W.P.Paton." G.B.Bryan was "knocked up" at Southwell, and W.H.Lancashire was forced to return from Newark by train. Of twenty seven club members, only eleven returned without mishap to tell the tale. Three cycles were destroyed. During the rest of the year, other problems occurred with strong headwinds, broken chains, broken spokes, buckled wheels, loosened tyres, poor road surfaces, falls, smashes, hills too steep to ride up, and on March 30th, a thirty minute blizzard between Melton Mowbray and West Bridgford.

The afternoon of Tuesday, June 3rd 1890

The school's sports day was held at the Castle Ground in dull and windy weather. Nevertheless, a large crowd attended, and enjoyed a day of "very fair sport", and a selection of music played by the Nottingham Borough Police Band, under the leadership of Bandmaster Redgate. The prizes were presented by Miss Goldschmidt. The most interesting event was the hundred yards Medley Handicap. In this boys competed in a number of heats over one hundred yards, and the handicap consisted in the means by which they had to cover the distance. The methods included skipping, sack race, three legged, pick-a-back on all fours and, most spectacular of all perhaps, on stilts. The final seems to have been a normal foot race as the winner's time was fifteen seconds. It is difficult to imagine any methods of locomotion as being as fast as this!

The afternoon of Saturday, June 28th 1890

The Cycling Club held their sports day at the Castle Ground. There were five events, including a five miles open race, an open one mile race, an Under-15 one mile race, an Old Boys' Race, and a slow riding race, over one hundred yards.

Wednesday, July 2nd 1890

The Nottingham High School Junior Fanciers Association held their first "fat stock" show in the Fives Court. There were sixty one pets entered, the most common being rabbits, pigeons and poultry. Other participants were white rats, doves, a dog, a cat, a parrot, a greenfinch and some guinea pigs. Special commendations went to Lewis's cat and Goddard's guinea pig.

Midsummer Term 1890

In a fine example of how languages are constantly changing, *The Forester* reported that the term had been "unusually gay".

Saturday, March 7th 1891

Tinsley Lindley, arguably the most talented footballer ever at the High School, represented England for the last time in a 6-1 victory over

Ireland. He had scored fifteen goals in thirteen international appearances, at least three of which were as captain, a record which was to stand for a number of years. Always wearing ordinary walking shoes rather than football boots, Lindley played for Nottingham Forest on 98 occasions and scored 82 goals, the best strike rate of any forward in their history. In cricket, he managed to take the catch which enabled Nottinghamshire to defeat the Australian tourists in 1888. He played rugby for Old Leysians R.F.C., and at Cambridge, represented the university as a sprinter on numerous occasions as well as playing cricket for them. He captained the football team there for at least one season and even turned out for Oxford University when they were a man short. In the late 1880s, Lindley became a barrister, and then lectured in Law at Nottingham University. Shortly afterwards, he became a county court judge and in his spare time reported on Nottingham Forest games for the *Daily Mail*. During the Great War he organised the Nottinghamshire Special Constabulary and received an O.B.E. for this work. He died of pneumonia in 1940 at the age of seventy-four.

August 1891

For the first time, the School List was published, containing a prospectus, a full record of forms, sets, scholarships and prizes and a large plan of the school and grounds. It was mainly the work of Mr Corner, who was now the Usher.

Tuesday, July 26th, 1891

Following the success of the 1890 show, the annual pet show was held in the Fives Court. The boys' animals included twenty-five pigeons, ten rabbits, eight dogs, various fowl, rats, doves, canaries, ducks, guinea-pigs, dormice and a thoroughbred goat "of a savage disposition. Last, and also least, was a diminutive but lively tortoise." The "champion" prize was awarded by Dr Gow to Hugh Browne's "celebrated Newfoundland, Nero." This was an extremely popular event during this era and attracted many entries from the boys. It was frequently reported in local newspapers, such as the Nottingham Daily Express.

September 1891 - December 1897

An Old Boy, R.J.Willatt, wrote down his reminiscences of the High School. He remembered that Dr Gow, or "Jimmy", was immensely popular, despite being: "rather reserved and possibly shy. His popularity may have been due to his absolute fairness and his interest, not only in the School generally, but in individual boys. I remember his keeping goal in a "Masters v Boys" match and being loudly cheered as he came in to Prayers the following morning. He blushed furiously but his delightful smile broke out and he was obviously pleased."

Young Willatt began in the Second Form with Mr L.C.Wilkes, who was inexplicably called "Demi". Other members of staff were "Jumbo" and "Nipper" Ryles, the Reverend T.W.Peck, and the Reverend T.B.Hardy, who was later to win a Victoria Cross in the Great War "a very quiet but efficient form master, and not at all the type one would have expected to win high military honours."

In the Upper School were "Carey" Trafford, and "Sammy" Corner. The latter "by no means an ideal form master, was invaluable to the School. He was completely wrapped up in it, and lived for it." Sammy was extremely generous, and whenever he heard of a boy who was interested in a particular subject or personality, he would buy him a book about it. The writer still had Ranjitsinghi's *Jubilee Book of Cricket*, which he was given shortly after he left school. The school's other character was Sergeant Holmes, a "smart little figure with his peak cap and grey moustache". He took every form for squad drill, and had charge of the sports gear. Every morning, prayers were held in one large room. The Drawing Room, with its extraordinary roof, was used for school functions such as concerts or dramatic presentations. First XI football matches were still played at the Gregory Ground but all other football, and all cricket matches, were played on the Forest. The playground was a "sandy waste" with a small football pitch on the eastern side. This was used to play the Football Sixes competition. To take a corner kick, the door of the school's north entrance had to be held open, so that the kicker could get the necessary run-up.

January 16th 1892

On a "piercingly cold" Saturday, Nottingham Forest played Newcastle East End at the City Ground. When the crowd arrived at Trent Bridge, they were surprised to see "skating in progress on the old course of the River Trent." Because of the recent introduction of the penalty kick, the frozen football pitch had some new markings, which in this case were made of broad strips of black soot. Newcastle changed from their normal crimson shirts into black and white stripes. Hopefully, before the game, Old Nottinghamian Tinsley Lindley, Forest's centre forward, was able to walk across the Trent to the game, just like Brian Clough used to do.

December 1892

Dr Gow again petitioned the Governors about a pension fund. He pointed out just how well he had performed in his seven years in the school. It was all in vain and nothing was done.

1893

The High School was formally admitted to Whitaker's Almanac's list of *The Great Public Schools*.

1893

Dr Gow presented the Governors with a detailed scheme for staff pensions. Nothing further was heard about it.

Thursday, July 27th, 1893

In the school pet show more than fifty animals participated, among them pigeons and dogs "of unusual excellence". Prizewinners included a St Bernard bitch called "Lassie", a fox terrier bitch called "Jennie", and in the miscellaneous category, an owl and a hedgehog.

Wednesday, January 24th 1894

The First XI played Mansfield Wednesday in an away game, and it may have been unfamiliarity with local custom which led two of the High School players to "linger in the pavilion" at the start of the match. Mansfield duly kicked off, and scored the only goal of the game while just nine of their naïve young opponents were on the pitch.

1894-1895

This year was picked by Dr Gow as the best of his reign. Three boys won Open Scholarships to Cambridge, one to Durham, and one to the London Hospital. F.C.Boon, who had already won a scholarship to Cambridge, qualified for a London University BA while still at the High School. Old Boy, Harold Knight won a National Gold Medal, a prize, three National Silver Medals and two National Bronze Medals for various sorts of drawing and painting. While Harold Knight was a famous artist in his own lifetime, his renown is somewhat eclipsed nowadays by the international success of his wife, Dame Laura Knight.

The Evening of Sunday, July 15th 1894

Mr Charles Bray died in his 68th year. He had visited a friend at Radcliffe-on-Trent that day and, having felt unwell, consulted a local doctor who performed a minor operation on him to relieve his discomfort. Mr Bray then felt much better so he returned home. He caught a cab at the station and asked the driver to take him to his home at 51, Bentinck Road. When the cab arrived however, the driver found that poor Mr Bray had died. His death was due to natural causes.

Mr Bray had worked at the Free School since 1859 and then in the new High School where he was Master of the Third and Fourth Forms. As he grew older he was given lighter work but had been in school as recently as the Monday before his death. That day he had been photographed with the rest of the staff and had ironically remarked that it was "for the last time". John Russell reminisced that Mr Bray was "a stern disciplinarian and a most energetic teacher" with "a striking personality and kindly nature." In the Free School, "his record is one of faithful, zealous, ungrudging service to the school through evil report and good report for nearly forty years. He taught well all that he knew."

His funeral left his house at 2.30 p.m. on July 19th, and proceeded to the Church Cemetery where the Reverends H.de B.Gibbins and T.W.Peck conducted the service. Both boys, staff and Governors were present and the gathering was so large that Superintendent Billington of the Nottingham Police was there to direct operations.

January 1895

For a period of ten days the River Trent was completely frozen and was safe enough to support skaters. One can only imagine how many boys must have taken advantage of this severe weather on their journey between the High School and their homes in West Bridgford.

Saturday, March 9th 1895

Madame Lionnet, the school's French teacher, died of pneumonia supervening on influenza. She had taught at the University College as well as the Girls' High School and was buried in the Church Cemetery on the following Wednesday, the Reverend Peck conducting the service. During the Franco-Prussian War both her husband and father had been killed in the battles around Paris and she had come to England after these sad events. In later life she was to lose her life savings when the Liberator Society failed.

Midsummer Term 1895

The High School stopped using teachers as players in their First XI at cricket. They were one of the very first schools in the area to do so.

1896

Dr Gow complained to the Governors about the Forest:

> "No play was possible there on either Thursdays or Saturdays, or after 6p.m. on any day. Furthermore, when we do play, we are instantly surrounded by a crowd of unemployed persons, who sometimes steal our clothes, and use the vilest language."

1896

Around this time there was what became a legendary fist fight for "physical supremacy" in the school. It was between S.H.Hill and Vernon James Steedman. The latter eventually became a private in the 54th Battalion of the British Columbia Regiment. He was to be killed in action on October 25th 1916, and his sacrifice is commemorated on the Vimy Ridge Memorial in northern France.

3 p.m. on Thursday, April 16th 1896

The school Prize-giving took place in the Albert Hall. Dr Gow announced that the High School now had the top boys in three of the subjects at the recent Cambridge Local Examinations. Furthermore among five thousand junior candidates they had "the top boy of all the world in Latin. (Applause)."

Among the seniors J.H.Towle was first in both Latin and Greek and was awarded a scholarship and sizarship to St John's College, Cambridge. Among the junior boys Dr Gow's world champion was L.S.Laver who was classified first in England for Latin. Two years later in December 1898, Laver was, as a senior, to be placed first in England in Latin, first in Greek and to be awarded his own scholarship of £60 to St John's College, Cambridge. He subsequently gained a Class I in the Classical Tripos of 1902. He became a schoolmaster at Calday Grange Grammar School on Merseyside, Wyggeston School, Leicester and Stourbridge Grammar School where he became Second Master. From 1912 he was Headmaster of Altrincham County High School for Boys but died suddenly in 1933, while still only in his fifties.

December 1896

The Governors began to negotiate for the use of a small piece of land in Mapperley Park on Mansfield Road, just outside Sherwood.

February 1897

The Mapperley Park playing fields were secured on a very short lease and a groundsman was recruited from the Grange Park Club, Edinburgh. He was Mr Albert Onions who was to work at Mapperley Park for over thirty years. He was an accomplished bowler and cricket coach and many successful High School cricketers over the years were to owe him a great debt. Mr Onions was also to able to run the line and to referee in a number of school football fixtures.

Thursday, March 11th 1897

Dr James Gow sent to all "Past and Present Boys" a circular appealing for money to provide "a pavilion and the nets and other apparatus necessary" on the recently acquired Mapperley Sports Ground on Mansfield Road. The Headmaster contributed £25 himself and the staff gave almost £40. In total, a sum of £215 2s 6d was collected and a pavilion, "a remarkably pretty and convenient edifice", was purchased from Boulton and Paul of Norwich at a cost of £158. The pitches were found to be "rather crumbly" and needed a good deal of attention, not having been used for several years. Nearly £40 was spent on the hire of horses and weeders, some heavy equipment and a shed to put it all in.

Wednesday, June 30th 1897

The very first fixture at Mapperley Park was against Newark Grammar School. It was not an auspicious start as Newark scored 90 in their innings and the High School were dismissed for 29. As *The Forester* said, "they broke down utterly, and made the lowest score of the season".

September 1898

School numbers reached 381, the largest they had ever been and just over twice what they had been when Dr Gow took over in 1885.

Chapter 9: The D. H. Lawrence Years

Wednesday, September 14th, 1898

In 1898 the High School welcomed its most celebrated student; a boy who would one day go on to be one of the most notorious writers ever, a controversial figure whose genius both challenged the world of literature and also created the most accomplished works of the twentieth century.

On Wednesday, September 14th, having won a County Council Scholarship, David Herbert Lawrence entered the High School at the age of thirteen. He was allotted the school number of 1733, and was normally known to the other boys as "Bert". Lawrence had been born on September 11th 1885, and his father is listed in the register as Arthur Lawrence, a miner of 3, Walker Street, Eastwood. At the High School D.H.Lawrence was a fairly average student, and performed best in Mathematics, where he won at least one prize. His performances could not have been helped by the great distance between his home and the school, which often meant a day which lasted from seven o'clock in the morning until seven o'clock at night. Indeed, in later years, Lawrence himself was to blame the long train journeys to and from Nottingham every day for the lung troubles which were ultimately to prove the cause of his death. "Train boys" were often late in the mornings, and frequently missed the morning assembly. Quite often, boys who were late would be able to hear the caretaker tolling the school bell as far away as the bottom of Waverley Street, or even occasionally as far away as Shakespeare Street. This sad feeling of impending punishment and eventual doom was later to be described by the great author himself. In the evening, "Train boys" invariably had to rush off to catch their train, and thereby missed any after-school games in the playground, and the chance to develop firm friendships. Not only the train journeys would have prevented Lawrence's full integration into the main body of school life but he was also unable to make his mark on the games field. He was a delicate child, and had never joined in with rough childhood games in Eastwood. Nor was his frail constitution helped by the damp and foggy climate of the city.

The main obstacle, of course, to Lawrence's ability to make friends would have been the wide difference in social background and class between himself and his school fellows. At such an early age, Lawrence would still have had a thick working class accent, and this would have made his origins very obvious to everybody. At least one boy, for example, is known to have invited him home for tea with his family, and then discovered that Lawrence was the son of a miner. The invitation was immediately withdrawn, and Lawrence told that any friendship between them was out of the question.

The young D.H.Lawrence was almost a complete outsider. He no longer fitted in with other children at home in Eastwood because he was schooled far away in Nottingham and to a far higher level of education than the people in his hometown or social class would expect to achieve. Neither did Lawrence belong completely at Nottingham High School. As a "train boy" he arrived late, which made him stand out from the other boys and would limit his opportunities to socialise, and he also had that broad Eastwood accent. Accents have always been an indicator of a person's origin and social class, and Lawrence's working class Eastwood accent would have quite easily betrayed his birthplace in a mining village. Continually mixing with the sons of the wealthier families of Nottingham would no doubt have made Lawrence acutely aware of his own humble origins.

Although little is known about the experiences of the young Lawrence at Nottingham High School compared to his later life, we can see how his experiences as an outsider may have shaped one of the great literary works of the twentieth century. In 1928, Lawrence, already dying from the tuberculosis that would finish him off some two years later, wrote his last major work, *Lady Chatterley's Lover*. There is a strong autobiographical thread throughout this novel, particularly in the character of Mellors, a working class man who is educated above his status and lives his life as a social outsider; an educated man who becomes a gamekeeper and fits in neither with the working class servants nor with the upper class gentry. In Mellors and his love affair with Lady Chatterley, we can see a young D.H.Lawrence and his love for Frieda Weekley. When Lawrence met Frieda in 1912, she was already married to an academic in Nottingham, but she decided to leave her husband and elope with Lawrence. This has significant parallels with the story of Mellors, a working class man bringing life to the unhappy existence of Lady Chatterley, a married, upper class woman who is bored with the intellectual circles she mixes in. There are further parallels between Mellors and Lawrence, such as when Mellors feigns a working class Nottinghamshire accent (or speaks spitefully in full dialect) to make himself appear like an outsider when mixing with the middle and upper class. Perhaps the most direct indication of Lawrence projecting his own experiences onto the character of Mellors is found in Mellors' own name. "Mellors" is nearly a perfect match for the surname of Dame Agnes Mellers, the foundress of Nottingham High School. Indeed, while there is only one letter of difference between the two names, we should be aware that the names sound absolutely identical when spoken aloud. With a working class Nottinghamshire accent both the "e" in "Mellers" and "o" of "Mellors" produce an "uh" sound, making the pronunciation of the two spellings indistinguishable when spoken.

In any case, there is also some further evidence which suggests that in the years of the late nineteenth century the name of Dame Agnes Mellers was spelled with a letter "o" rather than an "e". There recently came to auction a solid silver school prize medal awarded to FPC Walker of Ilkeston for his prowess in Mathematics in 1896, just two years before D.H.Lawrence entered the school. In the inscription around the medal, what would nowadays be spelled "Mellers" is rendered "Mellors". When Lawrence himself won his own prize for Mathematics, a ripping yarn entitled *Fights for the Flag* by W.H. Fitchett, that spelling is found on both the cover of the book and the inscription inside the cover: "Nottingham High School founded by Dame Agnes Mellors."

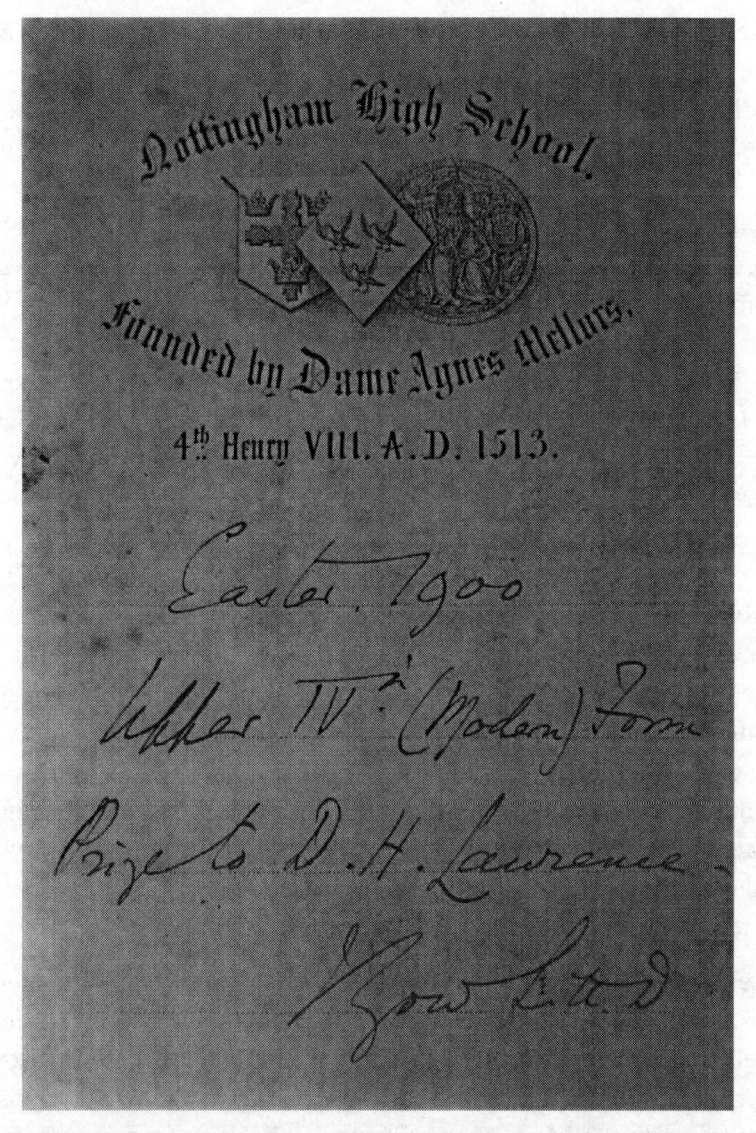

The young D.H.Lawrence must have flicked through these pages a number of times, seeing the name "Mellors" in connection with Nottingham High School over and over again. This further strengthens the argument that Lawrence used his experiences at Nottingham High School to help shape one of the most important autobiographical characters in his final literary masterpiece. If we can read the experiences of the author in the character of Mellors in *Lady Chatterley's Lover*, is it also possible to see another shadow from Lawrence's youth in the figure of the upper class, land-owning authoritarian, Lord

Chatterley? There is an intriguing connection between the date of the school's foundation and the name "Chatterley". Nottingham High School was founded in 1513 and the sum of the integers of this date (1+5+1+3) is 10, the same number of letters found in "Chatterley". In 1898, Lawrence, a young working class boy from a mining village, was faced with the prospect of Nottingham High School; an austere and imposing building representing the land-owning class, towered above him and subjected him to its authority for a number of years. As a "train boy", Lawrence would have walked from the Victoria Station to the High School every morning and his vision of Nottingham's skyline would have been dominated by the towers of Nottingham High School, just as Mellors' view of the countryside he presides over is overshadowed by the towers of Chatterley's colliery. In the late Victorian era, Nottingham High School was one of the very tallest buildings in Nottingham and its position on the top of a hill made it by far the most imposing aspect of Nottingham's vista. Defined by its huge tower with accompanying wings either side, its silhouette must have seemed similar to that of a colliery's winding tower flanked by buildings... especially to someone from a mining community like Eastwood. As the son of a miner, Lawrence would have grown up surrounded by collieries, immersed in the fabric of mining life, watching his father and the other miners trudge up to the looming tower of Brinsley colliery every morning – is this how he came to see his own walk up the hill towards the tower of the High School?

Lawrence evokes these earliest experiences as a boy when he renders the formidable character of Lord Chatterley as the antagonist to his Mellors, a rebellious outcast who rails against (and ultimately defies) Chatterley's authority and the imposed constraints of society. Tracing the opposition and antagonism of Mellors and Chatterley back to Lawrence's days at the High School allows us to appreciate the extent to which the school shaped *Lady Chatterley's Lover*, a work which is widely regarded as one of the finest pieces of twentieth century literature. In addition, as Lawrence evokes his experiences at Nottingham High School in his own swan song, an autobiographical work written when he was dying of tuberculosis (and self-published in Florence to ensure its survival and circulation after the rejections of British publishers), the author also acknowledges that the High School played its role in creating him as one of the great authors of all time. Nottingham High School gave Lawrence an exemplary education; the tools of the trade for any author. With such an education he was able to articulate and express his experiences as an outsider through his writing. It could be reasonably argued that Nottingham High School provided a young Lawrence with an invaluable springboard and that, if he had never attended the High School, we would not have the benefit of his great literary works today.

Lawrence began his school career in the Lower Modern Fourth Form with Mr.Crofts. In 1898-1899, he finished fifth overall in the form, and was third in English, tenth in French, fourth in German, 16th in Writing and third in Drawing. In Mathematics Set VIb with Mr.Hodgson, he was third in Arithmetic, ninth in Algebra and sixth in Euclid. Overall, he was fifth out of thirty-nine boys. In Science Set 4, with Mr.Trotman, he was fortieth out of fifty-two boys. The following year, 1899-1900, Lawrence was able to make friends with George Neville, the second boy to win a scholarship from the Beauvale School in Eastwood. The two travelled back and forth on the train together. Lawrence was now in the Modern Fifth Form with Mr.Gaskin. Listed in error as "H.D.Lawrence", he finished sixteenth overall in the form, and was thirteenth in English, seventeenth in French and thirteenth in German. In Mathematics Set IV with Mr.Crofts, he was again third in Arithmetic, and second in Algebra and Euclid. This made him overall first in the set out of twenty-one, and for this excellent performance, he was awarded a prize, an historical book entitled *Fights for the Flag*. It was written by W.H.Fitchett, already famous as the author of *Deeds that Won the Empire*.

A minor anomaly occurs in the fact that inside the book, the date is written as Easter 1900, and Lawrence is recorded as being in the Upper Modern Fourth Form. According to the School Lists, which are complete, and where Lawrence's career can be followed through from year to year, he was never a member of this form. The real truth, if it is other than just human error, will probably never be known. In Science Set IIB, with Mr.Hodgson, Lawrence was fourteenth out of twenty-three boys. From his school rankings, it appears that Lawrence must have been a late bloomer.

In 1900-1901, he spent his final year in the Modern Sixth Form with Mr.Corner. He finished fifteenth in the form out of nineteen, and in Mathematics Set II, again with Mr.Corner, he was seventh overall out of seventeen boys, eleventh in Arithmetic and Algebra, and sixth in Euclid. He remained for a second year in Science Set IIB with Mr.Hodgson, and was eighteenth out of twenty-six boys. Lawrence left the High School in July 1901, when the three years of the Scholarship were finished. According to F.R.Leavis, he had received "...a better education, one calculated to develop his genius for its most fruitful use, than any other he could have got." Lawrence had not necessarily been the most prominent of pupils, however, despite his fame in later years. Over the years, few teachers or fellow pupils have ever come forward with their memories of the future author. Only the Chief History Master, C.Lloyd Morgan, was left to recollect..."I think I just missed D.H.Lawrence, but I knew the woman he ran off with."

Indeed, what seems to be the only remaining story about the young Lawrence does not actually bear rigorous investigation, when the details are compared with the School Record. According to one source, therefore, Lawrence had a peculiar obsession with death. One day, his Form Master, the Reverend T.B.Hardy, who was later to win a Victoria Cross in the Great War, noticed how the young boy was not paying proper attention to the lesson, but was more interested with the contents of his desk. Naturally, the teacher walked over, and looked into the boy's desk. Inside was a vast collection of tiny coffins, gibbets and miniature skeletons. Later, Lawrence took his revenge on his Form Master by firing a paper pellet at him while he had his back turned, as he wrote on the blackboard. Another more ludicrous version of what is obviously the same story has the aggrieved Lawrence bringing a pistol to school, and then firing it at Hardy, the bullet shattering the board. Whatever the precise details of the incident, it seems that the young Lawrence had started his career as a rebel.

Lawrence has left three relics of his stay at the High School behind him. In the School Archives, there is a form photograph which has a very young Lawrence on it. I discovered this previously-unknown photo in the 1990s while researching the history of the school's many years of involvement in Association Football. I immediately checked the extensive school lists to ascertain which forms Lawrence had been in, and I then investigated whether any photographs had ever been taken of these classes. There was just one, a form photograph which dated from 1898. Careful examination revealed a likely candidate, tucked away on the next to back row. Further comparison with other photographs available elsewhere indicated that this was indeed the youthful D.H.Lawrence. The clinching factor in the identification was the way that Lawrence's ears were very fleshy and turned forwards. The second relic of the great man is his Maths prize, which dates from his days in the Modern Fifth Form in 1899-1900. It is entitled *Fights for the Flag* and was written by W.H.Fitchett. This spectacular find was again made during my own research for a book about Association Football.

Most spectacular of all, perhaps, is the third item, where the young Lawrence has carved his name on an old stone fireplace in what is now the Examination Officers' Office, on the first floor near the staffroom:

A leading academic was apparently relatively unimpressed by Lawrence's graffiti, and I was told after their visit that they thought it most probably to be a forgery. Careful examination of the contextual evidence, however, indicates a different possibility. In the first place, therefore, great care has been taken over nearly a hundred years not to paint over the carving, but to preserve it carefully for subsequent generations. Clearly this would not have happened if the people who started off this century-long process of preservation, all those years ago, had not had reason to do so. In other words, they must have thought that the initials were the genuine article otherwise they would have removed them. In addition, the other names and lettering on the fireplace all seem to date from the same fifteen or twenty year span of history around the end of the nineteenth century. They are regarded as genuine graffiti, as indeed are the names carved on a similar fireplace one floor lower down, on the Ground Floor, between the General Office and the entrance to the Assembly Hall. It must also be said that the names surrounding D. H. Lawrence's are very closely positioned together, indicating that they were carefully carved in relation to each other. It would be highly unlikely that a group of boys carving their names at the turn of the century would leave a space in the middle of the group for a forger, fifty years later, to add another name. The initials next to D.H.Lawrence include "AJO", "WB" and T(F?)M, as well as the name "R.Devey 20", which was presumably a reference to the date when young Devey carved his own particular contribution. In actual fact, Reginald Devey was born on May 31st 1905 and entered the school on May 27th 1918 at the age of twelve. His father was James Edward Devey, a civil servant, and the family lived at 22, Ebury Road, Sherwood Rise. He left the High School in August 1922. One of the other complete names carved on the stone next to that of Lawrence was actually quite a famous person within the context of the High School, even at the time when he added his name. He was L.S.Laver, a junior boy who, in 1896, achieved first place in Latin in the Cambridge Local Examinations. Dr Gow, the Headmaster, duly proclaimed him "the top boy of all the world". Two years later, in December 1898, Laver was, as a senior, to be placed first in England in Latin, first in Greek, and then to be awarded his own scholarship of £60 to St John's College, Cambridge. While no one can ever prove the authenticity of these initials (short of producing photographs of the boys vandalising their own school), the contextual evidence does appear to indicate that D. H. Lawrence left his mark on the school alongside his contemporaries. My only slight area of doubt is the fact that it would certainly be possible to argue that the letters "awrence" have been added later to the original "DHL", but that is not outrageous, and does not preclude the genuineness of the first three letters. For instance, "L.S.Laver" has itself been comically modified to "L.S.Laveri". People certainly still seem to be aware of the existence of the initials. Even nowadays, over a century later, tourists from as far afield as Tokyo and Toronto have come to see the name of D.H. Lawrence on the fireplace, a fitting piece of graffiti for the boy who later adopted as his emblem the fiery image of the phoenix rising from the ashes for his last major publication, *Lady Chatterley's Lover*.

Wednesday, January 18th 1899

Thomas Ignatius Joseph Gillott, the young boy who was one day to carve his name on the stone fireplace near the North Entrance, entered the school on this day. He was to leave after four years in July 1902. He died on Sunday, July 6th 1913 after an operation at the London Hospital. Thomas' brother, Bernard Cuthbert Gillott also entered the High School on this day. He was destined to remain a pupil only until the end of this academic year in July 1899. With the advent of the Great War Bernard was to join the army, serving as a Captain in the 6th Northamptonshire Regiment. A very brave man, he won both the British Military Cross and the French Croix de Guerre. He was eventually severely wounded and was invalided home to England.

1900 - 1901

This year the Gymnastic Club had sixty-four members. They were divided into four sections with promotion between upper and lower groups. An annual competition was established with four members chosen to represent each of the three parliamentary wards of the city and four more to represent those who lived outside the city boundaries. They then competed for four bronze medals. An outstanding gymnast might even receive a silver medal. This particular year the West Ward were the winners and both S.Hoyte and P.C.Sands achieved silver medals.

Saturday, February 3rd 1900

At a meeting of the Debating Society the idea was broached of forming a company or half company of the Robin Hood Battalion of the Sherwood Foresters. The Governors and Headmaster gave it strong support and recruiting quickly began. Soon more than sixty boys between the ages of fourteen and seventeen had been recruited by the Sixth Form recruiting sergeants and, when the Headmaster allowed Third Formers over twelve to join up, numbers increased to 87. The teacher in charge was Samuel Russell Trotman, the Head of Science and the Commanding Officer with the rank of Captain, He was described by a former pupil as "a chemist, biologist and gymnast. His shoulders proclaimed a mighty physique and he taught us the German system of gymnastics."

Thursday, May 17th 1900

The Cadet Force began drilling under the watchful eye of Sergeant Hartshorn. Their activities were to include rifle practice, inspections, route marches (up to twenty-two miles), church parades and a special service in the Market Place on the day of Queen Victoria's funeral.

Saturday, May 19th 1900

The Siege of Mafeking had been relieved the previous day, so school was dismissed at 10.20 a.m.

Thursday, May 24th 1900

The boys all had a half day holiday to celebrate the birthday of Queen Victoria, and the opening of the new Victoria Station in Nottingham.

The afternoon of Monday, May 28th 1900

Just after school recommenced for the afternoon, all the boys went out to see an eclipse of the sun. Most of the morning and the dinner hour had been cloudy, but, luckily, the skies cleared just in time and everyone had superb views. The eclipse began at 2.54 p.m., and was finished by 4.54 p.m. It was at its maximum at 3.52 p.m. The boys used coloured glass, smoked glass and cards with pinholes to observe it, but the idea of using a bucket of water so that the reflection of the sun could be seen did not work as too many boys crowded around.

Wednesday, October 17th 1900

At football, the First XI defeated Leicester Wyggeston School at Mapperley Park by a margin of 23-0. The goals came from Sands (10), Clayton (3), Sim (3), Thurman (3) Spencer (2), Kirby and Burden. The overall total, the number of hat-tricks and the number of different scorers, all remain records. Sands' personal scoring feat, amazingly enough, remained a record for only seven days.

Wednesday, October 24th 1900

At football, the First XI defeated Newark Grammar School by 17-0 at Mapperley Park. The goals came from Sands (11), Sim (2), Thurman (2), Kirby and Clayton. In scoring eleven goals Sands broke his own record of ten goals in a game, established only a week earlier. As far as I can trace, this new record of eleven goals has never been broken.

Wednesday, January 22nd 1901

Queen Victoria had died the previous day. Dr Gow was away in London so it was Mr Corner who addressed the school during morning prayers. He compared the dead monarch to King Alfred and spoke of how "none has reigned so long, none has reigned so gloriously." *The Forester* spoke of how "All the boys' games were stopped and all matches were postponed and in the playground boys stood in groups, talking of the Queen or walked quietly and orderly." At noon the boys assembled again in the Prayer Room and after a telegram from the Headmaster was read out, school was dismissed for the day.

Saturday, March 16th 1901

The most successful High School football team ever finished the season with a record of sixteen victories, two drawn games and seven defeats. They had scored 145 goals and conceded only 47. Margins of victory included 23-0, 17-0, 13-1, 12-0, 11-0, 8-0, 8-1, 7-1, 7-2, and 6-0. The team was usually selected from Heald, Wilkinson, Donnithorne, Lindley, Willatt, Gamble, Spencer, Burden, Thurman, Sim, Sands, Kirby, and Clayton. The chief goalscorer was Percy Sands, who, during his school career, is known to have scored a minimum of 106 goals in only 61 games spread over three seasons.

The afternoon of Friday, March 29th 1901

For the first time the School Sports took place at the new sports ground at Mapperley Park. A large number of boys, friends, parents and Old Boys attended but the day was spoiled by the bitterly cold weather, "the turf was naturally affected by the overnight fall of snow which made the going heavy." Nevertheless, W.A.Donnithorne still managed to run the hundred yards in eleven seconds.

June 1901

Dr Gow, known by the boys as "The Doctor", left the High School to become Head of Westminster School. Academically, standards had been raised dramatically during his seventeen years and boys were now quite regularly finishing in high positions in national examinations and then going on to great things at either Oxford or Cambridge. The school was attracting well over four hundred boys by the excellence of the education it offered. Facilities were equally impressive with Gow having improved everything from the boys' toilets to school administration, teachers' salaries and advertising. The majority of the school's societies were founded during Gow's reign, and school sport, whether football or cricket, was thriving on its new sports ground at Mapperley Park. The Cadet Corps had been established in 1900 and other school institutions such as the Sports Day or the Pet Show were inaugurated during this period. Dr Gow was to have similar success at Westminster, and soon became a national figure as Chairman of the Headmasters' Conference. He became President of the Association of Headmasters and in 1900, he was appointed as a member of the Consultative Committee of the Board of Education. In 1904, the Reverend W.G.Cruft was to deliver a famous verdict on Gow's reign, namely "he found a mob of schoolboys, and left a Public School." In *The Forester*, Sammy Corner wrote that "by energy, and ability, Dr Gow has converted Nottingham High School from an unpopular institution into one of the finest day schools in the kingdom, doing probably greater work now than at any time in its long history of five hundred years and upwards."

Dr Gow was, by a very large margin, the greatest headmaster that the school has ever had and indeed, is ever likely to have. The school's debt to James Gow, even now, is almost incalculable.

Tuesday, July 23rd 1901

Dr Gow was presented with a silver tobacco jar by the Assistant Masters.

Thursday, July 25th 1901

Dr Gow was presented with a silver bowl by J.Kentish Wright on behalf of the Governors. Unfortunately, the Duke of Portland had a prior engagement and could not be there nor could the Bishop of Southwell nor Sir William Blain.

On behalf of the boys of the school, Mr R.B.Brown gave Dr Gow a massive candelabra and a silver inkstand, decorated with the school crest and bearing the legend "To Dr James Gow, from the boys, past and present, of the Nottingham High School 1885-1901". The boys had collected just over £120 and the balance was spent on a silver glove box for Mrs Gow. The current Head Boy, P.C.Sands, made a short speech, but could not "find words to express my feelings". Indeed, it must have been a very emotional occasion, as the school bade farewell to "the best Head Master in England".

September 1901

There were thirty eight candidates for Dr Gow's job, and he was finally succeeded by Dr George Sherbrooke Turpin, one of the very few Old Boys ever to be appointed to this office. When he left the High School, Turpin went to Owen's College (Manchester) and then to St.John's College (Cambridge) where he gained a double First in Natural Sciences. He was a Doctor of Science from London University and had spent a year at Berlin University. He was the first "non-Classic" to become Headmaster of the High School. During the six years before his arrival at the High School, he had been Headmaster of Swansea Grammar School. Under his leadership, the High School was to introduce classes based on ability for certain subjects, to adopt rugby as a sport, and to build a separate dining room.

9.55 a.m. on Monday, June 2nd 1902

The previous day, a peace treaty had been signed between England and the Boers. After prayers the Headmaster said that the school would celebrate this great event and a notice was sent round that the school should reassemble at 9.55 am. Dr Turpin read aloud the proclamation and the telegram which Lord Kitchener had sent to England. The school formed a procession and set off to march around the town. Over three hundred boys with every flag they could find, made their way down Waverley Street to University College, the Guildhall, and the Market Place. They sang the national anthem at the College, the Guildhall and the Exchange Buildings. The procession went on to the Castle, where the anthem was again sung, and Mr Corner made a speech. The boys then made their way back along Mansfield Road stopping to sing the anthem for one last time outside the Girls' High School. Finally, Dr Turpin addressed the school from the front steps of the High School, photographs were taken and much to everyone's great joy, a half-holiday was proclaimed for the afternoon.

Autumn Term 1902 and Spring Term 1903

A new system was adapted whereby each form went down to the Forest to practice their football on one afternoon a week rather than going all the way to Mapperley Park. The latter venue was reserved for school fixtures, which allowed the boys more time to play and standards throughout seemed to improve. The same system was later introduced to cricket in the Summer Term of 1903.

Autumn Term 1902

A change was made to the school cap. Instead of the previous design (which remains, in actual fact, unrecorded), boys were to wear a plain black cap, with the school badge either in silk or enamelled silver.

The afternoon of Wednesday, December 17th 1902

The "Hare and Hounds Club" held its first meeting through Gedling and Lambley. Sixteen boys took part as hounds, chasing the hares, of whom J.F.Haseldine and L.T.Wootton were almost caught.

The afternoon of Monday, December 23rd 1902

The "Hare and Hounds Club" turned out again. The afternoon was not an unmitigated success, however, as the strong wind blew most of the paper trail away and the hares, A.F.Johnson and F.R.Simon, escaped their pursuers with ease. To compound this disaster one of the hounds attempted to cross a pond on a plank but then fell in when the plank came loose from its supports.

1903

Alderman Bright, one of the Governors, bought the Mapperley Park playing fields for £5,800 just as houses were about to be constructed on the whole area by a large building syndicate. He sold them on to the High School for the same price.

1903

An Old Boy, G.W.Brewill, became Champion of England over 200 yards.

The afternoon of Friday, January 2nd 1903

The "Hare and Hounds Club" met with further problems, this time starting off from the "Three Wheat Sheaves Inn" at Lenton and trying to continue through Bramcote and Wollaton. The hounds soon lost the hares' original trail of paper but then found some other paper discarded on a previous occasion. They followed this until they found, quite by accident, their own outward trail from today. Not recognising it for what it was, the hounds followed it and arrived back home before the hares.

1.30 p.m. on Tuesday, March 24th 1903

The school was rocked by a noticeable earthquake. Furniture, pictures and other objects were distinctly shaken and rattled, and small trees were seen to shake. It was around this time that the area around the school was the subject of a relatively serious smallpox outbreak.

The afternoon of Saturday, April 4th 1903

Everything was going well for the "Hare and Hounds Club" through Lambley, until the hares ran out of paper, and everyone had to go home.

Monday, November 23rd 1903

Mr John Suttill Jones, Master of the Junior Form, died after only a week's illness. He had been at school as normal on November 16th and was "very popular, willing to do any service that lay in his power. He maintained the best of discipline with scarcely any recourse to punishment, a good talker with a fund of good humour and amusing conversation, able to sing a song well, either in English or French, a reciter of very considerable dramatic power."

November 1903

Old Boy, John Dane Player became a co-optative Governor. His acceptance was typically modest: "Nothing would give me greater pleasure than to be a Governor of my old School; please convey to the Governing Body my thanks. I much appreciate the honour they have done me." His first gift was a cheque for £300.

December 1903

In Northern Nigeria the British authorities were keen to restore the King of Ankina to his rightful position, after he had been ousted from the throne by a usurper. A force was sent out under the command of Old Nottinghamian, Lieutenant Cyril Amyatt Wyse Amyatt-Burney of the

Police, and Captain O'Riordan, a local resident. Sadly, both men were murdered as soon as they reached the native village of Deckina.

Burney had previously fought against the Boers in South Africa, before a spell in the office of the Chief Constable of Glamorgan. It was from here that he had moved to North Nigeria as "a zealous officer and a young man of promise and energy."

Immediate punitive operations for the murder of Amyatt-Burney and O'Riordan were duly carried out by a force commanded by Major G. C. Merrick of the Royal Artillery. He had 11 European soldiers and 262 Africans along with two Maxim machine guns and a three inch field gun carried by 307 native bearers. This was an isolated area of heavy forest and thick bush, at a time when cannibalism was rife in the northern regions of Nigeria. Lieutenant Amyatt-Burney's body was never found, but on December 15th, a bundle of some of his blood stained clothes was discovered, secreted away in a native hut. His mysterious disappearance was never explained. The village was then completely destroyed as retribution for whatever may have happened there.

3.21 p.m. on Sunday, July 3rd 1904

The whole of Nottingham, including the High School, experienced an earthquake, which lasted two or three seconds with "rumbling noises, and the shaking of doors, windows and furniture."

August 1904

Mr R.E.Yates took a party of boys on what appears to be the school's first ever trip abroad. They stayed at the Collège Universitaire de St Servan near Saint-Malo in Brittany.

Friday, July 1st 1904

The whole school was granted a holiday to commemorate the four Old Boys who had won First Class degrees at Cambridge.

Wednesday, October 5th 1904

For the second time, the First XI defeated an unfortunate Leicester Wyggeston School at football by the extraordinary margin of 23-0.

Probably towards the end of the Christmas Term, 1904

John Francis Haseldine carved his name in rather florid handwriting on the stone mantelpiece of the fireplace between the General Office and the entrance to the Assembly Hall. Haseldine was born on December 28th 1886 and entered the High School on May 4th 1896, at the age of nine. His father was Frank Haseldine, a lace manufacturer of St.John's Grove, Beeston. John Francis was a very good footballer and made his début for the First XI on Wednesday, March 26th 1902, in an away game against Loughborough Grammar School (0-2). That particular spring Haseldine had been in the team which had won the Football Sixes. On Wednesday, February 14th 1903, Haseldine scored his only goal for the school in a 4-1 victory over Mansfield Grammar School, "a rather poor and one-sided game", played at Mansfield. As pretty much an ever present in the team he won his football colours and was then Captain of Football in 1903-1904. He was awarded a "Standard Medal" for Football at the end of this year. He then spent the Christmas Term of 1904 at the High School but he left half way through the academic year in December 1904. In the Great War Haseldine was a Major in the Royal Engineers, Special Reserve. He was mentioned in dispatches on June 3rd 1916, and received the Military Cross on January 1st 1917. By 1929, he was living at Northdene, New Barnet.

Among the other more legible names on the same stone mantelpiece are "A.E.Anthony" and "G.Devey". What is apparently "R.Salew" is also there, although there are many layers of gloss paint to obscure the lettering. Another seems to read "B.Abel 1905-190" as if the young man had been interrupted as he came to the end of his carving, but did not ever return to finish the job. Alfred Edward Anthony was born on June 12 1906, and entered the school on September 18th 1918, at the age of twelve. His father was F.W.Anthony of 120, Radcliffe Road, West Bridgford. He was the Managing Director of Gotham Co Ltd (apparently sic). Alfred left the school in December 1922. "G.Devey" was the elder brother of Reginald Devey, whose own name was already carved on the fireplace upstairs, alongside that of D.H.Lawrence and L.S.Laver, the High School's very own Latin Champion of the World. These initials were Gerald Bertil Devey who was born on June 10th 1903. Gerald entered the school on May 27th 1918 at the rather late age of fourteen. His father was James Edward Devey, a civil servant, and the family lived at 22, Ebury Road, Sherwood Rise. Gerald left the High

School in July 1919. John Rylett Salew entered the school on May 4th 1916, aged fourteen. He left in December 1918. John was born on February 28th 1902 and his father was Joseph William Salew, an "agent" of 19, William Rd, West Bridgford. Bertram Albert Abel was born on July 31st 1889, and entered the school on September 13th 1905, aged sixteen. His father was William Jenkinson Abel, a clerk to the Nottingham Education Committee. The family lived at 99, Waterloo Crescent, and Bertram left the school in July 1907. The fact that "S.Vasey" has carved his name in two different places on the stone, one of them complete with his own personal dates, namely "1917" and "1917-1922" shows not only that he had an extremely strong desire for immortality, but that, within the context of the High School, it has been fulfilled. Stanley Vasey was born on June 5th 1905 and he entered the school at the age of thirteen on September 18th 1918. His father was Alfred Vasey, a shop inspector, and the family lived at 15, Glebe Road, West Bridgford. He left in December 1922.

It is actually possible to best guess friendship groups among these carved names. John Rylett Salew and Stanley Vasey both lived very close to each other in West Bridgford, for example. Messrs Anthony, Devey and Vasey all joined the school in the same year of 1918 and they all left in the latter half of 1922. Given their similar ages they must surely have known each other. Did the three boys seal their friendship by carving their names into the surface of that ancient fireplace? Did two of them keep watch while the third scratched his name on the unyielding stone?

Saturday, June 3rd 1905

Playing cricket against Loughborough Grammar School, R.G.Cairns performed the hat-trick.

Saturday, July 22nd 1905

In a Second XI cricket match at Mapperley Park, against Leicester Wyggeston School, W.Taylor succeeded in splitting a bail when he bowled one of the batsmen. It was knocked some twenty five yards beyond the wicket.

Chapter 10: Major General Mahin: A Yank at the High School

The end of the Summer Term, 1905 onwards

Another notable boy has carved his initials on the much vandalised stone mantelpiece of the ground floor fireplace between the General Office and the entrance to the Assembly Hall. He is "F.C.Mahin".

Frank Cadle Mahin was one of the most interesting of the school's pupils. He was born on May 27th 1887, in Clinton, Iowa, the son of Frank W. Mahin, who was a retired United States Consular Officer at the time. Young Frank entered the High School on September 15th 1902 at the age of fifteen. The family lived at 7, Sherwood Rise and his father was the United States Consul in Nottingham. Despite his comparatively short stay, Frank seems to have been an accomplished sportsman and appeared for the school First XI at football in fixtures against Loughborough Grammar School, Notts. Magdala F.C. 2nd XI and Worksop College. He performed as a linesman in First XI football fixtures on several occasions. Frank was perhaps a better cricketer than footballer and was the regular captain of the Second XI. In addition we know that on Saturday, June 24th 1905, Frank finished in equal first place in the Open Long Jump on School Sports Day, managing a jump of fifteen feet nine inches, exactly the same distance as C.F.R.Fryer. In the academic world, Frank won the Mayor's Prize for Modern Languages and reached the rank of sergeant in the newly formed Officer Training Corps. He left in July 1905 and returned to the United States where he was in the Class of 1909 at Harvard University. His close contemporaries included Franklin Delano Roosevelt and two sons of the current President of the time, Theodore Roosevelt. They were called Theodore and Kermit. Theodore was to die in France a month after leading the first wave of troops on Utah Beach during the Normandy landings in 1944. Kermit was a distinguished soldier with the British in the Great War and won the Military Cross.

During his time at Harvard, Frank represented the University at football on a number of occasions, playing as a goalkeeper. After Harvard, Frank joined the Regular Army in 1910 after service with the New York

National Guard. Two years later he received his first commission. Frank and thirty eight others took an examination and were all made Second Lieutenants. At the time he was listed as being at Fort William Henry Harrison in Montana. Frank was married to Mauree Pickering in 1913 and they had four children, including twins named Margaret Celestia and Anna Yetive, both born in the Philippines.

Frank soon became a Major and served in France in 1918. He was wounded at St. Mihiel in the Meuse-Argonne campaign. Resuming his formal military studies after the war, Frank was a "distinguished graduate" of the Command and General Staff School in 1925. He graduated from the Army War College in 1929 and became Inspector-General of the Panama Canal Department. He was placed in command of the 3rd Infantry Division (1937). Frank then organized the 60th Infantry Regiment, the "Go Devils", commanding them until October 1941 when he was promoted to Brigadier General. He became a Major General after assuming command of the 33rd Division at Camp Forrest Tennessee in May 1942. Before his appointment he had been assistant commander of the 45th Division called "The Thunderbirds" at Camp Berkley in Texas.

Sadly, on Friday, July 24th, 1942, Frank Mahin and two Army flyers were killed near Waynesboro, Tennessee when their observation plane was sabotaged by a mechanic and crashed. Frank was commanding officer of the 33rd Division at Camp Forrest, Tennessee. Mrs. Walter Brewer, the wife of the Wayne County Sheriff, said "The plane struck a tree five miles west of here, but did not burn". The three occupants were en route from Tullahoma to Fort Sill, Oklahoma. The two others killed were Second Lieutenant Robert F. Turk of Wichita, Kansas, and Sergeant John Camerford of Alamo, Texas, both attached to the 127th Observation Squadron at Tullahoma. Memorial services were conducted at Camp Forrest, Tennessee and then the General's body was sent to Washington for burial in the National Cemetery at Arlington. Major General Mahin is buried side by side with his son Colonel Frank Cadle Mahin Junior, a graduate of the West Point Class of 1944. The General is also commemorated in the Memorial Church at Harvard University. He is the only Old Nottinghamian to be awarded the Purple Heart and the only one to be interred in the National Cemetery at Arlington. I would also argue that Major General Mahin is the highest ranked Old

Nottinghamian of all time. Incidentally, I believe that Mahin's surname was pronounced "Márr-hin". Certainly at the United States Military Academy at West Point his son was often teased by his fellow cadets who all called him "Ma-Heen".

The other names on the fireplace include "O.Gillot", "F.B.Ludlow", "N.G.Peet", "Littler", "Meigh" and "Holmes". The latter was perhaps the George Chudleigh Holmes who regularly represented the school in the First XI football team during the 1902-1903 season. Born on June 15th 1887, George had entered the school on January 17th 1900, aged twelve. His father was George H.Holmes, a Lace Manufacturer of Gregory Street, Old Lenton. George left the school at Easter 1903. Oswald Cornek Gillot was born in Ripley on July 22nd 1890 and entered the High School on September 12th 1899 at the age of nine. He left in March 1907. Oswald's father was Thomas Gillot, M.I.C.E., a civil engineer whose address was given in 1899 as variously either, Upland House, Eastwood, or Langley Mill near Ilkeston. Fred (sic) Ball Ludlow was born on April 28th 1891. He entered the High School on May 1st 1900 at the age of nine. His father was William Ludlow, a clerk in the Gas Depôt. The family lived at 10, Willoughby Avenue, Lenton. Fred left in June 1907. Noel George Peet was born on December 26th 1901 and entered the High School on April 26th 1917, at the age of fifteen. His father was William George Peet, a "general agent", and the family lived at 413, Mansfield Road. Noel left the school in July 1919. Samuel Littler was born on May 16th 1891. He entered the school on September 16th 1903 at the age of twelve. The family lived at 8, Appleton Gate, Newark-on-Trent, and his father, a veterinary surgeon, was also called Samuel Littler. Samuel junior left in July 1908. Vincent George Meigh entered the school as an Agnes Mellers scholar on September 12th 1899 at the age of ten. His father was George Meigh, a schoolmaster of 3, Willoughby Avenue, Lenton. Vincent left the school in December, 1903.

On the mantelpiece, one set of letters to set the heart a-flutter is "(illegible)BALL 1900-1907", but this cannot be the famous air ace, Albert Ball, as there are clearly a fair number of letters before the B-A-L-L. In any case, Ball did not stay long in the High School, being expelled after an incident when he disrupted school assembly with a large bag of bullseyes, gobstoppers and other sweets. The best fit is probably Oliver Herbert Ball who was born on August 13th 1891. He had entered the school on January 17th 1900 at the age of eight, the third of three brothers. Oliver was to leave the school in July 1907. His mother was called Emma and his father was Alfred Holmes Ball, the "Laundry Man" of "Sunnyside", Daybrook, Notts. Presumably this was the company which was eventually to become the massive "Daybrook Laundry". It was situated opposite the Home Brewery and was only recently demolished in the first decade of the twenty first century to provide land for a large supermarket. Oliver Ball's elder brother was Walter William Ball, the second son of three. To hear his story, the reader should read "Wednesday, November 24th 1915"

One of the more notable objects on the mantelpiece is perhaps the school badge which has been carved relatively large and in primitive style with the lozenge and the three birds still recognisable even now, the best part of a century after it was executed by some unknown, juvenile artist.

Less time proof perhaps, are the boys who managed to carve only their initials, namely "JL", "MV", either "WA" or "WR", and either "BFW" or "SFW". It is just so difficult to be certain about whose initials they might be. In some cases there are literally dozens of possible candidates and it becomes a pointless effort to try and guess who has carved them. Some boys have been able to make only part of their name legible. We appear to have, therefore, a group of letters which seems, perhaps, to form "H-LLF". Similarly, I have tried so hard to turn "----NGTON" into Victor George Darrington, one of the very few young men to have captained the school at both football and rugby. The time is right (he entered the High School on September 23rd 1909 at the age of twelve) but the fact is that the blurred and painted-over letters just do not look like they were ever meant to spell Darrington.

Even more striking is the young member of the "Chambers" family who did not manage to carve his initials clearly. Just a cursory perusal of the school registers reveals the existence, between 1897 and 1926, of "E.Chambers", "W.", "P.", "N.", "J.F.", "J.S.", "A.", "C.G.", "J.", "B.J.", "C.C.", "S.H.", "D.B.", and a second "W." No doubt a really thorough search would reveal even more members of the Chambers clan who were presumably one of the High School's best customers. It would be nice to think though, that the perpetrator was the (uninitialled) Chambers of Form IVb, whose doings are reported on Thursday, February 1st 1912.

Here again, it is possible to guess at friendships between the names in the stone. Two of the boys for example, Fred Ball Ludlow and Oliver Herbert Ball, both joined the school in 1900 and their entries are virtually next to each other in the School Register. The use of the surname of one as the middle name of the other may hint at a blood relationship as well as mere friendship. Coincidentally, a third name on this single ancient page of the register is that of Harold Binks who also entered the school in 1900 although Harold was never to carve his own name on the fireplace. From his reminiscences, published in in April 1935, however, we know that one of his best friends in the Senior School was called Ball. (see the entry for October 19th 1981). It seems likely too that another of the friends was Oswald Gillot who was already in the school when Ludlow, Ball and Binks arrived. All these boys were of the same age and they all left the school in the latter part of the academic year 1906-1907. Gillot lived in distant Ilkeston, but George Holmes lived in Gregory Street, Old Lenton, very close to Fred Ludlow and Vincent Meigh who themselves both lived in the same street, namely Willoughby Avenue, Lenton. Surely two of them kept careful watch while the third carried out the evil deed.

September 1905

The Preparatory School was set up in a house at 11, Waverley Mount where Dr Dixon had lived so many years before. The Main School then established a small Physics Laboratory where the youngest boys had previously been taught. There were thirty two pupils, making up a senior form taught initially by Mr R.Dark and then soon afterwards by Mr H.A.Leggett. Two ladies taught the other form, one of whom "lived in", acting as a housekeeper as well as a teacher.

Summer term 1907

According to the school magazine, *Highvite*, it was during this term that the system of school prefects was revived, after a lapse of several years. At many of the top public schools such as Rugby and Marlborough the prefects virtually ran the school from the discipline point of view and acted almost as an independent body. Although it was not a boarding establishment the High School does not seem to have differed significantly from this system and on numerous occasions in the Prefects' Book, the School Captain has written that he will go and see the Headmaster about various judgments that the prefects have reached as if they expected the Headmaster, either Dr Turpin, or his successor, Mr Reynolds, merely to rubber stamp their decision. In a similar way, members of staff, when they encountered misbehaviour outside the classroom, would frequently report it to the prefects so that they could deal with the culprits. The Prefects always wore a tassel on their caps and were usually referred to by smaller boys as "Pre's"

Chapter 11: Albert Ball and the High School Go to War

Thursday, September 19th 1907

Albert Ball, the future ace fighter pilot, entered the High School at the age of eleven as boy Number 2651. According to the school register, he was born on August 17th 1896 although on his birth certificate the date is given as August 14th. Later in life, Ball was to countersign a certificate from the Royal Aero Club on which his date of birth was written as August 21st. Originally the family had lived at 301, Lenton Boulevard (now 245 Castle Boulevard). Just a few years later they moved to Sedgley House, 43 Lenton Avenue, The Park, Nottingham and this is the address given in the school register where his father is listed as Albert Ball, a "land agent". The family lived in moderately wealthy fashion. Albert had a brother Cyril and a sister Lois. Their parents were always "loving and indulgent". Albert Ball Senior was originally a plumber, but he was ambitious and soon became an estate agent and a property speculator as his fortunes improved. He was elected as Mayor of Nottingham in 1909, 1910, 1920 and 1935 and was eventually to be knighted. As a boy, Albert junior was interested in engines and electrics. He had experience of firearms and enjoyed target practice in the garden. Thanks to his wonderful eyesight, he was soon a crack shot. On his sixteenth birthday Albert enjoyed a day as a steeplejack as he accompanied a workman to the top of a tall factory chimney. He was completely unafraid and strolled around, not bothered by the height.

Initially Albert went to Lenton Church School but then, for some unknown reason, he was sent to Grantham Grammar School along with his younger brother Cyril. Albert next entered the High School from which he was eventually to be expelled in 1910. Contemporary sources reveal that Albert enjoyed misbehaving in music lessons. The Third Form music master was a Mr Dunhill who had one eye which was straight but the other looked outwards at an angle rather like half past ten on a clock. Boys always used to make fun of him. Whenever he shouted "Stand up you!!!" and looked at a certain naughty boy, four others would get up elsewhere in the room. "NO! NO! NOT YOU!!

YOU!!" The original four would then sit down, and another four completely unrelated boys would stand up elsewhere in the room. Albert Ball specialised in misbehaviour during these singing classes. He and his brother Cyril would invariably "kick up a terrible row", and then be sent out of the room. According to one Old Boy however, Albert's actual expulsion came from an incident which took place at morning prayers. Albert brought with him a huge bag full of boiled sweets, which at one point he allowed to burst, and hundreds of sweets were all dropped onto the floor. The whole school assembly then became one seething mass of boys, all scrabbling about on the floor, "heads down and bottoms up, completely out of control", trying to pick up as many sweets as they possibly could. That did not necessarily mean, however, that Albert misbehaved with every single teacher. The Chief History master, C.Lloyd Morgan, was to recollect in later years "I think I taught Albert Ball but can't recollect him." Albert later moved to Trent College where he was a boarder. He eventually left there at Midsummer 1913 and he seems to have been for the most part relatively happy, although not everything was perfect by any means. On at least one occasion, for example, an unhappy Albert ran away to sea and he was only apprehended at the very last moment, "covered in coal dust, in the engine room of an outgoing steamer".

Thursday, December 12th 1907

In this era, the Prefects ruled the school with an iron cane. The Prefects' Book records that:

> "A meeting was held in the interval. Hemsley reported that he had been asked to report R.J.Thominet (Form 3c) for smoking on a tramcar on the night of the 3rd. Thominet pleaded guilty. Punishment to the amount of 12 strokes was inflicted and a severe reprimand as to his general behaviour was administered. Present were Heald, Hooton, Wootton & Wright."

Thursday, May 28th 1908

The Prefects had to deal with the most inappropriate of behaviour:

> "L.G.Lee was examined as to his behaviour on Forest Road in the evenings. He had several times been observed philandering in female company towards dusk; it was considered by the

prefects to be derogatory to the School and a bad example to the juniors. He was given to understand that such behaviour must discontinue, and that any further recurrence would make him, L.G.Lee, eligible for punishment."

Wednesday, June 17th 1908

Very often, threats about a boy's place in the cricket team were enough to stop his wandering hands:

> "A meeting was held in the Library on this date after the interval. All the prefects present. C.R.Attenborough reported having seen C.W.Goddard put his hands on the shoulders of a girl seated in a chair at Mapperley Cricket Ground. Under discussion, there were differences in the Prefects' ideas as to the enormity of the offence and this fact, coupled with the fact of a misunderstanding between Attenborough and Goddard, saved Goddard from corporal punishment. He was therefore allowed to depart with some good advice as to his future behaviour, the Cricket Captain pointing out that a recurrence of such behaviour would involve his dismissal from the First Eleven."

Saturday, October 24th 1908

Frederick William Chapman appeared in the Great Britain football team which played in the Olympic Tournament held in London. The Great Britain team won the final 2-0 against Denmark and Chapman scored the opening goal. He thereby became the only Old Boy ever to win an Olympic gold medal and, given the limited number of countries who were playing football at this time, Chapman had good reason to consider himself a champion of the world. Chapman had already appeared three times for Nottingham Forest in the First Division and he went on to win twenty amateur international caps for England, captaining the team on at least one occasion.

Tuesday, October 27th 1908

As gangsterism raised its ugly head, the Prefects had it all under control:

> "A meeting was held at 2.30 p.m. in the Library. All the prefects were present. M.M.Lyon was reported for bullying A.W.Barton during the preceding day. He had tried to make Barton

accompany him home & as Barton refused, he dragged him along Forest Road towards Waverley St. Lyon also hit Barton with the knob of his umbrella on his head just behind the ear. This blow had raised a big lump on Barton's head. Lyon only allowed Barton to go home on receiving a promise that he would bring him a penny in the afternoon. As Barton did not bring the money, Lyon thrashed him again in the afternoon. Lyon admitted the offence, and (as a first offender) received 6 strokes.

On the next day, however, Mr Woodward told the school captain that Lyon had treated other boys in a similar way, & had obtained 2d, from J.B.Cooper. Dr Turpin stated that he had warned Lyon previously, & threatened him with expulsion on a repetition of the offence. Mr Dark had also complained about Lyon's bullying propensities. H.J.Hoyte reported Lyon at the end of the summer term for swearing, but Lyon had not been punished as he was away from School. Taking all this into consideration, the prefects offered Lyon the alternative of 15 strokes or expulsion by the Doctor. Lyon chose the strokes."

Monday, November 23rd 1908

Now it was trouble at a school football match. An emergency second extraordinary meeting of the Prefects was held after afternoon school. The Captain of Football, Mark Thompson, reported:

> "C.E.Newham for barracking at 1st XI matches at Mapperley. He stood on the touch-line instructing each member of the team how to play, as though he were the best exponent of the game in the school. He used particularly disgusting expressions to R.S.Tonkin. He received 3 strokes, in preference to 150 lines."

1909

Dr Turpin introduced the house system. It was designed to give every boy the chance to participate in school sport in a meaningful way and to bring a long term element to the competitiveness of sporting events.

Wednesday, March 31st 1909

Smoking in the Library? That doesn't sound very likely, at least, not for an English boy:

> "J.W.Wootton reported that after afternoon school on the preceding day he had found Thominet and Fernandez in the Library, and that there was a strong smell of tobacco smoke in the room. When questioned by Wootton, both boys denied that they had been smoking. At the meeting on the following day Fernandez admitted that he had been smoking and that Thominet had not, so the latter, after being questioned, was dismissed. Fernandez pleaded ignorance of the School rules on smoking, and said that Thominet had not told him of them until after he had smoked; in consideration of this, and the fact that he was a foreigner and was leaving the school on that day, he was let off with a caution."

Obviously, the prefects had forgotten the events of December 12th 1907!

Saturday, May 27th 1911

In a cricket match against Denstone College, the High School scored a record innings total of 276. R.S.Tonkin and R.L.W.Herrick put on 116 for the first wicket, with Herrick going on to make 118, and Tonkin 56. Throughout the first half of this century the school magazine makes repeated reference to boys awaiting their turn to bat. Traditionally they seem to have eaten bags of fresh cherries. Perhaps this was a plentiful fruit at the time, or perhaps it was fun to spit the stones afterwards.

Saturday, July 15th 1911

Very often, simple crimes deserve simple punishments:

"Rushton (4c) was found bullying. It was decided to whack him. The prefects present were Turpin, Ballamy, Goddard & Saxton".

Monday, October 23rd 1911

This time, it was the most magnificent, the most surreal crime in the High School's long history:

> "The prefects minus Towers assembled at 10.45, place as usual. An old offender was summoned, e.g. R.G.Lawson; this time he had failed to do the lines set by E.Newham for signalling words of an indecent nature by semaphore. As regards the imposition, it seems that Lawson had accomplished the lines, but had not conveyed them to school, - a doubtful excuse. He was therefore

lectured on the folly and disgracefulness of his buffoonery, and ordered to bring the required lines + an additional 25."

Tuesday, October 24th 1911

The surreal theme continued with a miscreant from the First Form:

> "Owbridge of 1A was reported for throwing acorns at a motor-car in Waverley St, hitting a gentleman in the motor-car on the forehead. It was decided to inflict corporal punishment to the extent of 2 strokes."

1912

Dr Gow's portrait, painted by the distinguished Old Nottinghamian, Harold Knight, was exhibited in the National Gallery. Two years later Knight was to be a conscientious objector. He spent the war working safely as a farm labourer in Cornwall, a fashionable and convenient place of retreat for many artists during the First World War.

Monday, January 29th 1912

Now it was time to call the Fashion Police:

> "Edwards (3c) had been seen by Towles wearing a large cap with ear-flaps, his excuse being that cycling made his ears cold. He was given 50 lines, and was told that he must get permission from the Headmaster if he was compelled to wear such a cap."

Thursday, February 1st 1912

A dark day in any school's history is the day when a pupil brings a loaded firearm into class. Luckily for the High School, such a day passed without any fatalities:

> "A meeting was held before afternoon school, Towles and Haubitz being absent. Chambers (4b) had been reported for carrying a loaded revolver in his pocket. He admitted the offence, and produced the weapon, which proved to be loaded in four chambers. He was requested not to bring it to school again, and the School Captain decided to interview the Headmaster."

1913

According to the reminiscences of Roy Henderson, the boys played games according to their years:

> "In Form 1a, for example, everybody always had pockets full of marbles. They played in the covered sheds near the Forest Road entrance. To the left as one entered the playground via the Forest Road entrance, there was some extremely dirty sand. This was used as a football pitch, with rough and ready goalposts at either end. Every year, around Easter, a competition was held among teams of eight players, each one of which was captained by a different member of the First XI. The main game in the school playground at this time was called "relievo". It was a particularly thrilling game to play in one of the era's many dense fogs. Form 2a enjoyed a game called "rempstick". A member of one team would stand with his back to the wall, while one of the other members of his team stood with his head between the first boy's legs. The next team member would then put his head between the legs of the second boy, and so on, until a long caterpillar-like scrum structure was formed, just one person wide. The members of the other team then took a long run-up, and, one by one, jumped onto the top of the human caterpillar. If they caused a collapse, then their team was allowed to have a second go. If the caterpillar held up, then its members were allowed to do the jumping. In Form 3a, the main game was football, which was played on the left hand side of the playground, looking from the Forest Road entrance, right at the very far end. In Form 4a, football was played again to the left, but not as far along as in the Third Year. The Fifth Form played their football under cover in the sheds along the Forest Road wall, kicking the ball against the wall in an effort to get past their opponent. Among these boys, Lancelot Wilson Foster was remembered as a particularly good full back. The Sixth Form spent their free time walking and talking on the lawns at the front of the school.
>
> Nobody was ever allowed inside the school during breaks, but it never seemed to rain! In any case, all the boys were always very keen to get out of the building. There was a tuck shop, near the south eastern corner of the present day West Quadrangle. It was run by Robert, the School Caretaker. The small shop which boys

at the end of the twentieth century called "Dicko's" was at this time called "Baldry's", and it was a sweet shop. A female member of staff, a Mrs Digblair, lived above it. She was one of the school's first ever mistresses, and members of the Sixth Form loved to go and have tea with her. Nobody was ever allowed to speak to or approach girls from the Girls' High School. For this transgression, boys were punished by being confined to school. Attitudes at this time were very Victorian."

Sunday, February 2nd 1913

The school celebrated its four hundredth anniversary. The main act of commemoration was to "found a club for poor lads in Radford." This was largely at the urging of G.N.Brown and J.A.Dixon, who already worked regularly at Dakeyne Street Lads' Club. Very quickly, over £5,000 was raised, and a site was selected in Norton Street, Radford. Any other celebrations were put off until the summer.

Monday, June 16th 1913

The four hundredth anniversary celebrations began with a special service at St Mary's. A procession was formed at the Shire Hall, consisting of the Mayor and Corporation, the Headmaster and his staff, and members of the Old Boys' Association. The churchyard was lined by the members of the school's Officer Training Corps. The entry of the dignitaries was made to the strains of the hymn *Glorious Things of Thee are Spoken* and the lesson from the Book of Ecclesiasticus was read by Dr Turpin. The sermon was preached by the former Headmaster, the Reverend Dr Gow.

In the afternoon, a garden party was held in the grounds of the school:

> "The weather was perfect, and much entertainment was derived by visitors from the inspection of the boys' pets and hobbies which were on view in the class-rooms and playground. The laboratories were thrown open, and chemical and physical experiments of an interesting nature were carried on during the afternoon." Of particular interest was W.N.Hoyte's double pendulum, tracing out designs of remarkable regularity in accordance with laws said to be known to an esoteric few."

Hundreds of visitors visited the school to view the various exhibition stands or just to sit in the sun and chat. Mr Corner could show them the original charter and other mementos of the school's history. At Mapperley Park, a number of races were held in front of a large crowd, along with other sporting events. In the evening, there was a dinner for the Old Boys at the Exchange Hall, where Mr Kentish Wright presided as Vice-President of the Governors. The Duke of Portland was unfortunately unable to attend. Archdeacon Wild proposed the health of the school and mentioned the fact that Mr Corner, in his history of the school, had shown him how Dame Agnes Mellers had ordered that the vicar of the parish be paid an annual sum of twenty shillings to say a requiem mass for her husband and herself on June 16th of every year. The Mayor and aldermen were to be paid fourpence and the bell ringers were to receive eight peoles. The Guardians were to be careful to supply "fitting quantities of bread, ale and cheese." This moment, in actual fact, seems to be the first stirrings of the idea that some kind of Founder's Day be held on a regular basis. The Headmaster responded to the toast and congratulated Mr Corner on his compilation of the names and addresses of some three thousand Old Boys. This list, unfortunately, does not seem to have come down to us. Mr J.Lewis Paton proposed the health of the Old Boys' Association and expressed his difficulty in speaking on behalf of the Old Boys, so many of whom had now passed over to the astral plane, where even Mr Corner did not know their address. The toast was acknowledged by Mr J.A.Dixon who appealed for the remainder of the £5,000 required by the Working Lads' Club in Radford to be donated before Mr George Goodall submitted the toast of "The City of Nottingham". To this, the Mayor replied and Dr Gow proposed "the Universities". Mr P.E.Matheson acknowledged this and the Sheriff of Nottingham proposed the "Health of the Chairman". Mr Kentish Wright replied briefly to this.

Saturday, November 22nd 1913

The 1st XI played the City Asylum, in a match watched by the strangest crowd in the long, long history of High School football. It certainly gave *The Nottinghamian* an original excuse to offer for a heavy defeat: "perhaps the presence of so many lunatics unnerved the team, for it did not come up to its normal form" Team captain Price had put the school ahead but the Asylum then scored three goals to lead 3-1. Munks pulled a goal back and in the second half, Taylor managed another goal for the

High School, but the Asylum "kept running through and scoring", thus making the final score 3-7.

Christmas Term 1913

The Captain of Football was W.H.Price, the first goalkeeper ever to captain the school. At one point during the term Price was involved in a "cycle accident which occurred while he was giving an exhibition of fancy cycling, much to the delight of the Cadet Corps who were interested spectators".

Friday, December 26th 1913

On Boxing Day, the very first game of rugby in the long sporting history of the High School was played at Mapperley Park. It was the last Christmas and the last Boxing Day before the outbreak of the Great War. As a preliminary before the changeover from football (or soccer) to rugby the Old Nottinghamians played Notts Rugby F.C.. The Old Boys lost a closely fought game by 9 points (three tries) to 15 points (three goals). The tries were scored by H.A.Johnstone, C.G.Boyd and D.P.C.Grant. The referee was Mr Lionel Kirk. Presumably, this fixture was able to demonstrate the new sport to many people, particularly Old Boys, Masters, parents and current pupils, who, in the days before television, would probably never have seen the game played before.

The Old Boys' team was Stocks; H.A.Johnstone, H.S.Stocks (Captain), A.Willatt, R.L.W.Herrick, C.G.Boyd, W.Johnstone; D.P.C.Grant, F.Hardwick, J.K.Turpin, A.R.S.Grant, H.W.Ballamy, L.W.Peck, E.G.Hogan and W.S.Facon. A pleasant interval in the Christmas festivities, one might think, a short respite from roast turkey, Brussels sprouts, Christmas pudding, port, sherry, cigars and all the other indulgences of this lovely time of year. Except that nobody who was there on that fatal Friday knew that a World War was about to break out within less than eight months or that more than four years of fighting would leave almost a million British dead. In that number would be more than three hundred Old Nottinghamians. In actual fact, the eventual fate of the members of the Old Boys' team pretty much defies belief. As well-intentioned, patriotic, decent, optimistic, athletic young men, they were to run forward into the maelstrom of the Great War as if it were a blood spattered combine harvester.

Henry Archer Johnstone became a Major in the 152nd Brigade of the Royal Field Artillery. The beloved son of John and Ada Johnstone of Fairmead, Risley, Derbyshire, he was to die on Tuesday, May 21st 1918 at the age of only twenty eight. He is buried in Wancourt near Arras in northern France. His rugby playing days were finally over.

H.S.Stocks, who left in July 1904, was eventually to become a Lieutenant in the 7th (Service) Battalion of the Royal Sussex Regiment. He was severely wounded on Friday, July 7th 1916, in the Battle of the Somme, and rendered unfit for further active service. I would certainly have been very surprised if he ever played any more rugby matches with his young laughing friends.

John Riversdale Warren Herrick was a Captain in the 2nd King Edward's Own Gurkha Rifles (The Sirmoor Rifles). He was in the 3rd Battalion attached to the 11th Gurkha Rifles when he was fatally wounded on active service in Iraq. The son of Dr R.W.Herrick and Mrs Edith Herrick of 30, Regent Street, Nottingham, Captain Herrick was to die from his wounds on Sunday, October 24th 1920 at the age of only twenty seven. He is buried in Basra War Cemetery in Iraq.

Charles Gordon Boyd was a Second Lieutenant in the 7th Battalion of the Sherwood Foresters, but was attached to the 9th Battalion of the Leicestershire Regiment. On Thursday, May 3rd 1917, he was killed whilst attacking Fontaine-Les-Croiselles with 'D' Company at the age of only twenty four. He was the son of George Herbert Boyd and Sarah Louisa Boyd, of, initially, 13, Tavistock Drive, Mapperley Park. He surely got changed for this match in his own home nearby and perhaps walked along Tavistock Drive to the pitch in a laughing group of his fellow players. By the time of his death, his parents had moved to St Peter's-in-Thanet, Kent. Some details emerged much later from the great nephew of Lance Corporal Herbert Golder Marsh who said that "Lt Boyd "went down" early in the battle, well before dawn." Lance Corporal Marsh was seen later, wounded himself, trying to find help to get Lieutenant Boyd back to his own lines. He was unsuccessful and was last seen going back down towards the German Trenches "to be with his officer". Boyd's remains were not found until some six years after his death, in November 1923, when he was reburied in the Heninel-Croisilles Road Cemetery in the Pas-de-Calais in northern France.

James Knowles Turpin was a Second Lieutenant in "A" Battery, 241st South Midland Brigade of the Royal Field Artillery. On Tuesday, August 14th 1917, he was killed in action at Boundary Road behind the Brigade HQ at Hill Top Farm near St Jaan just west of the frontline. The beloved only son of Harry and Minnie Turpin, of 68, Henry Road, West Bridgford, he was just twenty five years of age. He was buried in Vlamertinghe New Military Cemetery, West-Vlaanderen, Belgium.

Allan Roy Stewart Grant, who, while he was at school as A.R.S.Grant, was nicknamed "Pongy", served as a Captain in the 10th Battalion of the Seaforth Highlanders, Ross-shire, Buffs, and the Duke of Albany's. He was awarded the Military Cross. He survived the conflict and returned to Nottingham. Not so his elder brother, Donald Patrick Grant, who was in the 7th Battalion of the Cameron Highlanders. He is listed as either a Lance-Corporal (by the Commonwealth War Graves Commission), or a Lieutenant (in the school lists of the fallen). He was killed on Thursday, April 12th 1917 at the age of only twenty seven. He had previously been the Manager at the British Crown Insurance Office in Nottingham. His remains were never found, but his death is commemorated on the Arras Memorial. Both young men were the beloved sons of the Reverend John Charles Grant, a Minister of Religion, and Ellen Jemima Grant who lived at "The Manse" at 16, Baker Street, Nottingham. The family was of Scottish origin. Donald had, in actual fact, been born at Loanhead in Midlothian.

Harold William Ballamy was a Lieutenant in "B" Battery of the 231st Brigade of the Royal Field Artillery. He was the beloved son of Mr Frank William Ballamy, a commercial traveller and Mrs M.A.Ballamy of 17a, Gedling Grove. He was killed on either Tuesday, August 14th or Wednesday, August 15th 1917, as part of the Third Battle of Ypres, usually known as the Battle of Passchendaele. He was twenty four years of age and is buried in Fosse No 10 in the Communal Cemetery Extension at Sains-en-Gohelle, in the Pas-de-Calais in northern France.

Leslie Wayland Peck was the son of Thomas Wayland Peck, a Clerk in Holy Orders, and a Diocesan Inspector of Schools, who had been, from 1885-1900, a Master at the High School. From 1886-1893, despite being a teacher, Peck Senior had played regularly for the school's First Team at both football and cricket. The family lived initially at 12, Arboretum Street, Nottingham and then in Gedling Grove. Leslie must certainly have known Harold Ballamy, a close neighbour. Perhaps the two boys used to make the short walk to school every morning, accompanied by Mr Peck. What could have been more embarrassing than walking to school with one of the teachers? Fortunately it was a very short walk. Leslie left the High School in June 1910 and joined The Bank, an establishment which was later to change its name to the National Westminster Bank. He had already served in the School Cadet Corps under Captain Trotman and joined the Sherwood Foresters Special Reserve, before being called up and sent to France quite early in the Great War. He was "Mentioned in Dispatches" but after being extremely badly shell-shocked, was invalided back home for a period in hospital. He was posted back to the Sherwood Foresters, but was not ever well enough to serve overseas again.

M.J.Hogan was a Sergeant in the 1st Battalion of the Grenadier Guards. He was severely wounded on an unknown date.

I have been unable to trace anything definite for W.S.Facon although according to the London Gazette, a Lieutenant W.S.Facon was promoted to Captain on December 21st 1921. There is also a mention of a W.S.Facon in the Air Force List for May 1939. He worked at the Air Ministry in the Department of the Permanent Under-Secretary in the Directorate of Contracts.

An unrecorded date in the Summer Term 1914

The 1st XI enjoyed what was probably its greatest ever escape from a heavy cricketing defeat. Playing against old rivals King Edward VII School, Sheffield, the opposition reached an impressive total of 209-6 declared, with the third wicket putting on 143. The High School, batting in deepening gloom, had reached 15 for 8, when a long threatened thunderstorm broke and the game had to be abandoned as a draw. Just as well perhaps, as the last batsman had a lifetime average of 1.5.

July 1914

Mr Samuel Corner retired after being at the High School since 1877. In 1891, he had become Second Master although he always preferred to be called Usher. Through his wide network of Old Boys and his careful examination of local records, he had become a great expert on the school's history. He edited *The Forester* magazine for many years and at one point it had contained a serialised history of the school. He also produced the School Lists, with up to fifty pages of news of Old Boys.

Tuesday, August 4th 1914

War broke out only a month after Mr Corner retired. For a couple of years he continued to help out at the school and despite being over sixty years of age, he joined up and went to France. After the war, Mr Corner moved to Croydon but his history of the school was to remain forever uncompleted, a source of very great regret, as he later told Mr Reynolds.

August 1914

Three members of staff were awarded commissions in Kitchener's "New Army", and a great many Old Boys joined up.

August 1914 onwards

The numbers of boys in the school increased dramatically although half a dozen members of staff had quickly left to join the army. They were replaced by lady teachers, the majority young and unmarried. The senior boys spent an increased time in Officer Training Corps activities. Gradually they too began to depart, in many cases at a premature age, as they left for the army. After about half a dozen teachers had gone, the Governors, fearing a full scale exodus, put a brake on the process. They decided that "the remaining members were performing their full duty in a scheme of national service and could not in the public interest be spared from their present work of education."

During the war, the Officer Training Corps took on a much greater importance. Messrs Leggett and Lloyd Morgan, the senior officers, were among the first to join up, becoming Captain and Lieutenant, in the 11th Service Battalion of the Sherwood Foresters and the 2nd Battalion of the Cambridgeshire Regiment respectively. *The Nottinghamian* hoped that "they will both have a "smack" at the enemy and return safely again." The Corps was now led by Captain Hood and Lieutenant Kennard, the latter taking over command when Captain Hood went off to the Royal Engineers in July 1918. At this early stage of the war, the O.T.C. was poorly equipped and frequently lacked sufficient rifles and bayonets.

Wednesday, November 25th 1914

The First XI played their last game of football for more than fifty years. It was an away fixture against Wyggeston School in Leicester and ended in a 2-7 defeat. This was the fifth defeat of the season, with only one victory, by 4-2 over Mansfield Grammar School and a single draw, 2-2 against Worksop College. After Christmas the main winter sport for the school became Rugby Union.

January 1915

The school duly switched from football to rugby with the two prime movers having been Mr Leggett of the Preparatory School and Mr Lloyd Morgan. When they volunteered for the Front, Mr Kennard took over. He had captained Lancashire and played for the North of England in an England trial. The decision to change sports was made by the General Committee on a two to one majority and both the Old Boys and the parents were in favour. The boys, however, by a substantial majority, would have opted for football.

Spring Term 1915

In contrast to the dwindling interest in football, more than fifty or sixty boys were turning up for rugby practice every Wednesday and Saturday at Mapperley Park. So far the school was not playing any fixtures but merely learning the game.

Christmas Term 1915

The First XV continued to anticipate their first ever victory but experienced another heavy defeat, this time at Newark by 0-43. Their best quality seems to have been their sportsmanship and they played at least one game without conceding a single penalty.

November 1915

The sons of those serving in the forces had their fees reduced by half.

Wednesday, November 24th 1915

Walter William Ball, the second son of three and the elder brother of the Oliver Ball who had carved his name on the stone fireplace near the North Entrance only some ten years previously, was killed at the age of twenty eight, a victim of the Great War. Walter had returned to the Yorkshire Regiment and the Western Front from his leave in

Nottingham on Friday, November 19th 1915. The *Nottingham Guardian* reported his death on Monday, November 29th 1915. He had apparently been shot through the head by a sniper while organising a firing party with his captain. The tragic news was communicated to his parents by his younger brother, Second Lieutenant Oliver Ball who by now held a commission in the same regiment. According to the *Nottingham Guardian* Walter Ball was "well-known in Nottingham and had a large circle of friends". He had received his commission as a Second Lieutenant a mere twelve months previously. Walter is buried in Houplines Communal Cemetery Extension in France.

Saturday, November 27th 1915

At the 354th meeting of the Debating Society, the motion was put to the House that "domestic servants are to blame for leaving their situations in such great numbers at the present time". The motion was introduced by G.Harrison, who explained that: "Owing to the numbers of men who have been called up by the authorities, domestic servants are leaving to work in munitions factories. A lady with a large family, knowing practically nothing about housework, had been suddenly deserted by her servants. Indeed, the situation is potentially so grave that boys in the Officer Training Corps will soon have to clean their own buttons".

Indeed, the view of the whole audience was that domestic servants had never had it so good, being in many cases able to earn wages of up to £14 per year. Present at this meeting was Harold Ballamy who had just returned from France. He was a Lieutenant in the Royal Field Artillery and said that:

> "My nerves are shattered when I return home to the more deadly perils of lady porters, lady ticket collectors, and lady taxi-drivers. Hence I think that servants should not leave their situations."

Ballamy had seen all the horrors of trench warfare at first hand and his words, although ostensibly meant in a humorous fashion, contained a large hint to stay safe at home. Certainly a man as intelligent as Ballamy could not possibly have failed to see the pettiness of such meetings.

December 1915

The 2nd Troop of the School Scouts were missing "very much" their scoutmaster, Mr Argyle. He had volunteered to join the Royal Engineers and was busy making poison gas. A temporary teacher, Miss Wood, had joined the Red Cross as a nurse. In the meantime Mr Leggett, who had volunteered for the Sherwood Foresters, had been thwarted in his desire to go to the Front, having had a serious accident when he fell off his horse and sustained concussion.

An unrecorded Wednesday in December 1915

Robert, the school caretaker, set up the Nottingham High School Pets' Club. He spoke to potential members for forty minutes at an inaugural meeting and kept them enthralled by his enthusiasm for the subject, offering advice on the care of pets or how to purchase them.

Tuesday morning, February 1st 1916

This morning, the boys woke up to find eight inches of snow blanketing the city. When they had all managed to make their way to school, seemingly every boy had a story to tell, for the previous night Zeppelins had attacked Nottingham:

> "Many and marvellous were the tales. it seemed as if everyone in the school was giving his experiences to everyone else as loudly as possible. Apparently, the aircraft had, at some time or another, been straight over the houses of nine out of ten of the boys."

In actual fact, the only bombs dropped fell well to the west of Nottingham between Stapleford and Ilkeston. They were dropped by one of nine airships of the German Airship Naval Division, carrying out a major bombing raid over the whole of the Midlands. The Zeppelin involved near Nottingham was the L.20 (LZ 59), commanded by Kapitan-Leutnant Stabbert.

This combination of thick snow and Zeppelins must have made this day perhaps the most perfect one ever, from a boy's point of view, in the long history of the school.

Thursday, September 28th 1916

Just over eleven years since he had carved his name on the stone fireplace near the North Entrance, Oliver Herbert Ball was killed, at the age of twenty five. After he left, Oliver had moved initially to University College, Nottingham. He then worked at the Nottingham Head Office of the Union of London and Smith's Bank. When the war began, he enlisted in the Royal Garrison Artillery and was quickly promoted to Bombardier. Five months later Second Lieutenant Ball was gazetted to the Yorkshire Regiment and he proceeded to the front in October 1915. He survived for less than twelve months and his death from wounds was announced in the *Nottingham Guardian* on October 14th 1916. He is buried in the Guards' Cemetery at Lesboeufs in Northern France. Poor Mr and Mrs Ball had lost two sons to the carnage of the Great War in less than a year.

Sunday, October 15th 1916

Lieutenant Garth Smithies Taylor was killed while his battalion were in the trenches near Le Transloy. His death was described in a letter to his mother from Second Lieutenant M. Marshall Shaw of 'D' Company, 2nd Battalion, Sherwood Foresters:

> "I was one of the last persons to speak to him. We had taken a section of trench in front of us from the Germans, and that night 'A' Company under Lieutenant Taylor was to relieve the Company which had taken the position. The German snipers were very active, and I was digging a communication trench for the relieving troops to use. He came to me and saw what I was doing and then went over to the new trench to get in touch with the Commander there. He came back shortly afterwards and as my trench was not ready for the relief, returned to the forward trench again. He was a little while there, and as the trench was being repaired walked with his servant on the top. The Germans shot at them, and he told his man to get down quickly. The man did so, and as he did so he heard his Officer say "I'm hit": Taylor lay perfectly still and closed his eyes so that his servant said that he looked asleep. They buried him and I believe the Adjutant has the reference to his grave."

During their six weeks on the Somme, the 2nd Battalion, Sherwood Foresters lost 12 officers killed and 152 non-commissioned officers and ordinary soldiers killed. Sixteen officers were wounded and 625 other ranks were wounded. This was an appalling total of 805 casualties in just 42 days in the Battle of the Somme. Originally, in September 1914, Taylor was a civilian clerk in the A.S.C., the same unit where his father had himself been a Captain. He soon applied for, and was granted, a commission. In October 1915, he had been promoted to Lieutenant, but found that his duties in the A.S.C. "afforded him insufficient time for the destruction of the Hun", and he soon applied for a transfer to active service in the front line infantry. In April 1916 Taylor became a Lieutenant in the Sherwood Foresters and enlivened the "many dreary tours of duty in the trenches" for 'A' Company by his frequent playing of a mandolin. He was twenty years of age when he was killed.

Christmas Term 1916

In a more successful term, the First XV won five of its six matches.

Thursday, May 3rd 1917

Charles Gordon Boyd, a young Second Lieutenant in the Sherwood Foresters, was listed as missing, believed dead. He was twenty four years old. Boyd was born on January 23rd 1893. He was the son of George Herbert Boyd and Sarah Louisa Boyd. His father was an insurance manager and the family lived at 13, Tavistock Drive, Mapperley Park during Boyd's time at the High School. Boyd was the School Captain in 1911-1912. He was the First Team's wicketkeeper, and he was an enthusiastic footballer, playing regularly for the First XI. His full record as a goalscorer was eleven goals in nine appearances. After he left the High School, on Friday, December 26th 1913, Boyd had played in the very first game of rugby ever played at Mapperley Park Sports Ground, when the Old Nottinghamians played Notts Rugby F.C.

Around 8.30 p.m., Monday, May 7th, 1917

Albert Ball was killed on patrol, shortly before his twenty-first birthday. For this last combat, Ball was awarded a posthumous Victoria Cross to add to his Military Cross, Distinguished Service Order, Distinguished Flying Cross, Légion d'Honneur, Croix de Chevalier, Russian Order of St George and the American Medal. These medals can be seen inside Nottingham Castle and outside is his statue.

Nowadays, Albert Ball is perhaps somewhat of a forgotten name. He was, however, one of the greatest air aces of the Great War. Ball was a natural fighter pilot and initially always flew French Nieuport fighters with a top speed of 110 m.p.h. although the English S.E.5 with its top speed of 138 m.p.h. was to gain a greater place in his affections in the latter period of his career. Unlike many of his colleagues in the Royal Flying Corps, Ball was to gain widespread fame for his achievements. Invariably flying alone, he shot down 44 enemy aircraft. In general, unlike the French or the Germans, the British did not use their aces for propaganda purposes but Ball was the first brilliant exception. The war weary English public loved the way he always attacked the enemy irrespective of the odds against him. Ball was genuinely fearless. His favourite prey was the German Roland C.II, the so-called "Walfisch". Most of his victories came by attacking from below, with his machine gun tilted upwards. It was very dangerous but remarkably successful. Romantically for his public, like a latter day Knight of the Round Table, Ball always flew alone.

There is no clear indication of what happened in his last combat although four German officers on the ground all saw his SE5 emerge from low cloud, upside down, and trailing a thin plume of oily smoke. Its engine was stopped and it crashed close to a farm called Fashoda near the village of Annoeullin. Ball was still alive and he was removed from the wreckage by Mademoiselle Cécile Deloffre. As she cradled him in her arms Ball opened his eyes once and then died. His death was later found to be due to his injuries in the crash. He had not been wounded. The chivalrous Germans gave Ball a funeral with full military honours on May 9th. The original white cross with which they marked his grave, No.999, is still kept in the chapel at Trent College.

Thursday, June 7th 1917

Just over ten years after he had carved his name on the stone fireplace near the North Entrance, Oswald Cornek Gillott was killed at the age of twenty six. After he left the High School, Oswald had moved to Teesside and he was an apprentice mechanical engineer living at 2, Woodland Terrace, Borough Road, Middlesbrough. With the advent of the Great War, Oswald joined the 68th Field Company of The Royal Engineers, who had been formed in August 1914 as part of Kitchener's First New Army. The Engineers trained at Newark before sailing for Gallipoli from Liverpool at the end of June 1915. They remained at Lala Baba in Suvla Bay until December 19th and 20th 1915 when they withdrew and returned to Egypt by the end of January. Oswald was recorded as having been wounded during this period.

In June 1916 the Division was ordered to France to reinforce the Third Army on the Somme. By July 27th they were in the Front Line and took part in the fighting around Thiepval. By 1917 they were fighting on the Ancre and then moved north to Flanders for the Battle of Messines. This fatal day, June 7th 1917, was the first day of the successful attack on the Messines Ridge. The assault was preceded by the detonation of a large number of mines. Oswald, as a Royal Engineer, may well have been involved in this activity when he was killed. He is buried in Messines Ridge British Cemetery.

Tuesday, August 14th 1917

Aged only twenty five, Second Lieutenant James Knowles Turpin, of 'A' Battery, 241st South Midland Brigade of the Royal Field Artillery was killed in action at Boundary Road behind the Brigade HQ at Hill Top Farm near St Jaan just west of the frontline. James was born in 1892, the beloved only son of Harry and Minnie Turpin. His father was a grocer and the family lived at 7, Claremont Gardens, off the Hucknall Road, but later moved to 68, Henry Road, West Bridgford. He was admitted to the High School on April 15th 1902 at the age of ten. He left in July 1911 and went to Cambridge University where he had won a scholarship at Christ's College. James was commissioned in August 1914 as a second lieutenant and promoted to lieutenant in 1916. His was known as the "Worcester Battery" and consisted of six 18-pounder field guns. His last leave to Nottingham was January 24th-31st 1916, so he had not seen his loving parents for nineteen months when he was killed. He is buried in Vlamertinghe New Military Cemetery, Belgium.

Tuesday, August 14th 1917

Harold William Ballamy was killed. He had already been wounded twice, but on each occasion had returned to active service, the second time just five weeks before his death. His Commanding Officer, Brigadier-General Herbert M.Campbell, who was present at Ballamy's funeral, wrote that he was "a gallant officer, loved by all who knew him, exceedingly capable and thoroughly reliable. The battery felt his loss very much, and he would be hard to replace".

Harold was twenty four years old when he died. He was born on July 5th 1893 and entered the High School on November 3rd 1902. His father was Frederick William Ballamy, a commercial traveller of 17a, Gedling Grove, Nottingham and his mother was Mrs M.A.Ballamy. Harold was to win many academic prizes in his time at the High School. They included Silver Medals for Mathematics and Science and Dr Gow's Prize for Geometry. In 1910 he became Vice-Captain of Football and in 1912, was Captain of Football, the same year in which he won a Standard Medal for this activity. He was Secretary of First Team Cricket in 1912, the year when he became Captain of the School. Harold was Colour Sergeant in the Officer Training Corps from 1911-1912, and in 1911 he was the School Librarian. In 1910 and 1911 he was the Secretary and Treasurer of the School Debating Society. In 1912, at the School Sports held at Mapperley Park, Harold won the 100 yards dash, a race held on grass and run in kit very different from that of the present day, in a time of 10.6 seconds, beating F.W.Goddard by several yards.

He left the High School in 1912 and went to Trinity College at Cambridge University, where he held the Bishop Open Exhibition of £75 a year for Natural Science. At the time, the philosopher Bertrand Russell was a professor at Cambridge, and, had he so wished, Harold could well have gone to hear his lectures. He might well have bumped into one of Russell's pupils, the soon-to-be-famous philosopher, Ludwig Wittgenstein. Harold was soon elected to a major Foundation Scholarship of £100 per year. He obtained a First Class degree in Mathematics and then changed to Natural Sciences where he was placed first in the whole University. At the same time he rowed for his college in their third boat and was a prominent member of the Cambridge University Officer Training Corps. Harold had obtained a B.A. degree by the time war broke out so he immediately volunteered, receiving a commission in the Royal Field Artillery. He reached the Front in February, 1915 and served in 'B' Battery of the 231st Brigade. By the time he was killed, Harold had seen the horrors of trench warfare at close hand. Surely, a man as intelligent as he clearly was could not possibly have failed to see the pointlessness of the Great War.

This bleak lesson, of course, is further emphasised by the fact that these two vastly talented academic young men, both from very humble backgrounds, Harold Ballamy and James Turpin, were both killed on the same day. One was the son of a commercial traveller, the other the son of a grocer, yet both young men were Captains of the School and both were educated at Cambridge University. What an absolute waste of the nation's future.

Thursday, August 16th 1917

Walter Leslie Howard, a Lieutenant in the Machine Gun Corps, died of his wounds. Like James Turpin and Harold Ballamy, Walter was from a very humble, working class background. Like Mr Ballamy, his father was also a commercial traveller. Like James and Harold, he too became Captain of the School before continuing his education at Oxford University.

Walter was born on April 20th 1895, the son of Walter Hermann Haubitz of 2, Regent Street, New Basford. He entered the High School on September 13th 1905, at the age of ten. Known throughout his school career as Walter Haubitz, he was eventually to become Secretary and Treasurer of both the School Debating Society and the School Literary Society. In 1913, after a year as Captain of the School he won an Open Scholarship of £80 a year for Classics at Wadham College, Oxford. Just after the outbreak of the First World War, in November 1914, he received a commission in the 176th Company of the Machine Gun Corps. He thereupon changed his name to the more anglicised "Howard". He was only twenty two years of age when he died, serving with the 7th Somerset Light Infantry. Walter is buried in Dozinghem Military Cemetery, Belgium.

These appalling three days in a freezing cold, rain swept, bleak August 1917 were surely the saddest, the most disastrous and the most poignant three days in the long, long history of the High School. But there was more to come.

Thursday, October 11th 1917

The slaughter on the battlefield continued as Captain John Wesley Wootton died of his wounds. He was twenty six years of age. "Jack" Wootton was born on March 25th 1891, one member of a fairly large middle class family of three brothers and three sisters but no servants. He was the youngest son of Arthur Wootton and Julia Emma Wootton. His father was a manufacturer of lace curtains and the family lived at 137, Foxhall Road on the opposite side of the Forest Recreation Ground from the High School. They were eventually to move to 30, High

Pavement. Jack Wootton entered the High School on September 17th 1901 at the age of ten, having won the Sir Thomas White Exhibition of £50 per year. He was to become Secretary of the School Society and Colour Sergeant of the Officer Training Corps. He became a Prefect and eventually was promoted to Captain of the School.

In July, 1910, Jack left the High School for Trinity College, Cambridge, to read History, having won a major scholarship of £120 per year. He was eventually to gain a First Class Degree after achieving First Classes in every examination he ever took at Cambridge. He won college prizes for History and Literature and the Derby Scholarship of £100 for historical research. He was an enthusiastic member of the University's Officer Training Corps and was commissioned in 1914 into the 11th Battalion of the Suffolk Regiment, the so-called "City of Cambridge Battalion". Indeed, by the time conscription was introduced at the beginning of 1916, some 75% of male students at Cambridge had already joined up for the "war-to-end-all-wars".

On the first day of the Battle of the Somme, July 1st 1916, Jack was one of a total of 120,000 men who "went over the top" at La Boiselle. Many years later, his erstwhile servant, a "Mr H. Allgood", described what happened that day:

> "We were going forward in rows. One row was leaving too large gaps, Captain shouts, Fill those gaps up. Soon after that I heard his voice. I looked back, he was on the ground, I went back & took off his boots, saw a hole through his ankle. He said, You will have to go, Allgood. I hope I shall see you again."

Jack had been wounded in the foot by a machine gun, and he returned to convalesce for nine months in Cambridge.

On September 5th 1917, "tall and dark and handsome in a rather melancholy-looking sort of way", he married Barbara Adam, whose father was Dr James Adam of Emmanuel College. In later years, she was to become a distinguished social scientist, better known as Baroness Wootton. Jack knew her because of his friendship with her brother, Neil. Just two days after his marriage, Wootton returned to his regiment. He was "a most conscientious and hard-working officer" who was well liked by all. By now, he had been married for a grand total of thirty-six days.

The Battle of Passchendaele took place in appallingly wet and muddy conditions. Men frequently drowned in shell craters or seas of churned up mud. Jack Wootton was destined not to drown, however. He was shot through the eye by a sniper while repairing a road on October 9th 1917. Around fifty men in his battalion were killed in similar fashion. Two days later, on October 11th, Jack died of his wounds as he was being transported on a French ambulance train. Some time after this, Jack's blood covered, mud encrusted uniform and personal belongings were sent back to his young wife. This appalling gesture was common practice during the First World War. Jack is buried in Longuenesse Souvenir Cemetery in St Omer, France. He is one of 2,874 casualties in this particular cemetery. His name also appears in the Roll of Honour on the War Memorial at St Mark's Church in Barton Road, Cambridge. Ironically, this was the exact same church where he had been married only thirty six days before his death. Barbara Adam continued to be known as Barbara Wootton and continued to love Jack with all her heart for another seventy years and three months. His photograph, wearing his officer's uniform with a neatly trimmed moustache and dark brooding eyes, stood on her bedside table as she died, an old lady in her bed. It is through his wife's unflagging love for him and her insistence on bearing his name (even though she later remarried), that Jack Wootton leaves a lasting legacy in Britain. During her celebrated career as a sociologist and criminologist Barbara used her surname when she wrote some of the greatest and most influential academic publications in the field of criminology in the twentieth century. The high point of her career was her spearheading a 1968 Home Office inquiry into the use of cannabis in Great Britain. *The Wootton Report* is still regarded today as one of the most daring and contentious of propositions, but its wide ranging fame and recognition ensures that Jack Wootton's name lives on in the work of his beloved wife, Barbara.

January 1918

The new school magazine, *The Highvite*, carried a list of the school prefects, with their nicknames. They were the Captain of the School, F.A.Bird (Dicky), A.W.Barton (Fuzzy), J.A.Saward, Captain of Rugby, (Seaweed), P.H.B.Furley (Dab), R.F.Parr (Fickle), N.F.Norris (Nigel), S.J.Buxton (Our Stan), T.L.E.Morley (Dreg) and J.King (Jabez).

Sunday, March 31st 1918

Harold Arno Connop died of his injuries. He was a Flight Sub-Lieutenant in the Royal Naval Air Service, and the son of Mr Arno B. Connop and Mrs Ada Connop of 33, Westwood Road in Sneinton. At the time, Harold was reckoned "the first Scholar of Corpus Christi College", and his death deprived the High School of its very best representative at Oxford University. Harold was also a very good rugby player, a fine three quarter and a very fast runner. For some reason though, however, Harold does not always seem to have been particularly well-liked, and he was not an outstandingly popular figure. He did have at least one close friend, however, and that was Francis "Dicky" Bird. This lack of popularity was perhaps connected with his rare combination of outstanding academic and sporting prowess and very humble origins. His father was a mere Elementary School teacher and Harold's education throughout his time at the High School was financed by his being both a Sir Thomas White Scholar and a Foundation Scholar. Harold was posted to Dunkirk on March 14th 1918 but he was dead only 17 days later. He is buried in Dunkirk Town Cemetery.

Saturday, May 4th 1918

Eric Inger Dexter, a Lieutenant in the 16th Squadron initially of the Royal Flying Corps and then of the R.A.F., was killed in action at the age of twenty two. This came almost exactly a year after the death of his elder brother, Harry Vincent Dexter, a member of the 43rd Battalion of the Manitoba Regiment who had been killed in the Battle of Vimy Ridge on May 24th 1917.

Monday, March 18th 1918

As the school flag fluttered permanently at half mast, the current pupils at the school had other things on their minds. The following rules were copied into the Prefects' book and formally adapted by A.W.Barton, the Captain of School, and the whole of the Corpus Praefectorum, who duly signed the relevant page.

1. The Prefects are charged to do their utmost to maintain a proper standard of behaviour on the part of all boys of the school, and may punish any offence likely to bring discredit to the school.

2. The Prefects may punish boys in any of the three following ways: (i) by reprimand (ii) by lines (iii) by caning.

3. No corporal punishment shall be administered by prefects except (a) after due and proper deliberation and (b) with the unanimous agreement of all the Prefects.

4. When announcing the decision of the Prefects to the offending boy, the Head Prefect is bound to allow him an appeal to the Headmaster.

5. Corporal punishment may be administered only in those cases which in the joint opinion of all the prefects render such punishment absolutely necessary, and only after a full opportunity has been given to appeal to the Headmaster; for this purpose an interval of at least 24 hours must elapse between announcing the decision of the Prefects to the offending boy and the execution of that decision. No instrument of punishment is to be used except that which is sanctioned by the Headmaster, and the number of strokes must not exceed three, without express permission from the Headmaster.

Thursday, July 11th 1918

The London Gazette recorded the brave deeds for which the Reverend Theodore Bayley Hardy was awarded the Victoria Cross. They had occurred on April 5th, April 25th, April 26th and April 27th 1918.

Hardy had begun his teaching career in 1890. He was Form Master of the Upper Second and was engaged in the teaching of English Grammar, Arithmetic, Algebra, Geometry, Geography, History, French and Latin. He spent seventeen years at the High School during which time he was later to be the form master of the Third Form, and from 1905, one of the three joint form masters of the Modern Sixth Form. He left in 1907 to become Headmaster of Bentham Grammar School near Lancaster. Hardy had been ordained as a deacon in December 1898 and soon became a curate at Burton Joyce. In 1899, he was ordained as a priest and shortly afterwards left his post at Burton Joyce to move to a curacy at New Basford.

When the Great War broke out Hardy, despite his advanced age of fifty-one, made numerous applications to join the Chaplaincy Department. He was refused time and time again, being given the excuse that there was a waiting list of some hundreds of younger men, all of them eminently more suited to the rigours of trench life on the Western Front. Hardy then considered joining up as a volunteer stretcher bearer and went as far as to sit and to pass, the final examination, after attending an Ambulance class in Kirkby Lonsdale. The carnage of 1916, however, created many vacancies for replacement chaplains and he was finally accepted for this post in the late summer of this year. Militarily, he became a captain and was attached to the 8th Lincolnshire Regiment and the 8th Somerset Regiment. Theologically, he was a Temporary Chaplain, Fourth Class.

Theodore Hardy's bravery was by now legendary. He had already won a Distinguished Service Order and the Military Cross. The citation for his Victoria Cross on July 7th 1918 read:

> "For most conspicuous bravery and devotion to duty on many occasions. Although over fifty years of age, he has, by his fearlessness, devotion to men of his battalion and quiet, unobtrusive manner, won the respect and admiration of the whole division. His marvellous energy and endurance would be remarkable even in a very much younger man and his valour and devotion are exemplified in the following incidents:

> An infantry patrol had gone out to attack a previously located enemy post in the ruins of a village, the Reverend Theodore Bayley Hardy, C.F., being then at company headquarters. Hearing firing, he followed the patrol and about 400 yards beyond our front line of posts, found an officer of the patrol dangerously wounded. He remained with the officer until he was able to get assistance to bring him in. During this time there was a great deal of firing and an enemy patrol actually penetrated between the spot at which the officer was lying and our front line and captured three of our men.

> On a second occasion when an enemy shell exploded in the middle of one of our posts, the Reverend T.B.Hardy at once made his way to the spot, despite shell and trench mortar fire which were going on at the time and set to work to extricate the buried men. He succeeded in getting out one man who had been completely buried. He then set to work to extricate a second man who was found to be dead. During the whole of the time that he

was digging out the men this chaplain was in great danger not only from shell fire but also because of the dangerous condition of the wall of the building, which had been hit by the shell which buried the men.

On a third occasion he displayed the greatest devotion to duty when our infantry, after a successful attack, were gradually forced back to their starting trench. After it was believed that all our men had withdrawn from the wood Chaplain Hardy came out of it and on reaching the advanced post, asked the men to help him to get in a wounded man. Accompanied by a sergeant, he made his way to the spot where the man lay, within ten yards of a pill-box which had been captured in the morning, but was subsequently recaptured and occupied by the enemy. The wounded man was too weak to stand, but between them the chaplain and the sergeant eventually succeeded in getting him to our lines. Throughout the day the enemy's continuous artillery, machine-gun and trench mortar fire caused many casualties.

Notwithstanding, this very gallant chaplain was soon moving quietly amongst the men and tending the wounded absolutely regardless of his personal safety."

5.00 a.m. on Friday, October 11th 1918

The Reverend Theodore Bayley Hardy was shot through the thigh by a German machine gun as he crossed a recently erected bridge over the River Selle near Briastres. He was evacuated over a hundred miles to the No 2 Red Cross Hospital at Rouen where he died of pneumonia on October 18th 1918. This was less than a month before the end of hostilities. During this time the 8th Lincolnshire Regiment and the 8th Somerset Regiment were to see only eight more days of combat.

Tuesday, October 15th 1918

Leslie Collins Woodward was the son of George M. and Alice Woodward of Nottingham. He was born on June 3rd 1892 and admitted to the High School on September 13th 1905, at the age of thirteen. His father was an estate agent and in 1905 the family was living at 65, Trent Boulevard, West Bridgford. Leslie left the High School in July 1907 and by 1918 his parents had moved to Raleigh House, 98, Raleigh Street,

Nottingham. At the outbreak of the war, Woodward volunteered immediately and quickly received a commission. He was twice mentioned in Dispatches by Sir Douglas Haig but on September 3rd 1918 was severely wounded in an incident for which he was awarded the Distinguished Service Order. He died of his wounds shortly afterwards and is buried in Heilly Station Cemetery, Méricourt-l'Abbé, France. On October 15th 1918 a ceremony took place at the Exchange Hall, Nottingham where the Mayor, Councillor J.G.Small, presented Woodward's Distinguished Service Order to his baby son who was aged at the time just two and a half. Normally such an award would have been given directly by the King to the widow of the recipient, but at the express wish of his wife, Mrs Annie S.Woodward, it was presented to Woodward's son. The medal was duly pinned to the little boy's breast, the latter saluting in a touchingly innocent gesture.

During his speech, the Mayor spoke of Major Woodward's: "...conspicuous gallantry and devotion to duty when in command of a brigade. Hearing that the enemy had broken through on his right, he brought up three guns onto a crest and for several hours fought his battery under severe artillery, machine gun and rifle fire, only stopping when it was no longer possible to see. Throughout the day, he displayed the greatest coolness and courage and the work performed by his battery was invaluable at a critical time."

The Mayor also read out a letter from Woodward's divisional brigadier-general, "deeply regretting the loss of a valuable officer and devoted friend, whose death created a gap which it was impossible to fill." According to the Mayor, "Major Woodward's gallantry and devotion to duty constituted a record of which any family might be proud and the City sympathised with them in their bereavement."

Monday, November 11th 1918

Just before midday, newsboys came along Arboretum Street, shouting "Paper, paper. Armistice signed!" Without permission, boys rushed to the windows overlooking the street and a number left their lessons to purchase a newspaper.

Just over 1,500 former pupils and masters had fought in the Great War. Two Victoria Crosses had been won, 124 men had been awarded other decorations, and 29 had been "Mentioned in Dispatches". Most important of all, though, was the fact that well over two hundred of them had died. This was from a school only half the size or less than what it is nowadays, a school whose numbers were never much higher than 400. For many years afterwards, a large number of photographs of fallen Old Boys were to be kept proudly on display in the lobby, among the first things to greet any visitor to the school.

There is, of course, no means of measuring the talent which was thrown away with such profligacy by out-of-touch upper class generals, comfortable in their châteaux miles behind the front lines and far from the horrors of the trenches. Suffice it to say, though, that the High School had lost five ex-Captains of the School. They were:

Harold Ballamy	Trinity College, Cambridge, First Class degree in Mathematics, first in the whole University in Natural Sciences.
Charles Boyd	Junior Appointment in the Civil Service and then became a Chartered Accountant.
Harold Connop	"The first Scholar of Corpus Christi College", Oxford.
James Turpin	Open Scholarship at Christ's College, Cambridge.
Jack Wootton	Open Scholarship at Trinity College, Cambridge, to read History. First Classes in every Cambridge examination he ever took and a First Class Degree.

In addition, when P.H.B.Furley was killed at Miranshah, North West India, shortly after the end of the Great War in Europe, he was the a sixth ex-Captain of the School to die. He was just nineteen.

Noon, Saturday November 16th 1918

The 395th meeting of the School Debating Society took place in the Prayer Hall. Mr Gaskin was in the chair and it was proposed and seconded that a letter of sympathy be sent to Mr William Henry Tonkin on losing his son, a prominent Old Boy of the school, Captain Frederick Cuthbert Tonkin M.C., D.S.O. of the 7th Battalion, East Yorkshire

Regiment. Tonkin had been killed on November 4th 1918, only seven days before the end of the war, aged just 24.

A vote of congratulation was then given to Mr Lamb for winning his rugby colours, the latter replying with a benign smile. Mr Towle proposed that letter of congratulation should be sent to Marshall "Fotch" for winning the war. Mr Lee seconded this, but pointed out that his name was Marshall "Fosh". Mr Coe then proposed the motion that "Warfare is a Necessary Accompaniment to the Human Race." He said that war brought out those noble qualities that were apt to be dormant in times of peace. Mr Kipping spoke of the good the war had done the country, and Mr Dunnicliff said that there had always been wars, and always would be.

What a pity that neither the father, William Henry Tonkin, nor his deceased son, Frederick Cuthbert Tonkin, M.C., D.S.O., had been available to speak.

Wednesday, December 25th 1918

Benjamin O'Rorke, who had served through the war as an unarmed padre and had been frequently in mortal danger, survived the fighting, only to die of influenza. He had been taken prisoner by the Germans in September 1914 but was released in 1916. He then returned to the conflict where he was "honoured by all".

Early 1919

The caretaker, Robert Knowles, wrote a poem to celebrate the end of the Great War. He had it printed and distributed to many boys and staff. Unfortunately, it does not appear to have survived to the present day.

Sunday, June 1st 1919

On this day, shortly after the end of the Great War in Europe, Second Lieutenant Percival Henry Biddulph Furley was killed in action at Miranshah, North West India at the age of only nineteen. He was fighting with the 1st Battalion of the 41st Dogras of the Indian Army. The School Magazine, *Highvite*, had spoken previously of the keenly felt losses of such talented young men such as Harold Ballamy, Charles Boyd, Walter Howard, James Turpin and John Wootton. This last death of all seems to have hit very, very hard, coming as it did when England was preparing to celebrate peace. How very, very foolish our nation had been to throw away the lives of so many hundreds of thousands of its most talented young men in this pointless conflict.

P.H.B.Furley's nickname had always been "Dab". He had entered the High School in 1907, the son of Willis and Bertha Furley. The family lived at 72, Cromwell Street, Nottingham. "Dab" was the "finest type of English boy, keen, intelligent and thoughtful; all manly sports gifted, hard-working, loyal and unselfish, straight and true, unfeignedly modest, of a stainless purity." He became a Foundation Scholar in 1912. In 1918 he was the Captain of Cricket and the Captain of the School. He was always one of the favourites of Sammy Corner, the Deputy Headmaster, and was a member of the First XI at cricket for three years. His other claim to fame was his talent in school plays. At this time, all the female parts were taken by boys, and, given his youthful good looks, Furley could always be made up into a very good looking girl or lady!

In the All-England Examination for the Indian Army, "Dab" had scored a record 10,000 points, over seven hundred more than the candidate in second place, and in India, was "specially marked as a man to keep on as a future adjutant. Officers and men loved him." Second Lieutenant Furley was buried in the garden of the local political agent at Miranshah. At the time of writing, this grave was not one of the many thousands to which the Commonwealth War Graves Commission is able to extend its protection, and "Dab"s last resting place is nowadays presumably neglected or may even be lost. Certainly, it would be a very brave and very foolish Westerner who would venture there to lay flowers on his grave, given the series of events since 9/11, as Miranshah, supposedly a hiding place for militants, has been repeatedly targeted for drone attacks by the C.I.A. and fierce ground fighting has continued in the hills around between militants and the Pakistan Armed Forces.

Chapter 12: The First Founder's Day and the Beginning of the Modern Era

September 1919

The School Magazine, the *Highvite*, announced that: "Miss Phemister has departed, but not, we suspect, without much weeping and gnashing of teeth by certain members of the Fifths and Sixths."

In actual fact, throughout the course of the First World War, the High School had been kept in business by a small army of strongly motivated unmarried women who came to teach its occasionally unruly male pupils. Nevertheless, they came through in determined fashion, all of them most worthy of our congratulation. They were:

Miss C.B.Forsyth (1918-1919), Miss M.Garwood (1920-1924), Miss M.H.Gunston (1915-1920), Miss M.W.Guy (1918), Miss H.S.Hall (1917-1919), Miss Hawkins-Ambler (1912-1914), Miss A.M.Kempson (1919-1920), Miss E.M.Larby (1915-1917), Miss I. McClatchie (1918-1919), Miss O.E.McCormich (1915-1916), Mrs S.Mottram (1915-1917), Miss F.M.Noble (1915-1917), Miss D.Oliver (1914-1915), Miss J.N.Phemister (1918-1919), Miss Place (1918-1919), Miss G.Prowde (1918-1919), Miss M.R.Shaw (1917-1919), Miss M.Williams (1915-1917), Miss R.G.Wood (1915) and Miss I. Woodward (1918-1920). Miss A.K.Wootton helped out from 1916-1918 but then, amazingly, returned in 1957 to teach his classes during the absence of Mr Ben Towers through illness.

September 1919

Miss D.E.Baker joined the Preparatory School where she was to work for many years. She joined Miss S.J.Webb, who had come to the school in 1917 and was to remain there for more than 30 years. At this time, of course, women teachers were not allowed to marry, and if they did so, they were forced to resign.

1919

The four houses in the Preparatory School were all named after fallen war heroes. They were Albert Ball, Theodore Hardy, Frederick Tonkin and Richard Trease.

The 1920s

Nottingham author and High School Old Boy, Geoffrey Trease, recalled "five minutes' breathless climb as the High School bell clanged its summons from the crest of the hill. Lawrence had climbed that hill, answered that summons, just twenty years before me, but as a "train boy", whose tiresome daily journey from Eastwood probably did his health no good."

The now unused bell tower still remains although few boys are aware of its original purpose. Fewer still realise that in an era unpolluted by the constant noise of road traffic, the school bell could be heard not just in Shakespeare Street, but also on the far side of Radford.

Saturday, February 5th 1920

The Prefects continued to rule the school with an iron rod, but by 1920 they had started to formalise how boys received their lashes:

> "Seymour (5C) and Vasey (5B) were given three and two strokes of the cane respectively this break. It had been decided at a previous meeting by a unanimous vote that, in future, offenders should be placed face downwards on the prefects' room table to be caned, instead of bending over a chair."

Wednesday, March 3rd 1920

Major Harold Ackworth Leggett, who had been a master at the Preparatory School since 1905, died of "trench fever". Born in 1873, he was educated at Shrewsbury School and began his studies at Pembroke College, Cambridge in 1892. In 1900, he had been gazetted as a Second Lieutenant in the 1st Worcestershire Regiment and on September 28th 1908 he was made a Second Lieutenant in the Junior Division of the Nottingham High School Officer Training Corps. He subsequently became an important member of this organisation. An equally keen Rugby Union player, Leggett had campaigned vigorously that the main school sport be changed from football to rugby. In August 1914, Mr Leggett was one of the first volunteers for the war. Eager to participate before it was all over by Christmas, he initially became a captain in the 11th Service Battalion of the Sherwood Foresters. In December 1915 however, Mr Leggett had been thwarted in his desire to go out to the Western Front for what the school magazine called "a smack at the enemy" when, in a serious accident, he fell off his horse and sustained severe concussion. He eventually reached France in April 1917, only to be wounded and invalided home in July of that same year. He then became the Commandant of the Officers' School at Ripon.

Mr Leggett was a top level sportsman and had played cricket initially for Shrewsbury School and then for Worcestershire, albeit in friendly matches against club sides, rather than the other first class counties.

Perhaps June 1920

The unpublished memoirs of Eric Penson tell how he sat the High School entrance examination:

> "I was entered for an examination which could lead to a free place for me there. When the day of this inquisition arrived I was taken to that seat of learning, where, with at least 150 others, I was allotted a desk in the huge Hall and set to work to answer the questions on the exam paper. In the hush of that impressive room, amidst the scratching of so many pens, I concentrated my efforts for the whole morning, at the end of which I was met and taken home to await the verdict in some six or eight weeks' time, the greater part of that period within the summer holidays."

Eric was to win a Dame Agnes Mellers scholarship, which meant free schooling and books and a grant of five pounds at the end of each term. He lived at 79, Port Arthur Road in Sneinton.

November 1920

The Governors decided to erect a monument to the fallen of the Great War at the front of the school at a cost of not more than £2,000.

The 1920s

Eric Penson's mother gave him 2s 6d pocket money per week (12.5 pence) but this had also to pay for his travel by tram from Sneinton to the centre of Nottingham and thence up Mansfield Road to Forest Road. Each leg of the journey cost a penny and, boys being boys, Eric was soon walking the whole distance to save wasting his money on tram fares. Using every short cut possible, the journey took him fifty minutes every morning and evening. Eric recalled how:

> "I saw then, and in the ensuing years when walking to and from the High School along the same route, young children running barefoot in the main road and the side streets, even in the depths of winter."

By his own admission, Eric had little impact on the school and did not join any of the many societies on offer or the Officer Training Corps. As he wore glasses, he was excused rugby and with his somewhat feeble frame, he found the exercises in the gym very difficult to accomplish. One interesting fact that he recalls, however, is that, despite his scholarship, he was never bullied or put upon. Nobody seemed to hold his humble origins against him and he was happy throughout his stay. The teachers were "invariably kind". Indeed, he remembered both "Nipper" and "Jumbo" Ryles as: "Dickensian characters, both were charming. At the close of my first term, Nipper had a few of us visit the flat he shared with his elder brother for sherry and conversation."

Friday, June 10th 1921

The Prefects were now using gadgets such as binoculars to aid their surveillance of the younger boys:

> "Vasey, Carnall, Mill and Craven were summoned for smoking (in school caps) and using bad language. Mr Watts, Mr Reynolds and Metcalf (left) had seen them, the first two through field glasses. All denied the charge of smoking in school caps and of swearing, but the latter charge was substantiated by the fact that a spectator at the match asked Metcalf to stop the use of bad language. They were sentenced to three strokes each."

September 1921

The school appointed the last of a cohort of thirteen teachers, more than half of whom were to spend their entire lives at the High School. To a great extent these young men replaced the young women who had kept the school going during the Great War. They were Messrs Brodrick, Cunningham, Hodgson, Parsons, Pike, Reynolds and Whitty (1919),

Annis, Betts, Bridge, Newbound (1920) and Duddell, Jackson and Wigfield (1921).

1922

The existing house system was given greater emphasis by the introduction of differently coloured sports shirts and different colours for school cap badges.

1922

The Rowing Club was founded by Mr Wigfield. The members struggled initially against cold weather and the raging waters of the Trent, but eventually they became for several decades one of the school's strongest sporting groups. It was normally performed as an alternative to cricket.

July 1922

The eccentric and beloved caretaker, universally known as "Robert" retired. Almost totally deaf and a great favourite of the boys, Robert was well-known for his poems, which he would have printed and then distribute himself around the school. Unfortunately, only one of his poems appears to have survived. On this occasion, he celebrated the first days of the Cadet Corps:

> If you look through them gates
> You'll see Captain Yates
> A-drilling of boys by the score.
> So come on, my lads
> Get leave of your dads
> And join the High School corps.

Autumn Term 1922

Under the auspices of Messrs Bridge and Reynolds, the house system was further modified to encourage a keener spirit of competition. Each house was to have its own room and noticeboard with meetings at least twice a term in school hours. A house cross-country competition was introduced and house rugby shirts were to be of one distinct colour. In the case of Cooper's, this was to be light blue, Maple's would be green, Meller's black, and White's red. The shirts would retail at 2s 9d (14p).

Saturday, November 11th 1922

The school war memorial was unveiled by the Duke of Portland. It was a life size statue in bronze, representing a young officer leading his platoon to the attack. It was designed by an Old Boy, Colonel A.S.Brewill D.S.O., the commander of the 7th Sherwood Foresters throughout most of the war. The statue was cast into bronze by Henry Poole A.R.A. Originally the school had asked Earl Haig to perform the ceremony but he was unable to attend.

The Duke of Portland arrived at the Forest Road gates, and was met by a party including the Mayor, the Sheriff and the Headmaster. The boys were all gathered on the east lawn, with the privileged ticket holders standing on the west lawn. In a reserved enclosure close to the statue sat the relatives of the fallen. The ceremony itself began with the singing of the original School Song. This was based on one of the odes of Horace and began with the words "Integer vitae sceleresque purus". It was accompanied by the City Police Band, and: "the sonorous Latin words floated sweetly on the crisp, autumnal air, and turned one's thought inevitably to bigger boys now lying dead in France and Flanders who had often sung the same song."

The Duke of Portland, at the top of the school steps, then made a short speech reminding everyone of the purpose of the memorial, namely to show "the respect, honour, and admiration which we feel for the Old Boys who laid down their lives in the Great War." He descended the steps, and pulled the Union Jack off the statue. A party of the O.T.C. saluted and the buglers of the Robin Hood Rifles sounded the Last Post. The Mayor laid a magnificent wreath, followed by boys who represented the Upper School, the Lower School, the Preparatory School, the staff and the Old Boys' Society. Principal A.R.Henderson read a passage from the scriptures. His son, Roy Henderson, sang a specially composed song *What are those which are arrayed in white robes?*, and the Bishop of Newcastle gave an address and dedicated the memorial. After the hymn, *O Valiant Hearts, who to your Glory came*, the *Réveillé* was sounded and the National Anthem sung. In what must have been a touching sight, the younger boys of the school then smothered the steps of the monument with Flanders poppies. Inside the school, an illuminated Roll of Honour, beautifully executed by the school's Art Master, Mr E.P.Betts, was put on permanent display. It records the full details of soldiers' regiments, their ranks and the dates of their deaths.

The High School's very wise choice of a statue to commemorate their Great War dead may well be viewed by later generations as one which occupied the moral high ground. Other schools were to behave in wholly unacceptable ways. At one school, the Bursar was given a new office and at another the Headmaster received a new house with a pleasant garden and four acres of land.

Friday, February 16th 1923

Dr James Gow died at his house, 40, West End Lane, Hampstead, at the premature age of only 69. By now he was nearly blind, and was suffering from "a distressing internal malady, which medical skill was unable to relieve." He had been forced to retire from the Headmastership of Westminster School in 1919 because of problems with his eyes and was much affected by the death of his son, Roderick, aged only 23, on H.M.S. Defence at the Battle of Jutland.

In his obituary, *The Nottinghamian* listed Gow's achievements. They included a reorganised syllabus, a new Chemical laboratory, a large number of Open Scholarships at Oxford and Cambridge and over a hundred boys who passed the various examinations of the University of London. Others obtained degrees in Medicine, Arts, and Science, winning numerous prizes and medals. In actual fact Gow did a great deal of teaching himself and always ended each lesson with his characteristic phrase, "I think that just about finishes our dose." On the sporting side, Dr Gow had started an Athletics Contest for senior boys which soon grew into a full Sports Day for the whole school. He regularly attended school football and cricket fixtures and organised a number of different venues for games including the Forest, the Gregory Ground and Mapperley Park. The Football Sixes, or later, the Football Eights, where teams were drawn by lot and competed for a trophy and medals was now a regular feature of the Spring Term. Dr Gow himself played football and cricket for the staff and on one occasion was playing against a local amateur team at Trent Bridge when he was struck a frightful blow by the ball. He was stunned, but returned to school the next day to be greeted by a great cheer of sympathy in Assembly. It was Dr Gow's idea to have school societies for Debating, Photography, Natural History and many other interests. It was in his reign that the Officer Training Corps was founded, the prefects were revived and much encouragement was given to a host of school activities including music and drama. On Monday, February 19th 1923, a memorial service for Dr Gow was held at Westminster Abbey, attended by many members, past and present, of both Nottingham High School and Westminster School.

Saturday, June 16th 1923

This year, largely at the behest of the Old Boys' Society, the school decided to introduce a Founder's Day service, presumably in imitation of the many larger public schools which had carried out such ceremonies for many years. Over four centuries previously, in 1513, Dame Agnes Mellers had laid down that a service of commemoration should be held every year on June 16th, the name day of her husband, Richard. The ceremony which Dame Agnes requested, however, was a solemn Roman Catholic Mass. It was probably celebrated for about thirty five years until such services were abolished by order of the Protestant monarch, King Edward VI. Although this type of Mass may have been briefly revived under Catholic Queen Mary, it disappeared for ever when the Protestant Queen Elizabeth I came to the throne in 1558. Nowadays, the only substantive connection between the ancient and modern ceremonies is that prayers are still said for Richard and Agnes Mellers.

I have found no real indication that the "bread, ale and cheese" distribution was ever connected with the Free School in the early sixteenth century. When this second ceremony was suggested by the Mayor of Nottingham, Alderman E.L.Manning, as another custom which might be revived, it seems that he was merely viewing it as an old tradition in the widest possible sense. And one, of course, to which the Old Boys would be ideally suited.

Present at the first Founder's Day service were the Mayor, the Town Clerk, a number of Governors and many Old Boys. Their president was Mr Herbert Durrant Snook who had been at the High School in 1876, and had made one League appearance for Notts County during their first season in the Football League in 1888-1889. Events took place in a "spirit of true gratitude and reverence". The service began with the hymn *O Merciful and Holy* and the psalm *I Was Glad When They Said Unto Me*. Dr Turpin read the Bible passage *Let Us Now Praise Famous Men* and the congregation then sang what was to become the boys' favourite hymn, *He Who Would Valiant Be*. Much to the boys' disappointment, the school censor had made an alteration in order to omit the lines:

> "Hobgoblin nor foul fiend
>
> can daunt his spirit"

After this came prayers, and an address by Canon Field. A collection was taken for the Dame Agnes Mellers' Lads Club while the congregation sang *Fight the Good Fight*. After the blessing Mr Vernon Read played Bach's *Toccata and Fugue* but by the time he had finished there were fewer than a dozen people left in the church. *The Nottinghamian* rather optimistically, perhaps, thought that everyone had probably gone off to the Exchange Building for the loyal toast to Dame Agnes and the many other benefactors of the school.

Summer 1923

Mr W.E.Ryles retired after forty one years at the High School. As he was very tall, he was always called "Jumbo". His brother, Mr W.T.Ryles, served the school for an equally long time, and was nicknamed "Nipper". William Edward Ryles was born on April 18th 1850. He came to the High School in September 1882 when his main subjects were English, Mathematics and Latin. He was the Master-in-Charge of football from 1885 onwards and he appears to have made his debut as a goalkeeper in 1888. He appeared only infrequently after this although it is known that he played as a right full back for the Masters' Team in a 1-6 defeat by the Boys, on March 23rd 1892.

As a teacher: "He was primarily a mathematical Master, and Form Master of 3a, and, when the Junior School was a separate department, he was in charge of it." "Jumbo" also had interests outside school, namely the study of insect life. This was well known among the boys and not infrequently at the beginning of a lesson, there would be one or two waiting by his desk with matchboxes containing specimens for identification, a service in which he always showed a very real pleasure.

Ryles always wore a mortarboard, and about a year before his retirement, was very amused by an unmistakeable caricature entitled *The Old School and the New*, published in *The Nottinghamian*. Ryles was described in affectionate detail by the famous author Geoffrey Trease:

> "Jumbo, who was my form master in my second year, was portly, comfortable, and generously moustached. Coming slowly down the street, he looked rather like a penguin. In school, he

was the last of the assistant masters to retain his mortarboard. The two brothers had joined the staff in the same year, but whereas four decades had not blunted Nipper's nervous edge, Jumbo was, to put it charitably, a more restful character. Indeed, he was known to fall asleep in class. The nearest to lively excitement he ever displayed was when a boy brought him a matchbox containing an insect for identification. He taught us Latin and Mathematics, but entomology was his enthusiasm. He was also reputed to enjoy his pint in the Vernon Arms, adjoining the school. Unlike Nipper, he was married, and in earlier days, he had taken boys as boarders in his home.

After a year with his high powered brother, it was pleasant to relax with Jumbo, who was so-easy going that one might have said that discernible movement had ceased. As his top boy I was regularly sent out on private errands in lesson time, to the tobacconist's at the foot of the steep hill or right down into the city centre to his bank - errands performed on foot, since, living so close to the school, I had not acquired a bicycle. On the tobacco expedition, I was told to buy toffee for myself. No higher authority ever questioned these absences from class, and, perhaps more remarkably, no boy ever accused me of being teacher's pet, or whatever it would have been termed in High School vocabulary. Jumbo never showed anything except the most correct and unsentimental detachment towards his boys, and probably had a secret preference for insects."

1923

The popular school caretaker, Robert Holmes and his wife both died. Robert had only retired in July of the previous year, 1922.

Summer term 1923

Under the directorship of R.S.Bridge and W.A.Parsons, the First XI cricket team remained unbeaten throughout the season. They were captained by J.S.McLellan and the leading players were V.A.Hodgkinson, D.W.Fletcher and D.J.Bowller. Hodgkinson took a phenomenal 53 wickets at an average of 4.92 and Bowller took 27 at only 8.11. This particular team was reckoned to be one of the best, if not the best, of all the First XIs that the school has ever produced.

Summer term 1923

The O.T.C. had what may well have been their first ever Field Day. They travelled by char-a-banc to Clumber Park and combined with the Trent College O.T.C. to fight an action against Worksop College and Sheffield King Edward's School who were the defending force. The contest took place in front of Clumber House but "was not a great success". In an ironic echo of the Great War, "if individual section commanders and platoon commanders had relied more on themselves and less on superior officers, better results might have been obtained."

Summer term 1923

Mr Woodward retired after twenty five years' service. He had been responsible for reintroducing Gymnastics to the Upper School.

1924

A new dining room with a capacity of eighty pupils was built to the west of the school lawns. There was a kitchen and an O.T.C. storeroom at one end, looked after by Captain Pollard. This building eventually became a Music School before being demolished in 1996.

December 1924

Throughout this period boys usually arrived at school by one of three methods. The first was, quite simply, on foot. In the 1870s and 1880s, a large number of boys came from the approximate area of Alfreton Road. In the early 1900s, many boys seemed to have lived even closer, in the streets adjoining Forest Road. During the period of the Great War a substantial proportion lived in Sherwood either close to Private Road or between Mansfield Road and Hucknall Road. A second category of boys used the trams which ran, for example, from West Bridgford to the Market Square and then from the Market Square up Mansfield Road past corner of Forest Road. A third group of boys, including D.H.Lawrence, used the extensive rail network which criss-crossed the county at this time. Local stations included the Midland and the Victoria Station from both of which there was a long walk, with a steep, tiring ascent of Waverley Street. Boys who were late could always hear the caretaker tolling the school bell. At the eastern end of Gregory Boulevard, on the far side of the Forest, was Carrington Station. Boys here could make use of the many footpaths which climbed the steep slope around the back of the Church Cemetery.

Whatever their route, however, "train boys" were famed for their ability to stroll in late at any time during the morning and then use the vagaries of the railway system as their excuse. This poem is by "Medusa":

SONG OF THE TRAIN BOY.

Oh who would be a train boy
On a murky, misty day,
When they wake you up at five o'clock
And bid you haste away,
With your breakfast half-uneaten
And your bootlace quite undone.
And with blinking eyes and a yawning mouth,
And your homework just begun?

Oh, it's nice to be a train boy
(When you've once got out of bed
And caught the train and reached your goal)
When the sun beams overhead
As you hear the school-bell ringing
When you saunter up the hill
And you think of the other boys hurrying fast,
And you crawl at your sweet will.

Oh, it's nice to be a train boy.
And to come in very late.
And to interrupt the masters
Oh, I think it's simply great,
As you knock at the door and enter
And begin to look for your books,
And reply with a smile of sweetest calm
To the master's peevish looks.

Oh, it's nice to be a train boy
If you are put in "D,"

> And you ask to do the work at home,
> And run off cheerily.
> Oh, these are the joys of the train boy
> And these are his miseries great,
> But you've got to take them together or none
> For such is the way of fate.

The mid-1920s

According to gossip, the Headmaster approached the Headmistress of the Girls' High School to see if she might allow boys to attend dances with the girls. Her reply was most definitely in the negative and the girls continued to dance with each other or with their teachers.

1925

The School was so short of funds that when Mr Betts and Mr Hood offered to install electric lighting in part of the school while their classes were taking examinations, this was eagerly accepted.

January 1925

Mr G.D.Day became the first Headmaster of the Preparatory School.

The evening of Tuesday, June 16th 1925

"Mrs.Reynard", a vixen who lived in the school grounds, was shot by Mr Hallam, the school caterer. The fox had been a particular favourite of the senior boys and had introduced them to "unknown parts of the shrubbery" where they had taken a keen interest in her activities. One prefect had even ruined his trousers by following her through the dense undergrowth. One day however, the fox went too far and attacked the caretaker's cat. The caretaker then asked Mr Hallam for help and the latter turned up one evening "in the playground armed to the teeth with a gun and two tame rabbits." The staff and their wives, playing on the tennis courts, were then rather amazed to see Mr Hallam leave the two tame rabbits on the lawn as bait and await developments. Sure enough, the fox soon arrived, attempted to eat the rabbits and was promptly shot. Luckily, no boys were following the vixen at the time!

Saturday, June 29th 1925

The Prefects' techniques of administering discipline were clearly improving by leaps and bounds, now that they had access to the most modern equipment. It was announced that "Mackirdy, Brierley and Butcher were well-beaten at the break. New canes, purchased the previous day, amply justified the confidence placed in them."

July 1925

Dr Turpin retired after twenty four years in office. He was the first headmaster to receive the nickname of "The Duke", and C.Lloyd Morgan remembered as "a very loveable man, essentially he was shy. I can see him playing croquet now, and he played a lot of golf." It was to Dr Turpin that the School owed the A, B, and C Form system and also the introduction of the "set" system in Modern Language teaching, in Mathematics and in Science. In 1903 form cricket and football on one school afternoon of the week was introduced as part of the curriculum. In the same year the Oxford and Cambridge Certificate Examinations were taken for the first time and the Preparatory Department was set up in Waverley Mount. This too was the year of the first prefects. Important changes were made to school games. Instead of football, "rugger" was introduced and the House system was brought in. A new canteen was built in 1924. Dr Turpin was succeeded by Cedric Lawton Reynolds, a Yorkshireman from Wakefield, and one of the few northerners ever to have held the office of Headmaster.

July 1925

Mr Wilfrid Tyson "Nipper" Ryles retired. He had been at the High School for over forty years, most of this time in the company of his brother, Mr William Edward "Jumbo" Ryles. "Nipper" was born on September 15th 1862 and came to the High School at Easter 1883. Like his elder brother, he specialised in English, Latin and Mathematics. According to reminiscences in *The Nottinghamian*, "Nipper": "must have possessed the temper of an angel to carry on so faithfully year after year the thankless task of trying to teach an always most unpromising collection of young ruffians something of the elements of learning."

In short, "Nipper" was "a very good Master indeed. I liked his lessons, he always made things so jolly interesting." "Nipper" carried out an extensive list of school activities. In the days when teachers played for the school at football, he was centre forward. In the years after that, he refereed school fixtures until rugby was introduced as the new school sport. He was a keen player of lawn tennis and fives, an ardent stamp collector, the treasurer of the Games Fund and the teacher in charge of the book department. Even just before his retirement: "he still retains the mental and physical alertness which have always characterised him, and we are glad to think that he leaves us with his energies unimpaired. In bidding him goodbye, we would assure him of our faithful appreciation of all that he has done for the School which he has served so long and faithfully, and offer him our best wishes for many years of happiness in his retirement."

Friday, July 5th 1925

The Prefects' Book records that "J.O.Coy, Upper 5B, had been reported by Mabbott for scaling the rifle-range wall. He had also put his clumsy feet through the asbestos roof of the cycle shed."

1926

Each house was divided into four tutor sets of about thirty boys, a system which allowed each individual to be directly supervised by the same teacher throughout his stay in the school. The new Headmaster, Mr Reynolds, had previously worked in a boarding school where this arrangement was normal practise.

Two further important changes were introduced. The first was to teach Biology as a separate subject and the second was to make Games compulsory. This had the immediate effect of raising standards as school teams were now selected from a larger pool of possible players.

The General Strike 1926

The school felt very little effect except for the loyal Sixth Formers who burned to enrol as special constables and wield truncheons on strikers' heads, or to borrow cars and transport young ladies around the city instead of the buses and trams. Some boys supported the strike and eagerly read *The Daily Worker*, keen for a chance to put a stone through the windscreens of strikebreaking local buses. During the absence of public transport, the school was overwhelmed with both bicycles and tricycles and "train-boys" could offer no excuse at all for their lateness.

Saturday, June 12th 1926

The whole school was given a holiday to see the Australians play England in the First Test at Trent Bridge. Unfortunately, rain fell almost without cease and Hobbs and Sutcliffe made just 32 runs before the game was washed out at lunch on the first day.

July 1926

The Old Boys' Society spoke out against the removal of the field gun from the front of the school. They felt that its barrel provided a wonderfully useful litter bin for the boys walking past.

July 1926

A number of Nottinghamshire Cricket Club members complained that High School boys were persistently dropping orange peel and toffee wrappers from the upper tier of the pavilion at Trent Bridge. When the Headmaster heard of this thoughtless behaviour, every boy who had been at Trent Bridge was questioned but nobody would confess. They were all banned from inter-form cricket for the rest of the term and had to remain at school to study. Around this time, many boys frequently spent their Wednesday half holidays either at the cricket or at Forest or County's midweek matches. Eric Penson remembered, for example, going to see Sam Hardy, England's goalkeeper, play for Forest against Oldham.

Thursday, September 23rd 1926

The very first boy appeared in the new Detention Book, recently purchased from Derry & Sons. He was North of 5A, and according to Mr H.E.George was guilty of an "impertinent noise". Rather typically the boy failed to turn up and had to serve his punishment on the following day. The very same detention book was still in daily use more than seventy years later although it was eventually forced to succumb to the Brave New World offered by computerised databases.

December 1926

The school started what turned out to be a very popular "Sing-Song Club" which met every Friday during the lunch hour.

April 1927

The Nottinghamian remarked how "new societies continue to spring up, flourish and then wither. The latest blossom is the Chess Club, which is so far showing no sign of decay." At the present time, all matches were friendlies but it was hoped to arrange some formal matches in the future.

July 1927

Mr E.P.Gaskin, the Second Master, and Head of Languages, retired. He was to pass away on Easter morning, 1931 after a severe illness of some six months' duration. For many years, a prize for Modern Languages was awarded in his name.

1927-1928

School fees increased to twenty seven guineas per term and an extra charge was introduced for books. It was probably for this reason, coupled with the effects of the Depression and the opening of Henry Mellish Grammar School at Bulwell, that numbers in the school dropped from 569 to 475.

Monday, January 28th 1928

H.H.Pockson was spotted by the Prefects: "coming to school with a girl. Pockson's defence was that without creating the need for an embarrassing explanation he could not detach himself from his companion." Pockson was allowed to choose his punishment, either two strokes of the cane or lines. He chose the lines.

Thursday, February 23rd 1928

The Detention Book records the punishment of Doar (4C). It was for "disobedience with a blowpipe".

The beginning of March 1928

After less than five years of retirement, "Jumbo" Ryles died. *The Nottinghamian* was sure that the announcement of his death would cause: "unfeigned sorrow. Those younger ones, who do not themselves remember him, should not forget his service to the School, a service such as is given to few to render. It is no exaggeration to say Mr Ryles gave his entire life to the School. It is for the School to remember and be grateful".

The end of March 1928

After fewer than three years of retirement, "Nipper" Ryles died, within a few short weeks of his brother. In his obituary, it was recorded that:

> "It would be a long task if we undertook to enumerate all the capacities, official and unofficial, in which Mr Ryles served the School. Everything he did was characterised by an untiring energy which even the smallest boy could recognise and appreciate. For his own Form 2A, he showed the pride and love of which only the great form-masters are capable. All those who had the good fortune to pass through it remember that year as one of the most pleasant and most interesting in their school careers. Those who, like the writer, entered it as new boys will agree that their introduction to NHS was one of the happiest. He certainly believed in hard work, but his lessons were never dull; nor did he forget us out of school hours, but took great interest in our form-magazine and other activities."

The Nottinghamian continued:

> "When, at the end of term, a presentation was made to him, he thanked us with quiet dignity. Even so, his self-control for a moment almost deserted him. When one had lived, he told us, for forty two years at a school, one became an inseparable part of it. This has proved true, for he enjoyed less than three years of his well-earned rest. But, regret it as we may, there is something fitting in his death. One cannot imagine him apart from the School and the boys he had served and loved."

Summer Holidays 1928

A young pupil, W.H.B.Cotton, was spending his holidays in Glamorgan. During his stay there, he managed to rescue two sailors from a ship which was foundering just offshore at Porthcawl.

Monday, October 1st 1928

Attitudes were very different in the not particularly distant past:

> "On Fri Sept 28th L. H. Jackson was seen in the company of two girls at about 4.20 p.m. For this offence, and because he was later seen with his two companions all on his bicycle at one time, he was sentenced to three strokes at a meeting held last period

169

this morning. The charge of riding down Waverley Street with the same cargo was not proven. Jackson attempted to wax eloquent on the troubles of being asked plain questions by one's female companions but when confronted with the alternative of an appeal to the Headmaster or a beating he sullenly accepted the latter."

Tuesday, October 2nd 1928

The Prefects' reign of terror continued. The very next day, the Prefects' Book records that "Jackson was well beaten today" almost as if they were enjoying it.

December 1928

In rowing circles, the school was now ranked alongside Eton and Shrewsbury, as having provided both Oxford and Cambridge with members of their Trial Eights. E.S.Abbott was cox to the Cambridge crew and S.Macdonald-Smith the Oxford representative.

1929

Using money provided by J.D.Player, the school bought eighteen acres of land from Colonel Seely for new playing fields on Valley Road. The total cost was £5,600, with a further £13,000 needing to be spent on levelling the site, returfing the surface, and then erecting a new pavilion. The Headmaster and J.A.Dixon had looked at over twenty possible sites before a decision was made. Interestingly enough, Johnny Dixon, for many years, continued to believe strongly that more land should have been purchased and that the whole school should then have been relocated to a new campus, surrounded by its own playing fields. On the other hand, the site had a marsh at the western end and it may have been the possible problems and expenses arising from this that led the governors to back away from buying any more of the available land. The old Mapperley Park ground was sold to the Corporation for £6,750, but the rest of the money for developing Valley Road, some £6,000-£7,000 was raised by the Old Boys, led by Sir Arthur Wheeler. It was at this time that a list of some 2,500 Old Boys, and their addresses, was compiled. It is kept to this day in the School Archives.

1929

S.Macdonald-Smith won a Blue for Rowing at Oxford. He did not actually row in the Boat Race, but was "spare man".

9.20 a.m. on Wednesday, April 10th 1929

In a slight drizzle, five adults and 20 boys waited on Platform 5 to leave on their school trip to Belgium. They were to visit Brussels, Antwerp, Ghent, Bruges and Waterloo. Many members of the original group were unable to go because of a local epidemic of mumps around this time.

Summer Term 1929

We still have a boy's timetable from this era. It was owned by John H.S.Firth of Form VB, and the subjects studied were Mathematics (6 lessons per week), Latin (5), French (5), Chemistry (4), English (3), Physics (3), History (3), Scripture (1), Drawing (1) and Machine Drawing (1). There appears to be no compulsory games or PE, although there is Saturday school with Wednesday off in lieu. There were six periods per day, and they were from 9.00-9.55, 9.55-10.45, Break, 11.00-11.55, 11.55-12.45, Lunch, 2.30-3.20 and 3.20-4.10. Every night there was an hour's homework in each of two subjects, with three subjects on Wednesday, and only one on Saturday.

Friday, October 18th 1929

Around the middle of the morning the enormous British airship, the R101, flew over the school. A few lucky boys were allowed out of their lessons to watch it sail majestically past.

1930

Mr Reynolds inaugurated the first Parents' Evenings, based on the house system.

Wednesday, February 26th 1930

Young Ward of 2B served a fourth detention, after three detentions in the previous five days, a situation not without a certain irony, perhaps.

Sunday, March 2nd 1930

D.H.Lawrence died at the Villa Robermond in France. Five years later, his remains were exhumed and his ashes interred in a small chapel on the Kiowa Ranch in the mountains of New Mexico.

The Nottinghamian carried a far from sympathetic (even sour) obituary for the great man, incorrectly described as a former Foundation Scholar. It was written by "G.T.", who may conceivably have been Geoffrey Trease, and spoke of his decay as a novelist, his fall from the previous great heights he had scaled, and the way that: "as disease pressed upon him, his writings became more and more tortured and obscure. He was degenerating into something like an ultra-modern painter, madly flinging his paint upon the canvas from far across the room. Certainly, he had forgotten that the main function of a writer was to be understood."

Begrudgingly, G.T. conceded that: "nevertheless, the critics are agreed that he was a great artist, and that the best of his work, both poems and fiction, will last. The School will be proud of her rebellious son long after those more conventionally honoured are forgotten."

Nowadays, of course, D.H.Lawrence is unquestionably the school's most famous old boy. It would be difficult to quote the name of any other Old Nottinghamian in, say, the USA or Europe, and expect that name to be recognised. And certainly, no other Old Nottinghamian is ever so widely studied in the universities of the world.

An unknown Saturday, early in May 1930

Thirty members of the Remove visited Stratford-on-Avon. They saw Shakespeare's birthplace and a performance of *The Tempest*. They were not impressed:

> "We realise that the same Company has to perform many plays, but that is hardly an excuse for forgetting speeches, or for the excessive loudness of the prompter. The man who played Ferdinand was particularly disappointing, while Miranda persisted in smiling all the time".

Summer Term 1930

The First Form went on a series of Nature Walks. 1A went to King's Mills but were disappointed to find that the ferry boat had been so damaged over the course of the winter that they could not cross the Trent into Derbyshire. 1C and 1D went to Fairham Brook, walking via Wilford Village, while 1B went to Wollaton Hall.

Tuesday, July 8th 1930

Problems with school uniform have their roots deep in the past:

> "A meeting was held second period this morning when Martin (5C), was brought up for wearing trousers of an extremely unpleasant pink hue. He said he was waiting for some ordinary flannels to be made. Such complete disregard for the School Clothing Regulations continued with Hickling (Rem A) who was found to be wearing a "Notts County" tie. He was told to sort himself out by the following day."

Thursday, February 12th 1931

A magnificent attempt to avoid the pain of a couple of strokes with the cane is recorded in the Prefects' Book which is actually rather ripped and dog-eared at this point in time:

> "Widdowson, who had been absent, was beaten by Carr today, with two good strokes which were rendered ineffectual by a quantity of vests. Widdowson was told to take the padding off. He said that he had appendicitis and the padding was to prevent injury to the affected part. The tale seemed plausible, but was unsatisfactory as Widdowson was playing Rugger. He pleaded an inability to obtain a medical certificate and was referred to the Headmaster who eventually said if Widdowson produced a note from his parents, (there would be no problem). However he deserved double the strokes without a certificate."

Thursday, April 30th and Saturday, May 2nd 1931

The Finals of the School Athletic Sports were held for the first time on the new Valley Road Playing Fields. Facilities included a new pavilion, largely paid for by the Old Boys. A.H.Bowman achieved a record of 10.9 seconds for the 100 yards and D.J.Lucking established another school record with a half mile run in 2 minutes 20 seconds.

Easter Term 1931

The School Four played a number of opponents at Fives. They included King Edward VII School, Sheffield, and the wonderfully named Lincoln Pariahs.

Easter 1931

A group of twenty seven boys visited the Great War battlefields of north-west Europe including Ypres, Vimy Ridge and Zeebrugge with visits to the place of Edith Cavell's execution and Waterloo.

Tuesday, June 2nd 1931

Fenton of 3C served a punishment from Mr Hardwick for being "a thorough nuisance".

Monday, June 8th 1931

John Auger Dixon died in a Park Row nursing home. He had been at the school from 1874-1876, and in his early years, played football for Notts County, the Corinthians and, in 1885, for England against Wales at Blackburn. He was more famous, however, as a cricketer and played as an all-rounder for both Forest Amateurs and Nottinghamshire whom he captained for many years with a highest score of 268 not out against Sussex and a hat-trick against Lancashire. In later life, he was a Governor, helping to select the Valley Road site for the new sports field. He was buried near the entrance to the Church Cemetery on June 11th and in 1933 the Dixon Gates were erected at Trent Bridge.

Friday, June 12th 1931

Young Widdowson had obviously shared his secret with his friends:

> "Healey was well beaten today, 6 strokes being delivered - the first three being useless as the culprit was wearing four pairs of trousers and one pair of pants."

Monday, July 6th 1931

And now, the supreme of all ironies: Burton of 2C received a detention from Mr Hood for receiving "too many detentions".

Wednesday, July 8th 1931

Batting for Nottinghamshire against Warwickshire at Edgbaston, Old Boy, George Vernon Gunn scored 100 not out. In the Nottinghamshire total of 521 all out, his father, George Gunn, had already scored 183. This is the only occasion in the history of cricket that a father and son have both scored a century in the same innings of a first class match.

Friday, November 7th 1931

More technical problems again with the administering of punishments:

> "Fawn was well beaten today at the hands of Lucking and Green. Owing to his obesity, some difficulty was experienced in folding him up. For the same reason he was little perturbed by his chastisement."

Friday, November 14th 1931

Roberts (Rem A) was reported to the staff by Mabbott for using rude and suggestive language. He had already been warned once this term and the number of convictions against him was innumerable. He pleaded that he would use the words he had used to Mabbott to his grandfather, and alleged that Mabbott had even taught him some of them. His record was so bad that as well as his punishment, he was threatened with expulsion by the Headmaster, if he gave any more trouble.

Saturday, November 15th 1931

The good old days? I don't think so:

> "Roberts received 3 good strokes at the hands of Jackson, Bowman, and Thompson at break today. He evinced signs of considerable agony."

The 1931 - 1932 Rugby Season

This was the first season when the new Valley Road playing fields were used. There were six full sized rugby pitches with a smaller seventh one and, for the first time, every boy could make use of the impressive changing facilities, rather than just school teams, as had previously been the case. Every boy could play rugby twice a week at least and many of the keenest played three times. These games occurred on the Wednesday half day as well as the usual sports afternoons. Many parents were now beginning to visit the playing fields to watch their sons perform. This had rarely been the case at Mapperley Park. Every boy now had a hooped school rugby shirt and a second plain white shirt. As a result, practice games were now much more "pleasurable and instructive".

December 1931

After twenty eight years' service, during which he was absent through illness for less than six weeks, John Allan Radley retired. He had been a teacher of Mathematics and a first form Form Master and, with characteristic modesty, asked that no official notice be taken of his departure. Instead he preferred just to leave at the end of term as normal, but never to return. At a subsequent prize giving, however, the Headmaster drew attention to his exemplary service and the school gave him "three special cheers". Despite his age, Mr Radley enjoyed "abounding health and vigour", was an "irrepressible gardener" and looked forward eagerly to using his free time for mountaineering.

1932

The school playground was finally asphalted, at a cost of some £1,000 after over fifty years of being just rough soil and sand. Even then a number of governors were opposed to it, fearing that there would be injuries if boys fell over on a hard surface.

January 1932

The Nottinghamian mentioned some of the boys' main diversions outside their schoolwork. They included snobs, snakes and ladders, Hornby trains, Tiger Tim annuals, and Edgar Wallace novels.

Spring Term 1932

The school play *Macbeth*, by William Shakespeare, attracted a record crowd of 422 people.

Tuesday, April 5th 1932

Thirty boys visited the Home Brewery Co Ltd, in Daybrook. They were accompanied by Messrs Hood and Houghton and saw the entire brewing process from barley to the finished product. At the end of the visit, the boys were given sandwiches and soft drinks, while the staff "sampled the real stuff."

Monday, November 21st 1932

The desire to avoid physical pain is taken to new, undreamt of, heights:

> "Pitt was due to be caned at the end of the break. He was wearing a pair of rugby shorts, and was told to take them off, which he did. When W.E.G. Payton had delivered the first

stroke - a hard beat - Pitt tottered and fell. Water was fetched and in a few minutes he had recovered so as to be able to walk. He said that he had been in a brawl the night before, and his head was plastered and his hand bandaged. In the Captain's opinion there was no question about the genuineness of his collapse and the other two strokes were not inflicted. He did not want to go home, and was hence allowed to return to his form room."

Wednesday, November 23rd 1932

Day two, the saga continues:

"The suspicions of the Captain being aroused as to the genuineness of Pitt's faint, Pitt was interviewed. There was no mark underneath the plaster on his forehead, and his hand seemed completely uninjured. Furthermore he had previously faked during a gym period of Sergeant's. His faint was therefore adjudged to be a fake, although he denied this. The Captain confesses himself completely taken in by the consummate artistry of Pitt's acting."

Thursday, November 24th 1932

Day three, Pitt is given his just deserts:

"The two strokes Pitt escaped were awarded at the break. He was sentenced to three more for the fake faint."

Pitt had apparently learnt very little. The next day, he "was well beaten at the break with a new cane, purchased from Morris, Wilkinson and Co (a factory near the gasworks) for sixpence."

Saturday, November 26th 1932

More problems with the rule book:

"Owen flinched at the first stroke, which was ordered to be repeated. This was not acceptable to Owen, who was therefore taken to the Head."

The Head made a judgement worthy of Solomon himself:

"Owen was offered the option of being beaten by the prefects or by the Head. He chose the Head."

December 1932

Various members of Form 5B were punished for a variety of different offences, including "wrestling in the form room", and "throwing rice about the Hall."

The first Saturday of the Summer Term, 1933

E.J.Dickenson threw the cricket ball a record distance of 96 yards 2 feet 10 inches. His throw broke a school record which had lasted since 1919. This traditional English event was excluded from the school sports only a few years after Dickenson's record was established, but his prodigious feat remains the best distance achieved in well over eighty years.

Summer Term 1933

An unknown member of staff outraged many of the prefects and sixth form by appearing at school in a "pale pink silk tie". Many of them accused him of accidentally snipping a section off his eiderdown.

Thursday, November 16th 1933

Mr William Carey Trafford died at Oxted in Surrey. He was eighty-five years of age and at the beginning of the month had gone with his wife to visit some friends. He seemed "wonderfully well, and was enjoying his visit immensely". On this particular morning he went out as usual to buy a newspaper but evidently fell down on the path by the roadside. He was seen by the driver of a passing bus and he and the conductor picked the old man up and drove him to a nearby hospital. A doctor examined him immediately but "death must have been instantaneous and painless".

In actual fact, Mr Trafford had always wanted to go suddenly so the end for him was "nothing but well and fair". He had worked at the High School from 1883-1922. Dr Dixon had appointed him as a science teacher and after being initially Form Master of the Upper Modern Fourth, he was a Fourth Form Master for many years. In 1909 he became Form Master of 3C where he remained until in 1918, in view of the strain being put upon him by his advancing years, Dr Turpin relieved him of some of his duties. Mr Trafford then taught Mathematics until he retired in 1922 at the age of 69.

Mr F.C.Boon remembered how Mr Trafford used to bring to school, "wire puzzles, which he gave to the boy who succeeded in doing them."

Despite his great interest in Mathematics, however, Mr Trafford was, for most of his life, a teacher of Science and when he did teach Mathematics, it was always of a very elementary standard. For this reason, he pursued more advanced Mathematics as a hobby at home. He used to try to find, for example, methods of discovering the factors of very large numbers and to find rational solutions of indeterminate equations. It was perhaps sad that Mr Trafford spent so much of his life not doing what he loved to do. At the same time though,"What he did succeed in doing was to earn the affection of all he taught; and that is a greater achievement."

July 1934

The games fields were so dry that they had all turned completely brown.

Saturday, July 21st 1934

Playing for the First XI against Loughborough Grammar School at Valley Road, A.G.Evans took nine wickets for eight runs.

September 1934

School numbers reached 513. They have never dropped below 500 since this time.

Saturday, October 20th 1934

The Prefects' Book records that "Fletcher was beaten - well beaten."

Monday, January 7th 1935

The Preparatory School was shocked by the first of two deaths during the first three months of this dreadful year, this *annus horribilis*.

The first death was Miss J.K.Richmond, who had an emergency operation but then succumbed to pneumonia (a disease known at the time as "The Captain of the Men of Death"). Despite being seemingly on the road to recovery, she died within a few days. Miss Richmond had been spending the Christmas holidays with her brother at Erdington in Birmingham. She had first come to the High School in 1911, when Mr Leggett was in charge of the Preparatory Department:

> "She served it faithfully for twenty-three years and her whole life was bound up in its welfare. During the very trying years of the

War from 1916 to 1919, during Mr Leggett's service with the army, Miss Richmond was in charge of the Prep, and steered it successfully through many rather difficult terms. She served us nearly a quarter of a century, yet she was not absent a month in all. A marvellous record!"

Miss Richmond's service was in an era when, if a woman wanted to be a teacher, she had to remain unmarried and forego the joys of having her own family. If she married, she had to leave the school.

Monday, March 25th 1935

After only nine days of illness, Mr George Duncan Day, the Headmaster of the Preparatory Department, died of pneumonia. Aged only forty nine, he had worked at the High School for just over ten years. From 1915-1918 he had been a Major in the Camel Corps and the rigours of his war service in Palestine had done much to weaken his general health. He had worked for the Egyptian Ministry of Education and came to England in January 1925. Day had an Oxford Blue for Association Football and his degree was in Classics and History. Throughout his life he had been a keen cricketer and a member of the Nottinghamshire Golf Club. His little son Patrick, a boarder at Shrewsbury School, was now an orphan, as his mother had herself died only recently.

April 1935

Although the school sports were no longer very much like their Victorian forebears, they still contained a number of events which would be considered unusual today. These included the 300 yards sprint, the 150 yards sprint, throwing the cricket ball, house relays, house shuttle relays, tutor set relays and junior tutor set relays, as well as a whole series of "House Tugs" and "Tutor Set Tugs".

Summer Term 1935

In 1935, the First XI remained undefeated throughout the entire cricket season. This was only the second time that this had happened, the first having been in 1923, although in the latter year the team had managed to win a greater proportion of its fixtures and had drawn fewer matches.

Thursday, September 19th 1935

The 1st XV went to Coventry to see the New Zealand All Blacks beat the Midland Counties by 9-3. Later in the season they were to watch Leicester play the same opponents.

October 1935

Captain Ernest Alfred Pollard, the school secretary, died at his house, 189, Perry Road. He had seen considerable service in the army, having joined the Robin Hoods as a boy and then enlisting in the 1st Battalion of the Sherwood Foresters. He suffered greatly in the Boer War, but did not hesitate to volunteer for the Great War, and served for five years in France and Ireland with the 2/8th Battalion of the Sherwood Foresters.

Saturday, October 5th 1935

The Prefects' Book records how: "Dodds, Bonello, Healey and Simpson received their strokes of the cane at break today, with the new Prefects showing considerable skill and vigour".

December 1935

The Nottinghamian, for perhaps the first time ever, actually included some remarks that might be construed as vulgar:

> "This term uncouth noises have shattered the calm serenity of the Prefects' Room. Do these emanate from the Orchestra's promised wind instruments, or do they have a baser origin?"

Thursday, January 9th 1936

Albert Grant Onion, the groundsman at Mapperley Park, died at the premature age of only sixty four. He had worked at the High School since 1897. Onion coached the High School cricketers with great enthusiasm and saw many of them go on to do very well with local clubs. In twenty-five years he did not miss umpiring a single First XI fixture and was famed for his fairness and impartiality. He and his wife and daughters were responsible, too, for preparing all the teas for the players. In 1929 he moved to Valley Road and was soon busy creating excellent wickets there. With the boys, Onion would "stand no nonsense", and set them an example of "straight, temperate and vigorous manhood". Many of them would not easily forget his strident calls of "Watch that ball! Bring that left across! Wait on the short ones! Lay on to the short ones!"

Monday, February 10th 1936

The new Assembly Hall was dedicated. It had been paid for by the ever-generous J.D.Player. After this, the East Quadrangle was turfed and provided with a covered walkway so boys could walk to assembly without getting wet. The Assembly Hall was equipped with a new organ, consisting of a pedal organ, great organ and a swell organ. The Assembly Hall was never consecrated as a site of worship, and this allowed it to be used for plays, debates, concerts and functions. It was the Headmaster, Mr Reynolds, who devised the system whereby if the School Bible was resting on its lectern, then the hall was a place of worship, but if not, then it was being used for secular purposes. Mr Reynolds wanted to call it the Player Hall, but this was resisted by Player himself who said that it should not be a "Player's Hall, but a Workers' Hall." To this day, Player's portrait remains in his hall.

An appeal for chairs for the new Assembly Hall was made around this time. Some six hundred were needed and each one had their name carved on the back of the chair and the dates when they had attended the school. Many of these chairs, despite being used almost every day of the school year, still survived more than sixty years later. The windows in the Hall were resplendent with stained glass coats of arms. They represented, on the north side, King Henry VIII, the Universities of Cambridge and Oxford, the City of Nottingham and the Diocese of Southwell. On the southern side, the shields were those of Sir Thomas White, the University of London, the Duke of Portland, Nottingham University College, Henry VIII, and Nottinghamshire County Council. The two shields on the balcony were early versions of the school's eventual coat of arms, recognised officially in 1949. Heraldically these two rather charming shields represented "Argent, three blackbirds rising proper" and "Argent, three blackbirds statant proper".

Saturday, June 27th 1936

The school was shocked to hear of the sudden death of Mr Clement Elphinstone Radcliffe Holmes. He had been at work as recently as Tuesday, June 23rd, although "for some little time he had not felt quite up to the mark." He was taken ill in the night and next day had an "urgent and serious" operation at the General Hospital. To begin with, he seemed to have made a slight recovery but "the struggle was hopeless" and he died within four days of first being taken ill. Mr Holmes had served the school for twenty one years as a teacher of Spanish and French. He was a keen supporter of the Old Boys' Rugger and Cricket Clubs and played golf and tennis in his later years.

Chapter 13: The Second World War

August 7th 1936

At the Berlin Olympics, Old Boy Arthur Willoughby "Fuzzy" Barton refereed the game between Norway and Germany at the Poststadion, Berlin, in front of some 50,000 spectators. Germany, anticipating an easy victory, rested three of their best players but lost by 0-2, having conceded a single goal in each half. Unfortunately, Referee Barton did not get the chance to socialise either with the Führer or with the German players after the match. During the evening, when the official Olympic party went to the German headquarters to commiserate with the gallant losers, they found that a furious Hitler had sent them all home in disgrace. This was the only football match that the Führer ever watched.

Christmas Term 1936

The Hobbies Club met throughout this term, with Meccano and stamps being the main interests. In addition, chess was also played. There were junior matches against William Crane School (lost 4-6), and a senior fixture against the University (3-3).

Monday, November 2nd 1936

The Economics VI and Remove visited the Rolls-Royce factory in Derby where they saw a large number of car and aircraft engines being constructed. They were completely deafened by a twelve cylinder aircraft engine which was being run continuously for six days. When they remarked upon just how loud it was, the boys were told, "You should hear it without the silencer."

Saturday, January 2nd 1937

In an unprecedented move, Old Boy H.G.Proctor resigned his curacy at St John's Church, Long Eaton. He explained that he could no longer believe in the fundamental doctrines of Christianity. He was definitely not an atheist, he still believed that God was good, and that men should strive to live good lives but, nevertheless, he felt that he could no longer accept the Christian faith. The only honest course was to resign. He became a farmer and moved to Durham.

Monday, March 29th 1937

A party of thirty senior boys left for Paris, which the school magazine described enthusiastically as "the gay city". They visited the Louvre, Les Invalides, Fontainebleau, Versailles, the Arc de Triomphe, and then Sacré Coeur, Notre Dame, and the zoo at the Bois de Vincennes.

Tuesday, July 20th 1937

The teaching staff continued to implement its strict policy of stamping out excessive happiness in any of its guises. K.W.Savidge received a detention for "whistling in school".

1937

This year the dining room was enlarged to seat two hundred pupils. John Player also provided the school with the money, on this occasion £50,000, to build the West Block, as a counterpart to the recently constructed Assembly Hall, gymnasium and East Quadrangle. Originally, the new classrooms were designed to house the Preparatory Department and the Second and Third Forms.

The rugby season, 1937 - 1938

The Captain of Rugby was J.F.Walker. He remains the only person in High School history to have captained the First XV for three successive years, having already performed this duty in the 1935-1936 and 1936-1937 seasons. Overall, his record was played 45, won 25, drawn 2, lost 18, points for 642, points against 516.

Christmas Term 1937

The Christian Union is mentioned in *The Nottinghamian* for the first time. They met at 4.20 p.m. on Wednesday afternoons and were one of the very few school societies founded at the request of the boys. Their meetings consisted of a hymn, a prayer, a Bible reading and a short talk. This term also saw, rather ironically perhaps, the foundation of the "World Peace Society". Meetings took place at 4.30 p.m. on Mondays and discussed topics as varied as how the teachings of Christ would prevent another world war and the successes of the League of Nations.

January 1938

A succession of international crises led the governors to examine Air Raid Precautions. They decided that the best course of action would be to provide an air-raid shelter for the entire Main School under the new science block, once it was built. In theory even a direct hit on the science block would be beneficial, since it would provide rubble to shelter from any subsequent bombs.

April 1938

The Nottinghamian published the following poem, written by N.E.S. of IIA:

MY LATIN.

Of all the lessons taught at school,
"Latin" takes the biscuit;
I think I'd rather learn Chinese,
Anyhow, I'd risk it.

With "pugnabis" and "pugnabat"
And second declensions,
I'm always getting a hundred lines
Or else a few detentions.

Why can't we study "botany",
And learn about the "daisies"
Instead of swotting "G.N.C."
And learning "Adverb Phrases"?

They say that Latin clears the brain,
That may be - but I doubt it;
I would not like to see in print
The things I think about it.

The memorising is the worst,
T'would make a Polar Bear grunt;
Fancy learning things like this: --
"Imus istis erunt."

Oh, Latin gives me sleepless nights
The Grammar - I could burn it.
The hardest task the Romans had

Was when they had to learn it.

Wednesday, May 11th 1938

The Deputy Headmaster Sammy Corner died at his home in Croydon aged eighty four. He had worked for thirty seven years at the High School, twenty four of them as Second Master. One of the most popular men ever to work in the High School, his obituary in *The Nottinghamian* is the most complimentary ever to appear in its pages:

> "He was a vivid personality, utterly devoted to the service of the School. No trouble was too great for him to take. Very rarely did his colleagues hear him speak disparagingly of any boy. He had indeed 'a soft spot' for boys. They were similarly affected in return, shown by the warmth with which mention of him is invariably received at any gathering of his Old Boys. Like Mr Chips, having no children of his own, he might yet claim to have 'thousands of 'em, thousands of 'em, and all boys'."

Mr J.Llewellyn Davies, the President of the Old Boys' Society, spoke of how he still had "a clear memory of the joy with which that master welcomed a visit from a former pupil. Such interest and kindness were heartily reciprocated."

Sammy was once described as "an elderly man who, in the winter-time, wore all day long two overcoats under his tattered gown, a woollen scarf round his neck and mittens on his hands, the whole crowned by a mortar-board which always seemed to be the worse for wear."

P.C.Sands, a Headmaster himself, recounted how he: "last saw him slowly proceeding up Waverley Street, books under his arm, spectacles on nose, lost in thought, but just waking up to look warily up and down before crossing the road to his house. To speak to him meant a long delay, for he loved to launch himself upon School memories, and his memory was capacious. So one had to stand, before button-holing him, for he was too abstracted to see you unless you stopped him. Of his editorial energy was the *Forester* born. It was as Chairman of the Debating Society that one remembers him best. His interests were so wide, he fell easy prey to those who preferred General Knowledge to Geometry. To get him to leave Euclid Book XI for a talk on meteors was almost too easy. Another way of getting relief from Geometry was to ask for a window to be closed. "Sammy" swathed himself in a scarf owing to a cold and liked all windows opened, and he would promptly call for a match to test the draught across the room, and demonstrate the absence of current. But what a kindly man! Those grey-blue eyes under bushy eyebrows, looking at you with such affection and humour, disarmed all schoolboy aggressiveness. Only good nature was felt for "Sammy". If he could not stick to the point in his lessons, he gave you a multitudinous number of hints on general affairs, including health. But his chief work was...how shall we put it? His old title of Usher does not embrace it, and he was hardly a Major Domo. Perhaps Remembrancer would be a suitable title for him. Anyway, he was the Spirit of the School, embracing all its best interests and affections, and pride of success."

Another Old Boy, F.C.Boon told how: "one man maintained a lone fight to produce what one knows as public spirit. Corner founded and nursed the Debating Society, ran the Library and started a Bicycle Club, which made every away match the objective of its run. Boys then did not watch school games, and Corner's cycle club was almost the only way to attempt to encourage them to do so. He spent much of his holidays in searching the City archives for material for a history of the school. He edited the annual School List. He seemed to follow the careers of every Old Boy. I learnt much about him, especially from his sister who told me how he endeavoured to save from the builders a piece of land adjacent to the School to serve as a playing field. He went round to the Governors and others, to urge the importance of this, but he was in advance of his time, and failed. Once a gathering of old boys were reviewing the promotions of their old masters. "And has Sammy Corner got his school yet?" "He has had one for years." "Really! What is it?" "Nottingham High School."

September 1938

During the Munich crisis, with the air-raid shelters still in the planning stage, the school was forced to dig a number of zigzag trenches across the lawns, tennis courts and shrubberies at the front of the school. This was done by Mr Duddell, Mr Palmer and a "host of senior boys". When Mr Chamberlain returned from Munich, however, the boys suddenly became extremely reluctant to continue the trench digging, and it was fortunate that the bulk of the work had been done. Shortly after this, Mr Reynolds was told that, in the event of war, the Board of Education or the Ministry of Health would either find a place to which the school might be evacuated or, a less likely scenario, perhaps, would give the school permission to remain at their traditional site.

This situation came about because the City Fathers, rather insulted by having had the "Queen of the Midlands" designated a "Neutral Zone", had protested to the government and the City's vulnerability had therefore been upgraded to "Dangerous", because of the presence of a gun factory near the Midland Station. On a national scale the plan was to evacuate all children in dangerous areas to safe ones. With this in mind, both Mr Reynolds, and Miss Merryfield, the Headmistress of the Girls' School, had viewed a number of properties to the north of the City. Eventually, the girls were to remove themselves to Ramsdale Hall between Arnold and Calverton but the boys were to have much less luck. Burgate House near Southwell was too small, Holme Pierrepont Hall was too spooky, and Bestwood Lodge, priced at £60,000 by the Duke of St Albans, was too expensive by a very large margin. Eventually the Headmaster and Governors decided on a deliberate policy of inactivity, which would put the ball firmly in the government's court.

September 1938

The newly completed West Block was ready for classes to move in. Initially it was planned to use it for older forms than was originally intended, the middle block having been demolished in a vast cloud of dust prior to a new round of construction work. It was to be rebuilt gradually as a science block over the course of the next five years. First to be completed was the air raid shelter, divided into a number of separate compartments, each one designed to hold some fifty boys. There were blast walls with electric motors to keep the air circulating, blast-proof steel doors and Elsan chemical toilets.

Saturday, October 22nd 1938

A group of boys went to Castle Donington to see the "greatest race of the year". It was started by the Duke of Kent although the boys missed this as they arrived after the first few laps had taken place. Even so, the race still had two hours to run. Contestants included cars from Auto-Union, Mercedes-Benz, Maserati, Delahaye, E.R.A., M.G., Alta and Riley. For the first twenty-six laps, Nuvolari led in an Auto-Union and the boys saw a number of near misses, crashes and skids, involving Nuvolari himself, Von Brauschitsch, Hasse, who missed a tree by inches and tore up a length of fencing, and Richard Seaman, the British driver of a Mercedes-Benz, whose car was eventually restarted for him by race officials. After around sixty laps the engine of Baumer's Mercedes burst into flames and Lang, who was leading, was passed on the straight by Nuvolari at 165 m.p.h. The latter was first past the chequered flag, the second consecutive time that Auto-Union had won the race. The team prize was won by the British team E.R.A., including Billy Cotton, the famous band leader. Only eight of the seventeen starters finished, with both Delahayes, the Maserati, the Riley, the Alta, and a number of Auto-Unions and Mercedes-Benz all being forced to retire.

Friday, January 27th 1939

The Detention Book records how Mr Gregg failed completely to see the funny side of the situation when J.A.Chambers of UVM was judged guilty of "having the impudence to snowball masters".

Thursday, April 13th 1939

Despite the evident risks of Herr Hitler's territorial demands in Europe, a High School party under the leadership of Messrs Beeby and Thomas travelled to Provence, visiting the traditional sites of Les Baux, Nîmes, Saintes Maries de la Mer and Avignon. At the latter location, the boys watched: "a harmless type of bull-baiting, accompanied by a blaring loudspeaker and Cuban tangos played by an unbelievable band of kettle-drums and obscure brass instruments."

Elsewhere, they were to see preparations for war including the grim faces of regular French troops, the red fezzes of the African zouaves and piles of machine guns behind the cathedral at Avignon.

Thursday, May 18th 1939

Playing against Notts Amateurs, the High School made a record low total of only seven runs. Shepherd was the top scorer with three, Mason and Knight made two, and eight batsmen scored ducks. D.H.Vaulkhard took five wickets for four runs, and W.A.Sime took five for three.

Sunday, September 3rd, 1939

The day war broke out, the Headmaster and many of the staff, despite the continuing international crisis, were not in Nottingham. The Ministry of Health rang up to say that the entire school could stay where they were, but unfortunately they did not bother to communicate this information to the Town Clerk who was the local billeting officer. He then allocated a gun battery of the South Notts Hussars to what he believed was an empty school. The Headmaster returned to Nottingham to hear the sirens for the very first air raid on the City. He was told of the Ministry's decision by Dr Blandy, the Chairman of the Governors, but when he entered the School Office, he was surprised to find an extremely rude army officer who proceeded to treat him as "one of the lower animals" because he was wearing a scarf over a boil on his neck rather than the more usual collar and tie.

Later in September, 1939

A compromise was reached whereby the army would take just the recently completed West Block and the dining room. This would mean the temporary loss of much new equipment, including the washing-up machine, crockery and cutlery with the school crest, and a tuck shop full of chocolate. The boys could have the rest, including the rubble of the recently demolished middle block. When it was suggested that the Army should have the older parts of the school, this was refused on the grounds that the condition of the older section was not up to the army's high standards. The following day, a party of gunners appeared and they painted blue every window in the occupied buildings. Unfortunately, the dedicated Mr Hubbuck was away on holiday but his assistant, Mr Boot, did much to rescue desks, chairs and other furniture from the military invasion. The army officers had wanted the chairs for their men and there was a prolonged argument between Lieutenant "M." and Mr Beeby. Overall, relationships between the military and the school were not as difficult as they might have been, as Captain D.M.Smith was an Old Boy, as were two of his subalterns, including Robert St C.Page who had been at the High School before the Great War and had written a novel based on his experiences there called *The Three Merles*.

Monday, October 2nd 1939

Because of the worries of both the Governors and the City Council, the school term did not begin until this date. In actual fact the Luftwaffe were not particularly quick to make Nottingham their number one priority and initial fears of immediate and intense aerial attack remained for the most part unfulfilled. A reduced total of only five hundred boys remained in the school, but nevertheless, to the great sorrow of the boys, for the whole term the school was open only in the mornings and Saturday lessons were cancelled completely. Throughout the day the army could be heard practicing their artillery drill in the yard and this would only stop for the boys' break. When the air raid sirens sounded the entire school would be in their shelters in less than five minutes. The prefects were a great help at this time and performed with great efficiency. After Christmas, when they were at Valley Road, their job was done equally well by the monitors of the Upper Fifth.

In theory, the soldiers were to use the trenches which had originally been dug for the Munich crisis, but in practise, when the sirens went, they were able to occupy the same underground shelters which the boys used in the daytime. They nicknamed the underground shelters the "Maginot Line". Surprisingly though, it was during this term that, by his own admission, Mr Reynolds "through lack of other occupation attained a higher standard of golf that term than ever before or since."

Early 1940

The weather during the first part of the year was of a ferocious severity with heavy snowfalls and severe frosts. Even in the city itself, travel by bus or car was extremely difficult and walking was the only reliable way of getting around. Added to this was an epidemic of influenza. On average, every day, eight staff and over a hundred boys were absent and every morning at prayers the Headmaster would announce an emergency timetable to allow lessons to proceed in a meaningful way.

Spring Term 1940

After an initial term without any afternoon school, a full timetable of lessons resumed from January onwards. Because of the risk of being caught in the streets during an air raid if they went out for lunch, all boys had to bring sandwiches which were eaten in their form rooms. The boys were supervised and cocoa was brought round by Mr Boot. It was two ingenious masters, namely Messrs Duddell and Kennard, who came up with an emergency timetable and the school's accommodation problems were thereby solved. The entire school was divided up into groups of forms and each group then spent just one day per week at Valley Road. In the mornings, they had normal classes and in the afternoon they had games. This killed two birds with one stone, since there was already a searchlight in the north-west corner of the games field and it was thought that the army had desires on the pavilion itself. Using the building not just for games, but also for teaching, was thought to be a sure way of preventing this. The masters, who in many cases were forced to commute between the main school and Valley Road by bicycle, were somewhat less than happy with the situation and their relations with the occupying military forces were frequently less than cordial. The tea brewing room at the back of the pavilion was now shared with the full time wardens of the A.R.P. post, which had been constructed at the back of the original building.

Spring Term 1940

The Nottinghamian deplored the decline in the use of the fives court due to the bitterly cold weather and darkness of the severe winter:

> "There is no more vigorous or enjoyable sport than fives when it is played properly."

Another problem was that because of the continuing ravages of Hitler's U-boat packs, it was becoming increasingly difficult to get good quality balls at reasonable prices. The only solution seemed to be to try to acquire balls in large quantities, but this would depend on demand.

Wednesday, February 14th 1940

The Detention Book records how Wrigley and Pennington (3A), Mason (3B) and Pennington (2A) were punished for what is surely the most surreal of all the misdemeanours over the years:

> "Throwing tapioca about in front of the pavilion. Nearly one pound was swept up!"

Presumably, there was concern on the part of the staff about the wastefulness of this behaviour during a period when food was rationed and the U-Boats had a stranglehold on the shipping lanes.

Thursday, May 16th 1940

Robert Percy Paulson died of appendicitis in the British Military Hospital, Jerusalem while on active service abroad as a gunner with the Royal Horse Artillery. He was nineteen years of age, and he had been training as a tailor.

Monday, May 27th 1940

Second Lieutenant Bruce Arthur Richardson of the Sherwood Foresters was killed in fighting near Dunkirk. He had previously captained the School Cricket XI, and played for the 2nd XV.

1940

What might have been a very serious fire in the new West Block was prevented by the ever vigilant caretaker, Mr Hubbuck. It started in the quartermaster's room, which later became the bookroom, and soon spread to the N.A.A.F.I., later to become the Prep Handicraft Room. Mr Hubbuck saw soldiers rushing up the stairs carrying buckets of water and promptly called the Fire Brigade. Minor damage was caused by the flames and, typically, much more by the water from the Forest Road hydrants used to put them out. Not long after this episode the school became a sorting depot for troops who had survived the Dunkirk evacuation and the South Notts Hussars departed, taking a large amount of school equipment with them. One evening in Arboretum Street, Mr Hubbock came across a group of youths who were stealing ropes from the gymnasium of the Girls' High School. He got the ropes back by pretending to be a plain clothes policeman, but was astonished to find that the military had left the school without even locking it. The Pioneer Corps then took over the school, "a tough set of chaps". They soon left and the anti-aircraft school of the Royal Artillery arrived.

Saturday, June 8th 1940

Sergeant Henry Guttridge, having been reported as missing, believed killed, was now reported by the Germans as a prisoner of war. He was "well and comfortable, and is being treated quite well".

Saturday, June 15th 1940

An ex-master at the High School, Edwin William Lovegrove, was killed near Dunkirk. He was 32 years of age, and held the rank of Lieutenant in the Sherwood Foresters, having joined up with his great rugby playing friend, E.M.T.Bunny. Lovegrove had moved to Framlingham College in 1937 after five years at the High School. He had been a popular figure with both boys and staff and left a widow, Helen, in Blythburgh, Suffolk.

Monday, July 22nd 1940

The Detention Book records how Mr R.D.Stewart gave Checkley of 2A a detention for "Blasphemy".

One minute to nine on the evening of Tuesday, September 24th 1940

Sergeant Leslie Hambleton Taylor was killed when his aircraft suddenly and catastrophically lost engine power on take-off from RAF Linton-on-Ouse. He was the observer in an Armstrong Whitworth Whitley (N1470, squadron letters G-EJ) and the crew's mission was to bomb Berlin. The aircraft barely cleared the boundary fence and crash-landed in a field near Youlton. Fire immediately broke out and the bombs all exploded, damaging a nearby cottage and farm buildings. Sadly three of the crew were killed although two, amazingly, escaped with just injuries. Leslie was nineteen years of age and had left the staff of Waring and Gillow's furniture shop in Nottingham, because, in his own words, "it was not a man's life". He joined Bomber Command and had flown many hundreds of miles over enemy territory before his untimely death. This was one of Bomber Command's earliest large-scale attacks on the Third Reich. Of 129 bombers sent to Berlin, just three aircraft were lost.

Wednesday, November 13th 1940

Second Engineer Officer Louis George Hore was "lost at sea as a result of enemy action" at the age of 56 when the M.V.Leon Martin, an oil tanker, hit a mine off Falmouth and went down in a matter of moments. After leaving the High School in 1903, Louis had gone to work at John Brown's shipyard in Glasgow, where he had helped construct the Lusitania. Only a week after the war had broken out, he was torpedoed by a German submarine but survived this traumatic event.

8.34 a.m. on January 10th 1941

Alan Robert Rose, an Ordinary Coder on a 'G' Class Destroyer, HMS Gallant, was reported missing, presumed killed, when his ship hit a mine some 25 nautical miles south-west of Pantelleria near Sicily. Alan was twenty-nine years old and "worked wholeheartedly, and his great cheerfulness and strength of character were always an inspiration". At home in Mapperley, he had founded the Sherwood Amateurs Football Club. He left a wife Elizabeth and a son, Christopher, aged two.

Saturday, May 3rd 1941

School Sports Day was held. The mile was won by Palmer in a time of 5 minutes 25.6 seconds. Even as late as this in the century, Sports Day events still included the Under-16 Cricket Ball (85 yards 6 inches) and the House Tug-of-War.

Saturday, May 24th 1941

Lieutenant Commander George Vernon Carlin died at the age of thirty-seven when the ship on which he was Paymaster, H.M.S. Hood, was sunk by the German pocket battleship, the Bismarck. George was the son of John James and Annie Carlin. He had an M.A. degree from Oxford University.

Friday, June 20th 1941

The School Spotters Club was founded with a membership of twenty-two, mainly junior, boys. The club was recognised by the Affiliated Spotters Club and given the number of 112. Aircraft recognition tests were quickly set up and lectures organised with an epidiascope.

Friday, July 4th 1941

E.R.Maltby of 2B was given a detention by Mr R.D.Stewart for: "throwing good food into the waste box at the Pavilion so as to save himself the trouble of taking home that part of his lunch which he did not want. Not thoughtlessness, for 2B has been clearly told of the difficulties and dangers overcome by those who bring the food to the country and had been cautioned that waste would be seriously treated".

July 1941

Mr H.Goddard retired after thirty-eight years at the High School. He had taught Mathematics, and became Senior Master after the retirement of Mr Gaskin. He was a man of: "quiet tact and a calm determination. Every member of the School and Staff, past and present, will, we know, wish him, from the bottom of their hearts, many happy and peaceful years to which he has been looking forward for some time."

Friday, September 5th 1941

John Hanley Faulkner died in an unfortunate accident at the age of only sixteen. He was very keen on aviation and aeroplanes in general and it was while experimenting in this area that the accident occurred. He had been a "quiet unassuming lad, popular with his fellows."

Tuesday, November 11th 1941

The Detention Book records how Phethean of the Remove was guilty of "obscene writing in another boy's book".

Thursday, November 27th 1941

Perhaps during a World War, there are more frightening things to fear than during more normal times. D.G.Lovett of 5B was punished for his excessive bravado when "laughing and talking in an examination".

The end of 1941

At this stage in the war, the air-raid shelter came into use, unfortunately, on many occasions. With the cold, the echoing of every tiny noise and the general boredom, the boys, not surprisingly perhaps, were often difficult to control. Every night until 1944, two masters and two senior boys spent the night on fire-watching duty on the roof of the school. Sometimes the watchers marked books, sometimes they did homework, played chess, or simply just talked. The boys slept in a little room on the bridge which connected the library with the west block, and the masters in the room which was later to become the Physics Laboratory workshop. There was a whole network of catwalks and ladders for the firewatchers and they made at least one tour of the rooftops before bed.

Easter Term 1942

Meeting at 16.30 hours on Fridays, the N.H.S. Spotters' Club had a quiet term, studying "with great interest" silhouettes of several different types of aircraft. Competitions were held between four teams, based on the *Spotters Bees* in *Ack Ack Beer Beer*. By now a number of boys had passed various official tests and had reached the level of third class aircraft identifiers.

Thursday, February 12th 1942

William Fraser Bland died in action against the Japanese in Singapore at the age of 34. The son of William Parlby Bland and Florence Mary Bland, he was a Major in the Royal Artillery and had previously escaped capture at Dunkirk. A solicitor, William was a member of the Law Society.

Thursday, March 19th 1942

The Detention Book records how Kirk of M4, presumably over eager for knowledge, was punished for "breaking into school during the dinner hour".

Sunday, June 21st 1942

Lance Bombardier Peter Frederick Paulson of 277 Battery (City of Nottingham) 68 Heavy Anti-Aircraft Regiment of the Royal Artillery was killed in action by enemy fire at Tobruk. Peter was the second of three High School brothers who all lived in Thorneywood House in Woodthorpe, a suburb of Nottingham. Peter had served for many months in the Western Desert yet was still only 23 years of age. He is buried in the Knightsbridge Cemetery at Acroma in north eastern Libya.

Winter, 1942

The army built a huge green shed in the north-west corner of the playground, hitherto used for cricket nets and practice wickets. They used it to store searchlight units and sound ranging equipment, which they brought out for drill during the daytime. Any unoccupied classrooms were used for theory lectures. Then the army began to dig the foundations for a second shed in the middle of the playground. According to popular legend, it was only when Mr Reynolds lined up the entire school and carefully explained that the boys might well pelt them with snowballs as they worked was the idea given up. Protests were also made to the War Office through more normal channels. Until the late 1980s, the exploratory marks left by the army could still be seen.

Tuesday, December 1st 1942

I.R.Whitaker was punished for "writing filth on the blackboard".

The early years of the war, probably the end of the Christmas Term, 1942

In Europe, Hitler stands on the opposite side of the English Channel, and Great Britain remains defiant, but largely unable to press home any significant advantage. There have been few victories so far for the British, and there seem to be few obvious ways forward to rid the continent of what will eventually become known as "The Scourge of the Swastika". These dark days are recalled on the pillars of the Forest Road entrance, where boys, or, more likely, young men, have carved their initials. Judging by the height of this vandalism, they may have been in, say, the fifth form, literally, upwards. They include "WH 1942", "DP" and "DP 1942", along with, possibly, "SS 1940", and the undated "MB", "HE" and "PFP". My subsequent researches, and best guesses, have revealed a few likely suspects. "WH" and "DP" may conceivably have been young colleagues in the Fifth Form A with Mr Whimster during the academic year 1941-1942. William Norman Hill was born on November 23rd 1927, and entered the High School on September 20th 1938 at the age of ten. His father was F.Hill, a School Master of 8, Lexington Gardens, Sherwood. He left the school on July 31st 1945. Dennis Plackett was born on October 22nd 1927. He entered the school on Monday, September 25th 1939, at the age of eleven. His mother was Mrs Ellen Plackett, a housewife of 7, Anthill Street, Stapleford. Dennis was a Nottinghamshire County Council Scholar and he left the school on August 1st 1944.

Another interpretation is that "WH 1942" was William Jack Harrison. This young man was, quite simply, outstanding. Born on December 5th 1924, he entered the High School on September 19th 1935 at the age of ten. His mother was Mrs E.M.Harrison of 53, Burlington Road, Sherwood. He was in the Upper Fifth Form with Mr Palmer in 1941-1942 and then in the Mathematical and Science Sixth Form with Mr Holgate during the academic year of 1942-1943. He stood out in two separate areas. In 1940 he was initially a lance-corporal in the Junior Training Corps, but soon became a full Corporal. In 1941, he won Mr Frazier's prize for The Most Efficient Junior NCO or cadet, and was then named Commander of the Most Proficient House Platoon. Towards the end of the academic year of 1941-1942, he was promoted to be the J.T.C. Company Sergeant Major. In addition, in the sporting world, by the time the School List for 1942-1943 was published, William had won his First XV Colours and Cap for Rugby and was Captain of the team. In the Summer Term, he became the Captain of Cricket and was awarded his Cricket Colours and Scarf. He was also, by dint of his sporting position as Captain of Cricket, a School Prefect. William left the school on December 19th 1942.

The reason that I myself would prefer this interpretation is that "DP" and "DP 1942" may well be David Phillips who was in the Economics Sixth Form with Mr Smyth during the two academic years of 1941-1943. He may have been carrying out some kind of school tradition when he carved his name on the pillar, expecting to leave the school in 1942, but then having to repeat the process all over again the next year, after he had unexpectedly stayed on for another year. David finally left at the end of that Christmas Term in 1943. He was born on May 2nd 1923, and entered the school on January 13th 1935 at the age of eleven. His father was P.Phillips, a Factory Manager of 45, Austen Avenue, on the far side of the Forest Recreation Ground. We have fewer details of David's career at the High School, but we do know that by September 1941, he was a Corporal in the Junior Training Corps. In the Christmas Term of 1942, he was awarded his Full Colours for Rugby and became a School Prefect. He was also awarded his Rowing Colours for his achievements with the Second IV.

Somehow I feel sure that these two young men were friends. Austen Avenue, of course, is arguably on the same cycle route home as Burlington Road, Sherwood where William Harrison lived. Perhaps the two walked down together across the Forest and David would then get on his bike and cycle slowly off towards Austen Avenue. William would continue down what would have been at the time an undoubtedly more traffic free Mansfield Road towards his home in Sherwood. David Phillips shared the same interests as William Harrison. They were both in the same rugby team and both loved sport, whether rugby, cricket or rowing. They were both in the Junior Training Corps and were clearly attracted to the military life. As regards their academic classes, they were a year apart, but I feel that their common interests might have overcome that, especially when the two rugby players, or J.T.C. members, realised that they could walk down across the Forest together every evening after a hard day at school. And when the end of 1942 came round, they may well both have left the school on the same day, December 19th. Were they both going into the Army together?

Not surprisingly, perhaps, it has proved impossible to trace any of the other initials in any meaningful kind of way. There were quite simply too many possible "SS"s in 1940, and "MB", "HE" and even "PFP" have all proved equally beyond my powers.

April 1943

Edward William Mitchell died at his home in Eire at the age of only fifteen. His parents had moved him from Nottingham to a boarding school in the Irish Free State where it was thought that he would be safe from German air-raids. It was at this school that he contracted the illness from which he died.

Tuesday, June 1st 1943

A certain Old Boy called Alfred Tregear Chenhalls was an accountant who dealt with many actors and theatrical people, including the famous Hollywood star, Leslie Howard, a man who was always eager to sign up for anti-Nazi propaganda. Chenhalls often smoked a large cigar and, given his cherubic physical appearance, he did look rather like Winston Churchill. Chenhalls was killed when the Dutch DC-3 of KLM Airlines, Flight 777, which was carrying Leslie Howard, with Chenhalls acting as his business manager, between Lisbon and London, was shot down by eight Junkers Ju 88 fighters. At the time, Churchill was known to be attending a conference in Algiers, and there was much speculation that German spies had seen Chenhalls getting onto the plane in Lisbon, and, mistaking him for Churchill, had then organised the aircraft's destruction. One additional detail is that Leslie Howard was also rather similar physically to Churchill's personal assistant. This was certainly one of the very few occasions when airliners were shot down on this particular route, and Churchill himself was certain that the Germans had believed Chenhalls to be the Prime Minister.

July 1943

The Nottinghamian included the following poem by T.J.N.Deaville of lB:

THE HOME GUARD

Daddy's in the Home Guard,

He's helping win the war.
He's donned a khaki uniform
Just as he did before.

He hasn't won a medal yet,
He hopes he will do soon.
He's only been a sergeant
This very afternoon.

His comp'ny's got a kitten,
He helps to feed it now.
It claws him every morning
And makes him call out, "Wow!"

I'm glad he's got promotion,
He has more leisure hours.
Commander says he's clever
(He's quite a friend of ours).

He hasn't shot a German yet,
He wants to get a chance.
If "Jerry" tries his funny tricks
He'll lead them quite a dance.

Wednesday, October 13th 1943

Captain Hayward Hastings Pockson was killed while serving with the 5th Battalion of the Sherwood Foresters (Notts and Derby Regiment). Hayward was the beloved son of Melville John Hastings Pockson and Blanche Hayward Pockson. He was 32 years of age. He had been a keen rugby player and enjoyed both badminton and rowing. Hayward's sacrifice is commemorated on the Cassino Memorial in the Provincia di Frosinone, Lazio in Italy, but he has no known grave. Presumably, Captain Pockson had by now more than atoned for the events of Monday, January 28th 1928.

Friday, October 22nd 1943

Sergeant Ivan Keith Doncaster of 166 Squadron, having taken off at 1812 hours from RAF Kirmington on Humberside, was killed when his Avro Lancaster Mark III bomber, EE196, was shot down by a night-fighter some fifty miles short of the target during a Bomber Command raid on Kassel. The stricken aircraft crashed at Brakelsiek on the western side of the Schwalenberger Wald, two kilometres to the northwest of Schwalenberg. This raid entailed 322 Lancasters and 247 Halifaxes. A total of 43 aircraft failed to return, an unsustainable loss rate of 7.6%. Five of the crew, including the mid upper gunner Ivan Doncaster, are now interred in the War Cemetery at Hannover. Only Sergeant A.I.Pilbeam was to survive the crash and after a period as a prisoner of war, he lived to be ninety two. This Lancaster, after 132 hours' combat time, much of it with Ivan Doncaster as a member of the crew, had already bombed Turin, Hamburg (Operation Gomorrah), Peenemünde (V-Weapons testing grounds) and Berlin. So experienced in warfare, Ivan was just twenty years of age when he perished. He was the beloved son of Raymond and Evelyn Mary Doncaster from Sandiacre. On his grave it is written, "To live in hearts, we leave behind, is not to die."

Saturday, December 4th 1943

Mr J.A.Radley died from heart failure. He had been a member of staff from 1904-1931. Mr Radley was a teacher with what would nowadays be considered to be ideas well before their time. He loved Literature, Art and Music and taught the boys about understanding and peace among mankind. Indeed, this was perhaps not particularly surprising for a man who knew French, German, Italian, Russian and Welsh. On one occasion, he brought an Egyptian into school to show his pupils that there were "other men than Englishmen and other creeds than Christianity." His obituary in *The Nottinghamian* ended with the words "Goodbye, Mr Chips!"

Early 1944

Three Old Boys, Kenneth William Herrod, G.R.Checkland and John Stewart Wibberley all succeeded in escaping from Italian prisoner of war camps, and managed to reach Allied lines in safety.

Tuesday, February 29th 1944

Signalman Peter Vernon died in hospital at Invergordon in Scotland as a result of illness contracted during naval operations in northern waters. Peter served as a member of the Royal Naval Patrol Service on H.M. Motor Minesweeper 260. He was the beloved son of Mr and Mrs Arthur Vernon of Radford in Nottingham. Peter was a keen cricketer and an enthusiastic member of the 2nd XI.

Tuesday, February 29th 1944

In Scotland, Private Richard Vernon Milnes of the 1st Battalion of the Sherwood Foresters (Notts and Derby Regiment) died of pneumonia while training as an Officer Cadet in Infantry. Richard was the beloved son of William Vernon and Florence Annie Milnes of Nottingham. He was the beloved husband of Barbara Milnes and he was only twenty-one years old. Richard had previously been in the High School's 1st XV during the 1939-1940 season. He is buried in the beautiful Stronuirinish Cemetery in Portree, the main town on the Isle of Skye.

Wednesday, June 7th 1944

During the first stirrings of a summer's morning, Flight Sergeant Frank Leonard Corner was killed in action over Caen in Normandy. His Avro Lancaster Mark III, NE150, squadron letters ZN-H, was one of sixteen bombers from 106 Squadron which took off shortly after midnight from RAF Metheringham in Lincolnshire. A member of the Royal Air Force Volunteer Reserve, Frank was the Flight Engineer. He and his crew were tasked with attacking "communications" in Caen, which consisted, for the most part, in bombing bridges, in the immediate aftermath of D-Day. Unfortunately, they were hit by anti-aircraft fire over Lison where a worker at the railway yard remembers how the German gunners celebrated the fact that they had shot down a bomber. The Lancaster finally crashed near the tiny village of St Jean de Daye.

Frank and the four other members of the crew were given a full military funeral by the French. The brave mayor and people of the commune of St Jean de Daye managed to find a Union Jack and a Tricolore to drape over the coffins and the village children all planted British flags around their grave. This was in brave defiance of the Germans who were not slow to kill innocent French civilians. Since then, Frank has been reburied in the Bayeux War Cemetery.

Frank was the beloved son of Captain Leonard Leslie Corner and Florence Edna Corner of Whiston in Yorkshire. He had been employed by the Notts War Agricultural Committee and had played rugby for the Old Nottinghamians' Wartime XV. He was just twenty years old.

Monday, June 19th 1944

Major Maynard Hastings Pockson received the D.S.O. for his services on the Italian Front. He had operated "a daring attack" with "skilful and fearless leadership." Major Pockson was serving in the Liri Valley with the Gurkha Rifles and the 8th Indian Division.

Friday, June 23rd 1944

Young John David Fletcher was yet another Old Nottinghamian to answer the "Call of the Skies" when the Second World War broke out. Initially a member of the Royal Air Force Volunteer Reserve, John became a Rear Gunner with 97 Squadron. He was involved mostly in bombing communications targets in France to prevent the Germans moving troops to oppose the D-Day landings. He had bombed such targets at Mailly-Le-Camp, Tours Airfield, Lille, Amiens, St Valery-en-Caux , Ferme D'Urville, La Peanelle, Argentan, Etampes and Poitiers as well as Brunswick and the Phillips Works at Eindhoven. By now, John was becoming quite a veteran with twelve "ops" behind him, a commendable total for a rear gunner.

Between half past three and four on a balmy afternoon, though, John was killed, not in action over Germany, but while practicing close formation flying with five other Lancasters over Deeping Fen in Cambridgeshire. He was just twenty-four years of age, and the beloved son of John Tabberer Fletcher and Dorothy Fletcher. John was also the much loved husband of Joyce Loretta Fletcher. His widow, in actual fact, only died in 2001.

John was in Avro Lancaster ME625, piloted by Flight Lieutenant Jimmy Van Raalte when a catastrophic training accident resulted in the deaths of 13 brave young men:

> "Six Lancasters were practicing formation flying this afternoon in two V formations of three, with calamitous results. Two of our aircraft piloted by F/Lt Perkins and F/Lt Van Raalte RAAF were flying in formation. Whilst attempting a gentle turn F/Lt Van Raalte's aircraft sideslipped over F/Lt Perkins' aircraft and dropped suddenly, removing the entire tail from F/Lt Perkins' aircraft and smashing the nose of his own. Both planes immediately spun to earth out of control. All of the occupants in both aircraft were killed with the exception of Sgt Coman, who managed to bale out when his aircraft broke in two at 1000 ft."

Sergeant Coman was badly burned when he landed almost in the middle of the burning wreckage. He owed his survival to the fact that he was blown upwards by the force of the explosion of the wreckage on the ground and was thus able to open his parachute and come down safely.

Roy Sturman, from Collingham was only ten when his brother-in-law, John Fletcher, was killed. He said that John was his hero. John had intended to make his living by farming poultry when he left the RAF. He is buried in Cambridge City Cemetery on the Newmarket Road.

Saturday, July 8th 1944

Lieutenant George Colin Brown was killed in action in the aftermath of the D-Day landings. He was in the 2nd Battalion of the Lincolnshire Regiment (3rd Infantry Division). George is buried in the Ranville War Cemetery near Caen in Calvados, Normandy. Ranville was the first village to be liberated in France. George was the beloved son of W. A. Brown and of Charlotte Brown of Chilwell near Nottingham. He was 24 years of age and at school, his "fast in swinging yorker on the leg stump was devastating on its day". He had appeared for the 1st XI in both 1936, 1937 and 1938. In 1937, he appeared in a fixture at Valley Road against King Edward VII School, Sheffield. George scored nine runs and took three wickets for 28 runs. Overall, though, that "fast in-swinging yorker on the leg stump" must have been very effective. In 1938, George took six wickets out of ten against Burton Grammar School and conceded a paltry fifteen runs. Later in the same season, he exceeded this, with a haul of seven wickets for twenty runs against Stamford Grammar School. Overall, George took 45 wickets at a cost of just 6.42 runs per wicket, the best performance by any High School bowler in that last, sunlit season before the war. Opponents included such old friends as the Old Nottinghamians, Ratcliffe College, Stamford School and Trent College, left hanging on by the rain at 50 for 3, chasing a winning total of 162.

Thursday, September 7th 1944

Acting Pilot Officer Warren Herbert Cheale, who lived with his family at 123 Church Drive, Burton Joyce, had moved to the High School in January 1944. He was appointed as an Acting Pilot Officer with the School Flight of the Air Training Corps. Warren was very popular; one of the boys described him as "one of the nicest people we had ever met".

While he was away at camp at Wenlock in Shropshire with the boys from the High School Air Training Corps, though, poor Warren was killed in a flying accident. He was 44 years of age, and he left a widow, Rose, and a teenage son and daughter. The official accident report said:

> "Flying accident at Wheaton Aston. An Airspeed Oxford LX509 of No 21 (P) AFU, with Flight Lieutenant Harrison as instructor, and Pilot Officer Cheale (Air Training Corps) took off for a night flying test from Wheaton Aston and was seen to dive into the ground shortly afterwards. Both occupants were killed instantly as a result of injuries sustained."

The crash location on the Accident Card was given as "at Colonels Covert, Hatton Grange, Ryton, just south of Hatton Grange, to the north of Ryton and just south west of RAF Cosford". The verdict of the inquiry was that it was "not possible to form a conclusion. Investigation has not revealed the cause of the accident."

Some years previously, Warren had volunteered for the Great War and eventually became a Sergeant Pilot in the Royal Flying Corps. At one point, he was involved in a mid-air collision at an altitude of over two thousand feet. British pilots were not allowed to wear parachutes, so Warren must have thought his death was imminent. The two planes, though, must have either have spun or perhaps fluttered down to earth, because Warren escaped with his life.

This time, though, Warren Cheale's extraordinary luck had come to an end. In 1918, he had somehow managed to avoid what must have seemed to him, as he fell earthwards for thirty seconds, perhaps a minute, an unavoidable death. But this time, the Gods of the Air had claimed him as their own.

Tuesday, September 26th 1944

Anthony Bertram Lloyd was born in Staffordshire. He was the son of Bertram Harold and Ada Lloyd, of Penarth, Glamorgan. Tony was a member of the High School from 1932-39 and was a promising boxer. He had an: "unswerving loyalty to the school, which he had revisited on several occasions during his military service. He was always in any mischief that was going, but under a seeming cloak of irresponsibility, there lay a deep respect for law and order. Here was a comrade to have at one's side in an emergency, a fellow whose courage steadied the nerves, and whose unfailing good humour showed a ray of hope in the blackest of moments."

Tony enlisted into the Royal Welch Fusiliers and began airborne duties in August 1942. In early 1943, he was engaged in fighting Axis forces in North Africa, during Operation Torch. On March 5th the Brigade handed this sector over to the Americans and moved eastwards to Tunisia. Three days later, a German force of divisional strength attacked the defensive positions of the 1st and 2nd Battalions. and it was at this time that Anthony was awarded a Military Medal for his bravery: His citation read:

> "On the 8th March 1943 in the Tamera Sector, Tunisia, Private Lloyd was a member of a counter-attack Company. During the advance Private Lloyd and two other men became separated from their platoon. They came under heavy machine gun fire and Private Lloyd ordered the two men to cover him while he himself attacked the post. He charged over country showing a complete disregard for his own safety and succeeded in capturing the machine gun post and three men. By this act of gallantry Private Lloyd prevented severe casualties being inflicted to the Company which was advancing."

On March 28th 1944, Tony was one of ten proud soldiers who received their Military Medals, all awarded for bravery in North Africa, at Buckingham Palace. Once Rommel was defeated and North Africa was won, Tony became engaged in heavy fighting in Sicily. Once Sicily was secured, he was then part of the sea-borne landings at Taranto in mainland Italy in September 1943. Pushing north, the Battalion fought their way as far as Foggia before they returned to the United Kingdom to prepare for D-Day.

On Sunday, September 17th 1944, Tony and his Battalion parachuted into Renkum Heath as part of the attempt to capture the Rhine crossings at Arnhem, codenamed "Operation Market Garden". Tony was by now the Second in Command of 8 Section, No 11 Platoon, T Company.

Tony and his fellow parachutists were to suffer severe casualties around Den Brink and the Queen Elizabeth Hospital as they tried to rescue the 2nd Battalion who were cut off and surrounded at the bridge at Arnhem, the famous "Bridge Too Far". Eventually however, Tony, along with the survivors, was forced to retreat to the Division perimeter which was now surrounded and besieged at Oosterbeek.

It is believed that Tony was wounded in the fighting at Oosterbeek, in the area near the Regimental Aid Post at Kate ter Horst's house. Unfortunately, Tony died from his wounds nine days later, on Tuesday, September 26th. He was one of 57 parachutists given a temporary burial in mass grave in the house's garden.

Young Tony was only 21 years old when he died. He is now buried at Oosterbeek War Cemetery in Arnhem, alongside many of his comrades, in the town he fought so courageously to free from Nazi occupation. Tony Lloyd was a very brave man.

The rugby season, 1944-1945

The 1st XV remained unbeaten throughout the season. They suffered a number of postponed matches, but these were all against opponents they had previously defeated. Overall, the school scored 225 points, and conceded only thirty-one. This was the first time that the 1st XV had finished the season undefeated. The feat has only been repeated on one occasion subsequently, in season 1986-1987, when the team, under the captaincy of P.L.Milton, won all eighteen of its matches.

Early 1945

The excellent Mr Hubbuck the School Caretaker died. He had worked for ten years at the High School, and proved himself to be: "a man of sterling character and remarkable adaptability...nothing was too much trouble for him...He had many an ingenious and adequate solution for the difficult problems of maintenance...We have lost a friend whom we greatly valued."

This time, because of a better economic climate than in the 1930s, and with so many men away at the war, fewer than fifty men applied for his caretaking job.

1945

The school gave up its grant aided status, and became independent. A small part of the cost of this was offset by the Nottingham City, County and Derbyshire Education Authorities who agreed to place twelve, twelve and two of their scholars respectively at the school.

Thursday, March 22nd 1945

Trooper John Arthur Finking died or was murdered while being force marched across Germany by the Nazis, who, between January and April 1945, decided to evacuate all Prisoner of War camps, to prevent prisoners being liberated by the advancing Soviet forces. Compelled to endure blizzards and sub-zero temperatures as they trudged up to 25 miles every day, huge numbers of men perished through cold, starvation, exhaustion or were quite simply shot without reason by their guards

Fellow prisoners of war describing John spoke: "with warmest praise of his courage and cheerfulness, and of his devotion to others, which contributed in no small measure to his death."

John was 39 years of age and had fought with the Royal Tank Regiment against Rommel in North Africa before being made a prisoner of war. He was the son of John Cyrus Finking and Emily Ellen Finking and the husband of Margaret Isabel Finking. They all lived in West Bridgford. John is interred in Hanover War Cemetery in Niedersachsen.

Tuesday, April 10th 1945

Flying Officer John Hopwood failed to return from a Bomber Command raid on Leipzig. He was thirty-two years of age, and left a widow and two sons. He was a Nottingham City police officer in civilian life and was in the Royal Air Force Volunteer Reserve. At the time of his death, he was a navigator with 630 Squadron. Flying Officer Hopwood took off at 18.23 hours from RAF East Kirkby in Lincolnshire. He was flying in an Avro Lancaster Mark I, RF122 with the squadron lettering LE-S. In company with 75 other Lancasters and 19 Mosquitoes, they were to bomb the Wahren railway yards. All of the crew were killed except the bomb aimer and the rear gunner, Flying Officer Fleming and Flight Sergeant Lynn respectively. They were able to sit out the rest of the war in captivity. One other Lancaster was shot down, ME739, LE-T. The eastern half of the railway yards was completely destroyed. John is buried in the Berlin 1939-1945 War Cemetery. He was the beloved son of James Alfred and Bertha Hopwood and the husband of Phyllis Irene Hopwood of Flanshaw near Wakefield.

Tuesday, May 8th 1945

The war in Europe ended, and this day and the following day were both declared public holidays. When the Second World War came to an end in August, total school casualties were less than half those of the Great War, but still numbered almost a hundred. The names of those who sacrificed their lives are commemorated on a carved list on the wall at the entrance to the Assembly Hall.

Saturday, May 26th 1945

Just days after the end of hostilities in Europe, Captain Eric John Hughes died from injuries received during manoeuvres in Germany. A member of the 7th Battalion, the Sherwood Foresters, Eric was serving in the Searchlight Regiment. He was thirty-three years of age, and at the High School: "on occasion, his bowling was devastating, having a nip from the pitch which completely deceived batsmen, and his fielding at cover-point was invariably excellent."

Eric was a prominent member of the Sherwood Amateurs Football Club, which he had captained for many years, and "wherever he went his infectious good humour made him many friendships".

Summer Term 1945

There was a good entry for the school's fives tournament, although, as *The Nottinghamian* pointed out, "the shortage of balls is a major problem".

June 1945

At long last, the army vacated the West Block. The final occupants were a school for instruction in the driving and maintenance of heavy vehicles. The Pioneer Corps had seen fit to fire guns inside the building and had left bullet holes in several of the rooms' ceilings. Even nowadays, some fifty years after the event, the staircases in this part of the school are still excessively worn down by the nails in the soles of heavy army boots. Perhaps the High School was lucky. Several large country houses and hotels on the east coast were so badly abused that they were beyond repair and had to be demolished. Large scale theft by the military was also a major problem.

Tuesday, July 17th 1945

The Old Nottinghamians inaugurated a golf competition for a cup donated by Mr S.J.Pentecost. The first winner was the Headmaster, Mr C.L.Reynolds, who defeated twenty-two other competitors.

Friday, July 27th 1945

Squadron-Leader Eric W.Partridge was mentioned in dispatches for his achievements in the Middle East. He had previously flown Bristol Beaufighters in the Bay of Biscay and before that he had worked at the Nottingham Building Society. At one point Eric had broken his back but made a good recovery and soon returned to combat flying.

Friday, September 7th 1945

The Nottingham newspapers all carried the remarkable story of Lieutenant John Henry Coleman, codename "Victor", who was shortly due to receive an M.B.E. from King George VI at Buckingham Palace. John had escaped with his father from Paris in June 1940, travelled to Biarritz and then embarked alone on a British troopship, arriving at Beeston in rags, and penniless. He joined the Royal Navy, and in 1942, as a Stoker Petty Officer, took part in the Dieppe raid.

John then volunteered for service with the French Resistance, and was accepted into their ranks. He helped sabotage bridges and trains, and reports were sent twice weekly to London, on radio sets that had to be moved every time they were used. Eventually, John became the Deputy Leader of the Résistance in Lyon and at the height of his unit's activities he was being sought by over 70,000 German troops, including the notorious Klaus Barbie, the so-called "Butcher of Lyon", convicted of horrendous war crimes many years later by a French court. When the Chief of the Lyon Résistance was captured a few weeks before D-Day, John took command and remained in that rôle until his chief escaped just after the invasion. On one occasion John was to reconnoitre a bridge while pretending to swim in the river. Shortly afterwards it was blown up. Just before D-Day his group moved their stores some eighty miles in a convoy of twelve trucks. They were not captured despite the fact that their eventual destination was a disused dye-works next to Gestapo headquarters and the entire operation was carried out in broad daylight.

John had married his wife Deirdre after his training as a parachutist and news of the birth of his daughter was given to him by a secret Résistance prearranged radio signal. The little girl's name, Antoinette, became the unit's code signal for a short while.

Christmas Term 1945

A new school subject was introduced with the arrival of Mrs Partridge from the University College to teach Russian to Sixth Formers. It was originally hoped by the boys that she might be a games mistress but she turned out to be a skilled linguist. As *The Nottinghamian* said "steppes must be taken to encourage the study of this all-important language."

Christmas Term 1945

A Boxing Club was started this term, with mostly senior boys attending the meetings. Mr Cruikshank was the instructor and referee helped by, when he had any free time, C.S.M.I. Fell.

Early 1946

The school was visited by two ex-prisoners of the Emperor Hirohito. They were R.M.Gunther and W.W.Peck. They had both recently returned home after their release from long spells in Japanese prisoner of war camps and subsequent periods of convalescence in hospital.

Saturday, April 20th 1946

Ex-member of staff, Harry Goddard died suddenly after an operation. He had retired five years previously after thirty-eight years' service as Chief Mathematical Master with fourteen years as Second Master. He was "well-loved by the boys as by his colleagues, the ideal of a popular schoolmaster." Mr Goddard had been an accomplished musician in the Sacred Harmonic Society and a keen player of both tennis and cricket. In later years, however, he had been much affected by the death of his wife and this was considered "a blow from which he never recovered".

1946

Reginald Thomas Simpson made his début in first class cricket, as a right handed batsman. He was to score 30,546 runs at an average of 38.32 for Nottinghamshire and Sind Province and to take 59 wickets and 189 catches. His highest score was 259 and he went on to play in 27 Test matches for England. He scored 1,401 runs at an average of 33.35 and took part in record first wicket partnerships with Len Hutton against New Zealand in 1949 (147 runs), and with Cyril Washbrook against the West Indies a year later (212 runs). His greatest innings was his 156 not out against Australia in the Fifth Test at Melbourne in 1951 and he made three other centuries in Test cricket. He remains, without doubt, the High School's greatest cricketer.

July 1946

Mr G.F.Hood retired after thirty-eight years' service as Senior Chemistry Master at the school. His departure was marked by a generous farewell in the school magazine.

The last day of the Christmas Term 1946

The first meeting of the Joint Sixth Form Society took place in the Girls' High School Hall. About a hundred and twenty members of both Sixth Forms attended a Christmas Party. They played a number of popular party games and there was a little dancing and a short sketch. The girls had also put together an excellent supper.

Tuesday, February 11th 1947

The Detention Book records how Mr R.B.Williams, always on the alert to the possibility of ever more sophisticated methods of cheating, had caught Skellington of 4B with his Chemistry text book open on the desk, while the class were taking a Chemistry test.

Easter Term 1947

The Photographic Society bemoaned the lack of attendance at their meetings. Most of the members had attended only three of the nine meetings during the term. Much more popular were the weekly copies of *Amateur Photographer* which were regularly circulated among the boys, so that each member could enjoy looking at the photographs at home.

Wednesday, February 26th 1947

The Locomotive Society viewed two films, *The building of an L.M.S. Pacific class engine at Crewe*, and *General Views of Railway Lines in the Peak District*. Members had previously visited railway sheds at Toton and Nottingham (L.M.S.R.) and Colwick (L.N.E.R.). Next term, plans were afoot to go to railway sheds at Derby, Doncaster, Annesley, and, conceivably, Staveley.

Summer Term 1947

For the first time ever, the staff fielded their own cricket team playing several friendly fixtures against the staffs of other schools.

Founder's Day 1947

As well as a religious service, the customary cricket match with the Old Boys was revived after the interruption of the Second World War. On the River Trent, the Old Boys' 1st and 2nd VIs were both successful and beat the school rowers.

End of the summer term, 1947

Messrs R.S.Bridge and W.A.Parsons retired simultaneously as coaches and organisers of school cricket. They had both completed twenty-eight years' continuous service in the position.

July 1947

Mr J.L.Kennard retired after thirty-seven years at the High School. He had joined the High School in November 1910 as a teacher of Modern Languages. His main role in the school was to introduce rugby when football ended in 1914. He was the master in charge of the new sport until 1939 but then, just as he was contemplating retirement from rugby, he was asked to take over school sport for the duration of the Second World War, while other, younger, teachers went off to join the forces.

Christmas Term 1947

The Nottinghamian reported how a large number of unauthorised newspapers and pamphlets had circulated in the school throughout the term. Their titles included *The Daily Wail*, *The Daily Shirker* and the twenty page *Butterflies Gazette*.

Friday, December 19th 1947

The Joint Sixth Form Christmas Party was held with a high standard of food, and dancing conducted by K.S.Collinson "with more gusto than audibility" on his "dubious microphone". The party games were "much enjoyed, and surprised the participators by their ingenuity". Highlight of the evening, however, was J.R.Turner, a conjuror "of great skill and confidence". He produced "pound notes from the most unlikely places".

1948

The Junior Training Corps and the Air Training Corps became the Combined Cadet Force.

Thursday, December 23rd 1948

Richard Edward Maddison died in Lagos, Nigeria, at the age of only twenty-seven, after twelve months' illness. During the Second World War, he had suffered great privations during his long years in Japanese slave labour camps in Malaya and it was thought that this had weakened his constitution. During his illness, he always "displayed great courage and fortitude, and always had a smile upon his lips." He left a young widow.

Chapter 14: Three Blackbirds Rising Proper: The School Grows

1949

The Kings of Arms made a formal grant-of-arms to the school. Previously the school had used what was thought to be the arms of Dame Agnes Mellers, namely three blackbirds on a lozenge shaped shield. The link between this design and Dame Agnes Mellers, though, is, at best, extremely tenuous. It relies on the supposition that Richard Mellers' family was related to the Mellor family from Mellor, a small village in north Derbyshire between Stockport and Glossop. The arms of the Mellor family displayed three black birds. Supposedly the heraldic name for blackbirds is "merle" and in this way, some kind of heraldic pun is created between the names Mellor and Mellers. On the other hand, there is no proven link whatsoever between the two families, who were separated by almost a hundred miles, a vast distance in Tudor England. Furthermore, my own research has led me to believe that, as far as I can discover, the term "merle" is never used in English Heraldry. This grant-of-arms to the school, for example, does not include the word "merle". The Kings of Arms could have done so, but preferred to call them "Blackbirds". And in actual fact, there is no proof that Dame Agnes herself ever used her supposed coat of arms, as was discovered when the grant-of-arms was made to the school. If the proposed coat of arms with the three blackbirds had actually belonged to Dame Agnes, then the school would not have been allowed to use it.

Where the black birds came from, of course, is a major puzzle. My own belief is that Dame Agnes was a staunch, devout Roman Catholic who did actually display on occasion a coat of arms with three black birds on it. They were not her arms, though, but those of Saint Thomas à Becket of Canterbury, the martyr the experts have called "the most important English saint, by a wide margin." Dame Agnes was presumably showing her spiritual solidarity with Saint Thomas, and a similar mark of respect is in evidence with a close contemporary of Dame Agnes, namely Sir John More, the pious father of England's second most important saint, the martyr Saint Thomas More. Given a totally free choice of heraldic design, Sir John chose for himself a shield with three black birds, no doubt to show his own spiritual solidarity with Saint Thomas à Becket.

One long-lived misconception was that the shield with the three black birds was first adapted when the school moved to Arboretum Street. In actual fact, it had been used as an unofficial badge for the school since at least 1808, and old photographs show quite clearly that this coat of arms was displayed on the wall of the Free School building, although the birds' wings were neatly folded rather than flapping ready for take-off.

In 1949, the so-called "merles", which were previously more or less unknown in eight hundred years of English Heraldry, became blackbirds. The full description of the new coat of arms is therefore:

> "Ermine a Lozenge Argent charged with three Blackbirds rising proper on a Chief Gules an open Book also proper garnished Or between two Ducal Coronets of the last. And for the Crest On a Wreath Argent and Gules a Squirrel sejant Gules holding between the paws a Ducal Coronet Or."

Such a precise description should prevent any future repetition of the apparent confusion such as, according to popular belief, had occurred when some new stained glass sections were put into windows in the Assembly Hall in 1936. On this occasion one set of blackbirds were depicted with folded wings, rather like the shield on the old Free School in Stoney Street. Alongside, however, three other birds had their wings flapping vigorously in the more dynamic modern fashion. The overall effect of such a seemingly simple contrast is, in actual fact, quite striking but such misunderstandings will never occur again, now that the school's arms are officially fixed.

1949

The School bought a Leyland thirty-five seater diesel semi-coach from the Midland General Omnibus Company, who were later to become part of the Trent empire. The bus cost £200 and was given a full overhaul and a new coat of paint. The school opted for all white with a black waistband, but as white was not available, the bus was painted cream. The bus' registration was "KRB 97" and it was to become one of the school's most memorable vehicles. The heavy diesel engine was noisy and the gear box had no synchromesh. The driver needed an HGV licence, and sat in a "half cab".

Easter Term 1949

To the relief of Bill Boot, the caretaker who ran the tuckshop, sweet rationing ended.

Easter Term 1949

The school suffered an epidemic of chickenpox, which affected many boys and some staff.

Easter Term 1949

Under the direction of Mr A.K.Smetham, Athletics made its début as an organised full school sport.

Christmas Term 1949

Extensive building works were required to install the school's new lift.

December 1949

The following poem appeared in *The Nottinghamian*. It was written by F.Martin Hall and John G.Golds, and was dedicated to the popular figure of the school caretaker:

> To Bill Boot on his 70th Birthday
>
> You are old, Father William, the schoolboy said,
> And your tooth is of marvellous length,
> Yet your tap on the door makes the whole building rock,
> Where on earth do you find all that strength?
>
> In my youth, said the Sage, when I fought for the Queen,
> Frequent exercise, Generals demanded,
> I chased Kruger each morning around Spion Kop,
> Do you wonder my muscles expanded?
>
> You are old, Father William, the schoolboy said,
> And your hair has long since turned quite grey,
> Yet your voice like a clarion round the School rings,
> How d'you manage such volume, I pray?
>
> In my youth, said the Sage, when I served with Lord "Bobs,"
> His commands could not travel by wireless
> So I bawled them (in code) right across the Transvaal,
> And my throat, by this means, became tireless.

> You are old, Father William, yet your eagle eye
> Seems as bright as the stars high in heaven,
> Pray, how does your eyesight thus function so well,
> With no help from Aneurin Bevan?
>
> I have answered your questions, the wrathful Sage said,
> And as sure as my name's William B.,
> If you pester me further, my patience will go,
> So be off, or I'll put you in D.

Early 1950

Old Boy J.W.Parsons captained the Cambridge University Ploughing team against Oxford University.

Thursday, April 6th 1950

John Dane Player died. He had been at the High School from 1877-1880 and had been the head of one of the country's largest businesses. A large proportion of his profits had been given back to the community and not only the High School had benefited from Player's enormous generosity. Nottingham's voluntary hospitals had been the recipients of many donations as had the Children's Hospital. He was one of the main supporters of the Dame Agnes Mellers Lads' Club. Much of this willingness to help children had surely come from the fact that he and his wife Margaret had never had children of their own. Player helped the church, and made regular donations to St Andrew's and other local churches. He paid for the building of St Margaret's in Aspley. Despite all this wealth, he was not a boastful man and he shunned all publicity, never appearing, for example, in *Who s Who*.

For the High School, he bought the Valley Road playing fields. It was probably the acquisition of this site which inspired Johnny Dixon to try to persuade Player to finance the rebuilding of the school on the outskirts of the city, surrounded by its own grounds. Player, however, thought that the old site was in the correct, central, position to serve a large number of widely scattered boys, even if the school was not next to its games fields. He paid for a new East Block and a Gymnasium. When the suggestion was made to convert the Drawing Room into an Assembly Hall, by giving it a new roof, he replied, "I don't believe in maccling, but I will give you a new Hall if you like." The Assembly Hall was duly built, and Player then paid for the building of the West Block.

A few years later he financed the demolition of the central block to build science laboratories. Even five years after his death the North Block was constructed largely with his donations.

In actual fact, very little of the major building in the school between 1868-1960 was not directly financed by John Player. The great irony, of course, was that John Dane Player was a very modest man. His own admiration was reserved for the brilliant scholars the school turned out. On one occasion he said to a fellow Old Boy, "I was no good at school. Were you?" Those brilliant scholars are largely forgotten nowadays, of course, but it was they who benefited from the High School. Exactly the opposite was true of John Player and one is tempted to wonder where the High School would be now were it not for him.

Sunday, July 2nd 1950

The memorial plaque to the Old Boys who fell in the 1939-1945 war was unveiled by the Duke of Portland who, on his arrival, inspected a guard of honour formed by the School contingent of the C.C.F. under the command of Captain Reid. The plaque was inscribed "In memory of the Old Boys of this School about one hundred in number who gave their lives for their country, 1939-1945". Underneath was a list of the fallen. As well as the plaque, the Old Boys had also endowed a scholarship fund in remembrance of the dead.

July 1950

Two long serving members of staff retired. The first of these was Miss S.J.Webb who had joined the staff of the Preparatory School in 1917, being mainly responsible for the teaching of Art and Handwork. The second was Mr L.W.Whitty who came to teach Modern Languages in 1919, after four years on the Western Front with the Lancashire Fusiliers and being severely wounded. For the most part he was involved with the teaching of, perhaps, the less talented scholars and he devoted much of his time to school rugby. He missed very few matches, home or away, in over twenty-five years and acted as both coach and referee. He was Housemaster of Cooper's for many years.

December 1950

William "Bill" Boot retired this year as school caretaker after twenty-eight years' service. He was replaced by Mr T.H.Briggs, who had previously worked as a policeman in the city. Bill Boot had fought in the Boer War and was famed for his rapid, shuffling gait and his extremely rapid speech, which, with his accent, was frequently almost unintelligible. His hobby was fishing and he travelled widely at weekends. When he retired, he received a small pension but, alas, he did not live very long to enjoy it as he was knocked down and killed crossing the road on December 7th 1952.

April 1951

A brand new system of bells had been installed in the school, and was used for the first time this term. It seems possible that before this, the beginnings and ends of lessons and breaks were marked by the tolling of the large school bell near to the tower.

Thursday, September 20th 1951

Kenneth Harry Clarke entered the High School as a Nottingham City Scholar at the age of eleven. He was born on July 2nd 1940 and had originally attended Aldecar Infants' School and then Langley Mills Boys' School, both of which were in Derbyshire. His father was Kenneth Horatio Clarke who was originally an electrician at the local pit but who opened a watchmaker and jeweller's shop after the family moved to the Highbury Vale area of Nottingham, just before young Kenneth's tenth birthday.

Shortly after this he took, and passed, his 11+ examination. Instead of going to the local grammar school, however, Ken came to the High School which, at the time, took scholarship boys from all over Nottinghamshire and a number of the neighbouring counties. In the register his father's address is listed as 25, Highbury Road, Bulwell. Ken was to leave the High School on March 25th 1959.

During his time here, Ken was, among other things, a Sergeant in the C.C.F. and the Captain of Fives. He was described by one of his teachers as "a confident, relaxed, cheerful individual, he worked hard and had a real sense of humour." Ken was to win an Open Exhibition at Gonville and Caius College, Cambridge, where he became President of the Union and was awarded a scholarship on the basis of the results of his first year examinations. In a short article about him in the *Daily Mail* in late April 2012, the seventy year old cabinet minister revealed some more personal, details about his career in the High School, explaining that the school was always very much geared to achieving the maximum number of successful applications to Oxford and Cambridge. He saw the Sixth Form in particular as being very similar to *The History Boys*. David Peters was "a great teacher in my life" who gave him "a lifelong love of history". By his own admission, he did not excel at sport, and was by no means a model pupil, or a prefect. It was his ability to do well in examinations which kept all of his teachers happy. In an interesting conclusion Clarke praised the school highly for the possibilities that it offered for upward social mobility. Otherwise, he explained, he would "have probably ended up working down the local pit until it closed."

Summer Term 1953

A particularly violent summer storm left the Headmaster's study and the Prefects' Common Room ankle-deep in water.

Summer Term 1953

The school tuck shop began to sell ice cream and various fizzy drinks.

End of the Summer Term 1953

Mr R.S."Beaky" Bridge retired at the age of seventy-one, after forty-seven years as a schoolmaster, nearly thirty three of them at the High School. Mr Bridge was Chief History and Geography Master, and House Master of White's. He was: "a fierce martinet, and could hold a class of boys, of any age, hushed and motionless with a stare, until his lip began to quiver, and the familiar grin would appear and snap the tension. His teaching was unconventional, but inspiring. His fund of stories was endless. His knowledge was vast and his memory remarkable. In his younger days, he had been a very good rugby footballer and cricketer. His twisted finger and bowed legs gave substance to the story that at one time or another he had broken almost every bone in his body. He was truly a "character". In later life it was remembered as a privilege to have been punished by him, and to have been called a "Nark", his name for any undesirable character was as memorable as a decoration."

Eric Penson too recalled how much he enjoyed Beaky Bridge's teaching of Shakespeare, Wordsworth and the *Ancient Mariner* in the Lower School. Beaky was: "very keen indeed on school cricket. He often exhibited his skill in class, as his aim with the dusty felt blackboard-rubber, flung without warning at the head of any boy he suspected of inattention, would have done credit to any professional cover-point."

The Nottinghamian's valedictory article spoke of his: "unremitting efforts, shrewd and often caustic criticisms, firm insistence on the old-fashioned virtues of strict discipline and hard work and outstanding ability. Few masters can have made a greater personal contribution to the school's success or that of its pupils."

Near to midnight, Monday, August 10th 1953

A group of thirty-two boys, accompanied by Dr Thimann, met at the Victoria Station Hotel to set off for their exchange visit to Belgium, the train leaving Nottingham's Victoria Station at 1.45 a.m. on August 11th. For the first time ever, the party included a girl, the daughter of Mr Thomas. One of the members of the party was later to note that: "Belgian sanitation is much better than that of France, the people are more friendly and work much harder, and, to me, the food seems more wholesome, for the Belgians, like most of us, dislike fancy food."

Christmas Term 1953

A new score box was built on the playing fields at Valley Road. It was the gift of Mr and Mrs. E.B.Armitage, the parents of Alan K.Partridge, "as an expression of all the School did for Alan during his ten years there". A major contribution to the building was made by Mr E.A."Eddie" Marshall.

Friday, November 20th 1953

The Debating Society debated the motion that "The construction of a Channel Tunnel would be in every way beneficial". The motion was defeated easily, by 58-8. And quite right too.

Sometime before Christmas, 1953

D.G.Kaye of Hucknall returned home from a prisoner of war camp in North Korea. Captured while serving with the Gloucestershire

Regiment, he had initially found it difficult to adapt to rich English food. Nevertheless, he had put on a stone within weeks of his release.

December 1953

By the time Mr Cedric Lawton Reynolds retired, school numbers had risen to a record 785. He had done much to encourage those boys who were not among the academic high fliers by keeping their classes deliberately small and making every effort to bring out the best in them. Mr Reynolds was replaced by Mr Kenneth Imeson.

Monday, February 15th 1954

An old servant of the school, Mr R.E.James, died at the age of eighty-two. He was born in 1872 and as a boy had been a coachman before getting a job at the City Hospital, driving a horse ambulance. In later life he became a gardener and groundsman, coming to work at Valley Road when he retired from the City Hospital. He worked at the Games Field for seventeen years, with few boys realising that he was over eighty years of age when they saw: "his portly figure as he carried out his valuable, if unspectacular, duties on the outskirts of the playing fields. He had a great heart. Would that there were more of his kind in the world!"

April 1954

The following piece of original work was published by *The Nottinghamian*. It was written by J.A.Bush of 3B:

SCHOOL DINNERS

(with apologies to Matron and Thomas Hardy)

This is the dinner the teachers like
And so do I!
When potatoes are floury and meat is tender
And not too dry.
When the fragrant smells draw us to the hatch,
And the sight of the food is hard to match,
When pudding is light and melts on the tongue
And in sampling the custard you never go wrong,
And neither do I!

This is the dinner the prefects dislike
And so do I!
When gristle is left in the shepherd's pie

> And we daren't ask why.
> When the veg is a mess, and the gravy is thick,
> And the taste of the spuds makes one feel sick.
> When the custard is lumpy and rhubarb is coarse,
> And the cheese walks off as though in remorse
> And so do I!

July 1954

The end of term saw the retirement of two long serving masters. Mr M.J.Brodrick had taught Modern Languages, and German in particular, since September 1919 as well as being a tutor and founding the "Hobbies Club". Mr J.F.Newbound had joined the school in January 1921 and had been a teacher of Science and Mathematics, as well as a tutor and the person in charge of the Photographic Club. Both men had participated in school rowing, and had performed as starters at the School Sports for more than twenty-five years.

Thursday, September 30th 1954

Miss Jane Place Farmer died at the age of eighty-one, in a nursing home in Nottingham. She had previously lived at Old Hall, East Bridgford and had been a music teacher at the High School from 1901-1935 as well as taking a carpentry class in the evenings at her home.

Saturday, February 26th 1955

The County Youths' Cross Country Championship was held in two feet of snow at Berry Hill, Mansfield. The weather made "overtaking difficult and extremely hazardous". The school team finished second.

Half term of the Easter Term 1955

Up to 80 members of the Historical Society, in five parties of about sixteen each, descended into the caves under Nottingham City centre. They were required to wear protective clothing such as miners' helmets and even woodwork aprons although nothing could compare to the magnificent blue overalls of Mr J.D.Powell. The boys saw medieval pottery and broken Tudor and Stuart clay pipes.

Easter 1955

Beaky Bridge, who, after his retirement, had continued to work in the school library, passed away. *The Nottinghamian* paid generous tribute to his talents as a: "Historian, painter, musician, cartographer, numismatist, philatelist, geologist and student of heraldry, a skilled player of cricket and of rugby. As a teacher, all know of the tweaked ear, the pulled tie, the croaky voice and the underlying chuckles. The board would rapidly fill with armour, or coats of arms, or older weapons, or faces, or a campaign. At the bell "Beaky" would tell his boys to go that evening into the Library where he was at his happiest directing them to this book or that, in which they could themselves dig for information on the current work. His lessons always ended there; a boy had to think and read for himself. As well as books, he collected slides, well over two thousand. These, together with his huge private library and some pictures, he left to the school."

A forgotten, sunlit morning between 1953-1956

An urban myth tells the tale…

> "The Headmaster, Mr Imeson, was conducting a completely normal, ordinary morning assembly in what is now called "The Player Hall", but was then referred to as just "The Assembly Hall". As was sometimes the case, "Imey" was not particularly happy about a certain example of misbehaviour, and was giving the school a good talking-to. As he addressed his pupils, what he did not know was that some mischievous Sixth Formers were already hiding high above his head, up near the ceiling. Slowly, slowly, they lowered a string of sausages down towards their unsuspecting victim. Everybody in the audience could see what was happening, of course, while the angry Headmaster remained blissfully unaware of what was the source of their merriment. Eventually the continuing stifled titters among the boys and, presumably, the upward glances of members of staff, made him aware of what was happening. There is no record of what happened to the perpetrators."

Further research among today's grandfathers reveals that a belief certainly exists that when Mr Imeson finally retired in 1970, some daring young man wrote "Bye, Bye, Imey" in weedkiller on the grass lawn of the West Quadrangle. This is probably just one of the many weedkiller stories which abound in schools and colleges, but it would be nice if it were true and it is included for that reason.

Wednesday, August 10th 1955

Nine boys left Nottingham Victoria Station for a visit to Ludwigshafen in Germany. The party experienced "extraordinary and often terrifying sausages of every size and colour, but we are all still alive." They were surprised that "the German does not eat until he feels satisfied, but continues until he cannot possibly swallow another mouthful." Nevertheless, the town and shops were meticulously clean, with no "queues, Teddy Boys and school uniform." Indeed, the German boys were "shocked" at the High School uniform, and preferred their more natural dress of lederhosen and shirts.

Wednesday, November 9th 1955

The newly formed naval section of the Combined Cadet Force appeared in uniform for the first time.

1955?

The school inaugurated its Duke of Edinburgh scheme, one of the very first schools so to do.

Monday, February 6th 1956

Young revolutionary, New, of U5G served a detention for "telling a master to shut up".

Monday, March 26th 1956

The school visited the Houses of Parliament on the very same day as the Soviet leader, Mr Malenkov. They heard speeches by Sir Anthony Eden, Hugh Gaitskell and Aneurin Bevan as well as Sidney Silverman, introducing a bill to abolish capital punishment. Among the party was a sixteen year old Kenneth Clarke.

Summer Term 1956

The Locomotive Society had fewer meetings than usual this term because of the pressure of work on its officers. One of the latter was Kenneth Clarke, who was destined to hold even greater office than Honorary Secretary of the Locomotive Society in the years to come, when working as a Member of Parliament or as the Chancellor of the Exchequer, the Home Secretary, the Lord Chancellor, the Justice

Secretary, the Education Secretary, the Health Secretary or as a Minister without Portfolio, all of which posts he has held at one time or another.

Summer term 1957

Fire drills were introduced, although the first efforts were apparently "far from successful". Even so, the boys appreciated the disruption of their "long uninterrupted periods of work".

Tuesday, October 1st 1957

Because of an outbreak of Asian flu, 347 boys were absent from the school. This represented 46% of the total complement.

Christmas Term 1957

The Astronomical Society was limited to a maximum of thirty members. After paying their dues of 2s 6d for the year, they were then entitled to view the film, *Project Moonbase*, for free. Non-members were asked to pay 1s 0d, a venture which provided a secure financial basis for the society for many months to come.

Friday, January 10th 1958

The Nottinghamian announced with great sadness that Mr Palmer had passed away after a long illness. He had spent a remarkable forty-four years at the High School, serving the school with great loyalty and devotion throughout this time.

Richard Arthur Palmer entered the School at the age of ten in September, 1913 and had a great deal of success both academically and as an athlete. Richard was a Foundation Scholar and won a great many prizes, especially for Mathematics. Eventually, he became Captain of the School, Captain of Cricket, Captain of Football and Sergeant-Major of the O.T.C., as it then was. He finished his school career in December 1921 by winning an Open Scholarship for Mathematics at Queens' College, Cambridge.

Unfortunately, Richard was unable to go to Cambridge for family reasons but Doctor Turpin immediately suggested that he join the staff as a teacher and he started in the Summer Term of 1922. Although he was a very young Old Boy, Richard was soon one of the main driving forces behind the Old Nottinghamians' Society which was being reformed around this time. Similar levels of commitment and enthusiasm went into establishing the O.N.'s rugby and cricket clubs. Richard was both a keen player and captain of each club during their first few years. Not surprisingly, he was appointed President of the Old Nottinghamians Society in 1941 and 1942.

In the school he was soon promoted to become one of the first tutors and an officer in the Corps, becoming the Commanding Officer from 1933 to 1939. When the war broke out, he took on extra coaching duties in Games and in 1941 was given the job of Acting Head of the Mathematics Department. He resumed his post as Commanding Officer of the Corps from 1942-1947 and, in actual fact, spent every single one of his summer holidays from 1940 to 1949 running the School Harvest Camps. Outside school, he was in charge of a company of the local Home Guard. In 1947, two years after the war ended, he was promoted to Housemaster of Mellers and shortly afterwards became the Master in charge of the Playing Fields.

Richard's character was always quiet, modest and unassuming, and, as his record shows, he had a great devotion to duty and an unwavering loyalty to the school. Nothing was too much for him and everything was always done meticulously, right down to the very least detail. He was not a teacher at the High School for any personal financial gain, and when he was presented with a gold watch by the farmers of Car Colston, he did not prize it for its monetary value, but valued it rather because they were his friends. Richard had always worked hard for the good of others, and he would surely be sadly missed at the High School.

Half term of the Easter Term 1958

Mr Fell died suddenly after a short illness. He had officially retired from the C.C.F. as recently as the previous December, but he had returned after Christmas in a part-time capacity.

Joseph Henry Fell joined the Sherwood Foresters as a regular soldier before the 1914-18 War, throughout which he served and in which he was wounded three times. He was proud to be one of the "Old Contemptibles" and came to the School to take charge of the Physical Training and to act as Sergeant Instructor to the School Contingent of the Officers' Training Corps in July 1920. He retired from the C.C.F. in July 1957 after thirty-seven years' service which had been recognised by the award of the Cadet Force Medal and the British Empire Medal, although he continued to work in the gymnasium. As his obituary in *The Nottinghamian* was to relate how: "Sergeant-Major Fell gave much to the School, but he took much from it in happiness, in friendships, and in the satisfaction of work well done, and he leaves with all who knew him a lasting example and the memory of a fine character; of him too we can say in all sincerity : Lauda Finem."

Half term of the Easter Term 1958

The Model Railway Society was formed. It extended the school's great interest in trains, and membership quickly reached the half century. Meetings were held in the Biology Laboratory every Friday lunch-time between 1.15 - 2.30 pm.

Easter 1958

A party of boys stayed at a hotel near Jouy-en-Josas near Versailles:

> "Some foolhardy individuals even tried swimming in the open air pool one morning. It was learned afterwards that it had not been cleaned out for a very long time."

Friday, May 23rd 1958

After several months' illness, Mr C.L.Reynolds passed away. *The Nottinghamian* spoke sadly of his "valuable and full life" and his "so brief a retirement".

Summer Term 1958

There were so many school swimming fixtures that it would have been difficult to accept many more. As the school had no swimming baths of their own, these fixtures were mostly evening matches at other schools while Mr H.V. "Chalky" White took the Second Forms for practice either to Radford or Meridian Baths.

Summer 1958

A party visited *Expo 58* in Brussels, enjoying the funfair, the Russian Pavilion and the "extremely impressive British pavilion".

Christmas Term 1958

The school chess team finished third in the *Sunday Times* tournament, after beating Colfe's Grammar School from London, but losing to Varndean Grammar School of Brighton. Perhaps the most exciting moment in the competition was the school's first ever "telephone" chess match against King Edward VI Grammar School in Southampton. This started at 6.30 pm., and finished five hours later. The school won by 5-1.

The evening of Monday, March 9th 1959

The first ever Staff v Prefects football match took place. The staff triumphed by a single goal.

Tuesday, June 9th 1959

Mr J.D. "Sandy" Powell thwarted a determined attempt by U4G to stink out the school. T.Dilks served a detention for "dropping a stink bomb before class." J.C.Morrell was convicted of "having a stink bomb in his possession" and T.J.Moore served his detention for "dropping a stink bomb in the corridor." Presumably, he was trying to dispose of the incriminating evidence.

Early 1960

Mr W.A.Parsons passed away in the early part of the year, having retired in 1949. Known always as "Wappy", Mr Parsons had been a teacher of Geography and English and, along with R.S.Bridge, had coached school cricket for nearly thirty years. He was himself a very competent bowler but had been severely gassed during the Great War and he had suffered constantly in the many years since that event.

Monday, February 1st 1960

The boys of the school were allowed access for the first time to the new block on the northern side of the West Quadrangle. The extensive school building scheme financed by J.D.Player was at long last completed. The new buildings consisted of two spacious Geography rooms, two junior form rooms, and four sixth form rooms. At half term, the members of staff moved into their first ever purpose built Common Room. The rooms on the second floor came into use in the half term after this. They were originally designed to be a music rehearsal room, a prefects' room, a general science laboratory and a biology laboratory. This was considered by Mr Neville to be the finest in the county.

April 1960

The House Prefects introduced a swear box to their proceedings. Within three weeks, it had raised fifteen shillings for World Refugee Year.

Chapter 15: Don't Let Examinations Ruin your Education

Saturday, June 18th 1960

Showing great bravery, young R.F.Barker saved the life of a two-year old child, diving into the Nottingham Canal to carry out a rescue. The City Police described it as "a noble effort".

Wednesday, June 29th 1960

The Valley Road playing fields, with a series of "carefully constructed ruins", hosted a Civil Defence rehearsal of a Soviet nuclear attack. As the photographs in *The Nottinghamian* show, the school dealt with such an emergency as an atomic bomb blast without any real problems.

At least the 1960s onwards

We forget nowadays, such is the high standard of the buildings of the present school, that in years gone by, rooms were often divided in two by wooden partitions and that many boys would see it as a challenge slowly and quietly to open up a gap between two individual panels and then make their escape. Rooms E1 and E2 were like this and many a teacher would remain blissfully unaware that his class was either melting away with time or perhaps slowly morphing into the class next door, as boys changed places, subjects and teachers, moving back and forth between the two rooms. In a similar way, there was a trapdoor under the floor at the back of the old Language Lab in what is now W1. Many a class has diminished in size over the years as boys slid gracefully under the floor and then "Down, down and away!" into the cellars.

Summer Term, 1961

A large number of school societies continued to flourish. During this term, there were Societies for Automobiles, Chess, Christian Discussion, Debating, History, Jazz, Locomotives, Modern Languages, Music, Photography, Science and the Third Year Sixth Form.

Monday, November 27th 1961

Mr D.N.Aspin gave a detention to the anarchic Williams of 2M for a "wilful attempt to trip up a Prep boy carrying a pile of plates in the dining hall". The detention book does not record whether total disaster was averted.

Saturday, May 5th 1962

Leg-spinner P.D.Johnson, the youngest player in the side, took a wicket with his very first ever ball for the 1st XI. It came in a match against Welbeck College and he finished with figures of 6-21.

1963

Celebrations were held for the 450th anniversary of the school. Marquees were erected and portable flowerbeds brought in. There were fountains and hundreds of tables and chairs were set out. Classrooms were converted into dance floors and in the assembly hall a huge mural with life size figures depicted the history of the school. The geography department became the "Caribbean Room". Two commemorative balls were held with professional dancers, three bands and an army of caterers being hired. There were two garden parties, a special service and, over a short period of time, a large number of dinners and private functions. Over ten thousand guests were catered for, many of them being temporarily accommodated with either parents or old boys. At midnight trumpeters emerged at the top of the tower and a fanfare was sounded over Nottingham. As soon as this music had died away Ukrainian dancers emerged onto the south steps and the festivities, temporarily suspended, resumed their frenetic course. The school took advantage of the influx of well-wishers to launch an appeal fund, the aim of which was the building of the Founder Hall which would incorporate the school's very first swimming pool.

Summer Term 1963

A French dictionary was returned to the book room after an interval of some fifty-seven years. It had been borrowed in 1906, but it is not recorded if any fine was levied on this forgetful pupil.

Summer Term 1963

The Community Service scheme began, initially with the Sixth Form, but soon spreading to the Fifth Form. Boys were variously digging gardens or decorating kitchens. Others helped at a club for mentally handicapped people or went on a Red Cross camp for the physically handicapped. A brave group took Borstal boys to Alsop and a holiday club was set up for children in the Meadows. There was a widespread desire to visit O.A.P.s, but unfortunately there seemed to be a shortage of suitable candidates, as "it seems very difficult to get names and addresses of people who need visiting".

Friday, July 26th 1963

The Head of English, Mr Ben Towers, died from the debilitating effects of asthma. He left a wife, Joyce, and twin sons, Bob and David. He had lived long enough to see them receive their degrees.

Tuesday, July 21st 1964

D.C.Haywood and P.A.Warsop put on 173 for the second wicket against King Edward's School, Sheffield. Haywood scored 137 not out and Warsop scored 71. This was the highest partnership since 1911, and the highest individual score since the same year.

Friday, July 2nd 1965

The First XI played a touring cricket team, Shawnigan Lake School from Canada. Much to everyone's embarrassment the latter were all out for a grand total of some 19 runs, the lowest total ever recorded against a full High School side. A.B.Palfreyman took five wickets for only 14 runs and P.H.Moody had the amazing figures of four wickets for one run.

Saturday, October 16th 1965

The Founder Hall and Swimming Pool were officially opened by Sir Stanley Rous. Although he was the President of F.I.F.A., and in charge of football for the whole world, Sir Stanley was present on this particular occasion in his capacity as Chairman of the Central Council for Physical Recreation. The building had cost somewhere in the region of £200,000. Rather imaginatively, perhaps, it was originally planned to call it the "Dining Hall and Swimming Pool", but the name "Founder Hall" eventually emerged, in the absence of any better suggestions.

December 1965

Inspired by Sir Stanley's visit to his old school, D.C.Haywood won a blue for Association Football, appearing for Cambridge against Oxford. He had the honour of scoring the third goal in a 3-2 victory, thereby becoming the only Old Nottinghamian, in almost a century of trying, to achieve the ultimate feat for a footballer, namely of scoring the winning goal at Wembley.

8 a.m. on Saturday, New Year's Day 1966

The High School's first ever ski-trip left for Hintertux, in the Austrian Tyrol. They were supervised by Messrs. Wilson and Littler, and after nine days practice, had become "quite proficient skiers".

Wednesday, February 16th 1966

When William Seeley Hughes passed away in West Bridgford at the age of 102, he was reckoned to be the oldest Old Nottinghamian. Born at Tipton in Staffordshire in October 1863, he came to the High School in 1876, when his father opened a shop selling paraffin lamps in Exchange Walk. On November 27th 1878 he played football for the Second XI against University School, enduring heavy rain in a dreary 0-0 draw. William left the school in 1879 and became a lace designer draughtsman. In later life he was to win more than seventy trophies for hurdling. A keen cricket fan, he attended Nottinghamshire matches at Trent Bridge until well after his hundredth birthday.

April 1966

In *The Nottinghamian*, the newly formed "Angling Society" boasted of being the most unofficial club in the school. They had visited the River Trent on a number of occasions although their catches to date had not been spectacularly successful. More than forty boys, however, had attended a film supplied by the Irish Tourist Board.

Summer Term 1966

The Astronomy Society's "Star Dome" which duplicated the movements of the stars, sun, moon, constellations and planets, was at last in operation. It had been built by its members and was to be visited by parties from a number of neighbouring schools.

May 1966

Four members of the Sixth Form, S.Davies, S.P.Hardy, R.E.D.Storer and P.A.Warsop appeared on *Talkback* on B.B.C. Television, discussing the Arts with four young ladies from the Girls' High School.

Thursday, January 5th 1967

P.R.Castles appeared on ATV, talking to Reg Harcourt about origami. His fame lasted for 3 minutes 35 seconds, preceded by an item about the animals at Dudley Zoo and a pensioner explaining advanced weaving techniques. When he had finished his explanation of the gentle oriental art, the camera went back to Reg Harcourt who proceeded to explain why he had a macaw perched on his finger. Nevertheless, an appearance fee of five guineas made it all very well worth while.

Every Easter holiday since 1967

For an almost unbelievable number of years, Martin Jones has taken countless members of the C.C.F. to test themselves against some of the highest, coldest and toughest mountains in the country. Here, Martin talks about the magic of being a mountaineer:

> "The main reason for myself, and several others to join the C.C.F. as section officers was the attraction of the Adventurous Training programme. I joined in 1967 as a very junior officer, with no ambitions of promotion, just a desire to explore the mountain areas of Britain. After three years, various senior officers either left or retired and I was suddenly in charge of the R.A.F. section and the Adventurous Training programme. The next thirty years would find me in Wales or Scotland, often a week in both places, every Easter holiday, with, usually, about twenty five boys and five members of staff. We had some fantastic times, climbing Munroes (peaks over three thousand feet tall), often in winter conditions, using ice-axes, crampons and ropes, scaring ourselves at times, but feeling proud of the boys', and our own, achievements."

Thursday, April 18th 1968

A small group of birdwatchers left for Lindisfarne with Mr and Mrs Curtis. They were to spend nearly a week there, seeing almost a hundred species of birds and visiting the walled city of Berwick-upon-Tweed.

Summer Term 1968

The Library held its first ever book sale. More than four hundred volumes were disposed of, and nearly £12 was raised.

Summer Term 1968

P.D.Johnson made 1,061 runs in the season, a school record, as was his feat of achieving five hundred runs and fifty wickets for the second successive year. His total of seventy-five wickets broke a record which had stood since 1899, and his career aggregate of 2,445 runs was another milestone in school cricket. Johnson was not the only cricketer to achieve new standards, however. R.J.Hartley took nineteen catches, breaking the record for any fielder and for the wicketkeeper, the latter figure having stood since 1898. Indeed, the team's overall total of 112 catches was a record for a single season.

September 1968

The new school year began unlike any other, with no Saturday school for the first time ever. In addition, Sandy Powell became Senior Master and Oswald Lush became the House Master of Cooper's House. These two gentlemen were two of the most respected, and most imitated, of the masters of this era.

September 1968

The Language Laboratory came into operation. At a stroke, according to *The Nottinghamian*, this: "freed the teacher of all strain, allowing him to doze at the console, or read "Reveillé" while his pupils obey and imitate an authoritarian foreign voice on tape (although nothing could be farther from the truth)."

The hockey season, 1968 - 1969

Playing a new school sport for the very first time, the 1st XI lost every match they played without scoring a single goal.

Tuesday, October 4th 1966

Rowing persisted as a school sport until 1979. Martin Jones was involved in it from 1966 onwards. He tells the following tale, which deserves to be quoted verbatim:

> "The First IV, keen to get in as much practice as possible, persuaded me to coach them on this Tuesday evening, in the dark, on the River Trent. A bicycle lamp was attached to the bow of the boat, I rode the bike, now minus its front light, on the

tow path. Close to the Wilford Bridge, I rode into a step whilst watching the crew, went over the handlebars, and landed on my chin. There was blood everywhere and I told the boys to carry on without me in the pitch dark. I then pushed the damaged bike up to the police station in the Meadows. I ended up in the General Hospital with five stitches and multiple grazes to the face. I got absolutely no sympathy from my colleagues at school the following day."

One wintry November evening, 1968

Association Football was played once more after an interval of some fifty-four years since the sport was abolished. This time it was an option for Sixth Formers which meant that boys would be able to play for their last two years before they left. In addition, as rugby was still the school's senior sport, the First, Second and Third XVs would continue to have prior claim on any players they wanted. The latter would continue with their rugby as before. Only those who were not needed for rugby would be able to play football. For their first match, the High School wore the very same colours that had first been seen as early as 1870. When the eleven young men, proudly wearing their black and white shirts, took the field at Bilborough Grammar School, sporting history was being made. Not for more than fifty years had a team represented the High School at this sport.

1968

A League table based on the ratio between the number of Sixth Formers and Open Awards at Oxford and Cambridge and published in *The Times* placed the High School in the very top position, making it theoretically the best school in the whole country.

Saturday, December 14th 1968

Mr M.J.Brodrick died in hospital as result of burns and shock caused by an accident in his home. He had worked at the High School from September 1919 until his retirement in 1954. A teacher of Modern Languages, he was for many years the form master of a Lower Fourth Form. He had helped with the coaching of the Rowing Club and was the Official Starter in the School Sports, as well as the man who introduced woodworking to the school.

1969

The school participated in the Business Game, competing with almost a hundred schools nationwide. In Round One, they won with an overall profit of £1,412,570, and in Rounds Two and Three were again successful, this time with scores of £1,137,160 and £1,261,140. In the final, the school's profit of £4,633,760 however, was eclipsed by Cheltenham College, who managed a staggering £5,366,140.

Spring Term 1969

The school continued to play Rugby Fives, with a victory over Q.E.G.S., Mansfield and a narrow defeat at Heath Grammar School, Halifax, as well as two defeats by larger margins and, unfortunately, three cancelled fixtures.

Spring Term 1969

The Aeronautical Society went from strength to strength. A number of films were borrowed from the R.A.F. and talks included *The Structure of an Aircraft*, and *The History of the Henschel 129*. A competition was held to identify forty aircraft featured in miscellaneous advertisements. It was won by A.J.Ross of 3A2.

Sunday, January 5th 1969

"Guts" Kennard died at the age of eighty-seven after a short illness. He had worked at the High School from 1910-1947 and was chiefly remembered as the master who introduced Rugby Union to the school in 1914. He taught Modern Languages and was also involved in the O.T.C., eventually becoming House Master of Mellers', Head of Modern Languages, and finally Second Master in 1941:

> "Sentiment had little place in his character, and his guiding principles were devotion to duty, loyal service and firm discipline".

Saturday, February 8th 1969

The Headmaster, Mr Imeson, punished Bowden of 6A2 with a detention for having "long hair".

The Easter holidays, 1969

The German Exchange party went to Hamburg. The group was under the aegis of Mr McMurchy, a proud Glaswegian whom the German boys insisted on always calling "Archibald", claiming that this was a typical English name, and that he was the most typical of Englishmen.

Friday, July 18th & Saturday, July 19th 1969

P.D.Johnson's final match for the school came against the Canadian Colts XI. Typically, he made 40 runs, and took 5-32. In this, his last, year at the High School, P.D.Johnson had set records which may well never be beaten. As a batsman he scored a career total of 3,502 runs at an amazing average of 46.08 and in one year managed a record 1,061 runs. As a bowler he took 473 wickets at an average of 12.39 with a record total of 93 wickets in 1969. In 1967, 1968 and 1969, he achieved the double of five hundred runs and fifty wickets, and on two occasions made more than a thousand runs in a season. His total of five centuries was more than any other batsman and his career total of forty catches was also, not surprisingly, another record.

The hockey season, 1969 - 1970

In their second season, the 1st XI won their first ever victory, by a convincing margin of 4-0 against Beeston 4th XI, to whom they had already lost 0-5 earlier in the year. Overall the team scored a total of six goals in their other matches, having failed to score at all in the previous twelve months.

The football season, 1969 - 1970

The First XI won at least four of their matches this season, scoring forty-two goals and conceding just twenty. In only their second year "remarkable progress has been made from humble beginnings". Team spirit, especially, was very strong with the team recovering from 0-3 deficits against both Mundella and Becket to draw 3-3. Most of this was due to their skilful and attractive play and the obvious enthusiasm of the team captain, R.R.Matthews. At the end of the Autumn Term they played their first match against the Old Nottinghamians, a revival of a fixture which dated back to September 29th 1877.

Probably 1969

In the 1960s very many people used to smoke cigarettes including a large proportion of the High School staff. Every morning at break, Martin Jones would join his fellow smokers. When the bell went, he would quickly snub out his cigarette by nipping the end and then save the rest for later. It was fashionable at the time for members of staff to wear a heavy tweed sports jacket with leather elbow pads. Halfway through the next Maths lesson one boy persistently had his hand up. As was also the fashion at the time, Martin just ignored him. Eventually he yelled out, "What do you want?" The boy replied "Please sir, your jacket's on fire!" The cigarette had started a smouldering fire in the tweed and this had gained momentum over the course of time. Smoking jacket indeed!

An unknown date during the Christmas Term 1969

Mr Whitty died at the age of eighty-two, having taught French and Scripture at the High School from 1919-1950. He had enjoyed a happy and active retirement and, indeed, on the very day of his death had spent the morning tending the roses in his garden.

7 p.m., Wednesday, December 17th 1969

The Christmas Concert took place with works performed under the direction of Kendrick Partington. They included three excerpts from *Swan Lake* and the *Dance of the Villagers* by Smetana. The School Choir, enlarged for the occasion with a number of co-opted members, sang a Fantasia of Christmas Carols by Holst as well as a large number of more traditional carols. The Bell Ringing Society gave a short performance before proceedings came to an end with the Band performing, among others, the *Grand March* from Aïda with Edwin Harris "expertly wielding the baton"

The end of the rugby season 1969-1970

The final game saw the retirement of N.J.Peel, who had been the 1st XV touch judge for the last three seasons, having previously performed this function for every age-group side throughout his time at the school.

July 1970

Mr Imeson, the Headmaster, retired. During his tenure of the office, the school's buildings had improved enormously, whether from the point of view of mere lighting and furniture, or the more spectacular equipment and facilities in the science laboratories. The West Quadrangle had been completed and the Founder Hall had been built. A Physical Science Laboratory and a Nuclear Science Laboratory had been brought into existence and a Language Laboratory had been constructed. A new Music School and Drama Room had been erected and fitted out and there were new premises for the Scouts, the C.C.F. and the Sixth Form. The Pavilion at Valley Road was also extended.

Thursday, July 9th and Thursday, July 16th 1970

A century of school cricket was commemorated with two special fixtures. The first was a game against an "Invitation XI", who scored a total of 163-8, in reply to which the school just held out at 128-8, the game finishing in a draw. A second match followed this game against a "Former Captains' XI". The school managed only 119 all out in reply to the opposition's 213-7 declared, and therefore lost by 94 runs.

1970

By the time Mr Imeson retired, the school had over forty different societies, from the Christian Discussion group to the Origami Society. On one occasion, the latter exhibited their work in Japan and their creations were viewed by the Emperor Hirohito. Despite the great interest shown by many boys, however, ten years later the society had folded.

Saturday, October 17th 1970

It would fall to a new headmaster, Dr Witcombe, to deal with the problems of a new era. The first of these was probably the outrageous behaviour of C.R.Fish of 6 History 1, who had been punished by Mr Lush, for "disrupting private study by playing his guitar."

Christmas Term 1970

The school's C.C.F. rifle shooting team proved itself to be the best in the country, winning the final stage of the C.C.F. Schools' Staniforth Trophy and receiving eight silver medals in the process. For the fifth year in succession the school had finished either first or second in this competition. The scores in the final stage were S.C.Cragg 100, R.M.Kruze 100, R.G.Sturton 100, E.M.Jackson 99, R.W.S.Whitby 99, J.K.Borley 98, P.R.Sallis 97, and J.D.Hale 96.

The Easter Holidays 1971

A group of boys, under the aegis of Messrs Thimann and Hayes, visited Dinard in Normandy. They caught the ferry at Southampton after a journey of some nine hours down the M1. Every morning the boys had an hour long French lesson before excursions to such places as the tidal power station and Mont St Michel. During the first week seven members of the group were confined to bed with a bug but fortunately when their accommodation lost its lighting and hot water, Mr Hayes repaired the gas and electricity supplies. *The Nottinghamian*, however, ever optimistic, called the trip "enjoyable for the most part, and very worthwhile".

Summer Term 1971

In the world of school athletics, the A.A.A. Five Star Award Scheme continued to run with great success. Boys chose their best three events, two track and one field, or vice versa, and could then win between one and five stars, depending on their performances. Nine boys in the school won five stars. They were P.Adey, D.A.Cragg, G.A.R.Cormack, S.Earl, F.O.Oniya, D.N.Palmer, S.C.R.Skill, J.M.Waddell and G.R.M.White. In the school as a whole, 494 boys won awards. Paul Adey went on to participate in the National Schools' Championships at Crystal Palace. He finished third in the pole vault, after only three weeks' practice with his new fibreglass pole.

Summer Term 1971

The Sailing Club went from strength to strength with matches at Trent Lock, Welbeck Lake, Beeston Sailing Club and Worksop Lake. There was great disappointment, however, when, having ordered a film called *Sail to Win*, they settled down to view it but found that they had been sent a substitute film entitled *Modern Dam Building Techniques*.

Summer holidays 1971

The 34th Nottingham Scout Troop went to summer camp in rural Radnorshire in the depths of Wales. They enjoyed hiking, mountain walking in the Brecon Beacons, cooking on wood fires and pony trekking. The only negative moment came when the boys decided to play a football game against a team of local lads who, bearing in mind the accents of the opposition, clearly took it as more akin to an international fixture than a friendly game. Their bad language, lack of sportsmanship and dangerous play led to the match's being abandoned by the referee, Mr Phillips, with the High School winning 4-0. Later in the evening, the same group of miscreants was observed creeping towards our lads' tents but they were routed with a well-timed charge across the field.

7.30 a.m., Thursday, October 28th 1971

A group of boys, led by David Peters, and driven by Bill Neville, visited the Houses of Parliament. They were shown around by recently elected M.P. and Old Boy, Kenneth Clarke, although they were unable to visit the Members' Gallery because of lack of space, it being the day when Great Britain's entry to the Common Market was due to be debated.

The rugby season, 1971-1972

The season was notable for the outstanding captaincy of J.M.Darke, a player: "who can kick sixty yard penalties, deflate opposition with even longer punts and who is also very difficult to put on the ground. (He had) the ability to motivate a very young side". Darke's great sporting abilities had been discovered the previous season, when he had been captain of the school football team.

The football season, 1971-1972

Results included High School 10 Forest Fields 0, High School 17 Fairham 2nd XI 3, and High School 13 Bluecoat School 0. Only slightly more plausible were High School 4 Fairham 1st XI 4, and Bilborough School 2 High School 3. In the context of local schools' football in the early 1970s, the two latter results were outstanding.

Spring Term 1972

N.Lymn Rose established a record by becoming one of the youngest ever members of the British Institute of Embalmers.

The cricket season 1972

The groundsman at Valley Road, Ted Hunt, passed away suddenly. He had worked at Valley Road for twenty-four years and was "a man of keen intelligence, wide reading and remarkable perceptiveness." Traditionally, the last match of the cricket season had always been

E.Hunt's XI v. The School, and it was decided to keep this fixture as a "fitting memorial to a gentleman."

The rugby season 1972-1973

The captain of the First XV, N.E.G.Johnson, established a school record by scoring 34 tries during the course of the season. This total easily beat the record of 22 tries which Johnson himself had scored the year before. Johnson was also to score ten tries in five matches for the County Schools' 1st XV, giving an overall total of 44 scores in the season.

Christmas 1972

Mr Kirby, the school's assistant gardener, died in the City Hospital after a short illness. He had worked at the school for eight years, and was a very quiet and rather solitary man. He had no family and lived alone in Arthur Street. Every Sunday morning, he could be seen walking along Waverley Mount as he came in to stoke the school's boilers. The school was his main interest in life, and he was "a well liked person, always willing to help others".

Tuesday, February 3rd 1973

It was a cold winter's afternoon, and Martin Jones was busy on the Embankment of the River Trent, coaching not one, but two, High School rowing crews. Let him tell the story:

> "I was using the only bike available, which had faulty brakes. Whilst watching the crews, the front wheel went down the first step on the Embankment. The back wheel then followed, pushing the front wheel down the second step...and so on. Along with the bike, I went headlong into the river. I was helped out, eventually, by a passer-by but without the bike. The two crews of boys displayed a mixture of worried concern and amusement. A police launch came by, and they decided to retrieve the bike with a rope and grappling hook. After ten minutes, a crowd assembled, in eager anticipation of a corpse being dragged from the freezing waters. They dispersed quickly though, when only a decrepit bike emerged. The next day at school, of course, everybody seemed to be aware of my swim in the river."

July 1973

Dr Thimann retired after 26 years at the High School. A colourful character, to say the least, he had been Head of Modern Languages and Current Affairs, as well as a keen tennis player and gardener.

End of the Christmas Term 1973

An inventory of the Library revealed that only 19 books had been stolen during the course of the year, as compared with the 51 in 1972. The cynic might justifiably argue, however, that there were few good books left, as the missing stock was by now well over two thousand volumes.

The rugby season, 1973-1974

The First XV entered the Under 19 County Cup and reached the final after beating Arnold Hill, High Pavement and Newark Magnus. The trophy was duly won with a 9-4 defeat of Carlton-le-Willows, three penalties being scored by Roy Dexter. This year's team, coached by Tony Bird, Geri Thomas and Chalky White, was overall very successful. They won seventeen of their eighteen fixtures, losing only against old rivals Q.E.G.S., Wakefield. In addition, K.M.Joy was selected for the England Squad Trial.

Thursday evenings, Spring Term 1974

The Table Tennis Club provided *The Nottinghamian*'s greatest ever linguistic tour-de-force. Its author's identity has, unfortunately, not survived, but it is worth quoting in full:

> "Under-the-table, pimply, spongy, chopping, slicing, you've guessed, it's the T.T.Club, led by this year's "King of Ping", A.R.Hodgkins. The team has enjoyed a sizzling season in the Sixth-form centre on Thursday evenings and given itself a position in the Notts Seventh League unassailable except by those in the Eighth. But with such stars as Andy Scull, pedant of the pingers' table, Dave Palmer, 'wee Jock' Smedley, the rafters have resounded to many a ding-dong ping-pong battle against opposition drawn from all over the City. Paul Stebbings has let his hair down and helped the team out when he could; but the bastion of the side was unquestionably the captain, whose wolfish howls greeted every losing point in a tight match, a

veritable King Kong of ping-pong, enough to make any opponent drop his points. The end of the season was celebrated in the customary fashion, with a tight match accompanied by King Kong's post-ding-dong-ping-pong-sing-song."

April 1974

One of the school's great characters from the 1970s, Adrian Noskwith, won *The Nottinghamian*'s prize for the best translations into English of the witty epigrams and mottoes which used to adorn many of its articles during this period. The majority of them came from Latin authors such as Martial or Virgil and French writers such as La Fontaine or Molière.

The cricket season 1974

One of the most famous incidents in staff cricket occurred when David Matthews "courageously stopped the ball with his head". It cost him a pair of glasses, and two black eyes. Other players during the season were Paul Dawson and Brian Hughes, batsmen David Padwick and Dave Phillips, bowlers John Hayes and Marcus Coulam, and Jimmy Sadler, who in one match took four wickets in the last over, to snatch an unlikely victory. John Hayes and Allan Sparrow were the usual umpires.

Summer term 1974

Over the course of this term, members of the Sixth Form studied computer programming with Dr Hughes. The Second Year Sixth tried to master COBOL, a business orientated computer language, and the First Year Sixth worked with BASIC, FORTRAN IV, ALGOL 60 and PLAN. Even the Fifth Form were able to participate, with an exciting early computer game called POLITICS, which simulated the ever changing popularity of the political parties in the opinion polls. According to this programme, the Liberal Party were destined to form a government within ten years.

September 1974

The High School greeted its new French *assistant*, Monsieur Jean Feydel, the first ever in a long line of French native speakers, each with their own peculiarities and vulnerabilities, and nearly every one of whom has remarked, usually in early October, at the relentless ferocity of the English winter.

October 1974

So great was the impact of the new ITV series, *World at War* that the school formed a "*World at War* Society", to "illustrate the hardships and feelings of World War II and to teach the members about different aspects of the War". They held several competitions and viewed episodes of the TV programme. Most of the members were First Formers, helped by Ted Kettell.

The hockey season 1974-1975

This year the First Team finished undefeated, with twelve victories and two drawn games. The most prominent players were the team captain, M.J.Price and the other forwards, D.H.Adams, P.J.Treadgold, T.F.Husbands, A.W.Allington, J.R.Pike and C.J.Orme. The half-backs were D.R.Morris, J.H.Diack and D.A.J.Stuart. In defence were M.Chadwick and D.J.Parker, and in goal was J.V.Morrissey. Highlight of the season was a 6-1 victory over Beeston Hockey Club.

Saturday, February 15th 1975

For the first time ever in six attempts, the swimming club, directed by Allan Sparrow, recorded a victory over Bradford Grammar School, by 204 points to 187.

Two weeks before the start of the Summer Term 1975

Practice at the school cricket nets was prevented by snow and frost.

Easter Holidays 1975

The school group who visited the Loire Valley found a half buried four-inch artillery shell. Only with difficulty were they dissuaded from bringing it back to Nottingham "as a souvenir".

A warm July evening in 1975

Four Junior Plays took place. They were *Charlottes Web* performed by 1M and masterminded by Roger Stirrup, a modernised version of *The Kraken* by 2AL, aided by Graham Powell, *Dillisclondes Saga* from Chris Smith and 3BT, *The Secret Life of Walter Mitty* by 3BS and Mike Royston, and the eventual winner *Liang and the Magic Brush* from Peter Norris and 1K, a traditional Chinese folk story, specially written for this occasion.

Friday, August 1st 1975

The first Junior Adventurous Training took place at Lake Bala in Wales. It has taken place every single year since then, at the same campsite at Pentre-Piod, right at the side of the beautiful lake. The boys were all in Year 9, and the staff, under the command of Martin Jones, consisted of Marcus Coulam, Paul Dawson, Ian Driver and John Hayes. There were approximately thirty boys, and the activities consisted of hill climbing, orienteering, canoeing, rock climbing, pony trekking and mountain biking. Catering has been provided every single year by the wonderful Barker family from Derby. Originally, they used Army Issue petrol burners (nicknamed "flamethrowers"), although they have now graduated on to Calor Gas stoves. Martin Jones, the man who started it all, has written:

> "The week has been attended, and mostly enjoyed, by more than one thousand boys. More than a hundred members of staff and Old Boys have also participated. That the scheme has run successfully for so long is a source of much pleasure and pride for me personally."

And so it should be!

Early September 1975

The second French *assistant* to arrive in the school was Gilbert Millat, with perhaps the most luxuriously styled sideboards since the schoolmasters of the Victorian era. Some of his fellow teachers, however, found his radical left wing views not quite to their taste. There was much spluttering into teacups on one occasion when unsuspecting Conservatives in the staffroom innocently asked him what he would do with Ian Smith and his Rhodesian white supremacists.

Monday, September 8th 1975

Adam Thomas died after only six years' retirement. He had worked at the High School for thirty-seven years, teaching mainly History but also on occasion English, Divinity, Economics, Biology and Music. He coached cricket and was in charge of the U-15 XV. In the early part of the war Adam was one of those who had to cycle down to Valley Road to conduct lessons, part of the main school buildings having been commandeered by the Army. Later on during the war he volunteered for service in the Navy and was a radar operator in the North Atlantic and the Mediterranean. After the conflict ended, he returned to the High School where he became Head of History and eventually Second Master. His greatest feat was his history of the school which built on the strong foundations of research carried out by Sammy Corner and which was published in 1957.

The afternoon of Tuesday, September 9th 1975

The young teacher turns up for his first ever Games Day at Valley Road. He is cordially invited up to the changing room to put on his pathetically poverty stricken games kit. As he changes slowly, trying to avoid revealing the truths of his body, he looks down and sees a recently arrived Much-More-Important-Person. The latter is sitting on the bench, taking off a succession of brand new garments all immaculately clean. His jacket. His tie. His shirt. His trousers. His highly polished shoes. His brilliant white string vest shines in the sunshine. Only then does the young teacher notice his underpants. They are not the usual Y-fronts, but have long legs in them like modern cycling shorts. They too are brilliant white, clean and gleaming. And he has ironed them. Or perhaps his wife has.

Mondays at 1.10 p.m. in the Chemistry Lecture Room 1975

Although interest had not always been fanatical, the Railway Society survived to celebrate its 30th anniversary. The model railway had been restored and visits were made to the Middleton and the Keighley and Worth Valley Railways as well as a short season of foreign railway films.

Saturday, December 13th 1975

The U-12 XV contrived to draw 0-0 at Abbott Beyne School in Burton-on-Trent. That they did not win was the direct fault of the current author who at the time was in charge of this team. When we were awarded a penalty two yards from the opposition line, right in front of the posts, a couple of minutes from the end, the young man taking it, Richard Briggs, was unable to lift the ball high enough for it to go over the bar for the winning points. Had I but known the rules of Rugby Union properly, I could have shouted to the boy what to do. Do you know what I should have told him?

Every break and lunchtime, Spring Term 1976

After four years' existence, the Wargame Society now met, more or less, on every single occasion when it was possible. They needed all their spare time of course, as, deep in the cellars with over 3,000 pieces they were simultaneously re-enacting the Decline and Fall of the Roman Empire and Hitler's invasion of the Soviet Union.

One damp Wednesday in April 1976

The school's first ever Biology Field Course took place at Malham Tarn Field Centre, in Yorkshire. The bus was driven by Bill Neville, and Paul Dawson was the second member of staff. The boys studied the distribution of plants in a limestone pavement and made an auto-ecological study of the sex distribution of Dog's Mercury which is a widespread plant in this area.

The Easter Holidays 1976

Nineteen boys and three masters descended to the bottom of Mansfield Colliery, some two thousand feet below the surface. *The Nottinghamian* called the account of their day "Journey to the Centre of the Earth".

The Easter Holidays 1976

A group of some thirty students, led by David Padwick, spent a fortnight in Rodez, a town in southern France. They visited Cordes, Albi, the Gorges du Tarn and the Cévennes National Park. At a large picnic on the first Sunday, they watched a display of ancient local dances and listened to bagpipes and drums. There was an official reception at the Hôtel de Ville and, although the boys lost their basketball game, they did manage to scrape a win in both of the cricket matches.

The Easter holidays 1976

On the school trip to France, a very naughty young man indeed had decided to consume secretly a large quantity of the local red wine. Unfortunately, he decided to do this, not on his own in the hotel, but on the back seat of the coach as the group toured around the area. Around three or four in the afternoon, therefore, there came two loud cries from the back of the bus. The first was:

"Sir, Sir, I feel sick!" (**OH NO!**), followed thirty seconds later by

"Sir, Sir, I've been sick!" (**OH ******!**).

"Where have you been sick?" (**CLUTCHING AT STRAWS**).

"Sir, into a plastic bag" (**WHOOPEE!**)

"Does it have any leaks?" (**OVER PESSIMISTIC PERHAPS**)

"No, sir, it's okay" (**DOUBLE EVEN TRIPLE, WHOOPEE!**)

"Alright, bring your bag to the front of the bus, and we'll throw it out of the door as we go along". (**A PLAN, BUT NOT A VERY GOOD ONE**).

The very naughty young man indeed set off down the gangway of the coach which was now travelling at the best part of fifty miles an hour.

Two problems. The boy was still, shall we say, rather shaky on his legs, and, secondly, the bag was absolutely brimful of *a naïve domestic Burgundy without any breeding but I think you'll be amused by its presumption*.

A slight lurch by the coach, and he dropped the bag. **TSUNAMI!!!** A red foaming tidal wave washed down the middle of the coach with the very last little waves lapping gently at our feet in the front, rather like *King Canute goes to the Bargain Booze Shop*.

The end of May 1976

Jack Mells suddenly passed away. He had worked at the school from 1931-1969, mainly teaching woodwork. After his retirement, Jack had continued for many years as the school's Book Room Steward, often in dreadful conditions as the plaster collapsed off the ceiling while he worked below. Jack was: "a fine Christian gentleman who embodied the old concept of service, courtesy and sympathetic understanding toward his fellow man".

The Summer half term holidays 1976

When the French boys arrived from Rodez to spend some time in England, a very silly young man indeed decided that, during his hour in the school's swimming pool, he would dive down to the bottom and sit for as long as he could on what in an ordinary bath would have been the plughole. Then he would swim back up to the surface and, as quickly as possible, climb up to the high diving board, towering vertiginously above the water.

JUMP IN! DIVE DOWN! SIT ON THE BOTTOM!

SWIM TO THE SURFACE! CLIMB UP TO THE TOP BOARD!

JUMP IN! DIVE DOWN! SIT ON THE BOTTOM!

SWIM TO THE SURFACE! CLIMB UP TO THE TOP BOARD!

REPEAT UNTIL YOU COLLAPSE IN A HEAP

His rather strange illness was subsequently diagnosed by the staff of the newly-built Queen's Medical Centre as certainly their first ever case of The Bends, if not the only case ever in Nottingham.

August 1976

The announcement of the results of recent public exams showed that T.Pike and S.Hawkins had become the school's first ever pupils to gain qualifications in the field of computing. Both candidates got Grade As at Computer Science A-Level, although most of their studies had to be carried out at a nearby College of Further Education. Other boys continued to work away at the computer languages of the day, including IND, CALCOMP and FORTRAN.

The end of August 1976

The school caretaker, Eric Oldham, collapsed and died as he walked round locking up the gates of the school, one sunny Saturday evening. He was "one of the school's finest servants and a warm hearted friend".

A forgotten day in September, around 1976 perhaps

At a recent reunion, Ian Jallands told me how I selected players for the Under-12 rugby team. Apparently, I walked out onto the pitch with a great big bag of rugby balls and just kicked one high into the air. A little boy ran after it and caught it cleanly without any problems. I shouted to him and then kicked a second ball as high as I could into the early autumn sky. Again he ran after it, kept his eye on the ball and caught it cleanly a second time. I shouted that the third ball was to be launched. I kicked it high into the sky. For the third time he caught it without any problems. "Right!", I said, "You're the full back! Now for the other fourteen!" A rough-and-ready method, perhaps, but Ian Jallands was to play full back throughout his career at the High School, finally winning his full Rugby Colours as a regular member of the 1st XV.

The rugby season 1976-1977

The Under-12 rugby team completed a memorable season when they won every single fixture and conceded only one try, in the last game against Newark Magnus. The team was captained by Richard Shotton and its most prominent members were Lawrence Bird, James Fawcett, Ian Gates, Tim Jackman, James Noonan, Murray Simpson, Peter Ward and Nick White. They finished the season by winning the City Schools' Rugby Sevens competition, scoring 118 points without reply.

1977-1992

The Dame Agnes Mellers' Lads' Club Charity, formed in 1912 under the ægis of Johnny Dixon, began to be used to help specific individuals rather than just to run a club. During the fifteen years under the new system, recipients included Darren, a boy of fourteen with cerebral palsy, who received a computer which allowed him to learn to write and then to gain several passes at GCSE. He went on to FE College and in his letter of thanks, he said "You have changed my whole life."

The Easter holidays 1977

As a mark of their esteem, the teachers of the French secondary school with which we were twinned presented David Padwick with a typical product of the region, an enormous Roquefort cheese. Keen to take it back to England intact he carefully wrapped it in several layers of towels, padding and various pieces of cloth and placed it almost reverentially in the very middle of all his clothes, packed carefully around it in his suitcase. **(A PLAN, BUT NOT A VERY GOOD ONE)**.

"The best-laid schemes o' mice an' men, Gang aft agley", as the poet says. It was a hot Easter. The coach had a rear engine. It was the best part of a 350 mile journey. The coach boot was next to the engine. Work it out for yourselves.

Summer Term 1977

In tennis the School First VI were very successful, reaching the east of England Area Final where they lost narrowly to Westcliffe High School.

Wednesday, May 18th 1977

Martin Jones continues his one man war with the vehicles the school has asked him to use:

> "John Hayes drove the School Coach for the Duke of Edinburgh expedition. Approaching the camp site at Wetton, he changed gear, and the gear stick snapped off at the base. We managed to get the boys to push the coach into a layby and get a Skill's coach to take us back to Nottingham. The following day, Marcus Coulam and I abandoned our classes, left school and travelled back to Dovedale, where the gear stick was to be welded back into place by the local blacksmith. Unfortunately, the two teachers provided the blacksmith with the wrong location, and the gear stick was therefore welded into the wrong place. The next step was to saw through it with a hacksaw, and then weld it for a second time, in the correct place. After this, Martin drove back to school with no further problems."

The cricket season 1977

There was a report of staff cricket in *The Nottinghamian* which was, many years later, to be requoted by William Ruff in his *From the Archives* section of the school magazine. It told of Tony Slack, "our benevolent dictator", Dave Phillips who "wields the straightest golf club in the business", Phil Eastwood, "for whose particular torture the LBW rule was invented", Clem Lee, "whose pectorals imitate the motion of the sea as he runs up to bowl". The regular umpires this season were Allan Sparrow and John Knifton, although the latter did play in one game, "and took an impossible catch to win the game". The more often I read that, the less possible it seems.

The summer holidays 1977

The 34th Nottingham Scout Group went to Chipchase Castle on the banks of the River Tyne. From here they visited Hadrian's Wall as well as swimming, fishing, studying the wildlife and, most romantic of all perhaps, digging the latrines for the Girl Guides in the field next door.

September 1977

Work started on the new Preparatory School buildings in Waverley Mount, after the demolition of a number of large Victorian houses. The one nearest to the school had been used as a Sixth Form Centre of sorts and for the teaching of small groups of sixth formers. On the wall of the Victorian family's parlour there was a full size, full colour rendition of Adam West and Burt Ward as Batman and Robin. It was a really great pity that there was no means of preserving it or that nobody even thought of trying to do so.

December 1977

The school play was *Macbeth*. The most famous performer, however, was not an actor or an actress but the prompter, who was a young lady from the Girls' School, Julie Pike. In recent years, she has grown to fame as Julie Myerson, the best-selling novelist.

The late 1970s

This period marked the final demise of the school's own "coach". It was an aging vehicle purchased from a local bus firm, Camm's, and therefore qualified as a "Camm's Collapsible", to use the expression current at the time in Nottingham. It was invariably parked in the old Green Shed, a vast cavern of a building which stood on the site of the present Design Technology block. Around six members of staff were quickly given the training needed to drive a PSV, including Martin Jones, who can now take up the tale:

> "Every time the bus was started, the Green Shed filled with vile-smelling, black exhaust fumes, which quickly flushed out all the naughty boys who were lurking in there when they should not have been. The road worthiness of that "coach" was highly questionable."

A forgotten, sunny late June in the late 1970s

The school examinations were over. So too were most public exams. Boys' reports were all written. Only the beautiful sunny weather and the blue skies remained to be enjoyed, before the end of the school year, and the beginning of the school holidays. What better way to spend a leisurely lunch hour, therefore, than to walk across to the Arboretum Pub for one of their legendary ham cobs and a pint of their *Ice Cold in Alex* lager? Tony Slack and myself, and a good few others whose names now escape me, had already finished off our food and our first pint. We leaned back comfortably in our chairs, our second pints ready, but untouched as yet on the table in front of us. Suddenly a Sixth Former burst in. It was Adrian Noskwith. He stepped forward with perfect poise, like Alfred the butler in Batman. He spoke quietly and clearly to me: "Mr Powell's compliments, but you should be invigilating an A-Level exam. Greek Paper IV." There was a laugh went up. In later years, young Adrian, of course, was to achieve eminence as one of the school's highest ranking military officers ever, when the glorious armed forces of Bolivia made him a Colonel in their Air Force.

The day the bus died, Wednesday, June 14th 1978

Martin Jones had a brilliant idea for a new initiative:

> "A day out in Derbyshire for the staff and their families! The coach, with its welded gear stick, and by now completely tried and tested, was completely full. Passengers included Headmaster Dennis Witcombe and his wife, Pat, with a large number of ordinary teachers. Just before Junction 28 of the M1, however, slightly after the crossing over into Derbyshire, the coach ground to a halt. There were vast volumes of smoke and black fumes. We immediately checked the oil. There wasn't any. The police had us all wait on the grass beside the motorway until, not for the first time, a Skill's coach came to take us all back to Nottingham, after a wait of a mere two hours. A few months later the school received its first minibus, and a new era began.

The evening of Wednesday, June 21st 1978

The staff cricket team had its two usual umpires, the young apprentice John Knifton, and the much more experienced Allan Sparrow. Whereas the first named umpire lived in permanent dread of having to make a decision which would upset his elders and betters by sending them back to the pavilion 96 runs short of their century, the senior partner, true to his own wonderfully analytical character, had no such scruples. This particular day in the very first over of the game, the opposition's opening bowler managed to trap, plumb in front of the wicket, with his score still reminiscent of a certain strain of wildfowl, a very important person indeed. Standing at square leg, the young rookie thanked the cricketing gods that he was not standing at the bowler's end. The shriek of "howzat" died away in the quietness of the evening. Umpire Sparrow waited for a moment. Then he raised the dreaded digit to the skies. The sad trudge back to the pavilion. That was the bravest thing I have ever seen in the history of sport.

July 1978

Phoenix, the school's magazine of imaginative writing and drawing, which was edited by David Matthews with artwork assistance from Terry Satterford, appeared for the twelfth consecutive year.

July 1978

The Reverend Charles "Charlie" Stephens retired after thirty-three years at the High School. He had taught not just Geography but also Astronomy, Divinity, Mathematics, Modern Languages and Photography and he was an enthusiastic leader of the School Photographic Society. Always a very generous Christian gentleman, as a parting gift, he presented the school with a large edition of the Revised Standard Bible for use in the Assembly Hall.

September 1978

The school was visited by a helicopter which landed in the main playground and took Dr Witcombe on a short flight around the area.

The rugby season 1978-1979

The U-12 XV had a successful season under the leadership of Bob Howard and John Knifton. Among the team's members was Edward Balls, a fierce tackling and wholehearted player, who was later to play a large part in running the British economy during the administration of Tony Blair's "New Labour" government.

Tuesday, October 10th 1978

Martin Jones continues his reminiscences about the "School Coach":

> "Having just driven the coach full of boys down the 1:6 gradient of Mam Tor in Derbyshire, I realised, at the very bottom, that the brakes had now stopped working. Fairly worried, to put it mildly, we managed to negotiate a turn, demolish a wall and then proceed, thankfully at a walking pace, into the Edale Car Park. As we found out later, a brake pipe had fractured, and all the fluid had emptied. We returned to Nottingham by train."

November 1978

The staff put on *Joseph and the Amazing Technicolor Dreamcoat*. Let the star of the show, Les Wilkinson, tell the tale:

"The production was Roger Stirrup's idea. He and Stephen Fairlie had discussed the project before I arrived at the school in September 1977, but I was a willing recruit to the enterprise. I suppose we started with a nucleus of interested parties – mostly the younger teachers – whilst the rest of the staff room remained aloof and perhaps slightly cynical of the whole thing. We sang through the numbers during the first half of the autumn term, then cast the show and began rehearsing in some earnest in November. By Christmas, we had something ragged to show for our efforts, at which point David Matthews came on board and used his directorial skills to give the show a lot more polish. Then a strange thing happened over the course of the Spring Term: Joseph fever grabbed the school. Those teachers not already involved were eager to do anything to be part of the show – even become the back end of a camel. By now, almost everyone was involved, from the oldest member of staff, Norman Thompson (Jacob) to the most junior (probably me). Marcus Coulam built a stage big enough to take all the singers and dancers. Boys and parents were clamouring for tickets; excitement was rising. In the end, the demand was so great that we had to put on five performances, with two on the Saturday. Those who couldn't get tickets were invited to the dress rehearsal. We made a very good profit on sales, which all went to charity. And the first night arrived: Tony Slack and John Knifton on lights, Simon Jenkins on sound, Dennis Witcombe in the wings ready to be the Voice of God, the first notes of the overture... It didn't take long for us to realise we had a great show on our hands (though I say it myself). Phil Pallant astounded as Pharaoh – but had to hobble through the last few performances having twisted an ankle at Prep Games on the Friday afternoon. Sandy Powell turned in a wonderful cameo turn as Potiphar, complete with Havana cigar and fez (supplied, appropriately enough, by Ian Parker). Norman Thompson did his bit as Jacob. Why do I think Joseph was so important? To begin with, it gave a lot of people in the audience a lot of pleasure. The show gave all the boys who saw it something to talk about until the end of term; they were astounded to see so many of their teachers in a different light, and to realise that they were, in varying degrees, quite talented individuals. Perhaps most importantly, it worked wonders for staff morale. I don't think the staff has ever been so united as they were during the final stages of Joseph; the sense of camaraderie was overwhelming. I, and many others, made friends for life in that term – and all the time, the teaching went on, without a falter. By the end of term, we were exhausted – but it had been worth it. Ask anyone who was there."

November 1978

Harry Latchman moved into the pavilion accommodation at Valley Road. An ex-Middlesex and Nottinghamshire county cricketer, he was to be heavily involved in the coaching of school cricket.

November 1978

The Nottinghamian carried what must surely remain its most ill-placed, and bizarre of advertisements. It was for a corsetry company in Bridlesmith Gate, Chapel Bar and King's Walk. They were called "Phone-a-Bra" and promised that: "the garment (subject to availability) will be reserved for eight days pending payment. Choose from our extensive range of the best known British, Continental and American bras. Free fitting Service at all Branches by experienced Fitters." It remains unrecorded just how much interest this advertisement provoked among the boys of the school, or indeed, just how much they knew about British, Continental or American bras. Presumably, though, this was a field in which many of them may well have been very keen to learn, and the occupation of bra-fitter would no doubt have been a dream job.

Sunday, February 18th 1979

In chess, Graham Waddingham, who had already represented Great Britain at U-13 level, achieved the magnificent feat of beating Soviet Grandmaster A.Kotov who was, admittedly, playing eleven other English boys at the same time.

Spring Term 1979

The winner of the Junior Verse Speaking Competition was Edward Davey, later to find fame initially as a Liberal Member of Parliament for Kingston and Surbiton and then as the Party Spokesman on Economics. Eventually Edward was to achieve high status as a member of the Privy Council and Secretary of State for the Department of Energy and Climate Change in the Coalition Government led by David Cameron.

The cricket season 1979

Staff cricket continued on apace, among its stars such sporting luminaries as Chris Chittenden, Paul Dawson, Bob Dickason, Claude Dupuy, Phil Eastwood, Steven Fairlie, Simon Jenkins, Dave Phillips, Graham Powell, Tony Slack, Chris Smith, Roger Stirrup and Norman Thompson. Such was the fame of the team that a member of staff appointed for the following Christmas Term actually came along to play in a number of fixtures. This was Ray Moore, who at the time sported a fashionable Afro hairdo, unencumbered by any such refinement as a protective helmet. On one occasion Ray was facing an extremely wild fast bowler, whose main interest in life seemed to be scaring the living daylights out of opposing batsmen with bouncer after bouncer. After a series of whistlingly fast deliveries he finished his over with a very quick, lifting ball, which actually went through Ray's hair. The moment when Ray advanced down the wicket, shouting loudly, and waving a menacing cricket bat was the closest the staff team ever came to an actual punch-up.

A few weeks later in the cricket season 1979

Umpiring a staff team fixture, I was at the bowler's end for the very first ball of the match. It was bowled by a tall young man who seemed strangely familiar. Was he possibly the "extremely wild fast bowler" of previous fame, returned to haunt us all? To tell the truth, I can no longer remember, but he was certainly quick. The first ball thwacked hard against the pads of the staff team's finest batsman. As far as I could see, plumb LBW. Thank God, there was no appeal. That might have meant a bat through the window in the changing room and a thousand thousand apologies from myself. The second ball, just the same. Third ball, again, thwack!! Against those pads. The batsman must have been out three or four times in just five balls. What on earth was happening? Why didn't he appeal? The truth slowly emerged, as the bowling became gradually wilder and wilder. He didn't want to dismiss the batsmen. He wanted to injure them. He wanted to knock a few toffs' blocks off, while the revolutionary zeal still ran bright red through his veins.

I forget the name of the opposition, but if it were Havana-on-Trent High School, then this was surely the Ché Guevara of their team. If it were Moscow College, this was the Vladimir Lenin of their bowling attack. Thank goodness after three or four overs his revolutionary zeal ran out of steam before anybody was injured and we all went down to the Fox for a pint of lager and a ham cob.

July 1979

After fifty-seven years since its foundation in 1922, the School Boat Club finally came to an end. Despite gallant attempts by Martin Jones to keep it afloat, the dearth of any members of staff with sufficient interest in the sport led to its eventual demise. Prominent among the masters in the recent past history of the club had been "Noddy" Aspin, Cecil Dick, Dick Elliott, Bob Horner, Geoff Hunt, Peter Horrill, Alan Locke and Ted Kettell, many of them assisted by those stalwarts from before the war, Messrs M.J.Brodrick and J.F.Newbound.

The late 1970s

According to an ex-member of the Fifth Form, he could remember lessons with a French teacher who always taught his lessons wearing his football scarf, "to the delight of his pupils and to the horror of the senior members of staff".

The late 1970s or early 1980s

Walking around the streets outside the school many boys and members of staff were familiar with a rather gaunt young man who usually wore a heavy overcoat and who often had a dog with him. He was bearded with very long and wispy brown hair. What the boys and members of staff did not know was that this rather striking individual was actually the world famous climber and mountaineer, Doug Scott, who lived, as far as I remember, in Waverley Street. There was at least one, no doubt, apocryphal, story that he had once been apprehended by the local police as he climbed a high vertical wall of sandstone blocks down near the bowling greens on the Forest. Not knowing who he was the police had been reluctant to disturb him in case he was startled and fell off to his death. Probably not a true story, but it ought to be.

Geography Room B, 1.10 p.m., Friday lunchtimes 1980-1981

The Stamp Club continued to meet. They received a valuable impetus from an Old Boy, Harold Barker, who, after a lifetime as an engineer travelling the world, left his stamp collection to the club, who were then able to use it to initiate much more swapping than was usually possible.

Chapter 16: Out with the Old, In with the New: The Golden Age of Teachers

The early 1980s

Josef Goebbels, the Führer's Minister of Propaganda, always insisted that the bigger the lie, the more likely the public are to believe it. Boys, of course, are even more gullible. As a recent experiment, I remember telling a Year 9 class that my hobby was handicrafts with particular emphasis, because of my background in the Scout movement, on using string and rope to secure objects effectively. Given my huge interest in local history therefore, I would soon be bringing out a short book entitled *Knots in Notts*. They eventually realised that I was lying although I will always believe that I might well have sold a few advance copies.

On the other hand, no member of the Games staff has ever worn a toupée. This was a foul rumour started originally by Bob Howard and myself. I was highly gratified on one occasion, though, to see two boys leaning over a stairwell, peering intently at the top of the said member of staff's head, some fifteen years after the rumour was started. There is no truth either, in another well-known tale. No teacher in the High School has ever been a wrestler and neither has any member of staff ever had to give up the wrestling ring out of remorse because he accidentally killed an opponent during a wrestling bout. Similarly, no member of staff has ever been so clumsy that he was capable of dropping a calculator and in the same fluid movement smashing it to smithereens by treading on it. This story does have a grain of truth behind it, however, in that it is on record that, on one occasion, Chris Mann dropped a calculator which his colleague Brian Hughes was showing to him and being rather flimsy, it broke as it hit the floor. Chris' finest triumph, however, was as a member of the group of young teachers who would come together to help each other move house when the need arose. On one unforgettable occasion Bob Howard, who possessed a handsome MFI wardrobe, was desperately upset when Chris managed to walk through it, totally demolishing the, admittedly, rather delicate structure, rather like Godzilla on a walking holiday around Tokyo.

Tuesday, January 1st 1980

An amazing 250 boys left in three coaches to go to Briançon and Cesena on the school ski trip. The master in charge was Roger Stirrup under whose leadership the boys managed to avoid any serious injuries. Indeed, by the time *The Nottinghamian* went to press, 126 boys had already signed up for the following year's trip.

Spring Term 1980

The National Poetry Society sent two famous poets to visit the school. They were Geoffrey Adkins and Yann Lovelock. Geoffrey Adkins asked one of the boys what it was like to be fourteen. The young man replied that it was "like being stuck in the park railings, with somebody kicking your backside."

September 1980

The school purchased its first Apple computer. It was an Apple II Europlus microcomputer which had 48K bytes of RAM and contained the provision for BASIC in its ROM. The school also purchased two disk-drive units, an Anadex printer, and a Visual Display Unit, which enabled the operator to see "almost immediately" the progress of his labours. Games on the computer included *Mastermind, Bridge, Othello, Space Invaders*, and a programme devised by Nick Hammond to solve the Rubik Cube although this took place in considerably less time than Nick's own record of 37 seconds.

The rugby season 1980-1881

The U-14 XV completed an outstanding season, with twenty-four victories and just a single defeat. They scored nearly six hundred points and won the County Cup with a victory by 16-7 over Arnold Hill. Coached by Chris Mann and Bob Howard, the team's outstanding players included the captain Andrew Bailey, Gareth Collins, and future Labour Government economist, Eddie Balls.

July 1980

Norman Thompson, who, because of his initials, was universally known as "Stan", finally retired. He had taught Economics to hundreds of boys including Ken Clarke, the future Chancellor of the Exchequer. Much of his spare time he had devoted to the Venture Scouts. Indeed, on many occasions, Norman was fit enough even in his later years to walk many a younger man off his feet.

Thursday, December 18th 1980

The Joint Community Service Group held their annual Christmas Party for local old age pensioners. After a pantomime organised by Simon Stebbings, everbody enjoyed a traditional Christmas dinner. They all then received a food parcel, donated by the boys of the school.

Wednesday, January 21st 1981

On a dull, dreary, drizzly day in winter, the author stood with the team coach, Tony Slack, watching the First XI play a well contested match against High Pavement 2nd XI. We were on the Forest, at the side of a pitch which has now been partly covered by the all-weather facilities. Suddenly, Norman Garden, his sleeves rolled up in determined fashion, won the ball with a strong, vigorous tackle at the edge of his own penalty area. He came out with the ball at his feet, took a few paces forward, then looked up, and sent a curving, arcing pass out to Bert Crisp on the left wing. Bert trapped the ball, then ran forward ten yards or so, and looked across at the attacking possibilities.

Five yards outside the penalty area stood Chris Ingle, the team's centre forward in his usual pose, apparently disinterested, lacking commitment, without any apparent desire for physical involvement, a young man who only came alive when he saw the whites of an opposing goalkeeper's eyes. Chris began to move, slowly but purposefully accelerating from his standing start as he crossed the white line of the penalty area. Bert Crisp instinctively knew what to do. He clipped in a wickedly curving centre, about four or five feet above the ground. It was timed to arrive at the penalty spot at exactly the same time as the deadly young centre forward. Chris Ingle, as the ball flew in front of him, launched himself full length over the cloying mud.

He met the ball hard with his forehead, catching it a blow which rocketed it towards the top corner of the net. "Goal!!" we teachers both yelled in our minds. But it was not quite over. The opposing goalkeeper soared backwards and with a despairing left hand just managed to flick out at the ball. He diverted it upwards, and it flew onto the crossbar and behind for a corner. Chris Ingle got up and wiped the mud from his hands down the front of his white shirt. Tony Slack turned to me and said, "You wouldn't see anything better than that in the First Division." And he was right.

Spring Term 1981

For the first time ever the High School entered the Schools' Challenge General Knowledge competition. They began by beating Lilley and Stone School from Newark-on-Trent, although details of their subsequent fate have not survived. The team was usually drawn from J.Hicks, I.Allen, D.Beech, N.McLachlan, R.Nolan, A.Woodcock, S.Osborne and J.Siegel.

Late March 1981

The school's footballers achieved their only ever trophy by winning the Nottinghamshire Schools' Football Association Seven-a-Side competition. In their initial group they won two and lost one of their initial games and qualified for the next stage of the competition as the best losers. In the semi-final they beat Worksop A by 1-0, thereby reaching the competition final against Worksop B, a team who had already beaten them in the group stages. In this last game the score was 0-0 at full time and extra time had to be played. The score remained goalless at the end of extra time and penalty kicks were taken. Five were scored by each side before Worksop missed. The High School's winning penalty was scored by Norman Garden, whose effort went into the top corner, hitting both the bar and the post. The team was coached by Tony Slack and consisted of Raich Growdridge as captain, Tim Little, Neil McLachlan, Richard Mousley, Chris Peers, John Ellis, Simon Derrick, Chris Ingle and Norman Garden. Raich Growdridge was eventually to appear as a triallist with Derby County's 'A' Team.

April 1981

The school play was *A Servant of Two Masters* directed by Les Wilkinson. The star of the show was Paul Carter as the Servant but he was ably assisted by Erica Worth as Smeraldina, Steve Handley as Signor Pantaleone and Chris Cook as Doctor Lombardi. This was the first occasion that close circuit television had been used by the stage staff as, thanks to the architectural talents of those who built the Founder Hall, the stage was not directly viewable from their main control room.

Saturday, April 25th 1981

Paul Balen became the first Old Nottinghamian to marry a former pupil of Trent College. His wife, Helen Phillips, had been one of the first three girls to enter the college.

Monday, May 11th- Friday, May 16th 1981

During Christian Aid Week the Poverty Action Committee led by Stephen Field and Ruth Horsley raised £55 from the school.

June 1981

Murray Simpson (100 metres) and Nick White (pole vault) were both selected to compete in the National Schools' Athletics Championships at Yeovil. Twenty-four other members of the school had already represented Nottinghamshire at inter-county level.

July 1981

Bill Neville retired after more than thirty years at the High School. As well as teaching Biology, he had been heavily involved both with the C.C.F. and with a succession of school buses and lorries. In addition, Bill was the first person to introduce photocopiers to the school.

July 1981

Andrew McMurchy retired as Head of German. "A true character, universally liked", he had set up the school's first Language Laboratory and was the pioneer who evolved the pedagogical maxim that "If I can teach in my sleep, then you can learn in yours." In actual fact, in his role as Form Master of 6 Modern Languages, Andrew McMurchy had inspired enormous loyalty among his pupils who were deeply respectful of his warm eccentricity. They wore their own tie which they had designed and had had manufactured themselves. They were proud to make themselves separate from the rest of the Sixth Form in this way. Never the best at remembering who people were, Andrew McMurchy had spent several years having to call the young Gaynor Knifton "Toots" as he could never remember her name.

July 1981

At Bisley in the Ashburton Vince Grealy scored sixty-nine points out of a maximum of seventy, thereby taking first place in the competition, winning a School's Hundred Badge, and the C.C.R.S. Special Prize. This was the best performance ever by a pupil of the school.

Monday, October 19th 1981

Harold Binks passed away peacefully at the age of nearly ninety. Born on April 16th 1891, he had entered the school on March 12 1900 at the age of eight. His father was Charles Binks, a cycle manufacturer of 36, Zulla Road. Harold left the school at the end of the Summer Term, in July 1906. His reminiscences had already been published in *The Nottinghamian* in April 1935. At the end, he had written:

> "Should you be curious to know what I used to look like, just look at a 1st form Group of about 1901 hanging in the corridor leading to Nipper Ryles' room and in the front row in the right hand corner, there is a small boy twiddling with his watch chain. One day I pointed it out to my son Peter and he grinned."

At the time of writing, that photograph of the First Form still exists in the School Archives. It is still easy to find Harold Binks the boy, years after Harold Binks, the old man, has passed into history.

The rugby season 1981-1982

The U-15 XV coached by Messrs Mann and Holding won fourteen of its fifteen games including a 50-0 thrashing of Newark Magnus and a 42-0 defeat of Oakham.

Sports Day 1982

On an overcast and occasionally rainy day Peter Boot won the Long Jump, Triple Jump, 800 metres and 1500 metres. He set new records in the Long Jump and 1500 metres. For the first time with a new system of entry, more than half the school now competed in at least one event on Sports Day.

Friday, June 11th-Tuesday, June 15th 1982

The Community Service Group took twenty-five deprived children from the centre of Nottingham to Castleton in Derbyshire accompanied by Ian Driver and Stephen Field:

> "The children arrived at the centre in Castleton at about 6 p.m. on Friday, and by 4 a.m., they were all finally in bed. After a

refreshing three hours' sleep, the children were all awake, and after breakfast they began to explore the surrounding area with great interest. It was not until this point that we realised how few of the children had ever seen the countryside before, let alone stayed in it."

Friday, July 7th 1982

A chess team consisting of Richard Billington, Derek Blecher, Chris Dunworth, Jonathan Eastwood, Simon Eastwood, Dominic Oakes and Graham Waddingham lost to St Paul's School in the final of *The Times* National Schools' Chess Championships by the narrowest possible margin.

The early or mid-1980s

It is often supposed that in a building as old as the present High School there really ought to be a school ghost. Ray Eastwood, the school caretaker, once told me this story:

> "One year, a small number of boys were expelled from the school because of their bad behaviour. They made threats that they would return, and either vandalise, or even set fire to the school. Because of this, Tony Hatcher and myself were asked to sleep in the school to forestall any problems. In actual fact, we borrowed an Alsatian dog from a security firm that I had connections with, and all three of us moved with our camp beds into one of the rooms under Reception, on the ground floor. One morning, around 6.15 a.m., Tony and myself were sitting up in our beds having a cup of tea and a cigarette, when we clearly heard footsteps in the corridor above. They seemed to start near the staffroom, and then proceed around the corner, past the staff toilets, and along the corridor towards the offices. We both of us thought that this was the noise of somebody who had broken into the school, and rushed out of our temporary accommodation. We grabbed the dog, and threw him up the stairs to pursue the burglars. He wanted none of it, and slunk off back into the room, his tail between his legs. We ourselves went on, and rushed up the stairs and into the area near Reception. We could find absolutely nobody. We explored all around. Every window was secure. All the doors that should have been

locked were locked. There was no explanation of what we had heard. There was certainly nobody there."

In actual fact, Ray did offer me an explanation. He thought that the footsteps that both Ray and he had heard were those of Eric Oldham, a caretaker who had worked at the High School until some eight or ten or so years before. After many years of faithful service, poor Eric had collapsed and died as he locked up the school, one sunny Saturday evening at the end of August in 1976. When he unlocked the various rooms inside the school every morning, Eric always followed the same route, and he would have been walking along the same corridors, in the same direction as the mysterious footsteps, at around the same early hour of the morning. Perhaps it was him, still reluctant to pass the school into anyone else's care.

Saturday, July 15th 1982

The Captain of the 1st XI, Russell Poole, scored 113 against Edinburgh Academy. This particular cricket team was extremely talented and contained many fine individuals such as Robert Elgie, Norman Garden, Duncan James, James Morris, Richard Mousley, Robert Rhodes, Richard Sadler, and the explosive Richard Briggs, a young batsman whom many had likened to a teenage Ian Botham.

The rugby season 1982-1983

The U-14 XV, coached by Bob Howard and Ron Gilbert, won all twenty of their matches scoring 952 points and conceding just 61. In later years, Ron was to have similar success when he twinned up with Chris Mann as his partner. For some unknown reason, the players always nicknamed the pair of them "Tweedledum" and "Tweedledee".

The chess season 1982-1983

This was the most successful season to date for school chess. Only the U-15 B team lost any match whatsoever and the A Team won all of its fixtures by the maximum score of 6-0. In the zonal matches in The Times British Schools' Tournament, all of the fixtures including the final against Arnold Hill, were won by the same score.

November 1982

Mark Tedds received his Queen's Scout Award from the City Commissioner, Mr P.Mason.

The early 1980s

It is the era of Ronald Reagan, a renewed Cold War and nuclear arsenals. Tony Slack asks his Second Year Sixth Chemistry set what they would do if they had ten minutes left before nuclear annihilation. Many and varied are the suggestions made. Somebody then says that the class swot would just do his Physics homework. They all laugh uproariously. "No, I wouldn't," says the class swot. "Why not?" they all ask. "Because I've already done my Physics homework." he replies.

January or February 1983

It was a dreary, grey winter's morning and a General Studies lesson, possibly of Russian Studies. I was at the front of the class, pontificating away, and behind the ten or so attentive listeners was the pile of their heavy winter coats which they had all been wearing because of the extreme cold and which they had piled up together on the empty desks. All of a sudden after some ten or fifteen minutes of the lesson, there was a moaning at the back of the room and as I stepped forward tentatively to investigate, a large corpulent figure, groaning and swathed in what appeared to be a fur coat of some kind, emerged slowly and noisily from the pile of coats, like a bear leaving its den when spring has appeared. It was a very silly Sixth Former, indeed, Marcus Smith, to be absolutely precise. No doubt he immediately regretted the very, very silly prank he had thought up. Although he did repeat it a few weeks later on a Field Trip to Slapton in Devon.

Wednesday, February 16th 1983

In football, the Second XI once lost a game in which a teenage girl played for the opposition. Today, we reached a new low point when we lost 2-3 against Broadgate School, who fielded an 11-year old in goal. This season, the team's players were bolstered by the presence of an apprentice referee, Royston Masters, who explained to us in enormous detail many hitherto unsuspected rules.

Sunday, March 13th 1983

Gareth Collins appeared as a hooker in the England U-16 team against Holland at Hilversum. He was to go on to play international rugby on two further occasions, namely against Wales at Bristol, and against Portugal at Lisbon, both matches taking place in April of this same year.

Friday, June 18th 1983

Although aged only fourteen, Mark Saxelby took five wickets for ten runs, playing for the First XI against Ratcliffe College. Mark was later to play county cricket for both Nottinghamshire and Durham. On one occasion, he was a member of the unfortunate fielding side when Brian Lara scored a record 501 not out for Warwickshire against Durham.

July 1983

Ted Kettell retired after twenty-three years. He had taught at various times Geography, Maths, English, Drama, Scripture, Politics and Constitutional History and was much involved in school rowing and the newly formed Sixth Form Centre. Always innovative he introduced weight training to the school and inaugurated Form 6G, which taught Economics, Politics and Law to boys who had not been particularly academic at O-Level and who would probably go on to train for qualifications in banking or business.

July 1983

Sandy Powell retired after some thirty-four years at the High School. He had been, at various times, a Form Master, Tutor, House Master and Senior Master as well as the master in charge of Cross Country, Athletics, and the Valley Road Playing Fields. Sandy would long be famed for his commanding presence as Official Starter on Sports Day, when so often, after a long dramatic build-up, the gun would fail to fire. He was a: "combination of strict discipline with an impish sense of humour: to phone Common Room and be greeted with the cheerful reply of 'Chinese laundry at your service' or to find a curious figure parading down the corridor and discover it was the Senior Master wearing a long blond wig were experiences. He was our good friend and most respected colleague. For years in his French classes, boys would wait with eager anticipation to reach the chapter in their textbook which included the verb "haïr"." During the Second World War Sandy had been a pilot with Coastal Command and had flown the enormous Short

Sunderland flying boats. An active participant in the Battle of the Atlantic, it had been on a routine patrol that one of Sandy's friends and colleagues had refound the Bismarck after initial contact had been temporarily lost. Sandy also visited West Africa during the war years and when the British moved into Dakar in Vichy Senegal he had seen one of the enormous Dornier Do-X flying boats with its ten engines. A German aircraft, it had been lent to the French by the Luftwaffe.

The Senior School football season, 1983-1984

The Nottinghamian carried its usual collection of witticisms in the football report. One player, Duncan Murray was likened to "a camel when in full flight". The team were then allowed to provide their own evaluations of the season. They included:

> "most of all, football is different."

> "a minority sport, and that's why I enjoy it."

> "the only honest thing on my UCCA form."

> "the only viable alternative to gangland warfare."

> "watching Mr Knifton play makes me feel fit."

> "well worth waiting for."

The first day of the football season, 1983-1984

As I had just returned from a school trip to West Germany, the First XI Captain, Rick Stubley, was able to wear the blue, black and white elasticated Captain's armband which I had purchased there. Rick was the first school team captain to have an armband and was so pleased that he mentioned it specifically in his report in *The Nottinghamian*.

December 1983

Sixth Former Richard May won the strings section of the BBC's *Young Musician of the Year* competition. Richard was an enthusiastic participant in school music who gave ungrudgingly of his time to many different musical groups and recitals as well as always being ready to play in the annual Bridge Cup competition and earn valuable points for his house.

Tuesday, February 14th 1984

I asked to see the notes which one of my tutees had written in a Second Year Sixth lesson. They extended over almost three pages, and they read...."blah-blah-blah-blah-blah-blah-blah-blah-blah-blah-blah-blah-blah-blah-blah-blah-blah-blah-blah-blah-blah-blah-blah-blah-blah-blah-blah-blah-blah-blah-blah-blah-blah-blah-blah-blah-blah-blah-blah-blah-blah-blah-blah-blah-blah-blah-blah-blah-blah-blah-blah-blah-blah-blah-blah-blah-blah-blah..."

Friday, March 2nd 1984

The Simon Djanogly Science Building was officially opened by Prince Philip, the Duke of Edinburgh. Earlier in the day, the Prince had visited the Central Television studios and then a local brewery, although committed Republicans were encouraged by the heavy snow falls which preceded his imminent arrival at the High School. Escorted by Dr Witcombe, he visited various laboratories in the new block and met a number of dignitaries including the Deputy Headmaster, the Senior Master, the Bursar, the Headmaster of the Prep and the four Housemasters. Not surprisingly perhaps, he was particularly interested in the efforts of Messrs Driver, Jones, Nicolle and Thomas with the activities of the school's Duke of Edinburgh scheme. As a souvenir of the first ever royal visit in so many centuries of the school's history, he was presented by the School Captain, Edward Davey, with a record of the boys' work for the Duke of Edinburgh scheme, bound in a sumptuous leather cover.

Wednesday, March 14th 1984

David Gardiner played for the England U-16 XV against Holland at Ipswich. He was to make a second appearance against Portugal at Twickenham on April 4th. Although he played as a fullback for the First XV, in these particular games David played as a centre, the same position which he had already occupied for both Nottinghamshire and the East Midlands.

Thursday, July 12th 1984

The Under 14 cricket team coached by Tim Dibdin and Paul Morris played in the County Cup Final against Colonel Frank Seeley School. From their allotted 40 overs they reached a total of 142-8, although no single batsman made a particularly substantial score. The opposition seemed to be cruising with a total of 100-2 but inspired bowling and fielding restricted them to 128-8, the school winning by 18 runs. The key players in this young team were Neale Fretwell, Nick Levett, Nick Nocton, Jason Parker, Chris Parkin, James Ratcliff, Mike Smalley, Eddie Spick and Michael Willcocks.

Monday, July 23rd-Thursday, August 9th 1984

Rohit Hagji, as an R.A.F. cadet, participated in the International Air Cadet Exchange which took him from R.A.F. Lyneham firstly to Frankfurt in Germany. From here he travelled to Washington D.C. and the city of Portland in the state of Oregon before finally returning to R.A.F. Brize Norton after 15 days.

Friday, July 27th 1984

The First VI, coached by Roger Kilby, played in the final of the Youll Cup at Wimbledon, the furthest the school tennis team had ever progressed since the competition began in 1947. Earlier in the week, in successive rounds, they had beaten Rugby School, Sherbourne School, Uppingham, Bryanston and Reigate. Unfortunately the final was against an extremely strong Repton side whose first pair easily beat Jon Bird and Graham Spalding in straight sets with the school's second pair, Alan Dion and Richard Ellis meeting a similar fate.

The rugby season 1984-1985

The 1st XV, coached by Clem Lee and Geri Thomas, won sixteen of their eighteen matches, the only defeats coming in narrow reverses against Trent College (17-18) and King Edward's, Birmingham (10-12). The side was captained from fly-half by Andrew Bailey and the two key members of the front row were Gareth Collins and Andy Hopkin, ably assisted by first Daniel Bailey and then, after he was injured, Richard Billington. Richard Bijster and Graham Harding played in the second row with Jim Chambers and Richard Hathaway as flankers and the ever impressive Mark Saxelby was at No.8. Andy Floyd was a skilful scrum half and in the centre, both Richard Staniforth and Nick Kidd were fine and resolute players. On the right wing was the pacey Tony Jenkin-Jones and on the left, first Peter Boot and then Richard Drew played extremely well. At fullback was the ever reliable David Gardiner.

Overall, this team scored over a hundred tries, the second highest total ever in High School rugby.

The swimming season 1984-1985

The school swimming team, directed by Chris Mann, remained unbeaten in all their matches throughout the entire year. They retained all three City Schools' Championships.

Wednesday, November 14th 1984

In a football fixture against Bilborough College, Paul Ingram scored a goal from well over seventy yards out. This seems to be the longest successful goal attempt in the history of High School football although *The Nottinghamian* described it as "the greatest fluke the season saw."

Christmas Term 1984

The balloon debates of the Debating Society were replaced by "Just a minute", a popular Radio 4 panel game. The format of the activities allowed James Ruzicka to sing in Polish for 60 seconds, Ruth Horsley to explain how she was attempting to grow a beard, John Wood to tell the audience how to house train a yeti and William Ruff to reveal how he kept his legs so shapely.

A forgotten day in the early 1980s, perhaps

I remember on one occasion greeting one of my Sixth Form class, Duncan Muir, as he stood in the corridor. Duncan clearly wanted to say something to me but I rushed by, on my way to some very important, but now long forgotten event. I was in too much of a hurry really to stand and chat so I just paused briefly to listen to what he had to say. Duncan announced that he had seen a car in Sherwood, with a sticker in the back windscreen which read "My other car is a Porsche". I was far from impressed, and I said grumpily to him, "How witty, Duncan! Surely you've seen that sticker before?!" "Yes", he replied, "but this time it was in the back of a Porsche."

The end of the Christmas Term 1984

Jeff Leach retired after thirty years at the High School during which he had taught not just History, but also French in his earlier years. He was always sympathetic to boys of weaker ability, and seemed often to play the role of "the prisoner's friend". An extremely witty man, Jeff was very much a character and numerous anecdotes existed about his nickname of "The Gnome" and his activities as a test pilot for Airfix. His form room was always adorned with a large collection of garden gnomes which, although they often disappeared or were confiscated, always seemed to be quickly replaced. From 1956 onwards, Jeff was in charge of school cricket and he devoted enormous amounts of time to this sport, umpiring for many, many hours each season, often in the company of his friend Jimmy Sadler. On a much more serious note, though, Jeff had been in the army during the war and in 1945 had been one of the first soldiers to enter Belsen concentration camp. He did not ever dwell on the horrors he had seen there, but I do remember his telling me about a girl who was so traumatised that she had prematurely grey hair. She was about five or six years of age.

Saturday, January 12th 1985

In a competition held at Wollaton Park, the U-12 cross country team, which was coached by Peter Baker, were crowned City Champions.

The end of the rugby season 1985

With his retirement imminent, Dick Elliott watched the 1st XV for the last time as a High School Master. He had supported the team through thick and thin for thirty-five years including a number of away matches and was justifiably proud of the fact that he had seen more of the team than anyone else in the history of the school. For this reason at the end of the season Dick was presented with his 1st XV Colours.

The mid-1980s, perhaps

The selections for the following year's Prefects were always based, in part, on the opinions of the members of staff. The latter were asked to record their thoughts in special books, which contained a single page for each potential prefect. One such hopeful was a young gentleman called Matthew Duck. He was a splendid young man and teacher after teacher had written sentiments such as "Highly suitable", "An excellent candidate" or "Will make a fine prefect". Every teacher except one, that is to say. He had written "Yes, but will he take to it?"

April 1985

The U-16 Sevens team won the country's most important national Sevens tournament, hosted by the London Irish Club. In the group matches they beat Campion (18-0), Sotham (26-0), Cawston College (24-0), and St Edmunds (14-0) and in the quarter final Warriner (18-0), and in the semi final Barnard Castle (40-18). In the final, they beat the Bishop of Hereford's Bluecoat School by the impressive margin of 20-0. The squad of players was Bill Atkinson, Miles Astbury-Crimes, Simon Austen, Robert Brierley, Paul Briggs, Jeremy Harris, Peter Leman, Philip Milton, Philip Sanderson and Mark Saxelby.

Friday, April 12th 1985

The Biology and Geography Departments took Sixth Form groups on a week-long Field Trip to Slapton Ley in Dorset. Their activities were as varied as determining the food sources of snails by examining their fresh faeces, trying to tempt badgers into the open with peanut butter sandwiches and wading waist deep into the icy waters of the River Dart.

Easter 1985

Under the direction of Andrew Winter, a group of boys visited Grenoble. With the help of their French host families, the boys travelled widely, some as far as Paris, the Mediterranean or various Alpine skiing resorts. As a school group, they managed to visit Lyon, the Vercors, and the Hector Berlioz Museum at Grenoble where they were able to view the composer's uncle's foot stool.

Saturday, May 11th 1985

Two boys from the school, Dave Farmer and Steve Abell, travelled up to Bradford to see their favourite team, Bradford City, presented with the Third Division Championship Trophy. The Main Stand was due to be replaced after the match but less than an hour from the scheduled end of its seventy-seven year history, it caught fire and in the ensuing conflagration, fifty-six men, women and children were burnt to death, more than two hundred were seriously injured and countless thousands were traumatised for life.

The end of the Summer Term 1985

Oswald Lush retired after thirty-five years at the High School, having arrived there in 1949 after spells at Trinity College, Dublin, Oxford

University and the Royal Navy. He taught French and took many trips and exchanges to France. For twenty-one years he was in charge of school tennis, a period during which the school reached the regional final of the Glanville Cup twenty times and the national finals on six occasions. In 1955 Oswald became "Head of the Lower School" and in the 1960s was "Master-in-charge-of-Buildings". In 1970 he became House Master of Cooper's. Oswald was a very popular man, widely recognised for his wonderful, kind and gentle character.

The end of the Summer Term 1985

Dick Elliott retired after thirty-five years at the High School, having arrived there in 1950 after spells at King's College, Cambridge and then the R.A.F. where he had been a Lancaster pilot in Bomber Command. Dick was Head of Classics and, after rowing at university, soon became one of the prime movers in school rowing. Once he had revealed that his middle name was "Babington", he was immediately nicknamed "Babs". He was known to many boys because his room, D1, was a short cut between two different areas of the school and far too many of them were willing to interrupt his lessons to go through. Although always very patient and understanding, Dick could occasionally become exasperated and on one occasion he presented a teacher with a Mars bar as the fiftieth person to interrupt that particular lesson since the start of the term (and it was only October).

The cricket season 1985

Playing against the Western Australian Public Schools XI, the High School managed a mere 92-9 in reply to their guests 221 for 8 declared, although these scores say more about Australian strength than the High School's particular weakness. During the season as a whole Mark Saxelby was to average 45.86 as a batsman and the team captain, James Morris, scored 640 runs at an average of 40.00. Tim Deas took a very creditable 45 wickets at an average of just 19.29.

July 1985

William Collin participated in the XVIIth Chemistry Olympiad in Bratislava in what was then Czechoslovakia. He won a silver medal while the rest of the British team won bronzes.

Wednesday, November 6th 1985

I was manager of the school football team. We had agreed to a fixture against Bilborough College 3rd XI but arrived to find their 1st XI waiting eagerly to play us. We lost 0-9 and in the words of The Nottinghamian: "we were lucky to get the nil. Still, at least we crawled off with heads held high."

The old folks' Christmas Party 1985

Entertainment was provided by Captain Edwin Harris and his All Star Band with Simon Lowe as a bingo caller and Les Wilkinson and Stephen Field singing folk songs and Christmas carols. In town, more than £1,000 was raised for the N.S.P.C.C. by carol singing in the Victoria Centre at lunchtimes and taking collections in every available pub during the evenings.

An unknown Wednesday in January 1986

The First XI played Dayncourt School in Radcliffe-on-Trent. They were watched by the Headmaster, Dennis Witcombe who always took the trouble to come to see the team at least once in every season. He was always an extremely welcome guest in theoretical terms but from a practical point of view, he never ever saw eleven extremely nervous young players do anything except lose, usually by a wide margin. The score this grey, cold and drizzly afternoon was Dayncourt 3 High School 1, which, by the standards of the day, constituted a moral victory.

Spring Term 1986

The Sixth Form Centre now had an annual budget of some £1,200, which allowed for the purchase of table top football, three pool tables, a snooker table and a table tennis table.

The rugby season 1985-1986

The 1st XV, coached by Clem Lee and Geri Thomas, won sixteen of their seventeen fixtures, suffering defeat only at the hands of Stamford by the narrowest possible margin (6-7), just three matches from the end of the season when the team was significantly weakened by injuries to key players. The side was captained from scrum half by Andy Floyd and had a front row of Daniel Bailey, Peter Leman and Jeremy Harris. The lock forwards were usually Simon Austen and John Swannell although both Greg Firth and Edward Knight-Jones were to play later in the season. The back row consisted of James Morris and Lyndon Astill with Mark Saxelby as a fine Number 8. Philip Milton was fly half and the two wingers were Robert Brierley and Miles Astbury-Crimes. In the centre were Richard Staniforth and Niall Bamford, the latter eventually being replaced because of illness by Robert Atkinson. At fullback both Dave Gardiner and then, when he was injured, Tim Martin, performed extremely well.

The rugby season 1985-1986

The U-15 XV, coached by Tim Dibdin and Chris Mann won all fourteen of their fixtures scoring exactly five hundred points, and conceding only sixty. The side was captained from fly half by Nick Carr and had a front row usually drawn from Paul Baggaley, Rupert Dixon, Julian Harrison, Mark James or Tim Smith. The lock forwards were Roger Marshall and William Lord and the back row normally consisted of Tom Leman, Paul Hatfield and Simon Miller. Roger Gardiner was scrum half and the wingers were either David "Charlie" Brown, John Hepworth or Richard Marshall. At fullback Nick Lee was an extremely competent performer. The names of the centres, unfortunately, remain unrecorded, since the school magazine omits to mention them, although we do know that during the course of the season, both Richard Hawkins and Julian Luxton appeared as backs, most often as replacement wingers. Matt Talbot and Simon Hosking were reserve forwards.

The mid-1980s

Shortly after the idea of a school ghost was first mooted, it quickly emerged that there was another claimant to the job. Boys from the Preparatory School reported that as they walked down some stairs towards the Waverley Street end of the building, invisible fingers grabbed at their trouser legs, as somebody was trying to clutch at them. This story was told to me independently by boys of varying ages so it must have been well known at the time, although none of the teachers seemed aware of it. One person in the Main School knew of it, however.

My explanation does require a certain "leap of faith". The new Preparatory School was constructed on the site of a magnificent Victorian house which originally belonged to Dr Dixon, Headmaster from 1868-1884. On May 29th 1876, his wife, Ada, died "of the effects of a chill", leaving her husband with five children, "Robert, Charles, Harold, Sydney and one daughter to bring up".

My belief is that the clutching fingers belonged to Ada, who could see that her husband was struggling to look after their five children and she, unwilling to make her way to the spirit world with such unfinished business at hand, was attempting to reach out and embrace any child she could. The staircase in the modern building merely occupied the same site as her old Victorian house. Interestingly, this ghost disappeared after just a couple of years at most. Hopefully, this means that Ada had finally found her own children.

The football season, 1985-1986

The Nottinghamian carried an extensive report of the First XI's doings, prefaced by Jimmy Sirrel's description of Notts County's season, "disastrous, demoralising, unsuccessful". At the end the author reflected on whether young people should play a sport which had produced the carnage of the Heysel Stadium. His conclusion was that such events are not real football:

> "Real football is the weekly optimism that this time you might just win, but in the equal certainty that you probably won't. An hour and a bit in cold drizzle, watching two fairly untalented groups of people kick lumps off each other, presided over by a usually less-than-unbiased referee. Then, not being bothered that you lose, just having a laugh and succeeding in remembering that all sport is just a game."

The mood was lightened somewhat by listing the team's nicknames, including Steve "The Cat" Pearson, Rob "Temples" Crampton, Ian "Delicate" Dale, Ian "Tink" Dale, Jon "Fun-Boy" Fawcett, Alan "The Car" Fenelly, "Mark or Matthew" Fletcher, Tom "Gunner" Gould, Jon "Hatchet" Hampson, Seamus "The Refrigerator" Mulholland, Dave "Pumper" Powers, Mike "Overlap" Storey and, best of all Nigel "Varicose" Venes. The strangest was possibly Tim "All on Board" Deas but this referred to his being late for the team bus for the West Bridgford game and then missing the first twenty minutes of play and, indeed, the rest of the season.

A forgotten lunchtime in the 1980s

For most members of staff, lunchtime duties remain thankfully, for the most part, relatively trivial parts of their week. Occasionally there are accidents and incidents, but fortunately usually nothing particularly memorable happens. Not so one long-forgotten lunchtime when, out on yard duty, I ventured into the green, wooden toilet building which stood alongside the Forest Road wall where the Art and Technology block now stands. As I opened the door, I found a young boy standing in front of the sinks, his left foot lifted up on a wooden box. He was making what looked like a campaign speech to a group of some half a dozen or so extremely attentive listeners. What made it so memorable, though, was that in his right hand he held a huge, long Cuban type cigar. As he continued his speech he puffed on it every now and again like some fourteen-year-old Fidel Castro. That was in the golden heyday of "Sat'day D", and sure enough, he got one.

1986-1995

Simon Williams has been associated with hill walking at the High School, either with the Scouts or the Explorer Scouts, for some twenty six years. This has been his most pleasurable activity during his time in the school and the young men and women he has met through it have been, with just one or two exceptions, of the very best. From 1986 to 1995, expeditions every Easter to the Cairngorms in Scotland were particularly noteworthy and the very first group of boys in Year 13 which included Charlie Sermon and Andrew Toms all stand out, as does the time spent with Catherine Curnow, Philip and Jo Hampton, Matthew Kennedy, James Phillips and Lisa Thomas as well as Stephen Lewin and Jonathan Riley and their contemporaries. Time spent with members of staff such as Will Hurford, Graham Lewin, Mary Mills, Richard Nicolle and Ben Thomas has been most enjoyable. Indeed the full list of people, both staff and pupils, would be too long to include in the present work.

Easter 1986

The French Exchange, under the direction of Andrew Winter, returned to Grenoble, where, as well as visiting Avignon, they were again able to view the foot stool belonging to the uncle of Hector Berlioz. The traditional football match was lost 13-14 although "it was too hot and the grass was too long and we hadn't brought the right shoes, and they were a load of fouling Frenchmen, sir."

May 1986

Simon Adamyk of the Second Year Sixth kept readers of *The Nottinghamian* entertained with his short, yet pithy, poems such as:

Thought # 24

Just when I'm getting on top
Life goes all fuzzy
Round the
Edges.

Thought # 55

Why is it
When I let my mind wander
It never comes
Back?

May 1986

The Nottinghamian printed a suitable apology to one of the school's many Old Boys. He had been included in error in the previous edition's obituaries and, in the unforgettable words of Mark Twain, the "news of his death had been grossly exaggerated".

Wednesday, May 14th 1986

In their traditional fixture against the M.C.C., the 1st XI, chasing a total of 196-8 declared, scored 200-5 to win by five wickets. The winning total was built around the innings of Mark Saxelby who missed a well-deserved century, being left undefeated on 93 not out.

June 1986

George Taft broke the Nottingham City School League records for the 3,000 metres with a time of 9 minutes 17.7 seconds and for the 5,000 metres with a time of 16 minutes 23 seconds. Earlier in the season Graham Harding had established a new pole vault record of 3.80 metres.

Saturday, June 14th 1986

Playing for the U-14 side against Abbot Beyne School, Richard Court took six wickets for seven runs.

Wednesday, June 25th 1986

Roy Seely "Dick" Whitby passed away after a short illness at the age of 67. From 1955 he had been Clerk to the Governors and then, from 1975 onwards, a Governor of the School and Chairman of the Governors' Finance Committee. He was President of the Old Nottinghamians' Society in 1970 and, as well as his work as a Governor, gave enormous amounts of his time to school shooting.

Founder's Day 1986

School celebrations reached a climax when, in addition to the normal activities of the day, the school's first ever minibus was delivered.

The cricket season 1986

In the school magazine the craze for nicknames continued, with the Old Nottinghamians cricket report featuring players such as "Woody", "Pep", "Ackers", "OJ", "Ay Pee Bee", "Nelly", "Dobbo", "The Skipper", "EMPF", "Jacko", "Wob Woades", "Butch the Dog", "Bruce Lee"and "Wajid Khalil".

July 1986

The school tennis team, coached by Tony Holding and consisting of Richard Ellis, Stephen Hopkins, Graham Spalding and Simon Wilson, won the Subsidiary Finals held at Queen's Club putting them in fifth position overall in the country. They beat Eton, Reigate and then R.G.S.Lancaster in the final by a convincing margin of 3-0.

July 1986

The U-13 tennis team, under the direction of Roger Kilby and consisting of James Aveline, Miles Dowling, Jonathan Turpin and Matthew Widdall, won the Midland Bank / L.T.A.Tournament, beating Fairham School 6-0, Colonel Frank Seeley School "B" 6-0, Padstowe 5-1, and, in the final, Colonel Frank Seeley School "A" by 4-2.

The end of the Summer Term 1986

David Peters retired after thirty-three years at the school, the majority as Head of History. For three years he was an officer in the Army Section of the C.C.F. and he ran school swimming from 1956-1960 in the days before the school had its own swimming pool. In 1961 he became Senior Librarian and in 1983 House Master of Mellers' House.

Summer 1986

Both Graham Harding and Nick Hunt represented England at cricket. Graham Harding, who had left in 1984, played for Young England against Sri Lanka in three Test Matches and two one day games. Nick Hunt, having appeared in School, County and Regional Sides, was selected for the U-15 team against Wales, scoring forty-six and eight.

Summer 1986

The School Library was entirely refurbished with new shelving, more display space, and a special area where boys could read magazines. Two librarians were appointed, Mrs Clarke and Mrs Wrathall.

The rugby season 1986-1987

The 1st XV, coached by Clem Lee and Geri Thomas, won all eighteen of its matches, to finish a season unbeaten for the first time since 1944-1945. This season, though, the team had a large number of absentees who were away playing for representative sides such as Nottinghamshire or the Midlands. The team's victories were over Hall Cross School, Doncaster (23-0), Loughborough (32-13), Welbeck College (27-0), Oakham (6-0), Solihull (10-7), Ratcliffe College (50-0), Trent College (22-20), Q.E.G.S.Wakefield (22-16), K.E.Birmingham (9-3), Greshams (24-15), Abbott Beyne (74-14), King's Grantham (28-3), Worksop College (35-0), R.G.S.Worcester (23-17), Stamford (15-0), Newark Magnus (65-0), Pocklington (3-0) and Mount St Mary's College (22-0).

Overall, they scored 490 points and conceded just 117. They won the *Rugby World & Post Magazine* "Team of the Month" award for January 1987 and both *The Times, The Daily Telegraph* and *The Independent* named them as one of the best sides in the country. Their closest games came against Oakham, Trent College, Pocklington and, most of all, Solihull where the team were losing until the last five minutes when Mark Saxelby set up a breakaway try for Jock Brierley. The side was captained from fly half by Philip Milton and had a front row of Jeremy Harris, Pete Leman and Daniel Bailey all three of whom normally played together for the county side. The lock forwards, Simon Austen and Edward Knight-Jones, were highly mobile and could scrummage well and win lineout balls. There was a fine back row of James Morris, Phillip Sanderson and Dave Howard and an excellent Number 8 in the shape of Mark Saxelby who scored twenty tries during the season. Jason Parker at scrum half, was, on occasion, a place kicker of unbelievable ability. The two wingers, Miles Astbury-Crimes and Robert Brierley, managed thirty tries between them and at fullback Fraser Shearer was an excellent catcher and kicker. Andrew Herberts and Robert Atkinson were resolute defenders and Tim Martin, Paul Briggs and Rupert Dixon were all dependable replacements when they were needed to play.

The football season, 1986-1987

The Nottinghamian contained its usual stand-out report on the year's footballing activities. Prefaced by the wise words of Jasper Carrot, "you draw some, you lose some", it spoke of being "on the crest of a slump", with a game at Bluecoat School: "of fabulous quality, a sort of school equivalent of Rochdale v Halifax. The most interesting event was a man weeding his allotment next to the pitch, and the only goal of the game, a speculative shot that went in off the post on the 26th bounce." There was doubt whether the game at Bilborough College was lost by 1-7 or 1-9 as few people had kept an accurate count. A slightly more positive note came, however, when Team Captain Mark Fletcher finally scored a penalty at Beckett School, the first success from the spot after ten previously missed efforts (not all by him). In the last game the goalkeeper managed to punch a corner into his own net. Most of the team's difficulties came from a "chronic lack of fitness due to smoking, a tendency to basic errors that come from only a year or so's experience of football and the manager's complete inability, given an initial lack of knowledge of the players, to put the jigsaw into place until well after Christmas." Nevertheless, as "The Big Boss" stated in his way over-serious conclusion, "for the sizeable majority of the players, the Football Fixtures were the highlight of the week."

Thursday, October 9th 1986

The Debating Society debated the motion that "This House is ashamed to be British". It was narrowly defeated by 26 votes to 20.

Wednesday, October 15th 1986

The First XI football team, playing away, won their only victory of the season by 1-0. The winning goal was scored by Ted Lord and a last minute penalty was saved by goalkeeper Andy Belfield.

Friday, October 17th-Sunday, October 19th 1986

A Geography Department field trip went to the north of England, visiting High Force waterfall, Cauldron Snout, and the Eden Valley. Everyone climbed Easedale as far as the tarn and the final activity was some pot-holing at Dow Cave with much time pleasantly spent, neck deep in icy water.

Friday, October 24th-Tuesday, October 28th 1986

The R.A.F. Section of the C.C.F. led by Messrs Cook, Coulam and Jones went walking in the Cairngorms. They negotiated the Lairig Ghru pass, then the Chalamain gap, before ascending Cairngorm where they met a herd of reindeer who were, in fact, tame enough to be fed Rolos.

Thursday, November 27th 1986

The Debating Society discussed the idea that "This House believes that television is the opiate of the masses". It was defeated by the worryingly massive margin of sixty votes to fifteen.

The beginning of December 1986

The U-13 and U-15 tennis teams both reached the National Finals at Telford. The U-13 team consisted of James Aveline, Justin Crowther, Matthew Widdall and Andrew Carr, a last minute replacement for the injured Kieron Crowther. Eventually, the U-13s were to lose to The Royal Grammar School, Guildford, by 5-1. The U-15s, consisting of Gareth Dunn, Andrew Hursthouse, James Preston and Daniel Rhodes, with Fouad Qureshi playing in the earlier rounds, lost by 2-4 to the eventual winners, St Paul's School, Barnes.

The Spring Term 1987

Efforts were made to revive the "Joint Film Society", beginning with a showing of *The Producers*, a Mel Brooks comedy, followed by *The Rocky Horror Picture Show* which was a "make-or-break" since the society's financial viability depended totally upon its ticket sales.

March 1987

The U-16 Seven-a-Side rugby team was extremely successful, winning tournaments at Newark, Warwick, and London Irish, a competition which is normally acknowledged as the National Championships in this type of rugby. The winning team was Simon O'Brien, Nick Hunt, Bill Atkinson, Tom Leman, Tim Smith, Nick Lee, Andrew Herberts, Nick Carr and David "Charlie" Brown.

Sunday, April 5th 1987

Because of the nature of the landscape and the severity of the weather, it is inevitable that in any Adventurous Training programme there will be "incidents", moments when danger and even the risk of disaster raises its rather frightening head. The story is taken up by Martin Jones:

> "In Snowdonia in north Wales an inexperienced teacher (and C.C.F. officer) was leading a group of cadets with the help of an experienced O.N. A navigational error resulted in their attempting the descent of a very treacherous slope. One of the cadets slipped and fell down the rocky ground. He collided with a slab some hundred feet lower down. Some rock climbers in the vicinity came to help and alerted the Mountain Rescue. I was on a different mountain with a different group. When I returned to the road I was stopped by the police to be told that one of my cadets had been helicoptered to Bangor Hospital. They weren't sure if he was alive or not. I drove to the hospital with Marcus Coulam, both of us fearing the worst. Fortunately the lad was sitting up in bed, smiling. He did have broken ribs and was off school for six weeks. I was quizzed by the Mountain Rescue Team about our planning, preparation, safety equipment and experience. The conclusion was "fine, no worries, anyone can make a navigational error."
>
> Back in Nottingham, the press found out about the story and contacted the Headmaster, Dr Witcombe, who spoke strongly in

favour of the C.C.F. and the way the Adventurous Training was organised. The boy's parents, though shocked, made no negative comments whatsoever, and their older son, who had participated in previous Adventurous Training expeditions with us gave a glowing account to the press about our safety procedures. All in all, the school came out of a potentially negative situation extremely well."

Easter 1987

The Classics Department cruise, led by Messrs Bird, Curtis, Horril and Phillips, visited Athens, Ephesus, Cyprus, Jerusalem, Bethlehem, Cairo, Rhodes, Crete, Dubrovnik, Venice and Lake Garda.

Easter 1987

The Biology Department Field Trip took place with around fifty biologists and geographers visiting Nettlecombe Court at Williton in Somerset. They carried out a series of different ecoogical investigations at sites such as Exmoor and in various fields and streams close to the Field Centre, using instruments as varied as impellors, augers, soil testers and pebbleometers.

Summer Term 1987

The First Year Sixth athletes participated in a Highland Games competition involving a "through-the-legs" shot put, a hop-five-steps-and-a-jump, a five hundred metres steeplechase, complete with a water jump, and, of course, a caber tossing. The overall competition was won by Simon Burden.

Saturday, June 27th 1987

Playing for the 1st XI, Nick Hunt made 105 not out. Despite a challenging declaration at 222-1, the match was drawn.

Friday, July 3rd 1987

One of a team of four students, Matthew Earnshaw, won a bronze medal in the XIXth Chemistry Olympiad held at Budapest in Hungary.

Saturday, July 11th 1987

Mark Saxelby, playing for the 1st XI for the very last time, scored a quite brilliant 131 against Bedford Modern School, having shared in a partnership of 167 in 111 minutes with Richard Jones (56). The High School declared at 267-5 and won well, with Andy Belfield and Mark Saxelby himself taking the majority of the wickets.

The end of July 1987

Captain Edwin Harris retired after twenty-one years of "service which have added considerable colour and vigour to the life of the school." Before he arrived, Edwin had seen extensive war service in Pakistan and was probably the only High School teacher able to speak fluent Urdu.

The end of July 1987

Mrs Gaynor Knifton departed after nine years in the Art Department. She was the very first Assistant Master to leave the High School through reasons of pregnancy. Indeed, when she joined the school in September 1978, her contract of employment was exactly the same as those of her male colleagues and made no provision whatsoever for the existence of a second sex, let alone for the maternity rights which she (eventually) was to be the first Assistant Master to receive.

The end of July 1987

Simon Harding, who had been the Captain of the School, left at the end of his Second Year Sixth. He was the very last boy to study Ancient Greek in the High School, ending (if only temporarily) a tradition which had lasted several hundreds of years.

Thursday, July 23rd-Tuesday, August 4th 1987

A group of eleven sixth formers, together with Richard Willan and Mr and Mrs Jones, visited Ireland for a walking holiday. They saw the Giant's Causeway, climbed Caruntoohil, the highest mountain in Ireland and participated in the locals' traditional barefoot pilgrimmage to the top of Croagh Patrick.

August 1987

The Head Gardener, Geoff Whitelock, retired after fourteen years. Both his father and grandfather had been school gardeners. Geoff's uncle was a pupil at the High School where he had been a contemporary of D.H.Lawrence, a young boy also known to Geoff's mother.

The academic year 1987-1988

The Third World Society raised the enormous total of £3,132. Two Trivial Pursuit Marathons brought in £1,554 for Oxfam and on Non-Uniform Day, £568 was collected for UNICEF. In the spring, the school Red Nose Day *Comic Revue* managed £128 for Comic Relief.

The rugby season 1987-1988

The U-12 team won just one of their nine fixtures. Coached by Chris Curtis and Andrew Winter, more than thirty different players were used in an attempt to improve their fortunes but only towards the very end of the season did they begin to look like a viable team.

The football season 1987-1988

In *The Nottinghamian*, the football reports continued to be refreshingly different. Having on previous occasions provided pen pictures of the squad and then opinions from the players themselves, this time, the football report again contained the team's nicknames. They included such unforgettable epithets as Tim "Trendy" Deas, Neil "I've got the Riddings" Fretwell, Richard "All the Skills" Lamb, John "Chippy" Lang, Ted "Rushy Boy" Lord, Dave "Mr Interesting" Norwood, Chris "Five Pints" Parkin, Andy "Diego" Walton, with the most perceptive comments of all being reserved for the goalkeepers: Ashley "Roadblock" Mortimer, Andy "Lumbago" Belfield and John "Spud" Hepburn, who always seemed to catch the ball as if it were a hot potato.

Thursday, December 10th 1987

The Debating Society held a balloon debate with various members of staff in the slowly sinking dirigible. Despite his brilliance as Dame Edna Everage, Mr Ruff polled only seven votes. Next out was the Deputy Headmaster, Terry Willcocks as Arthur Daley, who managed nine votes, all of whom, were later, allegedly, made into prefects. The winner by a large margin was Les Wilkinson who was Oz. Presumably, in 1987, everybody knew just who "Oz" woz.

The end of the Christmas Term 1987

The school play was *The Nativity*, where Adam and Eve were played by Richard Simcock and Louise Harris. Immense interest was shown by the entire school as to what costumes they would or would not wear. The mystery was solved when they both appeared in white body stockings.

Friday, February 5th 1988

Organised by the Third World Society, the school participated enthusiastically in Red Nose Day. Members of staff as senior and important as Messrs Willcocks, Sadler and Parker, wore red plastic noses and more than three hundred boys did the same. Tony Holding taught while wearing his and charged the class to witness the event. Overall, Comic Relief benefited received over £200.

A forgotten Wednesday in February 1988

The First XI, under the direction of Stefan Krzeminski, beat Dayncourt School by 3-2. Victory was secured by Jon "Chippy" Lang who greeted his winning goal with "celebratory jigs and cartwheels more suited to the Big Top than a football pitch." Any regular viewer of the Premier League on *Match of the Day* will recognise here a young man at least twenty years ahead of his time.

April 1988

The Hockey Team retained their County Championship, beating Colonel Frank Seeley School by 1-0 after extra time, the winning score generally reckoned to be the best goal of the season.

Possibly the Easter Holidays 1988

A minibus with every seat occupied by a Venture Scout was accidentally left behind in the High School yard; an excellent start to a long trip to the Scottish Highlands. The teachers realised the error of their ways when they stopped for a break at a café near Scotch Corner some two hours later. It had taken the Scouts themselves the best part of an hour to realise that they had no driver for their minibus. Fortunately, this entire organisational fiasco took place at late 1980s' diesel prices.

Summer Term 1988

In the Preparatory School, Iain Higgins, who was already the Nottinghamshire County Champion and the Bullock Cup Winner, was selected to represent England at chess. His school team mate, James Redburn, was later to join him in the same squad.

Summer Term 1988

In the Preparatory School, the Swimming Team finished seventh in the National Finals at Highgate. This team had already won the Nottingham Champion Boys School for the eighth year in succession.

A forgotten day in the 1980s

The coat racks in the West Corridor were looking to be absolutely full, so the Head of Junior School, Chris Curtis, embarked upon a thorough search through all the coats which were already hanging there. Among many others, he found a heavy, brownish overcoat which was labelled, quite properly, inside the collar. It belonged to Robert Tyrrell who had left the school at least five years before. Since then his coat had remained, waiting patiently for its owner's return. Robert Tyrrell had been a legendary figure in the Fifth Form, a keen punk when punk was in its heyday, and he always took "correct school uniform" to be a challenge rather than a statutory requirement.

If my memory serves me well, it was a number of Robert's friends who went on a school trip to Germany and, inspired by their non-stop *Antmusic*, decided that they would all dye their hair a most brilliant scarlet red. Alas, being boys, they knew nothing whatsoever of hair dyes and therefore chose a non-fast product. The next morning their hair was still its normal colour but not, alas, their pillows, sheets or blankets, all of which looked as if they had been recently used to film the climactic ending of *The Rhine Valley Chainsaw Massacre*.

Friday, July 15th 1988

The under-13 cricket team, coached by Richard Cross and John Wood, won the "Andrews Air Conditioning" Under-13 Schools Cricket Competition. The final was played against Valley School at Trent Bridge and much merriment was caused when the electronic scoreboard revealed that one of the High School players was called "Milnes Hyphen James". The High School batted first, but managed only 87-4 in their innings. The opposition started well enough but were eventually bowled out for a total of 68, with Rose taking four wickets for just fifteen runs.

Saturday, July 16th 1988

The 1st XI scored a massive 256-4 against Abbot Beyne School, with Nick Hunt scoring 144, and Simon O'Brien a fine supporting 72. Abbot Beyne were bowled out for only 63, so producing a victory by 193 runs. This excellent innings allowed Nick Hunt to pass 1,000 runs for the season. He eventually finished with a total of 1,108, scored at an average of 73.9. This included five centuries, the other four of which which came against the XL Club (103 not out), Leeds Grammar School (113), the Old Nottinghamians (100) and Edinburgh Academy (111 not out).

Monday, September 12th 1988

The first mechanical digger appeared in the playground, starting the building work necessary for the new Sports Hall. The driver was to uncover, among many other things, a large quantity of long buried army boots. Both the Rifle range and the Green Shed had to be demolished. Eventually, the Sports Hall was to have enough space for two separate forms to have P.E. lessons simultaneously and for boys to play badminton, tennis, basketball, volleyball and indoor hockey. There was a fully equipped fitness training room and four cricket nets, all lit at a level to rival those of the National Cricket School at Lilleshall itself.

The late 1980s

This High School "X-File", comes from Mark Cleverley. It deserves to be quoted verbatim:

> "As teachers, we are duty bound to ensure that the teaching environment in which we operate is well cared for and does not deteriorate as a result of malicious intent. Since the Science Block was first opened in 1983, I have spent much of my teaching life in Chemistry Laboratory C2, and have been as watchful as one can be in ensuring that there is no place for graffiti or damage to the permanent fixtures within the room.
>
> It was many years ago that, following a day's teaching, I was mystified to discover two almost parallel fresh gouge marks, about two centimetres in length and one centimetre in width, on one of the benches in the back row of the lecture area of the room. During the next few days, my various classes continued to

report this peculiar phenomenon to me. They were just as curious about the origin of the marks.

It was not until the following week that the truth emerged, when I noticed one of my Second Year pupils (Year 8 in today's terms) with his head buried in the workbench. He was deriving great pleasure from gnawing away at the wood of the bench and it was his two front teeth which were responsible for creating the chiselled impressions within the wooden surface. When challenged, the red-headed pupil, whom I recall as 'Wallace', was mortified at being discovered. I may possibly have asked him whether he kept a guinea pig as a pet, although my aging memory does contain a few gaps nowadays."

The rugby season 1988-1989

The 1st XV, coached by Clem Lee and Geri Thomas, with twelve players remaining from the previous year, won sixteen of their twenty fixtures. Playing exciting fifteen man rugby, they scored a total of eighty-three tries, with the team captain, Nick Carr, contributing 161 points.

The rugby season 1988-1989

The U-13 team, which the previous year, as U-12s, had been so spectacularly unsuccessful, improved by leaps and bounds. According to Tony Bird and Dave Phillips, the side was "a real pleasure to coach. They have shown a total commitment to training, and a highly competitive approach to all their matches. They have always gone on to the field looking for a win." This year, they managed to taste victory in six of their sixteen fixtures.

Ten o'clock on an August morning, just before the start of the new football season, 1988-1989

The new football coach, Stefan Krzeminski, cannot wait for that first kick-off. He has been tasked with moving the team on to the next level, after the previous season's incumbent has had his contract cancelled by mutual consent. Permission is sought, and granted, for the members of the team to go down to the Valley Road playing fields to train. Stefan is surprised at this because "football" and "Valley Road" do not often appear together in the same sentence. A dozen or so young squad members arrive. The place is fresh and green, sunny and newly mown, expectant, but deserted. The groundsman soon arrives, though, with the news that he has just received a phone call from the Head of Games. The footballers could indeed spend the morning at Valley Road but under no circumstances whatsoever were they to make use of a football during their training schedule.

Saturday, October 15th-Sunday, October 16th 1988

The school chess team won the 6th Marlwood Chess Tournament at Marlwood School, Bristol. The team was coached by John Swain and Phil Eastwood, and scored 41.5 points out of a possible 60. Both Iain Higgins, Matthew Kennedy, Olivier Playe, Alastair Rose and Matthew Tailby won Best Board prizes and Matthew Kennedy, scoring six out of seven, won a prize for the best individual U-16 performance. The school received a complete set of *Encyclopedia Britannica* and an impressive cup. Each individual player received a shield as a memento of the weekend. This was to be the first of four consecutive victories at Marlwood.

Wednesday, October 19th 1988

In the days long before the invention of the "exeat", a piece of paperwork that can only be signed by a member of the Senior Management Team, all that a boy needed to have in order to take time off school was the permission of the teacher whose lesson he would be missing. One Tuesday morning, therefore, a "certain young man" came to see his French teacher and asked him a favour. He wanted to go to a football match, you see, and needed to miss French so that he could set off promptly and not be late for the game, which kicked off at 7.30p.m. The teacher was puzzled as to why the "certain young man" had to absent himself quite as early in the day as Period 5. "Well, sir," came the reply, "the game's at Hampden Park in Glasgow. I want to go and see Scotland play." And, as was the custom at the time, he was allowed to go. And he got there comfortably for the kick-off. Happily, they drew 1-1 with Yugoslavia and qualified for the European Championships.

Saturday, November 26th 1988

The 4th XV won one of their greatest ever victories, by 70-0 over Ratcliffe College. The opposition were unable to resist the urge to kick the ball at every opportunity, and this proved their downfall.

Thursday, December 15th 1988

The newest copy of *The Nottinghamian* carried a poem by David Dewshi. It was called *The Lesson*, and its sentiments must have been echoed by large numbers of boys in the school:

"Drone, Waffle, WAFFLE, DRONE,

Teacher, drone, drone, waffle

        Gurgle! drone...waffles in a monotone

Monotone, Drone, waffle, gurgle, drone, monotone

Monotone drone gurgle

        Waffle. Drone....Boy?

Boy, drone, drone

Stares at WALL. Waffle, waffle, drone at the scratches

        AND THE SCRIBBLES

                and the scrawls"

December 1988-December 1989

A teacher exchange took place with John Cullen arriving from Queensland, Australia to replace Tim Dibdin for a year. John taught Geography but, not surprisingly perhaps, was a keen sportsman and a patriotic extoller of his country's many sporting achievements. John came from Coffs Harbour in Queensland and, as a native of tropical Australia, experienced for the very first time a number of what to us seemed very ordinary things. They included the common cold (early January), snow (April 25th!), a start to the school year in September, Goose Fair (October), a coal fired power station (November) and boomerang throwing lessons with 2Y (December).

Wednesday, January 11th 1989

The First XI achieved a fine result when they drew 2-2 at Bilborough College. The latter had recently been County Champions and, after they had gone into a 2-0 lead, it was most gratifying to see: "the team display the kind of skill, character and commitment that would have transformed the season, had these qualities made more than a fitful appearance in our other matches.."

A forgotten day in the early Spring Term 1989

The General Studies Birdwatching Group visited Wollaton Hall. Unknown to the teacher, "a certain young man" had bet the majority of the group that he could walk across an arm of the lake from one side to the other without getting significantly wet. The group asked the teacher's permission and he, intrigued, was foolish enough to give it. Much to everyone's amazement the young man duly proceeded to walk out across the lake with the water barely covering his shoes. He lived next to Wollaton Park and was well aware of the old ruined wall across the lake at this point. It never came above the water, except at a time of drought. Then the rest of the group followed him until, to the casual observer, it looked like a deleted scene from *The Life of Brian*.

Spring Term 1989

The school's Schools Challenge team won their regional final against Oakham School having beaten, in previous rounds, Repton, Trent College and Loughborough Grammar School. The team consisted of Richard Genever, Alastair Holland, James Kennedy and Matthew Kennedy, the latter thought to be the fastest speller of "pterodactyl" and "mnemonic" in the history of the competition. As William Ruff recorded in his report in *The Nottinghamian*, this "caused two question-masters to pause to recover their breath." Nick Dove was the team's ever reliable reserve.

Spring Term 1989

Guy Gisborne was selected for England at Under-18 level at hockey. He had previously played for the High School and also for Beeston Colts, Nottinghamshire and the Midlands, at all junior age groups.

Saturday, March 11th 1989

The school hockey 1st XI won their semi-final tie against Queen Mary's School, Walsall by 2-1. They had reached this position by beating Colonel Frank Seeley School by 7-0 in the final of the County Cup and then going on to defeat Weston Favell School, Northampton by 4-1 in the next round.

Another forgotten day in the Spring Term 1989

The Birdwatching Group again visited Wollaton Hall. Unknown to the same gullible teacher, "a certain young man" had bet most of the group that he could run down the grassy field towards the lake and jump upwards, over the water-filled ditch, the so-called "ha-ha", and then land on the grass next to the lakeside path. And he did it. And if you're not impressed, then go take a look at the lake.

6.30 a.m., Saturday, March 25th 1989

The Senior Adventurous Training party left for Scotland, where they walked over Meall nan Tarmachan and then climbed to the tops of Ben Cruachan, Stob Ghabhar, Benn Eunaich and Ben Lui.

A third forgotten day, later in the Spring Term 1989

For a change, the Birdwatching Group visited Attenborough. They trooped along densely wooded paths, always eager to catch sight of that elusive rare bird. One member of the group was, for various reasons, particularly his conceitedness, rather unpopular and he soon fell victim to what might well be termed "natural justice". As the group walked along the narrow paths, therefore, anyone feeling especially helpful would call out "Dog-poo!" so that nobody trod in it accidentally. Except when Mr Bighead was next in the line, in which case, the correct call was "Eagle!" so that he would look up into the sky but then tread in the doggy-dos. It worked a treat, and more than once.

April and July 1989

Richard Slater and John Riley, taking advantage of a C.L.Reynolds Travel Award, made an interesting comparison of St Michael's Mount in Cornwall and Mont St Michel in Normandy. This entailed a week's stay in the West Country, and a fortnight working hard in the summer heat of France.

12.15 a.m., Saturday, April 8th 1989

The French Trip departed at their traditional unearthly hour led by Tony Holding and John Hayes who also drove the coach. The boys visited all the traditional sights of Paris and then went on to Normandy where they saw the Bayeux Tapestry and the D-Day Landing Beaches.

Saturday, April 15th 1989

A good number of members of the teaching staff and numerous boys travelled up to Hillsborough Stadium in Sheffield to see their favourite team, Nottingham Forest, play in an F.A.Cup semi-final against Liverpool. Their sun-lit optimism was to be brought to a premature end, however, when, early in the first half, in England's biggest football stadium disaster, 96 men, women and children were crushed to death in the Leppings Lane end of the ground.

Friday, May 19th 1989

Manoj Patel of the Second Year Sixth who had previously boasted luxuriant, flowing locks, went to Pepper's Hairdressing Salon to have a flat top haircut. This sacrifice raised more than £150 for the victims of the Hillsborough Disaster. It was rumoured that the idea came from John Auld and Steve Booth, Manoj's close friends and classmates, who had spent eighteen lessons studying Balzac's *Le Curé de Tours*, looking at Manoj's hair and wondering what could be done to improve it.

Wednesday, June 21st 1989

The 1st XI cricket team, coached by Jimmy Sadler and Paul Morris, won their most thrilling match of the season against Repton School. The latter had made 192 all out, thanks mainly to some excellent fielding by James Kennedy and his very creditable bowling figures of 6-71. When the High School batted, they eventually needed two runs from the last ball which Nick Hunt duly hit for four runs, taking his own personal score to 133 not out.

July 1989

The school decathlon was won by Bill Atkinson, with a record score of 5715 points. Bill was reckoned at the time to be "probably the best all round athlete the school has ever seen".

Saturday, July 8th 1989

The 1st XI played against Forest Amateurs who made 216-9 declared. In reply, the school reached 219-1, with Tom Leman making 90 not out and and Simon O'Brien 75 not out to win by nine wickets.

The end of the Summer Term 1989

Chantal Sanchez left after five years working as a French assistante. Before her appointment the assistant/e had usually been one of a succession of university students, all staying for just one year. They were of extremely variable quality, ranging from the excellent Gérard Hilmoine, to the eccentric and occasionally explosive Claude Martinet, who always seemed to live up to his name. Chantal, once her excellent qualities had been recognised, was engaged on an open-ended contract and this guaranteed that French conversation classes would henceforth run smoothly and well. She was the first long term French conversation teacher since Madame Lionnet in the nineteenth century.

Sunday, July 30th-Friday, August 4th 1989

Led by Roger Kilby, boys from the the Naval Section went to Fleet Tender on the River Clyde. They had many difficulties with the local accent, and Charlie Hill spent twenty minutes lecturing the landlord of the local on how to talk properly. For this, and a number of other triumphs, he received the *Wally of the Week* trophy, consisting of the box which had previously held the football presented to Joe Traynor as best cadet. Peter Corlett had given Charlie a close run for his money when he tripped over a molecule of wood, and fell off the bridge of the ship.

The academic year 1989-1990

The last change in the uniform of the scouts had taken place as long ago as 1957 when the wide brimmed hat was discontinued. This year the Scout Group was allowed to decide what they themselves wanted to wear. They decided upon a béret and expressed a desire to discard the old fashioned mushroom coloured trousers and to wear instead their ordinary grey school trousers.

Every lunchtime at 1.10 p.m., 1989-1990

The lunchtime Computer Club, run by Jim Clarke, was in full swing. Numbers were potentially so overwhelming that only boys with a valid card were allowed to enter. Once inside they could use any one of sixteen Archimedes, two BBC Bs, or two Commodore 64s. That meant approximately two people to each computer or, on good days, perhaps even fewer. More advanced features included sound digitizers, video digitizers, scanners which could copy either text or pictures and modems which would allow communication with computers in other schools.

A forgotten autumn day in the late 1980s

The Second XI were not doing well. In fact, they were losing game after game. In which case, Bilborough College is not necessarily the best place to improve an abysmal footballing record. The problem was certainly not keenness. As team manager, I knew for a fact that, at home, the team goalkeeper used regularly to put all his football kit on and then go out into the back garden to practice diving around, comfortably saving the ball that he had himself thrown against a convenient wall. And I knew all this because the goalie's mum had told me. Unfortunately this day Bilborough ran amok. Goal after goal went into the back of the High School net. Indeed, their players actually grew bored with proceedings to the extent that they started to attempt shots from a vast distance in an effort to show up our rather immobile young goalkeeper. After a couple of humiliating efforts had sailed way over his head into the back of the net, the goalie cracked. He stepped forward to the edge of his penalty area, took off his gloves, threw them to the ground, and proclaimed loudly to everyone, "That's it! I quit!!" And he stalked off to the changing rooms and he never played again. A pity really, because we have had worse goalkeepers.

October and November 1989

The U-12 XV experienced an almost unprecedented run of wildly fluctuating results. They were 0-56 versus Warwick School, 0-48 against QEGS Wakefield, 48-0 at home to Manor School, 32-0 at Quarrydale, 0-24 versus RGS Worcester, and 0-20 at King Edward's, Birmingham.

Sunday, November 5th 1989

Richard Thynne of Form 4P in the Preparatory School continued the strong traditions of High School poetry:

The Guy Fawkes Story

In Sixteen hundred and five,
Guy Fawkes hatched a plot
To blow up the House (sic) of Parliament,
The King, His adviser, the lot.

He hired a deep dark cellar
Under the House of Lords,
And there he hid barrels of gunpowder ;

>A truly villainous hoard.
>
>Now one of Guy's fellow plotters,
>Tresham was his name,
>He went and warned the King's men
>About their dangerous game.
>
>The soldiers captured lone Guy Fawkes
>At that eleventh hour.
>They questioned him about the plot
>And locked him in the Tower.
>
>So when we light a bonfire
>To remind us of that day
>We burn Guy Fawkes on top of it
>Because Treason doesn't pay.

December 1989

The school play was *Macbeth*. It was directed by Les Wilkinson and starred Jonathan Swain with Claudine Astles as Lady Macbeth. Matthew Hayden played Banquo and James Hillhouse was Macduff. Sterling work was done by Geoff Woolley who, according to *The Nottinghamian*, produced no fewer than a hundred and forty-four half joints for the stage staff to enjoy.

Early one morning in February 1990

The Fourth, Fifth and Sixth Form students of Art under the direction of Messrs Gardiner and Greenwood left for their annual visit to the Art Galleries of London. They enjoyed, among many other paintings, Constable's *Flatwood Mill*, Umberto Boccioni's *Unique Forms of Continuity in Space* and Salvador Dali's *The Metamorphosis of Narcissus*.

Sometime in the 1990s

Les Willkinson remembers a noteworthy ski trip:

>"Dieter Hecht and I were guiding two groups of boys back to the hotel at the end of the day. We counted them before we left, but unfortunately, Chris Harris had wandered off to take a photograph. Each of us thought he was with the other's group. Just as dusk was falling, I went out to post some cards and met Chris taking his skis off. He had come back to where the groups had been and found us gone, so he'd gone to the lifts, but

unfortunately taken the wrong lift. A helpful Frenchman had skied back with him and pointed him towards the hotel. All's well that ends well – but of all the skiers to lose, it had to be the one-legged one. To be fair, no one would have known about Chris's leg. When the instructors came to present everyone with their certificates and medals, Chris had already taken off his prosthetic so he hopped up to get his award. The instructors could not believe that he had only one leg, given the way he had been skiing all week. He was a remarkable young man; I am still full of admiration for him."

C.C.F. Inspection Days in the 1990s

Having spent so many years in the C.C.F., Martin Jones is uniquely equipped to tell the tale:

"One of the disadvantages of being a C.C.F. Officer is having to survive the yearly ordeal of Inspection Day, and in particular, the final parade in the school yard. Although it provided much entertainment for the non-C.C.F. members of staff, for the more militarily inclined, it can be a nerve racking experience! The cadets have to look as smart as possible and some succeed. Others really let you down, with long, lank hair flopping out of their berets, uniforms creased and pressed but in the wrong places, trousers at half mast, marching which is barely recognisable as marching, with so many cadets out-of-step. These are all sources of embarrassment. The worst ever year for fainting was a particularly hot one when seven boys succumbed. They all collapsed onto the hard surface of the playground, their rifles clattering loudly in the silence. One year, the heavens opened, soaking everyone, and silencing the band. On another occasion the R.A.F. contingent marched past the inspecting officer, almost in step, almost saluting at the right moment, much to my relief, only for one cadet to have his non-regulation shoe come off and be left behind, alone and obvious, on the ground in front of the podium."

March 1990

The Mathematical Gazette carried rave reviews of Peter Horril's Maths textbook, *Applied Mathematics*.

Spring Term 1990

The Design Technology Department held a Swamp Buggy competition for First Year boys in the Founder Hall pool. Armed only with a low voltage electric motor and a three bladed plastic propeller, each entrant produced a machine well capable of coping with problems in the pool which were designed to reproduce the conditions of the Florida Everglades as closely as possible.

Spring Term 1990

In the British Mathematical Olympiad, Andrew Twells won one of the twenty prizes on offer.

Monday, April 2nd 1990

Another moment of mountaineering peril came in Scotland. Martin Jones takes up the tale:

> "One foul day on the Mamores near Ben Nevis in the Highlands of Scotland, Hamish Gibb was leading a group of boys along an icy ridge in zero visibility. He stopped the group and, to look at the map, took one step back and disappeared. He fell about eighty feet, landing on a steep snow slope. He was able to shout up to the group to get the safety rope out to assist his climbing up to them. They reminded him that the rope in question was in actual fact in his rucksack. He did manage to climb up for himself but it took well over an hour, before he was able to lead a group who were now very cold indeed back down to safety."

Monday, May 14th 1990

First Year boys, in the shape of Form 1C, visited the White Post Farm where they were able not only to play with a wide selection of baby animals but also to climb into the pens with the goat kids and sheep and to meet the recently acquired llamas. The boys saw the mushroom growing area and selected individual boys were allowed to touch a live snail. The White Post Farm, of course, had been set up several years before by Tim Clarke, who had himself been a boy at the High School. In Art classes with Mrs Knifton he had many times talked of his dream of one day opening a petting zoo.

June 1990

Pavan Dhaliwal represented Great Britain in two tennis competitions in Italy. Playing on unaccustomed dusty red clay courts, he defeated the Poland No 2, the Paraguay No 5 and the Denmark No 6, but lost to the Venezuela No. 1 and the Italy No 2.

Summer Term 1990

The School Tennis Team, coached by David Lewis and consisting of Pavan Dhaliwal, Kevin Dhaliwal, Richard Smart and Jeremy Smith won the county stage of the Midland Bank U-15 Championship without difficulty. In the regional final they met Repton School who they beat on games, after the tie was drawn 3-3. The National Quarter Finals were then held on the same day after lunch and the High School triumphed over K.C.S.Wimbledon, again on games after a draw. The semi-final was held at the Moat House Hotel in Telford when the High School beat Hymers College by 5-1. The winning streak came to an end, however, in the National Final, when the team lost to Millfield by 2-4. One match was actually lost 6-7 on a tie break, the latter being conceded by fifteen points to seventeen.

Sunday, July 15th 1990

The U-13 cricket team competed in the Andrews Competition. They reached the final at Trent Bridge, and beat Toothill School, Bingham to win the Schools' Championship Cup which was presented to them by the Nottinghamshire captain, Tim Robinson. The team was coached by Richard Cross and John Wood and captained by Richard Brindle. The most successful players were Peter Dunn who scored more than 200 runs in the season as a whole, Chris Freeston who took 32 wickets, and Graham MacNaughton who scored 107 in a Saturday fixture against Carlton-le-Willows School.

July 1990

Jimmy Sadler retired, having been a pupil at the school from 1938-1949 and a teacher since 1960. He had originally taught General Subjects but was eventually to become Head of the Geography Department and then Senior Master. On the sports field, Jim was, for many years, the close partner of Jeff Leach and, together, they ran school cricket and a number of different rugby teams.

At the same time, the School Bursar, Gerry Seedhouse, a pupil at the school from 1936-1941, retired after having been the School Bursar since 1971. During these nineteen years the school staff had increased enormously in number. Educational equipment had ceased to be merely chalk or rugby balls, but was now computers, videos, satellite dishes, photocopiers and risographs. An ex-Royal Navy officer who had seen action during the Second World War, Gerry was accurately described by Headmaster, Dennis Witcombe, as "never anything but courteous and approachable, and this is how he will be remembered by colleagues, parents and pupils." Nobody who had the privilege of dealing with Mr Seedhouse would ever argue with that.

July 1990

Clive Cox, the school's popular Pool Steward, was invited to attend the Royal Tournament at Earl's Court where, as a member of the Guard of Honour, he was presented to the Duke of Edinburgh and the Queen. Clive represented 41st Royal Marine Independent Commando and his invitation came in recognition of his work as branch welfare officer of the British Korean Veterans' Association. During the Korean War, Clive saw active service and was, for a long period, a much abused and mistreated prisoner of war in a North Korean prison camp.

Every week of the swimming season, 1990-1991

The new Geography teacher, Vicky Bruscomb, attracted huge numbers of boys to the pool for coaching sessions in the new sport of water-polo.

October 1990

Edward Wheatley was selected to play football for the Nottinghamshire U-19 side in the game against Cheshire, a comparatively rare distinction for a High School pupil since they are in direct competition with so many thousands of boys from the county's state schools. This appears to be the first time that a High School player had managed representative honours during the modern era.

Friday, October 12th 1990

The Sixth Form Birdwatching Group visited the White Post Farm where they saw Eagle Owls and Common Buzzards, weighed themselves on the animal weighbridge, played with a wide selection of baby animals and had an invigorating twenty minutes on the children's swings.

Friday, October 19th 1990

Thirteen Sixth Formers and five staff left for Pitlochry on the annual R.A.F. Adventurous Training expedition. They spent three days walking over a selection of Scottish Munroes.

Monday, December 17th 1990

The Nottinghamian carried a poem by Matt Allen. It described, presumably, one of his teachers:

> An accent so foreign
>
> A beard so strange
>
> The tie so extravagant
>
> He must be deranged.

January 1991

The Community Service Group presented Julia Stewart, the NSPCC Appeals Manager, with a cheque for £2,300. This had been raised on the Thursday, Friday and Saturday before Christmas Day by volunteers who visited a large number of Nottingham's pubs, singing carols and waving collecting shakers at members of the public of varying degrees of charitability and sobriety, the two attributes not necessarily being completely unconnected.

The May Day Bank Holiday 1991

The Nottingham Orienteering Club won the National U-13 and the National Under Age Group Championships. Oliver Edwards and Andrew Preston were members of the three-man team.

Friday, June 7th 1991

The school held its first *Bumper Fun Day*, organised by Wendy Nicolle and the Community Service Group to raise money for Prince's House, a charity which helped people with learning difficulties. The most popular attractions were *Soak the Teacher* and the Karaoke Machine, along with the sponsored swim, a geography quiz, and a pottery smash.

Monday, July 8th 1991

Matthew Kennedy took part in the Chemistry Olympiad in Poland where he won one of the British team's two bronze medals.

Sunday, July 14th 1991

The Preparatory Department visited Arques-La-Bataille in France. Their most surreal moment came when the entire party of forty boys queued up at the Post Office and every single one of them bought just one stamp for his post card home.

July 1991

Mrs Rene Moon retired after thirty-one years working as a senior member of the school's domestic staff. She was a lovely, cheerful lady, always very popular with teachers and ancillary staff alike.

The academic year 1991-1992

The Politics Society continued to attract a succession of eminent speakers. This year, they were to include Kenneth Clarke, the Home Secretary, Judge John Hopkin, Chief Inspector Jackson of the Nottinghamshire Police Force, Mr Barrington of the League against Cruel Sports, and Andrew Mitchell, the Conservative M.P. for Gedling.

September 1991

After a gap of almost thirty odd years, the Railway Society was reformed under the aegis of Nathan Duckworth. During the year, they travelled over 3,000 miles and managed 140 m.p.h. on the latest InterCity train as well as a more sedate pace on the steam locomotives of the Severn Valley Railway.

Thursday, September 5th 1991

Following the demise of the Boat Club, Martin Jones was cajoled into looking after the Second XV rugby team. After a disastrous run of results over the course of the previous season, it was decided that a change of management was necessary and so he was promoted to being in charge of the Under-12 team. During his first day in charge, he quickly realised that things were going to be very different as he was required to tie and untie the players' boot laces and distribute the half time oranges individually, otherwise fights ensued between the players. After the very first fixture at Valley Road, the largest boy in the team was extremely upset. He had lost his blazer and the only one left in the changing room was five sizes too small for him. He was unable to insert even his hands into the sleeves. The problem was soon solved as Martin watched the smallest boy walk out of the gates, wearing a blazer five sizes too big for him. He was, of course, completely unaware of the misfit.

Wednesday, December 18th 1991

Dennis Usher retired after fifty-one years' association with the High School. He entered the Preparatory Department in January 1940 and remained in the Main School until the latter years of that decade, becoming a Prefect and Company Sergeant Major of the C.C.F. After a period at Oxford University, he returned as a Mathematics teacher in January 1959. He immediately took over the Scouts which was his main contribution to school life outside the classroom.

Wednesday, April 15th 1992

While accompanying the French Trip back from the Côte d'Azur, I found a rare sea duck in the waters of the harbour at Dunkerque. It was an American Black Scoter (*Melanitta americana*), and the record of this vagrant was submitted to the French *Comité d'Homologation National*, who duly accepted it as the first ever to be seen in France and only the fifth ever in mainland Europe.

The General Election 1992

Old Nottinghamian Members of Parliament were now the Home Secretary, Kenneth Clarke (Conservative, Rushcliffe), Geoffrey Hoon (Labour, Ashfield), James Lester (Conservative, Broxtowe), and Piers Merchant (Conservative, Beckenham).

Saturday, July 8th 1992

The school chess team, coached by John Swain and Phil Eastwood, had qualified for the Final of The Times British Schools Chess Championship by beating City of London School by a margin of 4-2, although the score was actually a somewhat flattering one for their beaten opponents. In the Final, they were paired against Truro School. Stephen Joseph won his game on the top board in brilliant fashion and both Geoffrey Hodgett and Philip Faulkner triumphed in their matches. The winning margin of 3.5 points was achieved when Steven Maxwell agreed a draw in his match and Matthew Tailby then won his game to achieve a final winning margin of 4.5 to 1.5. The cup was presented by David Hopkinson, the Deputy Editor of *The Times*, along with a Disk Drive and a CD worth some £1,600. Sadly, Stephen Joseph was to succumb to cystic fibrosis on December 18th 1993 when he was in Year 13. His courage was an inspiration to all, not least when he insisted on being "released" from the City Hospital in order to play in some of the school chess team's matches.

The end of July 1992

Clive Cox retired, having worked at the High School from 1973 when he was initially employed as a gardener. He had seen active service as a Commando in the Korean War and survived the horrors of incarceration in a North Korean prison camp. As Pool Steward, "his bark was always worse than his bite, although many boy will long remember his piercing whistle, wall shaking shouts, comb and handkerchief inspection, and penetrating gaze along a pointing finger. He could immediately command rapt attention". Clive taught literally hundreds of boys to swim and numerous weak swimmers gained immensely from his expertise and understanding.

August 1992

A party of some twenty-five boys thought to have the potential to be 1st XV rugby players went on a ten day tour of France. They visited the south west and won their initial match against Montfort-en-Chalosse by 8-5. In the next game, however, they lost by a fifty point margin to a powerful Dax side although they won their final game against the host club of Mugron by 15-5.

The academic year 1992-1993

The Information Technology Centre was rehoused in M7 with brand new furniture, an ergonomic table layout and more than thirty computers which were now networked to a hard disk drive of some 160 Mb. I wonder what our grandfathers would have made of the instruction, "It is now safe to turn off your Macintosh."

The academic year 1992-1993

A small number of boys were released from rugby and allowed to do climbing as their Wednesday afternoon sport. This took place on the climbing wall on the side of the Sports Hall and allowed many boys to achieve Levels One and Two with Gavin Daw and Matthew Shale reaching Level Three.

Saturday, November 7th 1992

The U-16 XV beat Welbeck College by 100-0. This seems to be one of the High School's largest ever winning margins.

Wednesday, November 11th 1992

The Harry Djanogly Design Centre was opened by Chris Patten. The building had cost £700,000 and the majority of that sum was from Harry Djanogly who had already given so much to finance the new science block. Other donations were from the Wolfson Foundation and the Friends of Nottingham High School, as well as "a substantial contribution" from an anonymous benefactor.

December 1992

Peter Horril took early retirement through ill-health. He had rejoined the school in 1964, having already worked there from 1958-1962. During his career he had been Head of Mathematics and House Master of Coopers. He had also performed the school's least envied task, namely that of drawing up the teaching timetable. In his earlier years Peter had been keenly involved in school rowing and was later to gain great renown as an author of Maths textbooks.

Field Day, Christmas Term 1992

Masterminded by the English Department, and in particular Les Wilkinson, a hundred and twenty boys of the First Form re-enacted *The Saga of Hiawatha* in the Founder Hall. The play told the story of the Native American tribes of the plains and mountains with six different groups of boys each producing a scene each. The performance included a complete forest of trees, a large lake, a number of tepees, and copious quantities of warpaint and feathers.

Spring Term 1993

The *Doctor Rock Concert* raised a sum of just over £900, which was presented to the Maplewell Hall School who decided they would spend the money on Outward Bound type activities for their pupils.

A forgotten day in a forgotten Spring Term in the early 1990s

Every year, what was then the Fifth Form used to go down to the Sewage Works at Stoke Bardolph on Biology trips. Prompted by his French teacher, one of the cheekier members of the audience took advantage of the *Any Questions?* section of the afternoon to ask the young female scientist just what had attracted her to Sewage as a career. She was not in the slightest bit fazed. "Well," she said, "after leaving university, I initially spent a couple of years teaching Biology in an all boys' secondary school, and after that, I thought that the next logical step would be Sewage."

Saturday, April 10th 1993

The Senior Adventurous Training Group set off for North Wales where, accompanied by Martin Jones, Mark Cleverley and Brian Best, the group climbed the Glyders, Carneddau and Snowdon.

A forgotten day in the early 1990s

There is an apocryphal story that a teacher new to the school interpreted *Non-Uniform Day* as *Fancy-Dress Day* and turned up for school in Highland costume, complete with a kilt. In actual fact, he had no real problems whatsoever at school until, at the end of the day, he had to go to catch his bus on Mansfield Road. This necessitated an unforgiving walk through what was at the time pretty much the red-light area of Nottingham. Things did not go quite so well then.

After school, a forgotten evening in the early 1990s

A six year old Lauren Knifton from the P.N.E.U. School was introduced with great solemnity to the Headmaster, Dr Witcombe. Misunderstanding slightly, but ever polite, she bowed and asked him about his job as the "ringmaster". What scope for Smart Alec replies came in those few seconds of silence! What opportunities for witty pronouncements! Thank goodness, none of them taken.

The last game of the season, the early 1990s

In football, the First XI lost a thrilling game by 4-5. The memory of the coach, Stefan Krzeminski, is now, some twenty or so years later, understandably, a little hazy but he is certain that it was against a school somewhere out in the environs of Newark-on-Trent. What made the match especially memorable, however, was that the opponents had a young lady playing at right full back.

Wednesday, July 7th 1993

A group of eight boys, accompanied by Martin Jones and Richard Willan, departed on their World Challenge trip to Ecuador where they visited the capital, Quito, attempted unsuccessfully to climb Mount Tungauhura, walked along the Inca Trail for three days and spent several days in a rainforest.

The tennis season, 1993

Marc Powell represented Great Britain at Under-16 level in both Italy, Holland and Germany. He was listed in fourth place in the national rankings. Kevin Dhaliwal represented the Public Schools against the All-England Club, a match which they won for the first time since 1984.

Just before 6 a.m., Tuesday, August 31st 1993

Nathan Duckworth, William Taylor and his father Bill set out from Thurso in an attempt to "box the compass" on Britain's rail network. This involved visiting the most northern, southern, western and eastern railway stations in the shortest possible time. After Thurso, they visited Arisaig (western), Lowestoft (eastern), and then finally Penzance. Their final train was twelve minutes late, but nevertheless, they had taken 71 minutes off the previous record of forty hours five minutes.

1994

A brand new organ was installed in the Assembly Hall. It was a large three manual instrument, built by the Bradford Computer Organ Company. This new organ was paid for largely by donations, notably from various parents and friends of the school, especially Mr Gordon Sztejer without whose help its purchase would have been impossible.

Spring Term 1994

Andrew Preston won the M17 category at the British National Orienteering Championships, becoming the school's first ever national orienteering champion in any age group. Following this, he was invited to participate in the British U-21 tour of Norway.

Wednesday, February 2nd 1994

With myself as team coach, the Second XI defeated Bluecoat by six goals to two. Having gone the whole of the previous season without a win, this was their first victory in 27 months. The goals came from Steve Bennington, Mike Gurbutt, Adam Lawrence and James Redburn.

Saturday, April 2nd 1994

During Senior Adventurous Training in the Scottish Highlands two groups were caught in a "white out" near the summit of Ben Wyvis. As Jim Cook reached the group in front, they told him in a state of total shock that Martin Jones and Eddie Deverill had just vanished before their eyes. On looking down at the snow next to their feet, they realised that there was a big bite sized gap in the snow and that a large crack had appeared between their feet. Messrs Jones and Deverill had fallen vertically through a cornice on the cliff without having time to shout or scream. Despite a fifty foot fall onto snow they were both uninjured but nobody could see them. As their would-be rescuers went to get help they later climbed a ridge and "bagged" the summit.

Monday, April 11th-Monday, April 18th 1994

The Under-16 Cross Country team was invited to represent England in the International Schools' Federation Championships in Beijing, China. The races were held over a distance of five kilometres in the National Botanical Gardens and the team finished eleventh out of sixteen.

May 1994

The Nottinghamian printed what seems to have been a unique photograph. It showed the Hockey First XI squad, all with their backs to the camera. For ten of the members, this was reasonable as they all had their names printed on the back of their shirts, just like professional ice hockey players. One team member, however, thought to be R.J.Milligan, had a number 15 without a name, and another, who was conceivably W.Parry, had a shirt with neither number nor name.

Early July 1994

The Classics Department took a group of boys to Housesteads to view Hadrian's Wall. For what may well have been the first time ever, a report of the trip appeared in *The Nottinghamian* in Latin. It remains unclear just how many readers or staff were able to understand it.

The evening of Bumper Fun Day 1994

The First Year put on dramatic versions of two narrative poems, *The Rime of the Ancient Mariner* and *The Pied Piper of Hamelin*. Every single boy in the year played a part in the evening.

The end of the summer term 1994

Stephen Fairlie left after some marvellously creative years as Director of Music. He had been one of the co-founders of the Nottinghamshire Youth Orchestra and had written two musicals for the school, *Paul* and *Theseus*. More importantly, Stephen was a lovely human being with great patience. I shall personally always remember his idea that we should treat with courtesy, kindness and respect everybody who is different or who does not fit the accepted norms.

The end of the summer term 1994

Gordon Wood retired after thirty years at the High School. He had taught Geography in the Junior School but had been most prominent as the Head of Economics, taking over from A.N.S. "Stan" Thompson when the latter himself retired. Gordon was also very involved in the C.C.F. and eventually became Contingent Commander. He always had a great sense of humour and was a very well-liked man. I am sure that Gordon will have long forgotten that when I was his Assistant Form Master, he was the one who taught me how to keep a form register, using a system of zeroes and forward and backward slashes.

Friday, July 15th 1994

During their visit to RAF Waddington under the command of Jim Cook, Marcus Coulam and Martin Jones, some cadets from the C.C.F. misbehaved. As a punishment for their bad behaviour they were made to clean the underside of the wings of a gigantic Avro Vulcan bomber (3,554 square feet), using long brushes, buckets and step ladders.

The summer of 1994

A no doubt saddle sore Simon Williams achieved what he was later to describe as "my greatest personal triumph" He cycled across Europe from Calais to Hungary, taking in France, Switzerland and Austria. He battled over a number of enormous Alpine passes in a journey which took almost ten days and covered a total of 1,109 miles. On his last two days he managed 160 and 162 miles respectively. The trip left Simon with an indelible impression in several different ways. He achieved a top speed of 53 miles an hour downhill in the Alps and cycled to the very top of one particular pass at 2350 metres. His longest climb lasted eighteen kilometres uphill.

The rugby season 1994-1995

The 3rd XV failed to win a single match during the course of the season. Despite the fact that they were commendably keen and dedicated, every single game ended in defeat, some by large margins, such as the 0-83 reverse against Rugby School.

The rugby season 1994-1995

Playing for the U-12 XV, Tom Morgan scored a total of sixteen tries during the course of the season.

Christmas 1994

The Doctor Rock Concert raised £865 to aid with the purchase of a spirometer for those suffering from cystic fibrosis.

Wednesday, January 25th 1995

The First XI football team beat Bluecoat School by 11-1, according to *The Nottinghamian*, an "exceptionally enjoyable result". One of the team members was Peter Campbell who was to become a regular player for the Nottinghamshire U-19 side.

Wednesday, February 8th 1995

The Senior Cross Country team, consisting of Oliver Edwards, Andrew Preston, Ben Trapnell and Matthew Wilson won the Sutton Coldfield Road Relay, beating some top schools in the country.

Wednesday, February 15th 1995

The Second XI football team drew 5-5 with Becket School. This is apparently the highest scoring draw by a school football team in the modern era. On this occasion the referee blew the final whistle slightly early, thereby preventing either side from losing what had been a splendid game of football.

The Easter Holidays 1995

The National Concert Band Festival was held at the Royal Northern College of Music in Manchester. The School Big Band played *Born to Bop* with a fine solo on guitar by Matthew McGeever and further solos from James Marshall, Matthew Parry and Simon Parry. For their performance they received the Gold Award with the School Concert Band subsequently receiving a Silver Award.

Sports Day, April 1995

Three boys won three separate events in their age group. They were Richard Brindle (U-15), Andrew Turner (U-15) and Simon Strange (U-13). Later in the year, Andrew Turner was to finish in sixth position in the National English Schools' Championships, held this year at Harvey Haddon Stadium.

May 1995

The Governors appointed Christopher Parker to succeed Dr Dennis Witcombe when he retired in September 1995. Mr Parker had graduated from Bristol University with a degree in Geography and had done his P.G.C.E. at Cambridge University. He had taught initially at Bedford Modern School, before becoming Head of the Geography Department at Bradford Grammar School at the very early age of only twenty-five. He was then promoted to be Deputy Head of Goffs School in Hertfordshire, before becoming Head of Batley Grammar School in 1986. Three years later Mr Parker was invited to join the Headmasters' Conference, bringing with it full public school status for his school. As well as Geography, Mr Parker was a distinguished 1st XV coach at both Bradford and Bedford, where his team won the Rosslyn Sevens, and at Batley he was a keen supporter of their football teams. Away from school, as a member of an H.M.C. Working Party, he strongly favoured the Government's Assisted Places Scheme and was also a member of the

Admiralty Interview Board, selecting potential officers for the Royal Navy. In this guise, he was featured on BBC2's *Situations Vacant*.

Friday, May 19th 1995

Sir Bernard Ingham visited the Politics Society. Other speakers during the course of the year included members of the Natural Law Party, Lord Longford, Matthew Parris and Kate Adie.

Saturday, June 17th 1995

Playing against Forest Amateurs, Richard Nicholson scored 129 not out. During the season, he was to score 545 runs at an average of 60.56.

Sunday, July 7th 1995

The Community Action Group took a group of pensioners on a mystery trip. As in every single previous year, the bus went to Oxton Village Hall but nobody actually seemed to notice as they were all very busy eating, drinking, talking and playing bingo. A good time was had by all, even Jon Healy, Andrew Hesselden and Matthew Shale, the Sixth Formers who gallantly did all the washing up.

July 1995

Three important members of the domestic staff left the school. They were Jenny Cooper who, having served in the tuckshop, had possibly sold more Mars bars than anyone in the history of the school. Beryl Edson had worked in the General Office for many years and Rosey Upton, with her Risograph machine, had printed literally millions of worksheets in the Reprographics Department.

July 1995

Dennis Witcombe retired after twenty-five years as Headmaster of the High School. Throughout these years he had given enormous support to a wide range of school activities from 1st XV rugby to Music, Drama, the Duke of Edinburgh scheme and a whole host of other events. He was responsible for a number of building initiatives such as the new Preparatory School, the Science Block, the Design Technology Block and the Sports Hall, although surely to every boy and to every parent the most abiding memory will be his almost legendary handwriting.

July 1995

In the Physics Olympiad, Chris Biggs was placed in the top forty-five candidates nationally, and won a Silver Award.

6.30 a.m., Monday, July 17th 1995

Sergeant Dana Faratian was roused from sleep to begin his day at R.A.F.Wittering, where: "despite being meant to be on holiday, I was shouted at for having my hands in my pockets, for not wearing my beret, for not having the badge on my beret exactly over my left eye". Advantages to life in the R.A.F. however, were three cooked meals a day and visits by the Red Arrows, the Battle of Britain Memorial Flight and a simulated attack on the airfield by the station's Hawker Harriers.

Thursday, July 20th 1995

During the World Challenge expedition to Tanzania the party, led by Jim Cook, Martin Jones and Richard Willan, was camping close to the volcano Ol Doinyo Lengai. They were accompanied by four Masai guides who, on one occasion, stayed up talking by the fire for the whole night. In the morning it was discovered that a man had recently been killed by a lion very close to the site where they were now camping. The party, of course, were never in any danger as they were armed with an antique single shot Martini-Henry rifle, a weapon certainly capable of dealing with a simultaneous attack by five or six hungry lionesses.

August 1995

In his Art A-level, Henry Nwume achieved one of the top five marks in the country. He received full congratulations from the Associated Examining Board.

Friday, August 18th 1995

As part of the World Challenge expedition to Tanzania, the members of the school party climbed Mount Kilimanjaro. Jim Cook, Martin Jones, Richard Willan and some twenty boys reached the ice cliffs on the summit crater at 6.30 in the morning, at a height of some 19,341ft above sea level. They were able to watch the sun rise over the curved African plain below. It was a truly unforgettable experience for all of them. As well as mountaineering, the group visited numerous wildlife sites and helped with building work at Msufini High School where, in keeping with school tradition, they lost the commemorative football match against Msufini Sixth Form by 1-3.

The academic year 1995-1996

The Climbing Club went from strength to strength. Tom de Gay and Tim Marsh both reached their Level 3 Proficiency Award within their first year of joining the club.

Sunday, September 24th 1995

The eleventh annual David Leicester Memorial Walk took place. It covered 25 miles along the Shropshire Way and participants included boys, staff, Old Boys, and members of David's family. During the previous year over £1,000 had been donated from the fund to help various members of the school to finance adventurous training activities.

The rugby season 1995-1996

The 3rd XV, in only nine matches, used a record total of thirty-five players. These included Olly Nickalls, whom *The Nottinghamian* described as "the team's silent leopard". Meanwhile, the U-13 XV, coached by Tim Dibdin and David Talbot, won every one of its fourteen matches, scoring 553 points, and conceding only fifty.

October 1995

The Concert Band, Big Band and Chamber Choir, a total of some seventy-two High School musicians, visited Venice in Italy. They gave six performances around the city, including one memorable evening when the Chamber Choir sang in St Mark's Cathedral.

Wednesday, October 4th 1995

Accompanied by Ken Clayton and Jim Cook, the 3rd XV were away to Rugby School for the first time ever. Everybody was extremely apprehensive, and with very good reason. Their coach was also the match referee and after each score he kept shouting loudly "Come on, let's get to a hundred!! Let's get to a hundred!!" The High School, however, defended the last ten minutes magnificently. The final score was Rugby School 99 Nottingham High School 3rd XV 0.

Friday, October 27th 1995

A party of eight Year 11 and Year 12 pupils, accompanied by Messrs Cook, Corbould, Jones and Rood, embarked on their journey to the Lake District. They climbed a number of mountains, including Kirk Fell, Looking Stead, Scoat Fell, Red Pike, Yewbarrow and Scafell Pike.

March 1996

Alistair Footitt represented England in Germany against five other orienteering teams. Alistair finished in fifth position overall, and was the fastest British runner.

The Easter Holidays 1996

Forty children from Forest Fields Primary School, seven Notts County footballers, fifteen Sixth Formers and Malcolm Saperia all assembled at Valley Road playing fields for a football coaching session. It was so successful that children from Berridge Road Juniors were able to have their own coaching session there in June.

The first Wednesday of the cricket season, 1996

In their traditional fixture against the school, the M.C.C. scored the extremely high total of 273-4. In reply, however, the 1st XI were able to win the game, thanks to a magnificent innings of 133 not out from Keith Tate, assisted by 59 from Andrew Parker and a cavalier 36 from James Hartley. Keith's innings was rightly judged to be the best of the season, and in recognition of this, he was awarded a commemorative bat and a miniature replica bat signed by past and present England captains.

The cricket season 1996

The Under 14 XI, coached by Roger Benson and Simon Turrill and captained by Andrew Saxton, won thirteen of their fourteen matches. Highlights included their dismissal of a previously unbeaten Macclesfield side for only 32 runs and an astonishing victory over Trinity School, Aspley, when the team scored 272-3 off 35 overs with Richard Pilgrim and Paul Riley achieving a partnership of 206 runs in 26 overs. Trinity were then dismissed for 32 all out, clinching a victory by 240 runs. The main batsmen in the side were the openers, Gary Middleton and Paul Riley, ably assisted by Richard Pilgrim and Andrew Saxton. The best bowlers were usually Lamin Marenah, Gary

Middleton, Vaqaas Mohbat and Paul Riley. Tom Shacklock was an excellent wicketkeeper.

The cricket season 1996

The Under 12 XI, coached by Leigh Corbould and Kevin Weaver, won eight of their nine matches, despite the relatively high total of some twenty-five players used in the team.

April 1996

The A-Level Politics set visited the House of Commons, where they were able to watch Michael Heseltine and John Prescott "exchange rapid fire for twenty minutes on a variety of topics." Unfortunately, both John Major and Tony Blair were absent from the house as they were busy welcoming Nelson Mandela who was in the country on a state visit. Other politicians that the group did manage to see included Geoffrey Archer, Tony Banks, and Roy Hattersley.

April 1996

Andrew Parker, the captain of the Hockey 1st XI, was chosen to represent Wales in the Under-18 Home Countries Tournament. Later in the year, he was to appear for the Wales Under-21 side.

Wednesday, May 15th 1996

The Summer Concert took place in the Albert Hall. For perhaps the first time ever, a pupil, Ben Sanders was allowed to review a school event of this type in *The Nottinghamian*. While he thought that "Charles Bain was brilliant singing on his own", and that, in "Playful Pizzicato", "the plucking of strings was brilliant", Ben was also allowed to venture the opinion that "the Chamber Choir I didn't like it", and the rather heretical "I'm not really fond of church choirs" and "I didn't enjoy this, as I'm not a real fan of classical music".

Wednesday, June 19th 1996

The 3rd XI alias "The Cluniacs", played a fixture against High Pavement who reached 92-8, with eight different bowlers each taking a wicket. "The Cluniacs" eventually won by nine wickets.

The beginning of July 1996

Members of the Community Action group spent two days at Alton Towers with thirty children aged between eight and eleven years of age. The most popular rides were Nemesis and the Bouncy Castle.

July 1996

The Under 14 XI won the County Cup at Trent Bridge, dismissing West Bridgford School for just 91 runs and reaching a winning total in only 21 overs.

July 1996

In the National Final of the Intel Chess Challenge, held at Nottingham County Hall, Rajesh Reddy held out for fifty moves, lasting for just over three hours, against Nigel Short, a World Championship contender.

July 1996

The highlight of the tennis season is the Independent Schools' Tennis Association Championships which are held at Eton College. The standard is always high with around fifty schools competing. Many competitors, including Tim Henman, have gone on to play at Wimbledon. This year the High School, coached by Malcolm Saperia, won the Thomas Bowl for Under-15s when the trophy was lifted by Jeremy Smith and Marc Powell.

Monday, August 5th 1996

Edward Brentnall, Russell Coxon, Leigh Jepson, Andrew Moore, Jonathan Polnay and Alex Sweeney left Nottinghham en route for the Alps. There, with the help of Will Hurford, a former member of staff, they succeeded in climbing Mont Blanc, the highest peak in Europe.

Winter term 1996

In the National Simultaneous Pairs Bridge Competition, Mark Goddard and Rowan Temple finished in a very impressive eighth position. Earlier in the season before a series of lectures from Tony Neale of the Nottingham Bridge Club the Team of Eight had lost heavily in every single game.

September 1996

Andrew Preston became the school's first ever Orienteering international, when he ran in Northern Ireland, finishing second in the Junior Home International. Later in the year he was to finish fourth in the British Championship and to visit Scandinavia twice with the U-19 tour.

October 1996

The school's Team of Four, in the persons of Robin Blaney, Mark Goddard, Naveen Kachroo and Adam Polnay, won the Midlands Open Team of Four Bridge Championship for Schools.

Wednesday, October 16th 1996

The Second XI opened their season by beating Bilborough College by an amazing ten goals to one. This was just the first of a grand total of three victories in the season, in one of which the goalkeeper, Sachin Gajree, saved a penalty, the first time that this had happened within living memory.

Monday, November 11th 1996

Thanks to the new Headmaster, Chris Parker, who had spotted a number of discrepancies between the names on the school's Rolls of Honour and those on the War Memorial, a total of five names was added to the inscription on the statue at the front of the school.

These were H.A.Johnstone (died May 21st 1918), J.G.Johnstone (died of wounds, May 1922), F.Parry (died of wounds, 1918), A.Riddle (killed March 24th 1918) and H.F.Senior (died of wounds, April 13th 1918).

November 1996

The 3rd XV lost so many players to an injury hit 2nd XV that they fielded a side of only thirteen individuals. They were narrowly defeated.

November 1996

The whole of Year 8 entered the Junior Mathematical Challenge. They won 22 gold, 32 silver and 29 bronze awards. Steven Dyke was first in the school by some considerable margin and was invited to take part in the Junior Mathematical Olympiad where he won a bronze medal.

Mid-November 1996

In the British Schools Orienteering Championships (held in Scotland), Alistair Footitt won M16 and was selected to represent the United Kingdom Schools in the World Orienteering Championships in Italy. In addition, Tim Blaney finished in a very creditable third position in M13.

December 1996

Demolition work started on the Music School in order to build a better one. The Music School had, of course, begun its life as a dining room.

December 1996

In the Intermediate Mathematics Challenge Jeremy Young scored full marks, one of the only two entrants in the whole United Kingdom to do this. He was then invited to participate in the International Intermediate Invitational Mathematics Challenge where he again scored full marks, the only contestant to do so.

December 1996

The Nottinghamian published a number of "haiku" about the various seasons. Alexander Smith wrote of autumn:

> Nature sheds its leaves,
>
> Ready to rest before,
>
> It dresses again.

And Tim Pickin wrote about winter:

> The trees are empty
>
> Skeletons standing alone
>
> In fields of snow.

Robert Horabin described spring as:

> Slowly melting ice
>
> In the Spring's warmer air
>
> Winter's wrath has gone.

Anthony Rawlins was slightly less optimistic about the English summer:

> The sweltering heat
>
> This wonderful weather

It won't last for long.

Wednesday, March 12th 1997

Having lost seven games out of seven, the Second XI played their very last football fixture of the season against High Pavement College. They duly won by two goals to one, the winning goal coming from Giles Ball, after an intricate build up involving three accurate passes.

April 1997

The Politics Society was entertained by Ian Hislop, the editor of *Private Eye* magazine, and a team captain in the satirical TV show *Have I Got News For You*. The demand to see this nationally known personality was so great that tickets had to be printed for the meeting, creating for the first and possibly last time, a black market in clandestine ticket sales.

The cricket season, 1997

The Under 13 XI, coached by David Talbot, won ten of its eleven matches. The main batsmen were Messrs Bratley, Davies, Foster, Sargent, Seaton and Tew, and Wright was a competent wicketkeeper. The best bowlers were the fast bowlers Foster, Karim, and Sood, the spinners, Bratley and Cardwell, and the seamers, Sargent, Seaton and Zaki.

The cricket season, 1997

The 3rd XI, coached by Colin Sedgewick and now officially christened "The Cluniacs", played only three matches during the season. They won just one of them, against High Pavement, when Stefan Flannery scored forty runs and Geoff Oxendale took four wickets for just five runs.

Saturday, May 10th and Sunday, May 11th 1997

Almost two hundred High School boys participated in the Notts A.A.A. Championships held at Harvey Hadden Stadium. In total, they won eighteen gold medals and a large number of silvers and bronzes, a feat which enabled the school to accumulate a massive number of points and thereby win every single age group of the competition by a large margin.

The day of the General Election 1997

Alistair Footitt left for Italy to represent the United Kingdom in the World Schools' Orienteering Championships. Individually, he finished in fifth position and the British Team won the competition overall. Alistair thereby became the first High School boy to win a Gold Medal at world level since Frederick Chapman won a Gold Medal for Association Football in the Olympic Games of 1908.

June 1997

Having already won the County Championship in the Intermediate 100 Metres Hurdles, Andrew Turner competed at national level in the English Schools Championship. He won the event in a new school record time of 12.98 seconds and received a gold medal. The following week he ran for England in an international match against Ireland, Scotland and Wales.

Thursday, June 26th 1997

The Junior Maths Club, led by Roger Kilby and Kevin Weaver, visited Green's Windmill in Sneinton, enjoying a number of mathematical puzzles and the impressive plasma ball.

Around 2.10 p.m., Friday, June 27th 1997

The coach, driven by John Hayes, departed on the Latin Year 10 trip to Hadrian's Wall. The boys spent a weekend based in Otterburn Hall and visited Housesteads and Vindolanda, spending their time not just in museums, but also in walking along the wall itself. They returned to Nottingham via Chester where they were able to visit the cavalry fort and the bathhouse.

July 1997

Cooper's House, encouraged by Martin Jones, raised no less than £2,700 to help in the fight against Multiple Sclerosis. The following year, they excelled themselves by collecting some £4,000, of which £2,500 was donated to the Play Centre at Sherwood, for disabled children and their families, and £1,500 went to the Hunter Trust, which provides educational opportunities for children in Malawi.

July 1997

Allan Sparrow retired after eighteen years, much of it as Head of the History Department. He was a keen photographer and was in charge of school swimming for many years despite the fact that he himself could not actually swim. Allan was an extremely academic man with a keen, analytical mind, whose opinion was often sought and always respected.

Chris Curtis retired after thirty-three years. He had taught Classics and was Head of the Lower School for many years. He was also the first ever Chairman of the Staff Common Room Committee. Chris took many Classics trips in this country and abroad, but one of his best claims to fame must surely be his twenty-five years of rugby coaching, mainly with the U-12 XV.

Ian Parker retired after thirty-nine years, much of it as Head of Physics or Head of Science. He was responsible for the initiative to take the science classrooms and laboratories out of the Main School and to house them in a separate, purpose built Science Block. Most boys, though, will remember Ian as the teacher who played the organ in Assembly or, in the case of the older ones, as the person in charge of Cross Country and Athletics and then in later years, of Shooting.

August 1997

The High School's World Challenge team accompanied by Jim Cook, Martin Jones and Richard Willan, visited Sulawesi in Indonesia. In the village of Wasu, they played a football match against the locals. The team was Mitchell: Bravant, Johnston, Lauder, Nickalls: Hands, Rogers, Pratt: Raven, Excel, Bilkhu. Aided by the presence of an Indonesian guest player at centre forward, the High School team, keeping up the school's fine traditions in this global sport, won by a heart stopping 7-6.

Monday September 15th - Wednesday, September 17th 1997

Having won the East Midlands heat a few months previously, Marek Nelken participated in the National Finals of the Young Engineer of the Year contest. He met various TV personalities including Carol Vorderman, Johnny Ball, Trevor Bayliss, Kate Bellingham, Bob Symes and Vivienne Parry and was judged the Best User of Computer Technology, winning the IBM Prize.

October 1997

The school bridge team finished second in the Team of Four Event at Rushcliffe. Mark Goddard, Naveen Kachroo, Graham Nelson and Rowan Temple almost won but were pipped into second place by a team containing their own bridge teacher, Mary Mills.

November 1997

In swimming, the Under-14 team won the regional finals to qualify for the Bazuka National Finals in Wolverhampton. In the latter event, Paul Webster of Year 9 was to win two silver medals.

Early November 1997

A number of school orienteering teams participated in the British Schools' Championships held near Winchester. The Year 7 team of Matthew Forester, David Simner and Tom Wilson won the M11 age class and Alistair Footitt won his age class for the fourth consecutive year. A team of Year 7 and Year 8 boys, namely Tim Bagguley, Martin Cox and James Seddon, won the M12 age class and, despite not being able to field mixed teams, the school finished in their best ever overall position of third in the country.

Wednesday, November 19th 1997

Lady Carol Djanogly performed the opening ceremony for the new Lady Carol Djanogly Music School. The building, which had taken only ten months to complete, contained a recital hall for a hundred and fifty musicians, ten specialist practice rooms, a percussion studio, and a music technology laboratory which offered an 8-track direct-to-disc digital recording facility.

Wednesday, December 10th 1997

The First XI, coached by Stefan Krzeminski, played Trent College at football. This fixture is a very long standing one and dates from December 17th 1870, when the High School won the first ever match in Long Eaton by 3-0. The two teams had not met since the match at Trent College on November 27th 1889 when the High School triumphed by 5-4 in a closely fought game. A return fixture in Nottingham was offered to Trent College, but they refused it, according to the school magazine: "making a very paltry protest against our playing four masters, while they only played three, the probable cause being that they were afraid of a beating." Fortunately feelings on both sides had calmed down somewhat in the intervening one hundred and nine years and, this time, the High School won a very sporting encounter by two goals to one.

Friday, December 12th 1997

The Politics Society was addressed by Anne Widdicombe, the shadow spokesperson on Health, and the most entertaining speaker of the year although only by a very narrow winner over Neil and Christine Hamilton who had recently appeared on television in the satirical quiz show, *Have I Got News For You* .

Sports Day 1998

Koby Gyasi won the Under-15 100 metres in a new record time of 11.39 seconds. Later in the year he competed in this event at national level in the England Schools Athletic Championships where he finished seventh.

7.30 a.m., Wednesday, April 15th 1998

Eleven pupils from Years 10 and 11, accompanied by Alison Griffin and Grahame Whitehead, left on the German Exchange to Gilching near Munich. They visited monasteries and breweries, Neuschwanstein Castle, the local Springtime Festival, and watched Munich 1860 play Hertha Berlin in an exciting Bundesliga relegation battle.

May 1998

Tim Blaney and Stephen Wright both went to Latvia to represent Great Britain in the World Schools' Orienteering Championships. It was a very difficult course, made up of dense woodland and sand dunes, but Tim Blaney was the first British runner to finish.

Tuesday, May 5th 1998

The High School's proposed "partnership" scheme with the Shepherd School was one of only forty-seven from nearly three hundred applications to be approved by the government. It would involve the establishment of a video conferencing facility so that staff and pupils at both schools could communicate easily for planning and conducting meetings. In addition, members of Years 10 and 11 from the School Community Action Group would spend time working with children at the Shepherd School, something which it was hoped they would find both challenging and enriching.

Saturday, May 9th 1998

The High School History Department, under the leadership of Matthew Bartlett, took a trip to the Heritage Motor Museum, just one of their many weekend days out during the course of the year. Boys were able to learn not just about the history of the car but also to have a session on the Land Rover Test Circuit and to try out some Quad Biking before moving on to view Blenheim Palace.

Sunday, May 10th 1998

The Senior Swimming Team, consisting of Chris Douglas, Richard Green, Bruce Lauder, Neil Pallender and Paul Webster competed in an Invitation Gala held at St Paul's School, London. They finished second equal with the City of London Freeman's School, beaten only by Campbell College. This was the high point in what was probably the best ever year in the history of school swimming.

Tuesday, May 19th 1998

The Year 9 Latin pupils went to visit Lunt Fort in Coventry to see how the Roman army used to operate. They were able to try on Roman armour, and to have mock fights with Roman weapons.

The cricket season 1998

The Under-14 XI won all eleven of their matches. The side's first five batsmen were usually Karim, Sargent, Sood, Seaton and Davies, with the middle order usually drawn from Bratley, Foster, Middleton, Morris or Perkins. Tew, Wright and Cardwell then frequently provided a sting in the tale.

The tennis season 1998

James Armstrong and Tom Day reached the last eight of the Public Schools' Tennis Championships.

The end of the Summer Term 1998

Marcus Coulam left the R.A.F. section of the C.C.F. after 28 years' service, six of which he had spent in charge of the C.C.F. as a whole.

The end of the Summer Term 1998

John Wood left the school after seventeen years as a Mathematics teacher, six of them as Head of Department. In this latter capacity, he was the inventor of the Departmental Handbook and was responsible for a number of other important initiatives particularly in the field of Information Technology. Outside the classroom, he devoted much time to Careers Advice, school music, Duke of Edinburgh expeditions and school cricket, as well as a Sixth Form General Studies Geology course.

Thursday, July 9th 1998

The Under-14 XI won the County Cup, defeating Rushcliffe by a narrow margin at Trent Bridge.

July 1998

Three different pupils took part in academic Olympiads. Tim Richards represented Great Britain in the 29th Physics Olympiad held in Reykjavik and came third in the British team which was 96th out of 350. Robert Wilson participated in the International Chemistry Olympiad in Melbourne, Australia, achieving a position of 71st out of 200 and receiving a bronze medal for his score of 78%. Although a year under age Jeremy Young went to the 39th Mathematical Olympiad held in Taiwan and won a bronze medal, finishing second in the British team. This was the first time that any school in the country had had three pupils participating in International Olympiads at the same time.

The England Schools Athletic Championships 1998

During the course of the season, Andrew Turner had broken school records at 100 metres (11.1 seconds), 200 metres (22.7 seconds), 110 metres hurdles (14.24 seconds), and long jump (6.93 metres). At national level in the Under-20 110 metres Hurdles, he won a bronze medal.

The England Schools Athletic Championships 1998

Already the Nottinghamshire County Champion, Oladipo Senbanjo came fifth at national level in the Under-17 Triple Jump.

Sunday, July 12th 1998

In cricket, the First XI played against the XL Club who set them a victory target of 235, Roger Kitching taking three wickets for 44 runs. The High School won by five wickets, after a partnership between James Hartley (63) and James Shacklock with his first century for the First XI.

Late July 1998

A party of thirty-two boys, sixteen staff and two Old Boys went to the annual camp at Bala, in Wales. They were able to enjoy canoeing, rock climbing, orienteering, and pony trekking.

Summer 1998

Simon King was one of only ten people nationally to be selected as Earthwatch Fellows in the ARCO Young Scientist of the Year Award. This enabled him to carry out his project on volcanoes in Skaftafell National Park in Iceland.

August 1998

In the Under-14 events Paul Webster finished in fourth position in the 200 Metres Butterfly in the National Age Group Swimming Finals at Leeds. In the U-13s, Kevin O'Loughlin came sixth in both the 100 metres and the 200 metres.

Friday, August 27th 1998

Alan Wheelhouse died after a long illness. He had been at the High School as a pupil from 1945-1953, and was both a Committee Member and President of the Old Nottinghamians' Society in 1981. From 1988 onwards he was a Governor of the School, and Chairman of the School Committee. In the words of *The Nottinghamian*: "many of the recent improvements in the school owe much to his hard work, and future generations will benefit from his energy and foresight."

Monday, September 21st 1998

Roger Kilby, Head of Mathematics, watched Jeremy Young and the rest of the United Kingdom International Mathematical Olympiad team receive their medals at the Royal Society in London.

October 1998

National Bag and Back Campaign Week proved to the boys, if, indeed, they needed it, that they were being asked to transport almost dangerous weights of homework around the county.

October 8th-17th 1998

Eleven pupils from the Christoph-Probst Gymnasium in Gilching near Munich visited the school as part of the German Exchange. They enjoyed a full programme of visits and activities including trips to Warwick Castle and Cadbury World.

October 22nd-28th 1998

Messrs Bird, Douglas, Spedding and Streets accompanied forty boys on the Classics Trip to Rome, Naples, Pompeii, Sorrento and Capri.

Sunday, November 15th 1998

In the British Schools' Orienteering Championships, Tim Bagguley, Tim Blaney, Matthew Winser and Stephen Wright all achieved top ten positions in the face of over 1,400 competitors. Tim Bagguley, James Seddon and Tom Wilson won the Year 8 Championship and Tim Blaney, Matthew Winser and Stephen Wright won the Year 11 Championship. No other school had ever retained a trophy for the second year but the High School won the Year 8 Championship for the second time and the Year 11 Championship for the third time. Previously, in early November, Stephen Wright had won the M16 Class of the British Night Championship, with Tim Blaney in second place.

December 1998

The Nottinghamian continued to publish poetry from the boys. This particular example, from Edward Aram of Year 7, was no doubt inspired by the hit film of the day:

> The Titanic with her mighty funnels,
> Has set sail from Southampton's great water,
> That would soon rush over her gunwales,
> And then kill the poet's favourite daughter.
>
> Titanic flew straight across the ocean,
> Her many passengers joyful with glee,
> But not one would have the slightest notion,
> That she would sink to the bed of the sea.

> But sadly that night came the fateful sight,
> From the head of the water poked up ice!
> Many people would drown that awful night,
> And force designer Andrews to think twice.
>
> Oh that horrid night when the death count grew,
> And little survived, not even the crew.

An unrecorded, damp and misty afternoon in late 1998

The First XI, coached by Stefan Krzeminski, played their County Cup semi-final against Christ the King School, Arnold, using facilities kindly provided by High Pavement College. Leading by three goals to two with just a few minutes left, Christ the King brought on their fourth substitute in an effort to counter the First XI's continuing attacks in search of a third equaliser. A fourth substitute, however, by the rules of the competition, was not allowed and a written protest was duly made. After lengthy deliberations by the Nottinghamshire Schools' F.A., and the English Schools' F.A. the officers of the Nottinghamshire Schools' F.A decided that: "although there had been a technical offence, in the spirit of schools' football, the original decision and result should be allowed to stand."

Wednesday, December 2nd 1998

Forty Year 10 boys went to the Carlton TV studios to watch the recording of *Mad for It*, a children's TV programme. Six boys were competitors and eventually Tom Fletcher of 10S was selected to go on a *Blind Date* type holiday at EuroDisney in Paris.

Wednesday, December 9th 1998

The 3rd XV, coached by Ken Clayton and Jim Cook, played their final game of the season away against Hall Cross School, Doncaster. They changed in a freezing, empty gym, played on a public park, apparently frequented by all the local dogs, and the referee was wearing a full all-white 1972 Leeds United kit. The opposition contained a large number of their 1st XV players, who had all been dropped down to their third team for some mysterious reason. At the first scrum our hooker shouted "Don't punch!" Immediately, their entire pack adopted a tea-pot stance and mimicked in an upper class accent "Oooh..downt panch". The 3rd XV's only consolation that day was to be allowed to use the girls' showers afterwards to wash the blood off. In actual fact, a grand total of forty different players was used during the course of that season.

Sunday, December 13th 1998

The High School featured prominently in the *Mail on Sunday* colour magazine. This tabloid interest came as a result of the political successes of Kenneth Clarke, Geoff Hoon, Ed Balls and Edward Davey.

Wednesday, December 16th 1998

The school carol service took place at All Saints' Church in Raleigh Street. It featured the Chamber Choir singing a selection of carols.

The late 1990s

Making the very first of what were to be several appearances on Channel Four's popular word game, *Countdown*, Stanley Ward (the school's Deputy Headmaster from 1969-1981), asked the beautiful but very brainy, Carol Vorderman, for his first ever letters. Amazingly, the first three turned out to be D, T and W, the initials of Dennis Trevor Witcombe who had been the Headmaster from 1970-1995, and whose period of service overlapped Stanley's tenure of the office of Deputy Headmaster almost perfectly.

Spring Term 1999

A revival of Ancient Greek began when Murray Streets started to coach a small group of volunteers during the lunch hour. The aim was that eventually, they would be able to work towards an A/S Level qualification during their General Studies time in the Sixth Form.

Sunday, March 21st 1999

In the Zone Final of *The Times* British Schools Chess Championship, the school lost only on age difference after a 3-3 draw. Their opponents, Oakham School, had the World U-18 Champion on Board 1 and his twin brother, an English international, on Board 2. Their Board 3 player was on a chess scholarship and World Champion, Gary Kasparov, had already selected him as one of the most exciting prospects in Russia.

Easter 1999

The very last Adventurous Training in Scotland took place this year. The school was unable to continue visiting the Highlands because of the very strict criteria governing the qualifications of group leaders.

Friday, April 23rd 1999

Headmaster Chris Parker was named a Commander of the Order of the British Empire in the Queen's Birthday Honours List for his "services to education", notably his role as Chairman of the Government's Advisory Group on Independent / State School Partnerships.

May 1999

For decades, dissecting rats was a mainstay of practical examinations in Biology. Jim Cook used to collect freshly killed rats from the Boots Laboratories in Pennyfoot Street in the middle of Nottingham. On one hot day in May, he rushed down to collect an enormously heavy bag of rodents for that day's exam. As he struggled into the Prep Room, the bag inexplicably ripped open, to spill a huge pile of pristine, but dead, white rats on the floor. The reason for the ripped bag suddenly became clear as one rat looked up and then made a dash behind the fridge. Obviously, Super Rat had chewed his way out of the heavy duty bag. Kim, the technician, and Jim Cook, were none too keen to drag the great escaper from his new den.

Chapter 17: The New Millennium

May 1999

Brian Best retired after more than seventeen years. At various times he had helped with audio-visual resources and run a car maintenance course, but most of all, Brian had been an invaluable member of the C.C.F. More than a thousand cadets were thought to have had direct contact with Brian and he had attended all of the twice yearly field days, annual Adventurous Training and the annual Central CCF camps. Brian was a "real character" and was always extremely popular with the boys, a very large number of whom would call in to see him whenever they revisited their old school.

Wednesday, May 9th 1999

The school received a Sportsmark Award from the Sport England organisation, for the quality of their physical education and sports provision. It was accepted by Clem Lee and Martin Smith.

Thursday, May 13th, and Friday, May 14th 1999

The senior swimming team, consisting of Leighton Cardwell, Chris Douglas, Richard Green, Kevin O'Loughlin, Neil Pallender and Paul Webster, became UK National Swimming Champions, beating Robert Gordon's College of Aberdeen and Campbell College from Ulster into second and third place respectively.

Tuesday, May 19th 1999

Non-uniform Day raised a total of £1,600 for the Kosovo Refugees.

June 1999

The High School Fencing Team finished third in the Stratford Foil (Public Schools') Competition.

June 1999

Paul Webster (Year 10) won six events at the ASA Midland District Championships. They were the 100m and 200m Butterfly, the 100m,

200m, 400m and 1500 m freestyle. He also came second in the 400 m Individual Medley.

Thursday, June 17th 1999

At the Independent and Prep School Relays Finals, held at Bromsgrove Dolphin Centre, a High School team of twelve and thirteen year olds won the 4 x 50 metres freestyle event. They were Tim Bagguley, Tom Griffin, John-Claude Hesketh and Kevin O'Loughlin and they broke the national record by more than two seconds. In the 4 x 25 metres medley relay final a team including James Thomas finished in second place but they too broke the national record for the event.

Friday, June 18th 1999

As part of their *Keep the Army in the Public Eye Tour*, members of the First Battalion the Worcestershire and Sherwood Foresters under the command of one of our Old Boys, Jim Ellis, brought a Warrior Armoured Personnel Carrier to school. A large number of boys were able to explore the vehicle and to see an extensive collection of weapons used in the Bosnia conflict.

Friday, June 18th 1999

A special parade was held to allow the Worcestershire and Sherwood Foresters to present Mr Parker with a framed memento of Albert Ball VC, the Great War air ace. The school had recently accepted a role as official guardian of the Ball VC Memorial at Annoeuillin, France where Ball crashed on May the 7th 1917.

Saturday, June 26th 1999

The History Department wound up their extensive series of weekend visits with a trip to Holkham Hall and Sandringham in Norfolk. During the course of the year Matthew Bartlett had organised twenty-nine history visits from Dover to the Firth of Forth with more than twenty members of staff helping out from a variety of different departments.

Summer Term 1999

In the County Championships, the School Athletics captain, Andy Turner, won gold medals in seven different events.

Sunday, July 4th 1999

Roy Henderson became one of the longest lived Old Nottinghamians ever when he reached the age of 100. During his time at the High School (1909-1917) he was in the First XV for three years and played cricket for the First XI for four years, captaining the team in 1917. He later became a Professor at the Royal College of Music and in 1970 received a CBE for his "services to the art of singing". On November 11th 1922, he had been the soloist at the dedication of the school's War Memorial when he sang a special song *What are those which are arrayed in white robes?*

Tuesday, July 13th 1999

Tim Dibdin left the school after sixteen years' dedicated service. He was a Geography teacher and coached junior sides in rugby and cricket. He went on an enormous number of school trips including Adventurous Training, the Duke of Edinburgh Award Scheme and departmental field trips. Tim always had "unbridled enthusiasm, a delightful sense of humour and infectious goodwill".

On the same day, Tony Bird retired after thirty-one years at the High School. He had taught Classics and been Head of the Classics Department, and Housemaster of Maples, as well as running school tennis for many years. In the winter, he was the coach of the Second XV and organised many trips to see Hadrian's Wall and further afield, cruises around the Classical sites of the Mediterranean.

Wednesday, July 14th 1999

The Under-12 cricket team coached by Kevin Weaver, won the Calypso Cup, the Nottinghamshire County eight-a-side competition. Their opponents, Portland, batted first and scored 105, but the High School ran out easy winners with an overall total of 166. This particular High School cricket team thereby finished the season undefeated.

The summer holidays onwards

An extensive renovation and modernisation of the Valley Road Pavilion began. This scheme involved a huge refurbishment of the changing and showering facilities and an extension of the hospitality area as well as a resurfacing of the drive.

August 1999

In the world of yachting, Thomas Pickles and David Steed became National Schools' Champions in the Laser 4000 class.

Thursday, August 19th 1999

The A-Level results were the best in the history of the school, with a pass rate of 99% and 95% of candidates obtaining at least four A-Levels. No fewer than 51% of passes were at Grade A and 96% of the Upper Sixth went on to University.

Thursday, August 26th 1999

When the GCSE results came out, they were just as impressive as the results at A-Level had been. Every single boy had achieved at least seven passes at Grade C or above and more than 97% of boys had passed in at least nine subjects. No fewer than 37% of passes were at Grade A*, and overall, the average boy achieved nine Grade As, and an A*. This was the highest standard the school had ever achieved.

September 1999

In Design Technology, Nima Mehdian won a Sir William Siemens Medal for his *Automatic Curtain Opener and Drawer*. This was the first year that schools had been invited to take part in the Siemens competition which is usually open to universities.

Thursday, October 7th 1999

In a Cabinet reshuffle, Geoff Hoon became Minister of Defence. He had previously spent several formative years in the Combined Cadet Force.

Tuesday, October 19th 1999

The Politics Society was privileged to welcome Neville Lawrence whose son, Stephen, had been murdered in an unprovoked racist attack in London in 1993, without the Metropolitan Police ever managing to bring the killers to justice. In an address of great dignity, Mr Lawrence spoke of institutionalised racism and racial prejudice. His talk, held in the Player Hall, attracted the highest ever attendance in the history of the Politics Society, a grand total of some 700-800 members of the Boys' and Girls' High Schools.

Friday, November 12th 1999

Old Nottinghamian Professor Brian Shaw died in Beeston at the remarkable age of 101. He was one of the last survivors of the Great War in the City, and had won the Military Medal at Passchendaele. In the Second World War, he fought with the Sherwood Foresters but then spent five years in a German prison camp. In civilian life, he was a Professor of Chemistry at Nottingham University, famous as a world expert in explosives. His lectures to High School boys are the stuff of legend. He would cause explosions that would leave the audience deaf for up to a minute, dip objects into liquid oxygen so that they shattered like glass and then burn swabs of cotton wool spectacularly using the freezing gas. Using an ancient musket, Shaw would pierce several layers of wood with an ordinary candle fired out of it. Witnesses to his displays say that they were utterly unforgettable.

March 15th 2000

Twenty-five boys from Years 10 and 11 went to King's College, London, to see a production of *Œdipus* by Sophocles.

Thursday April 6th 2000

The "Grecian 2000" trip flew out from Heathrow to Athens. Accompanied by, among others, Murray Streets and Stefan Krzeminski, the group were to visit all the usual sites, such as the Parthenon, Delphi and Olympia. Less expected was what *The Nottinghamian* described as "Mr Street's pole dancing in a nightclub. We now know how he occupies his time on those frequent weekend jaunts to London. By day, a mild mannered Classics teacher, by night the king of the dance floor."

Friday, April 7th-Thursday, April 13th 2000

The Year 7 French trip, led by Tony Holding, followed a well-worn path, visiting Paris and then Normandy. In the "City of Light" they saw all the familiar tourist attractions, including the Musée d'Orsay which, according to Joshua Butterworth in his diary of the trip, contained a painting used in the film *Mr Bean*. After Paris, the party visited Bayeux and its tapestry, and then the D-Day Landing Beaches where the boys explored the gun batteries. Disappointingly, all of them, with just one exception, contained water. The only one that wasn't flooded, unfortunately, seemed actually to smell of urine.

The last week of June 2000

School chess enjoyed a unique double. The U-15 team travelled to New York with David Woodhouse and Gerald Douglas to play the final of the World Schools Championships, sponsored by the then World Champion Gary Kasparov. This was just over a year before 9/11 so the team had the chance to do some sight-seeing which included the Twin Towers. Curiously, this was the only over-the-board match of the entire competition, the rest of the competition being held over the Internet against schools from as far away as Africa and Israel. The team lost the final against opponents from New York but were nevertheless declared U-15 European Champions and were given an outsize banner to prove it. The High School's Board One was then able to play Kasparov in a simultaneous display. The following day two of the team flew back for the finals of The Times National Schools Chess championship. In this competition the High School finished a very creditable third.

Friday, July 7th 2000

Bumper Fun Day was organised by Andrew Winter. It had all the usual fun of the fair, but this year one of the attractions was the almost unbelievably original *Living Fruit Machine*, consisting of Tom Heath, Paul Spedding and Murray Streets. Each one of the three had a bag which contained a selection of small plastic fruits. On the word of command, all three teachers pulled a single fruit out of their bag and that formed the winning, or hopefully, losing, combination.

End of the summer term 2000

Adam Henderson left the school after eight years of teaching French, although he also knew Russian, German and Spanish. *The Nottinghamian* called him "an open, friendly, considerate man... who is interested in a variety of artistic and intellectual areas—notably the literature, music and film of several cultures". International hurdler, Andy Turner, had nothing but praise for Adam:

> "I had a French teacher called Mr Henderson who seemed to understand me. I was different from most of the pupils as I was naughty, maybe because I wanted to be playing sport, but Mr Henderson had a way with me that I respected so I wasn't naughty in his class."

End of the summer term 2000

John Shepherd left after twelve years as a very popular teacher of Economics and Politics. He had breathed new life into the Politics Society, inviting speakers such as Peter Lilley, Anne Widdecombe and Ian Hislop. Not many people knew, however, that John was "an Internet whiz (sic) kid". He ran the leading politics website in the country and because of this, he was eventually to find both a job, and a wife, Tobey, in the United States.

Geri Thomas retired as Director of Marketing and Development, having worked at the High School, with a hiatus of around six years, since 1958, giving a grand total of some thirty-six years' committed service. During this time Geri was involved in more or less everything, whether it was the teaching of Biology, the Duke of Edinburgh Award Scheme or school sport, where his input to Rugby and Athletics in particular was, quite simply, immense. Chris Parker paid enormous credit to Geri and his attitude to the school in his Annual Report, given at Prize Distribution a couple of months after his retirement. The Chairman of Governors also spoke of Geri's "dedication and energy". For the vast majority of us, though, the abiding memory of Geri will be that ever smiling face behind his camera as he rushed round taking photographs at all of the school's public occasions.

John Hayes left the school after thirty-three years of teaching French and Latin. He had, however, done much more than that. He ran the school minibuses and was for ten years the editor of *The Nottinghamian*. He was one of the founders of the Junior Adventurous Training Camps at Bala and helped with many sports including cricket and even rugby, when he acted as a coach driver and interpreter for the Tour XV visiting Mugron in 1992. The school hockey players saw his departure as "the end of an era". John Hayes had managed the sport for thirty years and had personally umpired literally hundreds of games. With his encouragement the School XI had won the County Championship numerous times and on two occasions the Midlands Championship, enabling them to compete in the Hockey Association Youth Cup National Play-offs. John had trained three National players and one Oxbridge blue. John Hayes was a wonderful teacher, "a real character", as they used to say. But more than that, he was always "a real schoolmaster", and "a real gentleman".

The end of the cricket season 2000

In the traditional fixture against the Old Nottinghamians, on a scorching hot day at Valley Road, the Old Boys scored 260 for six, thanks mainly to Messrs Storr and Hartley. The school replied with an excellent opening partnership between Ben Worley and Richard Pilgrim, the former reaching 53. Richard Pilgrim then batted on and on and on, finally reaching 157 not out. He won the game with successive sixes.

The summer of, probably, 2000

The following account was provided by Gerald Douglas. I feel that it must be quoted verbatim:

> "Whilst tiring, music trips have always been a source of encouragement and inspiration. As one can imagine, carting PA systems, drum kits and instruments around Europe over the past thirty years has been a challenge! I remember one year particularly, when the Big Band and Concert band travelled down to Tossa de Mar, Costa Brava. After a long and tedious journey through France we arrived at the hotel hot and tired. After asking the boys to settle into their rooms I thought I would unpack and have a shower. Then the phone rang. It was Reception. 'One of your boys has brought down the ceiling in one of the bathrooms'. Not the kind of start to the tour I had hoped for! After reassuring the receptionist I would sort it out as soon as I'd had a shower, there was a knock at the door.
>
> 'Who's that?'
>
> 'It's me sir. Guy Kiddey.'
>
> 'What do you want?' (I'm about to step into the shower)
>
> 'I've been shot, sir.'
>
> Can things get any worse? I decide to peer out of the door to find three Year 8 boys, Guy Kiddey, Joe Jackson, and one other, who must remain nameless. Guy looked okay, which was a semi-relief.

'Who shot you, Guy?'

'He did sir', pointing to Joe, next to him (head bowed)

'With what, Joe?'

'With this, sir.'

Joe took from behind his back a rather smart looking air pistol.

'Where on earth did you get that from Joe?'

'From him, sir,' pointing to the boy to his left (head bowed in an even greater expression of shame)

'Where did you get the gun from?'

'Last school trip, sir.'

Generally speaking, musicians are tender, considerate, sensitive creatures, but in the past I have had to confiscate more than twenty catapults, several knifes of various shapes and sizes and one extremely impressive macheté. I thought the Japanese Samurai sword should perhaps be mentioned as well."

An unrecorded date in 2001

The School's Challenge team, organised by Kevin Weaver, reached the National Finals of the Senior Schools' General Knowledge Competition held at King's School, Worcester. In the first round, the team, consisting of Michael Dnes, David Owens, Dafyd Jones and Alex Rossiter, beat the Abbey School from Northern Ireland by 690-340. Things were a lot tougher in the semi-final, however, where they lost very narrowly to King Edward's School, Birmingham. This did guarantee, however, a final position of third nationally, a marvellous achievement.

Thursday, May 17th 2001

The Politics Society, organised by Peter Cramp, held a Mock General Election. The results were:

Sanjay Brown (New Communist Party)	33 votes
Michael Champion (Conservative Party)	175 votes
Samuel Downes (Anarchist)	106 votes

Oliver Kempton (Labour Party)	55 votes
Nicholas Myers (United Christian Dem. Party)	19 votes
David Owens (Liberal Democrat)	59 votes
James Rowland (Monster Raving Loony Party)	85 votes
Wayne Simmonds (UK Independence Party)	40 votes
Chris Sweet (Socialist Alliance)	29 votes
Richard Whitaker (Green Party)	67 votes

June 2001

In Athletics, the first ever Hardwick Memorial Trophy was awarded to Victor Tung. This new award was presented to the school by an Old Nottinghamian, Mr K.S.Green (1933-1939). He had won the school's first ever discus event at Sports Day in 1938. Mr Green did not present the trophy for his own personal vanity, however, but to commemorate Mr A.Hardwick, "Tubby", who had taught at the High School from 1925-1960, and who had been the first teacher ever to coach the discus.

A Sunday afternoon in June 2001

The Community Action Group took a group of Senior Citizens to Derbyshire where they all enjoyed a cream tea. The usual schedule of activities had taken place this year, including visits to local inner-city schools, the partnership with the Shepherd School, trips to Castleton and Alton Towers, the Christmas Party and work with the Nottinghamshire Wildlife Trust at a number of sites.

June-July 2001

The second half of the German exchange took place with the English boys visiting their German counterparts at Gilching near Munich. Conditions were tough, with every German family owning a BMW convertible, free periods in the pupils' school timetable and a school day that finished at 1.00pm. As Head of the Exchange, Alison Griffin had organised trips to see the Olympic Stadium, a salt mine at Berchtesgaden and the country's deepest lake, the Königssee. Nick Phillips summed up the trip as "overriding memories of German sausage, one-man bumper cars and pink pyjamas."

The end of the Summer Term 2001

Roger Benson left after sixteen years at the High School. He had managed to achieve a "challenging and enthusiastic presentation" of Physics. He had been in charge of the Naval Section of the C.C.F. and been very involved in the Shooting Team and in canoeing for the Duke of Edinburgh Scheme.

Philip "Phil" Eastwood retired after more than thirty years of dedicated service to the teaching of Chemistry. Indeed, in his final year, having been entered for a Salter's Award for Teachers of Chemistry, he was to win a Lifetime Achievement Award. Outside the laboratory, Phil played both for the staff football and cricket teams and devoted an enormous amount of time to Athletics (1968-1993), especially the coaching of hurdles and sprinting. He was in charge of school football from 1970-1977 and was a prime mover in the re-introduction of this sport to the High School after a hiatus of almost fifty years. Phil coached the Second XI from 1978-1993. His greatest achievement, however, was in chess which he managed from 1980-1986. During this time the school twice finished runners-up in the British Schools' National Team Competition. Whatever activity Phil was engaged in, however, the main quality which he brought to it was his own enthusiasm. Whatever he was doing, he gave it his all. And this dedication would invariably bring success.

September 2001

David Slater arrived to teach Latin. He would never be forgotten by any of his countless adoring fans. His most famous exploit concerned the class he conducted in his lunch-hour, teaching GCSE Ancient Greek to a small group of both boys and girls from NGHS. He made the promise that, if everybody achieved full marks in a test on Aorist Participles, he would jump out of the classroom window. The pupils all performed extremely well in their test and David duly jumped out of the second floor window onto the flower bed below. And he also had the good manners to apologise to the extremely irate, fist-shaking School Gardener for any damage he might have inadvertently caused.

The academic year 2001-2002

The Politics Society, under the masterful direction of Peter Cramp and now assisted by Darren Poole, continued to attract an outstanding selection of speakers. This year they listened to Martin Bell, the BBC War Correspondent and independent M.P., and Yvonne Ridley, recently released from her stay with the Taliban in Afghanistan. Old Nottinghamian, Ken Clarke, also paid a visit as did those high profile media figures, Neil Hamilton and Richard Wilson (alias Victor "I don't believe it" Meldrew).

History visits, led by Matthew Bartlett and accompanied by a large selection of other staff, spent the year at various sites, some famous and others not quite so well known. They included Auckland Castle and Killhope Lead Mine as well as Anfield Stadium, Buckingham Palace and H.M.S.Belfast, by way of Harry Ramsden's fish-and-chip shop and Sheekey's fish pie.

Spring half-term 2002

The Under-15 rugby Sevens Team won both the Doncaster and the Notts, Lincs and Derbys Sevens Tournaments, as well as being finalists at Solihull. The squad was C.Nembhard, D.Lambert, M.Perkins, M.Hallam, H.Pick, A.Johal, T.Elder, A.Leccisotti, D.Jones, N.Nesbitt and R.Mason.

The end of his last football season, Wednesday, February 20th 2002

The First XI's coach, Stefan Krzeminski, looked poignantly back on what he had achieved in his time at the top of the High School's footballing pinnacle. "Bald Eagle" had carried out exactly what he had planned to do when he started out all those years ago. The First XI had achieved a record ten victories in their very first season under his direction. A number of players had been involved with the Nottinghamshire Schools' F.A. U-19 team and had represented their county at inter-county level. By the end of his tenure, Stefan's First XI had reached three County Cup semi-finals. All this was down to having done the majority of their training with, rather than without, a ball.

The Easter Holidays, 2002

John Allen is accompanying four Lower School mathematicians by train to the National Final of the "Enterprising Mathematics" competition in Glasgow. "JJ", is one of them. He stands out from the rest because he has brought with him a family-sized bag of chocolate doughnuts to eat during the journey. Or, alternatively, to smear down the front of his nice clean shirt. The hotel has been taken over by hundreds of budding Isaac Newtons, but they are all held in equal contempt by the staff, however well they try to behave. The four High School contestants are practically asleep before dinner appears. It is spaghetti Bolognese, and "JJ" is able to make valuable additions to his shirt front. The next day, after a decidedly ordinary "Design-a-Poster" competition, the High School finish an outstanding second in the main competition. Amid high security they are allowed to shake hands with Princess Anne. On the way back, the train terminates at Stoke-on-Trent. There will be no more trains that day. Careful negotiations, however, secure the services of a local taxi driver, who takes them to Stafford at a frightening Formula 1 speed to continue their journey home.

Wednesday and Thursday, May 22nd and 23rd, 2002

Over two days, the whole of Year 7 visited the White Post Farm, where they were given the chance, according to Paul Dawson, "to handle young birds and mammals, not be missed at any age!"

Thursday, June 27th 2002

The Swimming Team, coached by Paul Spedding and Andrew Martin, competed at Millfield where the U-12s and U-13s achieved nine top eight finishes at national level. Swimmers included Hugh Jones, Phillip Gadsby, William Powell, Oliver Gott and Aidan Hewitt in the 50 metre freestyle. It was now six years since the school had lost to another school in a head-to-head gala. Legendary names included Leighton Cardwell, Chris Bowker and Rhys Davies who all came to the end of their school swimming careers. Kevin O'Loughlin swam for the Midlands and finished third nationally in the 50 metres Butterfly. Paul Webster was Captain of the English Schools' team during the year.

July 2002

The Classics trip, accompanied by, among others, Justin Stanley, Davinder Gill and Matthew Bartlett, visited Italy, taking in the historic sights of Rome, Herculaneum and Pompeii. They also climbed Mount Vesuvius.

July 2002

The last day of the Summer Term saw the departure of Ian Driver after thirty-five years of dedication to the High School. As a teacher of Mathematics, he had a particular specialisation in Statistics but he was also a popular Senior Master for twelve years and a tutor who was always willing to go to great lengths to offer his help to any of his many grateful tutees. More than any of this, though, Ian was a man who gave so much of his time to so many varied activities. He was a prime mover in the Duke of Edinburgh Award Scheme and worked hard with the Lake Bala Junior Adventurous Training Camps and the David Leicester Walk. He was for many years with the Community Action Group, frequently involved with the trips to Castleton. Ian's other interests were the Chess Club, the School Bell Ringing Society and, until it folded up, the Origami Club.

The last day of the Summer Term also saw the departure after more than thirty years at the High School of the much loved and respected Paul Dawson whose glittering career in Biology was sadly cut short by illness. As well as being the Head of the Biology Department, Paul had also contributed enormously to the Army Section of the C.C.F., and to school sport, not just coaching cricket and rugby, but also refereeing countless matches in the latter sport. Paul was always very happy to be Head of Year 7, but most of all, he was a really nice man and well-liked by all those who had the privilege of knowing him.

A third departure on this final day was that of Matthew Bartlett, the charismatic young Head of History. His trademark, of course, was the series of historical trips which crisscrossed the country almost every weekend in search of different historical sites. As *The Nottinghamian* so rightly said: "His energy and stamina mark him out as one of our more memorable colleagues. No four-star hotel was left unmolested as Matthew, with his usual panache and style, explored the menu and wine list for items and evidence of historical significance."

Wednesday, October 2nd 2002

The First XI, newly under the imperious command of John Knifton, had played the first half of their fixture with High Pavement with the mental and physical determination of a shoal of quivering jellyfish. At half time, he tore into them:

"There are four of you in this team who just aren't playing!!! If you don't pull your fingers out, and buck up, then I'll take all four of you off at once and substitute you. You four, you've got ten minutes!!!! "

What the forgetful fool omitted to do, though, was to tell the team exactly who the four players were. At the time, it seemed to be a total memory disaster, but it turned out to be a tactical master stroke. Every member of the team, including the goalkeeper, thought it was them. They all played as if they were under threat of public humiliation, in front of the rest of the team and both of the spectators. We soon turned the two goal deficit around and eventually ran out winners by 4-2.

Wednesday, February 12th 2003

The First XI played their very last game of the season away against Bilborough College. Things did not look good when both teams had to stand around, looking sheepish, for a good twenty minutes before it was realised that the appointed referee was not going to turn up. Somebody had the bright idea of making an appeal to the crowd, so all three spectators were asked if they could help. "Comes the hour, comes the man", and to everybody's visible surprise, a young man said, "Certainly, I'm an F.A. Referee." And he was the best referee we had all season.

A steady stream of goals hit the back of our net and with five minutes left, we were losing 4-1. There were four substitutes, all of whom had been picked so that they could say afterwards that they had played for the High School, even if it had been just on one occasion, for a mere five minutes. Fulfilling the ambition of a lifetime, all of them were put on at once, with the tactical instructions of "Well, we've already lost this game. I haven't got a clue what to do. Play where you want!"

In the next couple of minutes Daniel Storey made it 2-4 with a shot later described as a "rocket-powered banana". Two more goals soon followed and suddenly the score was an improbable 4-4. Five minutes later, the final whistle blew as Bilborough time wasted so as not to concede a fifth goal and be forced to drink from the bitter cup of defeat.

Tuesday, July 8th-Friday, August 8th 2003

Colin Sedgewick, Richard Carpenter and 17 boys went on the World Challenge Expedition to Tanzania. The party enjoyed a safari to the

Ngorongoro Crater but their main aim was to climb Mount Kilimanjaro which was duly done, although not by the two teachers. They were forced to descend to lower altitude when two boys began to suffer from acute mountain sickness.

The end of the summer term 2003

Rick Gardiner retired after twenty-one years as Head of Art. He was famous not so much for his artistic talents, however, but as a magician and conjuror. He was, in fact, the first member of staff to be a member of the Magic Circle. This interest in the unknown and the mysterious extended to cryptozoology and Rick was, in fact, the only member of staff ever to be in the Loch Ness Investigation Bureau. He spent the majority of his summer holidays watching attentively from the side of the loch but, as far as is known, he never saw anything.

September 2003

The Nottinghamian greeted the arrival of new members of staff. On the very same page there appeared, therefore, Henry Wiggins, a teacher of History and Yvonne Steinruck, a teacher of German who had been appointed to cover Alison Griffin's maternity leave.

Wednesday, November 3rd 2003

The First XI drew 2-2 with Bilborough College. What was probably goal of the season was scored by the team captain, Adam Jaffe. The new First XI fanzine described it thus:

> "There are moments in the life of a young footballer that will stay with them for ever. The moment at which the ball landed at the feet of our captain, the keeper was out of goal, both teams were preparing for the goal kick. However Jaffe kept his cool and glided a 35 yard lob into the empty net. The team gave him the hero's celebration he perhaps deserved…"

Thursday, November 4th, Friday, November 5th and Saturday, November 6th, 2003

Karen Mitchell directed the school production of *Hamlet*. Everything was of a very high standard with Nick Phillips as the young Prince of Denmark, ably assisted in other roles by Ross Ludlam, James Maclaine,

Martin Noutch, David Ralfe, Mia Reeves and Thirza Wakefield. The imaginative music was provided by the talented David Ibbett.

Wednesday, January 14th 2004

The First XI visited Bramcote College and won by 5-0. Irfan Zaki scored his "a landmark goal, his first and last". In the fanzine he was described as "a constant source of commitment", who "expertly mixed football and religion to play through a fast". Daniel Storey scored a hat-trick, the first being from a centre which he clipped delicately across the face of the goalkeeper and off the far post into the corner of the net, one of the most skilful goals I have ever seen. Daniel managed two hat-tricks this season, totalling thirteen goals in twelve appearances.

Wednesday, January 21st 2004

The First XI eventually visited Welbeck College where they managed a highly creditable 2-2 draw. One of the many articles in the new football fanzine was to describe beautifully the transport arrangements:

> "The bus arrived, the driver emerged with a fag in his mouth, looking like a cross between Ozzy Osbourne and Liam Gallagher. Those who know Mr Knifton instantly realised that this man would come under serious abuse, and rightly so. Laughter turned to agony when he then announced that he had no idea of the whereabouts of Welbeck College, but he did know where Worksop was (yeh cheers mate!)
>
> After an hour of randomly driving around, Storey announced that he had "seen" the school forcing a majestic three point turn. I am no Mr BSM, but any driver who mangles the gears three times and almost hits a fence, taking fourteen minutes in the process should perhaps have his licence checked. The school Daniel had seen was inspected by the resident cross-country champion, Tom Wilson, who came back with a tractor, hanging on for dear life. The team burst into tears of laughter. He explained that he had trespassed on some sort of stately home, and that Welbeck was three miles down the road. We finally entered the school an hour and a half after departure."

Friday, January 31st-Saturday, February 1st 2004

A group of some dozen or more boys, accompanied by Peter Dowsett and Justin Stanley visited Fountains Abbey, Marston Moor and the city of York. Most popular was the National Railway Museum, the flooded River Ouse, the Jorvik Viking Centre, the dizzy climb to the top of York Minster and the many implements of torture in the York Dungeons.

The football season 2003-2004

For what may well be the first time since the 1920s, the pupils of the school produced their own publication. It was a footballing "fanzine" with detailed reports of all the matches, and marks allocated to all of the team's players. It was a genuinely witty, indeed, laugh-out-loud publication. They paid thanks to their team coach, for example...

> "...without him the team would have been nowhere, or to be more exact, stuck sitting in the minibus with no driver."

At half-time of every game, the team were encouraged to drink Explosade™, a brightly coloured energy drink, bought in large quantities from the Aldi supermarket in Hucknall. The players were all very dubious but an analysis in the fanzine revealed that after half time they conceded a season's total of seven goals but managed to score a massive seventeen. The only drawback was the frequent and agonising leg cramps they all had to endure and which would quite often reduce the players to the status of overturned beetles, lying on their backs, kicking their legs painfully in the air, unable to move. This, though, was a relatively small price to pay for their success.

Spring 2004

Martin Jones and his colleagues, Paul Allison, Ken Clayton, Jim Cook, Carol Fletcher, Mary Mills, Simon Payne, Phil Rood, Ian Thorpe, and Henry Wiggins, along with Old Nottinghamians, Robert Swyer, Dougie Thomas and Nigel Walker, took part in the school's thirtieth visit to Bala in north Wales. The party was also accompanied by John Hayes who had himself been on the first ever trip back in 1974. The thirty-seven boys were able to enjoy canoeing, rock-climbing, hill walking, mountain biking and orienteering.

Saturday, June 26th –Sunday, June 27th 2004

A group of some dozen or more boys, accompanied by Justin Stanley and Peter Dowsett, visited Bath, with its Royal Crescent and Roman Baths. Next day it was the Clifton Suspension Bridge in sunny Bristol and the S.S.Great Britain.

Bumper Fun Day, Wednesday, July 7th 2004

Under the ægis of Andrew Winter and Cooper's House, the school was able, just for the afternoon, to enjoy fun, fun, fun. The twenty or so Activities included "Soak the teacher", "Teachers in the stocks", sumo wrestling, crockery smash, six-a-side football, table tennis and target golf. There was karaoke in the Large Lecture Theatre, a Penalty Shoot-out, photographs of the staff as babies and computer games. A sum of some £2,600 was raised for Jill Hunter's charitable works in Malawi.

July 2004

Martin Jones retired after just over thirty-eight years of dedicated service at the High School. He had taught Mathematics and been heavily involved in rugby, rowing, the Duke of Edinburgh scheme and the C.C.F. He participated in a vast number of trekking and exploring activities. Quite often he would return home from one expedition and leave on the next one the following day. As *The Nottinghamian* so rightly put it:

> "His contribution to the life and spirit of the High School has been amazing and many boys and staff are eternally grateful for the opportunities he has offered them over the years."

Dave Phillips retired after more than thirty-seven years of service to the High School. He had not just taught Mathematics but devoted enormous amounts of time both to school rugby and to the Scouts. Dave taught vast numbers of junior boys over these years and he was not just a thorough and hard-working teacher throughout the period, but a splendid, and important, role model for them all.

Richard Nicolle retired after some thirty-one years teaching Physics and as Head of Careers. He was heavily involved with the school Scouts and, initially inspired by Norman Thompson and Dennis Usher, was always extremely keen on mountain walking. "Trickie" participated in countless expeditions and extra-curricular trips and thereby gave countless boys their own chance to do so.

Clem Lee retired after some twenty-seven years as Head of Games. He had coached variously the School First XV, Nottinghamshire U-18s, the East Midlands, and the Midlands Division. He had toured Canada, New Zealand and Australia with the England U-18 rugby team in 2001 and had also been in charge of the school ski trip for many years.

The school year 2004-2005

The Politics Society, organised by Peter Cramp, and helped by Darren Poole, provided three well known speakers this year. They were Steve Green, the Chief Constable of Nottinghamshire, a local Member of Parliament, Vernon Coaker, and the charismatic Liberal Democrat Member of Parliament, often known in the popular press as "The Living Anagram", Lembit Opik. Most interesting of all, however, was the Mock Election. The results were:

Stephen Dnes (Monster Raving Loony Party)	174 votes
Oliver Henderson-Smith (Green Party)	71 votes
Edward Maile (Liberal Democrat)	145 votes
Robert Pinfold (Labour Party)	79 votes
Daniel Sedgewick (Veritas)	18 votes
Tim Sherwin (Conservative Party)	137 votes
Richard Vernon (Reform Party)	89 votes
Adam Winter (Anarchist)	57 votes

Friday, December 24th 2004

Barry Duesbury, the Head of English, unexpectedly passed away. He was a man with the most amazing knowledge of literature but to an outsider it was perhaps his precision with English spelling, grammar and punctuation which was the most impressive. Few people ever knew, though, that Barry had been a member of the King's College team which had appeared on University Challenge.

2005-2009

This was the "Golden Age" of High School Chess. Coached by Dr John Swain, "The Special One", the team won The Times National Schools Chess Championships for three consecutive years. In both 2005 and

2006, the stars were Balvinder Grewal, (captain), Ian Harris, Dominic Heining, Michael Keetley, Ankush Khandelwal and Kishan Lakhani. In the following year of 2007, the champions were Jonathan Day, Oliver Exton, Michael Keetley, Ankush Khandelwal (captain), Kishan Lakhani and Daniel Lin. In both 2008 and 2009, the High School came second overall in the competition. Michael Keetley had played in the team in each of these five years, and, fittingly, in 2009 (his last year) as captain of the team, he was to win the best game prize in the Final.

Wednesday, January 26th, 2005

The First XI visited Bramcote College where, for a good half hour, they were watched as they played by the police helicopter. Eventually, they ran out winners by six goals to three, with Leo Fisher scoring all six goals. Leo was one of the greatest goalscorers the school has had in modern times. This season, he was to score nineteen goals in nine games and was called in *The Nottinghamian*, "the manager's 'get-out-of-jail-free card." Leo clearly harkened back to the Victorian era of Arthur Francis and Percy Sands. If only he had been a player in the late 1890s when, in the three seasons from 1896-1899, for example, Arthur Francis scored a minimum of 76 goals for the High School even with the goalscorers unrecorded in 23 fixtures. Between 1898-1901, Percy Sands managed an overall career total of a minimum of 106 goals for the High School, scored in just 61 games.

February 2005

Robert Grant took a group of pupils to the Cambridge Arts Theatre to see an innovative production of *Œdipus* by Sophocles in the original Ancient Greek. All the principal men's parts were played by women and all the principal women's parts were played by men. The details of the production leave even the most dramatic of American soaps like *Dallas* or *Dynasty* far behind. Œdipus was "frenzied" and at one point "covered in his own blood". Teiresias was "upset at the abuse" and Creon "strutted across the stage with his riding crop in hand".

Wednesday, March 16th 2005

After two spells as manager of the First XI, John Knifton finally retired. "The Big Boss"'s final game came against New College where, for the only time ever, there was a concrete trainer's dugout. The opposition kicked off with only ten men as their star player was finishing an A-Level examination. Despite being a man down, New College quickly raced into a 2-0 lead. After some twenty or thirty minutes, the latecomer finally arrived and tried hard to play a starring role in central midfield. The High School duly won by the iconic score of 6-3.

Thursday, March 17th 2005

In one of the school's more unusual outings, Carol Fletcher took a group of nine students to Newmarket to the National Stud. They were able to enjoy finding out about "breeding techniques high-tech style using cloning and embryo transfer."

Tuesday and Wednesday, March 29th and 30th 2005

Organised by the Reverend Stefan Krzeminski, over the course of two days, the whole of Year 9 had the privilege of visiting the Holocaust Memorial Centre near Ollerton in north Nottinghamshire. In past years they had been able to listen to the testimony of Arek Hersh, but on this occasion the speaker was Josef Perl:

> "It was not long before the train soon stopped and the front wagons pulled up at a platform. The people inside, who had clearly come directly from their homes, were marched away and disappeared down some steps straight to the gas chambers. We were in Auschwitz.
>
> The doors of our wagons were unlocked and we had to jump down. There was a smartly dressed commandant deciding who would live and who would die. Waving his riding crop, he indicated "links oder recht" ("left or right") with a casual flick of the wrist. Those he sent to the left (over 70 per cent) went immediately to the gas chambers, those to the right had been selected, either for slave labour or human experimentation. I had just met Dr Mengele."

I myself well remember hearing this chilling story of an encounter with the Angel of Death. At lunch, I was able to ask Mr Perl the question about concentration camps which had burned in my mind for years, namely, "Why, if you were all going to die anyway, didn't you fight back and kill the Germans?" Mr Perl then asked me that, as a teacher, I should tell as many people as possible what had happened in the Holocaust, so that it could never happen again.

I have never forgotten Josef Perl, or his request. Once again, therefore, I am humbled to do as he asked. By the way, Mr Perl's answer to my question was that, as the inmates at Auschwitz were eating just five hundred calories a day, it was impossible to stand up, let alone fight.

Summer Half Term 2005

Grahame Whitehead took a group of Year 8 boys to the Rhineland. They visited Bonn, Rüdesheim, the striking castle of Burg Eltz and Germany's main amusement park, Phantasialand, where the Colorado ride met with general approval.

July 2005

Andrew Holman left the High School after some seven years. He was a teacher of Mathematics and the Head of Year 7, introducing the pre-High School Day for Year 6 boys and the Taster Day for Year 5s. Andrew was in the R.A.F Section of the C.C.F. and participated in numerous expeditions and camps. He ran the Junior General Knowledge team, a junior cricket team and two tennis teams, one of which won the County Final. Perhaps the best indication of his dedication, however, is the fact that he once broke his leg playing football with other members of staff and then spent the next six weeks teaching his classes with his leg in plaster, propped up on a chair.

Wendy Nicolle retired after more than twenty years as a teacher of Physics. She achieved great success with the Community Action Group, changing its name to reflect a more proactive attitude of its role. She introduced formal training for members, organised a Conference and oversaw mystery trips, Christmas Carol Singing in the Victoria Centre, Christmas Pub Collections, Christmas parties for the elderly, and visits to Castleton, the White Post Farm and Alton Towers for local children.

Summer 2005

Guy Kiddey spent six weeks on Svalbard living on dehydrated food, barely washing or changing his clothes. He wrote in *The Nottinghamian* of his "tearing loneliness" and his dreams of "Sunday lunchtime, sitting with steaming food piled high in our warm kitchen, safe and dry." He saw abundant wildlife, including eagles, reindeer, a young Arctic fox and the dessicated corpse of one of the island's many polar bears.

The school year 2005-2006

The boys of Community Action continued to help the more vulnerable and disadvantaged members of the community. Their activities were heavily featured in the Yearbook. William Gee was helping his granny's friend Kitty with her shopping so that she avoided the seeds to which she was allergic. Greg Beer was assisting the elderly in his area by valeting cars, putting out the wheelie bins and carrying heavy items. George Craig was with the Salvation Army in Arnold, serving in the shop and helping the full time staff in the tea bar.

Saturday, September 24th 2005

Fourteen members of the Community Action groups from the Boys' and Girls' High Schools, under the leadership of Davinder Gill, Andrew Martin and Malcolm Saperia accompanied twenty-five pupils and two teachers from the St Ann's Well school to Castleton in the wilds of north Derbyshire. As the Yearbook said, of the little children:

> "Many have never left the city, and some have never even seen a sheep. It all went very well. These children genuinely enjoyed their time, seeing the world outside the city, smelling the country air, walking and running about in ways that they simply cannot at home. How keen the children were. Not just to climb the mountain, but to make friends with us. Most disquieting was the number of the young girls who wanted to play happy families, pairing us off as mummy and daddy."

Sunday, October 9th 2005

The twentieth David Leicester Memorial Walk took place with a record number of more than eighty adults and children. As always, Marcus Coulam was there in the minibus to monitor the participants' progress and to offer lifts to those who needed them. These walks had been in memory of David Leicester (1962-1985), and this was the final one. As the Yearbook said, it was "a most fitting tribute to his memory".

The Orienteering season 2005-2006

One of the young orienteers, James Taylor of 9W, showed to what extent their mentor, Jim Clarke, had been capable of combining an extreme sport with cutting edge Mathematics in his summary of what it took to be a good orienteer... "15% running and navigating, 30% banter and singing on journeys, 15% spending money in various arcades and 50% generally having fun with the people around you."

January 2006

Peter Dowsett and Robert Grant took a group of pupils on a weekend trip to Manchester where the highlight of the weekend was a visit to Manchester United's home, the fabled "Theatre of Dreams" at Old Trafford. Everyone hugely enjoyed this opportunity both to explore the stadium and to be photographed in the home team's technical area, especially Liverpool supporter Robert Grant.

Tuesday, March 21st, and Wednesday, March 22nd 2006

Once again masterminded by Stefan Krzeminski, the whole of Year 9 visited the Holocaust Memorial Centre at Ollerton. This time one of the speakers was John Chillag who had endured living in Auschwitz with, apparently, no hope of survival. In a splendid testimony to the continuing dark side of humanity, the boys were also able to hear the equally devastating tale of Ebrahem Ibrahim Aziz, a refugee from Darfur (in what was then the Sudan) where Arab fighters, convinced that black Africans should not be allowed to live in this region, had burnt down his village and murdered his wife.

Thursday, March 30th 2006

The Hockey First XI played in the King Edward's School Bath Hockey Festival and, thanks to the coaching and encouragement from Ian Cowley, performed extremely creditably by managing to defeat Exeter, one of the strongest teams present in the competition.

The last Bumper Fun Day, Wednesday, July 9th 2006

For the very last time, thanks again to Andrew Winter and Cooper's House, everyone enjoyed fun, fun, fun. Once more, there was an enormous variety of activities available including the ever popular "Soak the teacher", "Teachers in the stocks", crockery smash and six-a-side football. Most notable, however, was the Penalty Shoot-out, which involved Kate Costante as the High School's first ever lady goalkeeper. Resplendent in her pink Juventus goalie's top, she defied all comers, facing up courageously to a selection of flying footballs.

The end of the summer term 2006

The School Librarian, Marilyn Clarke left after twenty years' faithful service to the school. During this time, she had quite simply transformed the previous library and moved it on to what it has become today. At the same time Marilyn had turned the library into a friendly, welcoming place, which now, thanks to her, houses one of the finest archive collections of any school in the country.

Véronique Winter, the French assistante, left the school after two periods of teaching, the first from 1988-1992 and then from 1999-2006. She was always helpful and unfailingly patient, even though every day she was forced to endure an ever changing parade of boys enthusiastically putting the most beautiful language in the world through a succession of industrial strength mincing, shredding and grinding machines.

The ex-ball boy from Bristol City, David Slater, left after four years at the High School. Like a meteor streaking across the dark night sky, he had become a legend in his own lifetime with his wonderfully eccentric behaviour. Like a pedagogical Lawrence of Arabia, his vast army of small boys worshipped him. When his departure was announced at the end of the year, it was greeted with a vast groan of genuine regret from the young audience. For years afterwords, his name was still mentioned by boys around the school. Few teachers can ever dream of achieving that.

August 2006

The School Rugby Tour went to South Africa, where they played a number of games against the locals. They visited Manenberg Township, Robben Island and Table Mountain, as well as seeing Ushaka Marine World in Durban and traditional Zulu dancing in Shakaland.

August 2006

A school expedition, led by Richard Willan and Jim Cook went to South America, where they visited Ecuador and the Galapagos Islands.

They swam with sea-lions, fished for pirañha and played a high altitude football match against the locals, losing by nine goals to two.

Monday, October 2nd 2006

A regularly visiting theatre group, "The Actors of Dionysus", spent a day in the school. In the afternoon they treated the Sixth Form Classicists to a drama workshop, and in the evening they performed an "exhilarating production" of Sophocles' *Œdipus*. The latter explored the whole range of emotions from "rage through to guilt", while Jocasta was presented as a "yummy mummy".

The rugby season 2006-2007

The Third XV, managed by Ken Clayton and Jim Cook, assisted by Neil Highfield, established what must surely be a record when they used forty-six different players during the course of the season. They won only four games and drank from the bitter cup of defeat on nine occasions.

A forgotten date in 2007

The tale was told that a member of staff departed on maternity leave. Her replacement, however, did not last too long because, presumably having had the idea put in her mind, she too became pregnant before she could take up the post.

January 2007

The First XI were drawn away to Garibaldi School, Mansfield, in the County Cup. Not surprisingly, despite a promising beginning and an even better second half, the High School lost by four goals to one. And that would have been the end of it, except that Garibaldi later owned up to having fielded, completely in error, an ineligible player. The young man in question did some of his lessons at Garibaldi School but his registration was held by a second, different school. It is an unfortunate aspect of professional sport today that such an attitude is almost unheard of. This was a wonderful gesture, and deservedly (but perhaps, predictably) Garibaldi won the rearranged game.

The first weekend of February 2007

The scouts had a lovely time with Ben Thomas on a Day Hike around Monsal Head. As the Yearbook said, it was "a fantastic day with blue skies and an ice cream to polish off a perfect day!"

The last Sunday of the hockey season 2007

Nils Lloyd-Penny, who had played for Midlands Representational sides and the Welsh National Junior Representative teams played his last game for the school. It was against Wallington County Grammar School and finished, fittingly enough, in a 7-0 victory for the High School.

The end of the Easter Term 2007

Headmaster Chris Parker retired. He had been responsible for a number of important initiatives such as the establishment of four new academic departments, namely Learning Support under Carla Brien, Philosophy under Stefan Krzeminski, Psychology with Andrew Martin and, last but not least, Spanish with Matthew Jackson. In terms of building he had carried out vast improvements to the library, the development of the Art Rooms above the CDT block and a new Large Lecture Theatre. New rooms had been provided for Philosophy and Religious Studies, and most exciting of all, he laid the foundations for the daring new building plan to infill the West Quadrangle with a brand new Dining Hall and Sixth Form Centre, the quality of which was, when completed, far in advance of the facilities in many universities. Most significant of all, though, and perhaps years ahead of its time, was Mr Parker's attitude to fund-raising for a private school. He maintained links with important donors, therefore, and as the Yearbook reported:

> "Chief among these in recent years has been Sir Harry Djanogly who has become a good friend of Mr Parker's."

On another occasion, Mr Parker visited the United States to raise funds and eventually one of these kind donors came to Nottingham and met the boy whose place he was helping to support. Most boys, however, will remember him for his frequent visits to the Valley Road Playing Fields where his Helly Hansen jacket was, quite literally, outstanding.

The first few days of the Easter Holidays 2007

Under the leadership of Ben Thomas, the scouts visited some extraordinary sounding places in Cumbria. They included Whin Rigg,

Illgill Head, Esk Haus, Nethermost Pike, Swirl How, Wetherlam and Pavey Arc, along with those sturdy characters from a Lake District version of *Emmerdale*, Sergeant Man, Harrison Stickle and their girlfriend, the delectable Dollywaggon Pike. All watched over, of course, and judged by, the Old Man of Coniston.

Monday, July 2nd onwards, 2007

The whole of Year 7 took part in a production of *Hiawatha*. Every single boy had a part and the entire scheme was to occupy twenty five periods of English. To get into character, the boys were helped by Adam Blackhorse, a real Native American, who taught them games, songs and dances. On the final Tuesday there was a dress rehearsal and the following day, in the afternoon, the play was performed for that most critical and scathing of all audiences, Year 8.

The end of the Summer Term 2007

The Yearbook bade a fond farewell to two younger members of staff, Henry Wiggins and Yvonne Steinruck, who appeared together once more on the same page. The story does not end there, however, as Henry and Yvonne were married shortly after their move to their new schools.

Geoff Woolley retired. He had been at High School for twenty years and was the man who introduced Design Technology as a subject, starting off in classrooms which were on the very top floor of the Founder Hall. By 1991 the subject was being offered at GCSE and the rest, as they say, is history. Only twelve months later Geoff helped design a new building where the old Green Shed had once stood and, financed for the most part by Sir Harry Djanogly, it duly opened in 1992. Outside the classroom, Geoff dedicated much of his spare time to the Army Section of the C.C.F. and, as he grew older, he started up a Young Engineers' Club and the Engineering in Education Scheme.

Marcus Coulam retired after thirty-seven years at the High School. When he first arrived, he seemed so young that he was once told off by a senior member of staff for not wearing his uniform. He had spent the last thirteen years as Head of Economics and Politics and numbered both Geoff Hoon and Ed Balls among his former pupils. Outside the classroom Marcus spent many years in the R.A.F. Section of the C.C.F.

and also enjoyed many other activities, ranging from the Duke of Edinburgh scheme to ski trips, Stage Staff and Adventurous Training.

2007-2008

Andrew Simner related how the Stage Staff, while, "not as glamorous as the C.C.F.", worked hard the whole year round. Highlights were the backstage visit to the Royal Centre and the amazing pizza count for the academic year. The group was ably supervised by Lisa Gritti and John Kennedy but most prominent of all was the newly arrived Tregi Scholes whose work rate was of a phenomenal level.

Wednesdays evenings, or perhaps Thursdays, 2007-2008

As part of his Community Action year, Jonny Hubbard helped out in the Edwards Lane Music Club, teaching guitar and drums to young people from less favoured backgrounds. William Clark helped out with the St John's Ambulance, at one point attending the Robin Hood Marathon. George Harvey, along with Charles Lea, helped at a local tennis club, and Anthony Brown lent a hand with a youth group for primary school children. Josh Ackermann worked in a local charity shop. These were just five of many, many boys trying to make the lives of people with circumstances much more difficult than their own, just that little bit easier, if only for a short period.

Lunchtime in W11, 2007-2008

The Bridge Club went from strength to strength in terms of numbers. Indeed, the Yearbook recorded "a sudden surge in Lower Sixth boys taking up the game this year." Perhaps not totally unconnected with the presence of Bryony Balen and Ana Yau from the Girls' High School.

Autumn Term 2007

The record for the "Forest Run" was broken by three seconds by a Year 7 boy, Michael Costante.

7.00 a.m., October 14th 2007

Year 9 departed on their large scale invasion of the London Docklands. They visited Canary Wharf, the Greenwich foot tunnel under the Thames and St Katherine's Dock as well as Tower Bridge and the "mysterious" Tobacco Dock. Almost a thirteen hour day!

November 2007

The four members of the Schools' Challenge team, namely Captain Benedict Nolan, Ted Pynegar, Kyle Lam and Adam McElhone, retained their crown as Cleverest Clogs in the East Midlands with victories over Warwick, Bourne Grammar School, and the Girls' High School. They were eventually to lose out to Perse School, Cambridge.

Friday, December 21st 2007

The school Cross Country team, managed by Paul Allison, having "kicked off" their season in October, ran against the Old Boys, despite their own admission that they had eaten far too many Wagon Wheels and mince pies. Craig Woods and James Taylor both achieved record times for the course.

Thursday, January 31st 2008

Ray Eastwood retired as School Caretaker after many years' valuable service. Always carrying what appeared to be the largest bunch of keys in the world, he was an unfailingly nice man who always did his very best to be helpful. Neither he nor his colleague, Tony Hatcher, will ever be forgotten by those who had the privilege of knowing them.

March, 2008

The four members of the school's Bridge team, namely Aron Iger, Simon Spencer, Ankhush Khandelwal and Ted Pynegar, won the National Schools' Cup at Loughborough. In the qualifying round they scored 127 imps, then beat Reading 'A' by 27 imps and in the final, Reading 'B' by 3 imps.

Spring Term, 2008

Five members of the school's Orienteering team, namely James Taylor, Peter Lynas, Harry Nicholson, Craig Woods and Daniel Hughes represented England in the World Schools' Orienteering Championship, held in Edinburgh. They finished fifth of the twenty countries.

Spring Term, 2008

Over two days the whole of Year 8 visited Burbage Brook in the depths of the Derbyshire Dales. After the heat of narrow zigzagging roads and the heat of walking over the moors, the majority of boys were only too happy to cool off, either deliberately, accidentally or deliberately accidentally, in some of the large quantities of cold water available. A muddy time was had by all, much to the dismay of the coach drivers.

Tuesday, May 6th, 2008

Four Year 8 boys, Messrs Chaldecott, Corke, Luong and Stothard visited the Salters' Festival of Chemistry Competition. They were accompanied by Kate Costante and lucky enough to see and hear "loud bangs and colourful explosions". Indeed there was so much chemical excitement that the smoke alarm was set off just before the lunch break.

Thursday, May 15th 2008

Year 7 visited Twycross Zoo, one of Europe's main specialists in apes of all sizes. The boys saw monkeys who ate in "such a near-human fashion", as well as chimpanzees, leopards, marmosets small enough to fit in a teacup and at the other end of the spectrum, hissing cockroaches, red-kneed spiders and skin shedding anacondas. Everybody had remembered to bring some form of photographic identification so there was no problem leaving the primates at the zoo and returning the boys back to school after a tiring, but lovely, day.

The Summer Term, 2008

The Summer Concert included Saint-Saën's *Carnival of the Animals*. The audience heard Edward McDonald as a "galumphing elephant" (double bass), Christopher Heining as an aviary (fluttering flute), Simon Durrant as a fossil (xylophone), and Dominic Basista as a lyrical swan (cello)

The Summer Term, 2008

Coached by Scott Boswell, the school cricketers enjoyed their first taste of the new format 20/20 cricket, in a competition held at Valley Road against Trent College and Repton School. In the more traditional format of two day cricket, the First XI managed to defeat Wellingborough by two wickets during the very last over of the game.

July 2008

In the Yearbook, Les Wilkinson revealed that, as a young man, he had seriously considered the Probation Service as a career. The best school play he had ever directed was *Macbeth* in 1989. He revealed the "healthy banter" in the staffroom and his dream of being Bob Dylan for a day. Most disturbing, though, was the fact that he admitted to having once bought a copy of *Snooker Loopy* by Chas'n'Dave. Most comforting, though, was the fact that he watched Coronation Street "religiously" every episode.

The end of the Summer Term, 2008

Garry Martin retired after teaching at the High School since 1992. He was a man who was in love with books and who had written "an impressive number of novels over the years". As his farewell in the Yearbook said, Garry was able to: "talk stimulatingly not only about literature, but about seemingly anything. He can dazzle with his erudition and often illustrates points by reference to the many lives he has led and to the wide range of astonishing people he has met. His absence from the English Office will not go unnoticed. The large armchair will now be empty, the chair in which Garry would think so deeply that some might even have supposed that he was asleep."

Graham Lewin retired after thirty-seven years' teaching at the High School. He was not just Head of the Physics Department but was also in charge of Cross Country, helped with Athletics and was Treasurer of the School Scout Group. He will always be remembered by those who knew him as the most pleasant and affable of men.

Down at Valley Road, the Head Groundsman, Terry Brown, retired after thirty years. He had prepared pitches for football, rugby and cricket to an amazingly high standard, given the general wetness of the area and the tremendous amount of wear to which the turf was subjected. A thousand boys' feet for five days of the week over forty weeks of every single year represent a good deal of wear and tear on the green sward.

Bob Brown retired as the school's Pole Vault coach. He was a world veteran gold medal winner and a world record holder. This represents one of the highest levels of sports ever achieved by anyone associated with the High School.

Monday, July 21st 2008

A group of fourteen Sixth Form pupils, accompanied by those indomitable teachers of Geography, Richard Willan and Colin

Sedgewick, left Heathrow Airport for Ecuador and the Galapagos Islands. Among many other unforgettable sights, they were to see Galapagos tortoises, iguanas, frigatebirds and blue-footed boobies as well as jaguars, spider monkeys, spiders and "millions of insects".

Friday, September 18th 2008

Grahame Whitehead and Susan Hills took a group of children from St Ann's Primary School for a weekend of various activities at Castleton. The Sixth Formers were astonished at just how much energy the little children had and were completely shattered after two days of climbing up castles, playing football, giving piggy backs, cooking, cleaning, and masterminding the party on the final night. Indeed, every single Sixth Former fell asleep in the bus on the journey back to Nottingham.

2008-2009

The Philosophy Society had a successful year. Stefan Krzeminski organised a succession of speakers including Robin Le Poidevin (speaking on the Philosophy of Time), Will Browne (cognitive robots), and Carrie Jenkins (the Philosophy of Mathematics and Logic).

2008-2009

The Politics Society had another very successful year. Darren Poole, now in charge after a regime change from Peter Cramp, was once again able to attract a selection of high profile speakers including Ross Longhurst (the eco-Communist), Michael Cockerell (the vintage documentary film maker) and Oliver Letwin (the Conservative Member of Parliament and Chairman of Policy Review).

The last kick of the football season, 2008-2009

Deep into injury time, Aaron Iger lashed the ball into the Welbeck College net to win a hard fought match by 3-2. This was the Second XI's first and only ever victory under the management of Simon Williams. At a special press conference after the game, "The Special One" said, "Forget the Champions' League - this was the stuff of legend!"

Friday, March 6th, 2009

It was Jazz Night with contributions from The Big Band with guest singer Oliver Metcalfe. A staff jazz quintet was there to play, along with

The Junior Big Band and, most popular of all perhaps, "The one and only" Neil Highfield, singing "his own inimitable *Blue Suede Shoes*".

Monday, March 9th, and Wednesday, March 11th, 2009

The whole of Year 8 visited Burbage Brook. They surveyed all the geographical and hydrological features but also had time for a game of pooh sticks, albeit with crunched up dog biscuits.

Thursday, March 17th, and Friday, March 18th, 2009

The whole of Year 9 visited the Holocaust Centre where they had the privilege of listening to Arek Hersch who had been a prisoner in Auschwitz. He reduced them to stunned silence when he showed them his camp number tattooed on his forearm. Everybody was able to add their own small stone to the huge pile of stones in the gardens, each one of them representing the life of a child who died in the Holocaust. Eventually, every single one of the one and a half million children murdered by the Nazis will be remembered here.

Tuesday, May 12th 2009

Four Year 8 boys were taken by Kate Costante to the Salter's Chemistry Competition at Nottingham University. According to Max Spalding-Gardner, the best part of the day was the: "presentation by a daredevil scientist on hydrocarbons. It was literally hot, many a sizzling explosion occurred—each more thrilling than the last!"

Saturday, June 6th 2009

In a closely fought cricket match, the First XI defeated Trent College, our nearest and dearest rivals. Trent scored 216-8, but the High School, urged on by Scott Boswell, edged home in the narrowest of finishes, thanks primarily to the runs of Arun Johal and Alex McDonald. Prominent players in the team this season had included James Godrich, Sam Johnson, James Reeson and Alpesh Tosar. Most important of all, though, was their team spirit.

The end of the school year, 2008-2009

After a gap of more than twenty years, Housemaster Roger Kilby led Mellers' House to a stunning triumph in the Wheeler Cup. Early in the year Michael Keetley and Ankush Khandelwal had excelled in the

Chess and Bridge respectively. James Taylor, Craig Woods and Alex Lloyd had sewn up the Senior Cross Country. Tim Walton had helped win the Senior Rugby and in the Bridge Cup, joint second place was achieved with outstanding contributions from both Tristan Ellis (junior percussion), Dominic Ader and Richard Cassidy (individual verse speaking), as well as Oliver Metcalfe and Ben Storey. After Christmas, Matthew Berrington guided the house team to a fingertip victory in the Swimming Gala, and on Sports Day, Jonathan Huggard won two events and Alex Lloyd all four of his.

The end of the summer term 2009

Davinder Gill left the school after eleven years as a teacher of Physics. Outside the Science Laboratory, he had been involved in many different activities including cricket and the school's Community Action Group. Davinder was always very hard-working and reliable, a modest person who did his job to the best of his considerable ability. As the Yearbook said, "one of the unsung heroes who makes the School tick."

John Rayfield retired after fourteen years as Director of Music. He had energised this part of school life, which was transformed by the Lady Carol Djanogly Music School, a building which John had supervised from its very inception. His favourite moment at the High School came when he was able to play the organ at St.Mark's Cathedral in Venice, Italy, high up under the magnificent, golden dome. In the Yearbook, he revealed that his favourite composers were Bach and Mahler.

Dieter Hecht retired after seventeen years as Head of German. He had displayed almost unbelievable levels of energy, enthusiasm and dedication to his job. Everything was planned in meticulous detail and every method of awakening his pupils' interest was fully explored. There were visits to the Rhineland and an exchange with the Gymnasium Paulinum in Münster as well as study groups for sixth formers. Outside the classroom, he participated in thirteen school ski trips, and coached various teams in tennis, rugby and cricket. Most important of all, though, Dieter was a lovely person with a great sense of humour and a genuine sympathy for, and interest in, his fellow man.

Stephen Barber retired after twenty years as Head of Modern Languages. He had expanded departmental resources enormously, from just a single cupboard to a Languages Centre with facilities for self-access in thirty-five different languages. Stephen was a talented musician and a member of such supergroups as *Hip Replacement*. He also supervised the Christian Union and its various incarnations over the years.

Tony Slack retired after thirty four years at the High School. He had started out as a Chemistry teacher but finished as the Director of ICT, responsible for the introduction of any number of technological innovations, including (most importantly) paying for food electronically at lunchtime. Outside the classroom Tony was in charge of cricket for many years, coached the Second XV and in the 1970s, ran school football. Few were aware that he was himself an accomplished footballer and had played for Rotherham United Reserves many times, being threatened with physical violence by Charley Hurley on one famous occasion. Tony was equally talented at cricket in his youth and, while playing for Yorkshire Colts, had once hit Freddie Trueman for a boundary. Tony was Yorkshire born-and-bred. He had all the best qualities of a Yorkshireman, and none of the worst ones.

Summer 2009

Eighteen boys, led by Ian Thorpe and Darren Brumby, went on a World Challenge expedition to Siberia. Travelling via Moscow, they eventually finished up at Tyungar after sixteen hours in "the world's oldest bus on undoubtedly the world's worst roads. Just when we thought the road surface couldn't get any worse, it didn't. It stopped. Among many other wonderful experiences, we played a game of football against a local team, on a pitch backed by snow-topped Siberian mountains."

On the other side of the world a party of young cricketers visited Barbados in the sunny Caribbean. They played six games in six days, against teams from Trinidad and Tobago, Guyana, Barbados, Dominica and England. In addition, they watched the floodlit final of the Sir Garfield Sobers Tournament and found some time to sail a catamaran, to go swimming with turtles and to enjoy a trip in a glass-bottomed boat.

In contrast, in Nottingham, a series of severe summer downpours left the Upper School Library severely flooded. Thanks to the efforts of Yvette Gunther, the School Librarian, and Mr Curtis, the after school supervisor, very little lasting damage was caused, although some 10,000 books had to be packed away and then put back on the shelves in time for the new school year. A Herculean task, accomplished with ease.

The school year 2009-2010

The Politics Society, organised by Darren Poole, provided a number of famous speakers this year. They included the Government Chief Whip, Patrick McLoughlin, Haven Roosevelt (the grandson of FDR), Ed Balls the Old Nottinghamian, and Vernon Coaker the Minister of State for Children, Schools and Families (and an ex-teacher himself).

November 2009

As part of the "Year of Reading", two eminent authors, Beverley Naidoo and Mark Wagh visited the school. Firstly, there was a presentation in the morning and, after lunch, a writing workshop.

Wednesday, February 10th 2010

In football, the First XI, coached by Peter Cramp with assistance from Kieron Heath, recorded an emphatic victory over New College by six goals to two. The goals came from Rohan Rana (2), Robert Sowter (2), Sam Storey and Tom Heath. This was the team's first victory in a little over two years and was thoroughly deserved as they totally played their demoralised opponents "off the park".

A weekend in early Spring 2010

A group of young Art students visited Newcastle-on-Tyne, taking in the Millennium Bridge, the BALTIC Centre for Contemporary Art, the Biscuit Factory (also full of pieces of Art), and a ghost trip around the city. Most impressive of all, of course, was the Angel of the North.

Thursday, April 27th 2010

Sports Day took place, as usual, on a lovely, warm spring day. Luke Dudley set a new record for the Year 10 shot put of 11.59 metres. The victors were White's House (756), and then Maples' (708), Mellers' (678) and Cooper's (669).

Tuesday, May 13th 2010

Four young chemists, namely Jacques Lachetta, Ben Mills, Sanjay Puri and Anouj Rajput, were taken to Nottingham University by Kate Costante to do a "forensic report on a murder". In the afternoon, they took part in an egg survival competition, but most striking of all was the last event, when a guest lecturer put a wax candle into a musket and proceeded to fire it, producing a deafening explosion.

Friday, June 25th 2010

The school held its first "Activities Day", when the vast majority of the junior boys participated in something not just educational, but also fun. Year 7 were entertained by the Black Cat Theatre Company. For the most part they spent their time in the Sports Hall and finished their day by presenting their very own little playlets. As far as I remember, every single one involved a shooting and many of them, gangland style executions. The whole of Year 8 cooled off at Holme Pierrepont where they had a chance to indulge their taste for water sports. Led by the Head-of-Year, Tony Holding, they spent a rather wet Activities Day with everybody offered the choice of sailing, kayaking, water skiing, or raft building, as well as an adventure assault course. Year 9 remained completely dry back in school as they were taught how to become filmmakers at the "One Day Film School". For Years 10-13, it was business-as-usual, with a normal Field Day. Various groups of the Army, Navy and the RAF sections tried out a number of exciting military activities. The Stage Staff painted the set for the school's next dramatic production and Community Action carried on trying to improve people's lives.

After the school exams 2010

The whole of Year 8 put on a production of Homer's *Odyssey*, with additional dialogue by Les Wilkinson, assisted by Rachael Pearson and Rhian Wheeler. A splendid backdrop was provided by Tregi Worsley and the Stage Staff. Everybody had a thoroughly wonderful time, although the Yearbook revealed that one of the main fascinations was "some boys having to wear make-up" and at least one of them was described as "disturbingly feminine throughout". Other stars were Ciárán Green and Robert Jackson as Odysseus, and George Cowen, typecast as the ferocious Polyphemus.

The end of the summer term 2010

Neil Highfield retired after fifteen years as a rugby and cricket coach. The Yearbook described him as being full of "not only expertise, but boundless enthusiasm which never diminished." It would certainly be very difficult to top his retirement speech, which combined the very best of "The Comedians" with the profundity of the idea that when we retire we leave as much behind us as does a human hand when it is pulled up out of a bucket of water. Neil had accompanied sports tours to South Africa, New Zealand, Portugal, Ireland, Barbados and Durham and it was not going to be too long before he was going on another one.

Summer 2010

A group of rugby players, accompanied by David Allerton, Neil Highfield, Ian Thorpe and Stuart Whitehead visited South America. They played games in Santiago, Chile, Uruguay and Argentina. As tourists, they visited the Iguazu Falls, but surely the most abiding memory will be Neil Highfield's innovative idea that every player should sing the song "Robin Hood" to their direct opponent and give him a Robin Hood hat as a souvenir.

The school year 2010-2011

The Arts Society organised by William Ruff continued to offer a huge variety of activities including drama from *Œdipus* to *She stoops to Conquer*, from ballet to opera with a wide variety of different orchestras and classical music concerts. Solo pianists included Stephen Kovasevich, Lars Vogt and Lang Lang.

Elsewhere, the Debating Society, run by Claire Sanford, went from strength to strength. This year they entered *The Mace*, the English Speaking Union's oldest debating competition. The team had practiced for this moment by debating sample motions such as "This house regrets the British have lost their stiff upper lip", "This house believes Religion is better left in the home than brought into school" and "This house would introduce quotas for women in cabinet."

Two dates in 2010-2011

After thirty four years of being involved in every single school play, Les Wilkinson bowed out with two very different productions, *The Threepenny Opera* and *Bugsy*, the latter work perhaps the lighter of the two. He described the highlights:

> "Paul Carter in *The Servant of Two Masters* and *Playboy of the Western World* was a remarkable actor; the ensemble who worked

on *On the Razzle* and *The Nativity* (1986 version) were a wonderful group of people. Jonathan Swain and Claudine Astles were outstanding in *Macbeth* in 1989. Ben Gibson gave a great performance as Eddie Carbone in *A View from the Bridge*. I loved working with Ollie Metcalfe, Richard Hill, Jack Noutch, Laurie Field, Camilla Burnside and Jess Nicklin in three plays. A really talented bunch of people.

The one photograph I wish I had is of Ed Davey (currently a cabinet minister) dressed as a French maid in a production of Ionesco's *The Bald Prima Donna*. A lot of people would pay good money for that one..."

The rugby season 2010-2011

The Second XV, coached by Ian Thorpe, lost only one of their twelve matches and won the rest, four of them by a margin of more than fifty points. With this record they were classified in the English Schools' Rankings as being the fourth best team in the country. The team's outstanding players included Matthew N.Brown, Pablo Egbuna-Ruiz and Conor Snape.

The hockey season 2010-2011

Under the inspired leadership of Ian Cowley, the U-14s were the County Champions, and the U-16s, were runners up, having drawn the final against Worksop College.

The swimming season 2010-2011

Adam Sperry was selected for the England U-15 Water Polo squad, the first time that a member of the school has excelled at this sport since the golden days of Vicky Bruscomb in the early 1990s.

Wednesday, October 13th 2010

The First XI, coached by Peter Cramp and Kieron Heath, had the pleasure of playing against Trent College at Nottingham Forest's training facilities at Wilford. There was a professional referee and a pitch like a grass covered billiard table. There were outstanding performances from Sam Johnson and Sam Storey as goals from Richard Brierley,

Robert Sowter, James Monk, John Kehoe and Roham Rana produced a 5-1 scoreline.

Wednesday, October 20th-Tuesday, October 26th, 2010

The school's Big Band and Cutting Harmony toured New York. There were 27 young musicians in the party accompanied by Gerald Douglas, Karl Leutfeld and Stefan Reid. Highlights included visiting the Hard Rock Café and a concert in Harlem. Outstanding personal performances included Jack Hadfield singing the spirituals *Nobody Knows* and *Deep River* at St Peter's Lutheran Church and Jake Hinson playing Artie Shaw's very own clarinet in the demanding *Concerto for Clarinet*.

Friday, November 12th 2010

The Politics Society, supervised by Darren Poole, invited Old Nottinghamian and Member of Parliament, Ed Davey, to give a talk. Other speakers this year included Ken Clarke, one of our other Old Nottinghamian Members of Parliament, as well as Tony Eggington, the first democratically elected Mayor of Mansfield, Stephen Bercow, the Speaker of the House of Commons and David Smith, the Economics Editor of the Sunday Times.

December 2010

The R.A.F. Section of the C.C.F. was now commanded by Flight Lieutenant Nigel Key of the R.A.F.V.R. One of the members of the section, Cadet Sergeant Roland Buchta, became the very first to gain the coveted yellow lanyard within months of the new award being set up. Roland was soon followed by a number of other members of the section.

Tuesday, January 25th 2011

The Valley Road Sports Ground was used by the Duchess of Cornwall's helicopter en route to the City Hospital and the Council House.

February 2011

Andy Lumley, a would-be teacher of Mathematics, became the first person at the High School ever to be interviewed for a teaching post via Skype. And he succeeded in his job application as covering teacher for Caroline Howat's maternity leave.

February 2011

Under the ægis of Wilma Robinson, Daniel Turner achieved third place in an essay competition run by the Royal Economic Society. The title of his essay was: "Has recent government policy towards banks reduced the chance of another big financial crisis -- or increased it?"

The beginning of March 2011

A Year 8 Fencing team, coached by Andrew Reid, reached the quarter finals of the National Schools' Fencing Championships at Brunel University. The team consisted of Philip Davey, Annanay Kapila and Sam Steele, and their final placing was fifth out of thirteen, a splendid achievement for such a new school sport.

Late March 2011

Will Burn and Ben Harrison directed *Iphigenia at Aulis*, one of what has now become a series of Classical dramas put on in recent years.

The Easter Holidays 2011

David Allerton took a small group of Sixth Form Spanish students to spend a few days at the K2 International School in Cádiz. They were able to live with a family during their stay and were taught by a teacher who spoke exclusively Spanish when they were in the classroom.

Friday, May 6th 2011

The Battle of the Bands took place in the Founder Hall, raising some £130 for the House charities. This event bade a final farewell to Les Wilkinson who sang for the last time on stage as a teacher. On this particular occasion, he was performing solo as the rest of the staff band, *Hip Replacement* were away backing the Rolling Stones on their tour of North America.

The end of the summer term 2011

Scott Boswell departed after five years of almost unbelievable energy levels as Director of Cricket. He ran trips to Portugal and Barbados and introduced 20/20 cricket to the school as well as two day games and a new house match programme, all of them, hopefully, little acorns.

Matthew Jackson left the school after nine years. He had introduced Spanish to the syllabus, and had been both Head of Spanish and then Head of French. Along with Paul Allison, Matthew devoted enormous amounts of time to Cross Country and to Athletics. But most of all, though, what both the staff and the boys would all miss very greatly was his characteristic vitality and *joie de vivre*.

John Lamb retired after twenty years in the High School. Initially a teacher of Maths, he was soon promoted to Head of Year 11 and Senior Careers Adviser. Outside the classroom, for ten years as head of cricket, he devoted vast amounts of time to make the sport possible and enjoyable.

Les Wilkinson retired after thirty-four years at the High School. During this time he taught English, producing a long series of school plays including the high spot of his career, namely *Macbeth* in 1989. Les was also Head of the Sixth Form and Senior Master and had organised many ski trips over the years. He had given any number of Founder Hall assemblies, the majority incorporating his trademark guitar and folk songs. Most important though, was the fact that *Uncle Les* was always without fail a polite, kind, and caring man, although this was with his fellow human beings, not computers.

Friday, October 28th 2011

A group of Sixth Form students from Mellers' House collected money in the city centre to raise funds for the Teenage Cancer Ward (E38) at the QMC. More than £300 was raised for this worthy charity.

Friday, December 9th 2011

A Non-Uniform Day for boys and staff raised more than £1250, which was divided equally between the four House charities. The Housemasters sportingly paid for the chance to wear specially designed House rugby shirts in their respective house colours.

Tuesday, December 13th 2011

The school's Barbershop singing group, *Cutting Harmony*, visited Oakfield Special School, in Aspley, and entertained the children, many of whom had physical and mental disabilities. Songs sung included *Yesterday, The Streets of London, Uptown Girl, My Everline,* and, appropriately enough, *Rocking Around the Christmas Tree.*

January 2012

After just over six years of part-time study with the University of Southampton, Rachael Pearson became Doctor Pearson as she was awarded her Ph.D. Her doctorate was entitled *Power and Politics in the Gothic Drama of M.G.Lewis*; an amazing achievement alongside a job as a full-time teacher.

January 2012

The Yearbook produced its first ever Nottingham High School A-Z. It was:

> Advice, Brasserie, Commitment, Determination, Exams, Football, Girls' School, Houses, Interests, June, Kevin Fear, Leadership, Music, Neil Highfield, Opportunities, Pride, Queue, Respect, Sport, Tutor, University, Valley Road, Wilkinson, eXtra Curricular, Your Year and Z (forget it)
>
> TEAM…Together Everyone Achieves More.
>
> Old School motto that really does hold true."

Saturday, January 7th 2012

The Cross Country team took part in the Nottinghamshire AAA County Championships. The Under-17s won Bronze medals, and the Under-13s finished fourth. The Junior School team came second in their age group.

Thursday, March 1st 2012

The school celebrated World Book Day. There was a visit from World Famous Author A.M.Crawford, whose first novel, *The Titan Prophecy*, was "climbing the young adult fiction charts". Ms Crawford gave a reading from her latest work and took questions from an appreciative audience of Year Seven pupils as well signing copies of her book.

Wednesday, March 7th 2012

The school hosted the EMACT Regional Latin and Greek reading competition. Three boys were highly commended. They were Ross Jackson, Ashhad Noor and Raghav Sudarshan.

Monday, March 26th 2012

The Senior Quiz Team went to Ampleforth College for the Inter-Regional Round and won handsomely by 950-380. The team consisted of the Captain, James Pell, Max Bowling, Robert Jackson and Luke Sperry and they moved on to the National Finals later in the year.

Lunchtime, Thursday, April 26th 2012

International guitarist, Adam Brown, gave a recital to a large and appreciative audience. They listened to the timbral possibilities of the guitar and heard pieces which reproduced the sound of gunshots.

Tuesday, June 12th 2012

The Valley Road Sports Ground was used as a landing and take-off point for the Royal Helicopter which paid a visit to Nottingham as part of the Queen's Diamond Jubilee tour of Britain. First of all, the Duke and Duchess of Cambridge arrived from Anglesey and then left by road to meet the Queen at the station. Later, the Queen ended her own visit to the city by leaving in a helicopter which shortly afterwards returned to pick up the Duke and Duchess of Cambridge.

Thursday, June 21st 2012

Despite being the youngest age group at which this challenge is aimed, four Year 9 students achieved Gold certificates in the Intermediate Maths Challenge. They were Annanay Kapila, Timothy Lee, Dayal Sekhon and Jack Wickham.

Friday, June 29th 2012

The whole school participated in an "Activities Day". Year Seven went to Drayton Manor Park. Year Eight went to Walesby Forest near Newark-on-Trent. Year Nine spent a day learning how to make films with the One Day Film School. Year Ten pursued their usual Monday evening activities with either the CCF, Community Action or the Young Engineers. Year Twelve visited the University of Nottingham for their Open Day.

The week beginning Monday, July 9th 2012

As part of a radical refurbishment of the staffroom work area, the magnificent wooden tables were sold off in an auction to members of staff. Opinion differed as to exactly how old they were. Some believed that they all dated from the immediate post-war period or the early 1950s, but my own, perhaps faulty, memory is that a refurbishment took place at the same time Dick Elliott's room disappeared for ever.

Certainly, the vast majority of the tables auctioned were relatively pristine, and they certainly had no graffiti.

There was, though, just one table which did. It must have been sited in a classroom at the very least in the 1980s because it bore the word "BIF". Presumably, this was an abbreviation of some kind, the perpetrator perhaps unable to complete his evil handiwork before his vandalism was spotted. It is certainly a matter of record that the teacher's full nickname was "Biffo", in honour of the character in the Beano comic, *Biffo the Bear*. Except that being occasionally a somewhat less-than-interesting teacher, he was often called *Biffo the Bore*. The table in question is certainly old. It has other carved graffiti which include "Boggins 1951-1962" and "Albert 1954-1962", and must surely harken back to those Cold War years.

Personally, I would like to believe that this was the very table around which used to sit throughout the 1970s and 1980s, those members of staff whose main concern before school began was to complete the Times Crossword. This élite group usually included Jeff Leach, Ian Parker, David Peters and Allan Sparrow. Golden days.

Thursday, July 12th 2012

Ron Gilbert retired after twenty four years in the High School, spread over two periods, from 1979-1983 and then from 1992-2012. In the interim, he had spent some time in the European School in Varese, in northern Italy. Ron had come from the humblest of beginnings in London's East End, to achieve a degree at Oxford University and then to be a teacher of Chemistry at one of the country's finest schools. His successes are a glowing testimony not just to his own character and determination but to the quality of the help afforded him at different points along the way. Ron dedicated enormous amounts of his free time to school sport. He coached the Under-14 and Under-16 rugby teams and in Athletics, he coached the discus. Ron enjoyed hill walking and took part in many expeditions to Scotland and Wales with Adventurous Training and the Duke of Edinburgh scheme. He also enjoyed his time with the C.C.F. and ran Chemistry Club for a great many years.

Stefan Krzeminski retired after twenty six years in the High School. He had succeeded in changing the Religious Studies Department radically and had established Philosophy as a Sixth Form option. Outside the classroom Stefan was the drummer in the staff band *Hip Replacement* but his greatest love was always football. He ran the school team for fourteen years and a number of his players were to represent their county at national level. By the end of his tenure, Stefan's team had reached the County Cup semi-finals on three occasions. At the quarter final stage, they once came within eleven seconds of beating High Pavement, who were themselves soon to be crowned Champions of England.

Stefan was unfailingly kind and understanding, and a man who, no matter what point of view you had, could always find an equal and opposite opinion that seemed just as valid. He made you think. He made you question your preconceptions. The boys loved him. They appreciated his treating them with respect and patience, no matter what their opinion. Stefan brought his career to an end with the best assembly I have ever heard. It was a privilege to watch. It stands as a wonderful testimony to the values that Stefan held most dear.

Afterword

And it is at that point, at the very end of that Summer Term in 2012, that I have chosen to end my story of the High School. Clearly, when the history of any ongoing organisation is being written, there will always be the problem of finding the exactly right place to stop.

And if I finish now, I will have made it so much easier for whoever writes the history of the thousand year High School in 2513. With the benefit of centuries of hindsight, and knowing that I have never touched upon it, they will be able to write about the momentous decision to admit girls to the school from September 2015. In similar fashion, they will be able to discuss the whole series of exciting, impressive and imaginitive events which celebrated the school's 500th birthday, knowing that they are presenting them to their readers for the first time ever. And with any luck, if that writer, so far in the future, has any imagination, they might even turn to the book which I myself wrote at the time of the school's 500th birthday. This modest effort allowed a huge number of teachers, pupils and ancillary staff to describe a single minute of their lives, thoughts, hopes and feelings during that momentous day of February 1st 2013.

It is fitting too that the last event in my history of the school should be the retirement of these two gentlemen. Despite being very different indeed one from the other, both still managed to encapsulate all the best qualities of what is now, perhaps, a dying breed; the old fashioned school master. In actual fact, Messrs Gilbert and Krzeminski were the first of quite a large number of teachers and support staff to retire between 2012-2015. This is no reflection on the school, of course. It just sometimes happens that way, whether in the realms of education or with the players in a professional football club. People grow inexorably older and sometimes their ages are similar enough for them all to retire together in a short period of time.

And so, soon afterwards, the High School bade farewell to Keith Brierley, Jim Clarke, Ken Clayton, Mark Cleverley, Jim Cook, Wendy Davies, Ro Doron, Gerald Douglas, Carol Fletcher, Susan Hills, Martin Jones, Roger Kilby, my good self, namely John Knifton, Jim Knight,

Andrew Martin, Mary Mills, Paul Morris, William Ruff, Paul Sibly, John Swain, Richard Willan and Andrew Wood.

That should give any future historian a great deal of material as they write about every single one of this group of retirees whose service to the High School and its pupils lasted (when added together) for an amazing grand total of more than 600 years. If they had served the school consecutively, a couple of these teachers could have helped Dame Agnes Mellers herself back in the early days of the school during the reign of King Henry VIII, and then handed the baton down through all the years to the present day. Equally though, their departure will allow the school to face the future with a fresh-faced army of young teachers all full of the vigour, optimism and confidence that comes with being young. Here's to the next 500 years!